Tradition and Innovation in Renaissance Italy

Peter Burke was born in 1937 and educated at St Ignatius', Stamford Hill, and St John's College, Oxford. After a period at St Antony's College, Oxford, he moved to the University of Sussex, where he is now Lecturer in Intellectual History in the School of European Studies. He is the author of *The Renaissance Sense of the Past* and *Venice and Amsterdam*.

D0949074

PETER BURKE

Tradition and Innovation
in
Renaissance Italy

A SOCIOLOGICAL APPROACH

FONTANA / COLLINS

First published in Great Britain
by B. T. Batsford Ltd,
under the title *Culture and Society in Renaissance Italy* 1972
Fontana edition 1974
Copyright © Peter Burke 1972

FOR SUE

Contents

List of Illustrations

Acknowledgments

In the course of writing this book I have received much help from many quarters. John Hale suggested it, encouraged it, and criticized the typescript. The Institute for Advanced Study at Princeton provided me with three months in congenial surroundings to get the research off the ground, and the University of Sussex gave me a term's leave of absence. D. H. Hitchin and J. D. Hargreave, programmers at the Centre for Social Research at the University of Sussex, processed the data on the creative élite. Different parts of the book have been scrutinized by Zev Barbu, Francis Haskell, David Herlihy, Hugh Kearney and John Larner; I do not wish to remember what the manuscript was like before their emendations. I have been encouraged, advised and warned by James Beck, Julian and Alison Brown, Marshall Clagett, Ernst Gombrich, Hans Hess, Millard Meiss, Alasdair Smart and Gerry Warden. Historical Association audiences have asked usefully awkward questions. University of Sussex students who have taken 'Introduction to History', 'Culture and Society', 'The Italian Renaissance' and 'The Sociology of Art' courses will recognize ideas I tried out on them; and others which they tried out on me.

When Fritz Saxl gave Ernst Cassirer a guided tour of the library of the Warburg Institute, Cassirer is said to have remarked: 'This library is dangerous. I shall have to avoid it altogether or imprison myself here for years.' I have done neither, but without frequent visits there this book could not have been written.

P.B.

The Author and Publishers would like to thank the following for permission to reproduce illustrations: Accademia, Venice, Pl. 19; Alinari, Pl. 1; Jonathan Cape for Pl. 15 (from Iris Origo, *The World of San Bernardino*, 1963); Kaiser-Friedrich Museum, Pl. 12; National Gallery of Art, Washington D.C., Pl. 18; Photographie Bulloz, Pl. 10; Princeton University Press for Pl. 14 (from Alfred Einstein, *The Italian Madrigal*, Vol. 1, 1949) and Pl. 17 (from Felton Gibbons, *Dosso and Battista Dossi*, 1968); Réunion des Musées Nationaux, Pls. 9 and 11; The Frick Collection, New York, Pl. 7; The Mansell Collection, Pl. 13; the National Gallery, London, Pl. 8; The Owner, Pl. 3 and the Vatican Museum, Pl. 16.

NOTE TO FONTANA EDITION

I have taken the opportunity afforded by a new edition to correct mistakes, clear up misunderstandings, and add references to books and articles published between 1971 and 1973.

P.B.

Major Towns of Italy

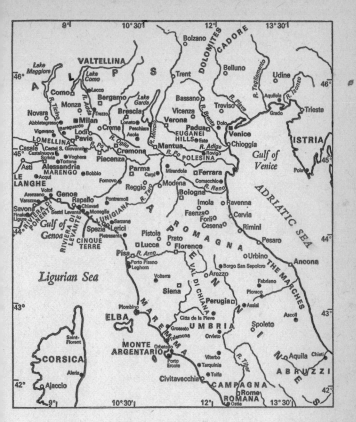

North and Central Italy

Introduction

Italy in 1420 was neither a social nor a cultural unit, though
the concept 'Italia' existed, and some educated men in other
regions could understand Tuscan. It was simply a geographical
expression; but then geography influences both culture and
society. Geography encouraged Italians to specialize in commerce and industry rather than in farming. Italy's position
in Europe, and good access to the sea, made it relatively easy
for Italian merchants to become middlemen between East
and West, whereas Italy's surface, one-fifth mountainous and
three-fifths hilly, discouraged agriculture. Thus it is not
surprising that during the commercial revolution of the
thirteenth century, Italian cities – Genoa, Venice, Florence –
were the economic leaders of Europe, nor that some 23 cities
in North and Central Italy had a population of 20,000 or more
apiece by the year 1300. Politically, city-republics were the
dominant form of organization in the twelfth and early
thirteenth centuries. A relatively high urban population and
a high degree of urban autonomy underpinned the importance
of the educated layman in medieval Italy, much greater than
in other parts of Europe. In the late thirteenth and early
fourteenth centuries, a number of city-states, not including
Genoa, Venice or Florence, were taken over by despots, and
in the mid-fourteenth century the Italians were hit by slump
and plague. But the tradition of the educated laity and the
urban way of life survived into the fifteenth and sixteenth
centuries. Italy then consisted of some nine or ten million
people. The majority were peasants, living for the most
part in extreme poverty and probably untouched by the
Renaissance. So this book, although a study in cultural history,
is principally concerned with a minority of the population,
the relatively educated. The illiterate majority also had a
culture and it is well worth study, but it is not the subject
of this book.

Writing in 1860, Jacob Burckhardt saw the Renaissance as essentially modern; a modern culture created by a modern society. In the 1970s, it does not look modern any more. This change is due in part to more than a century of research on continuities between the Middle Ages and the Renaissance, but much more to the change in our conception of the modern. Since 1860 the classical tradition has withered away, the tradition of representational art has been broken, and many rural societies have turned or are turning into urban industrial ones on a scale which dwarfs Renaissance cities and their craft-industries. In the fifteenth and sixteenth centuries, most Italians worked on the land, many were illiterate, and all were dependent on animate sources of power, which makes Italy 'underdeveloped' rather than 'modern' in contemporary terminology. This perspective makes the cultural revolution of the period more remarkable, not less so. It may also justify the attempt to write a book on the subject on which Burckhardt produced a masterpiece.

The great economic historian Sir John Clapham once wrote that, 'Of all varieties of history, the economic is the most fundamental. Not the most important: foundations exist to carry better things.' Similarly, the social history of art might be regarded as the basement of art history.

I

The Historians

It is Nature's custom, when she creates a man
who really excels in some profession, very often
not to make him by himself.   *Vasari*

What causes creative epochs in the arts? It has often been
remarked that great achievements in art and literature tend
to occur not singly but in clusters. In the history of the drama,
Aeschylus comes close in space and time to Sophocles and
Euripides, Corneille close to Racine and Molière, Shakespeare
close to Marlowe, Jonson, Webster, and others. Similarly in
Italian painting, Leonardo, Raphael, Michelangelo, Giorgione
and Titian cluster together. The fact of such clustering makes
it useful to speak of a 'creative epoch', suggests that creativity
cannot be explained solely in terms of the genius of the
individual (why should geniuses tend to appear together?) and
also that it cannot be explained solely in terms of the internal
history of painting, the drama or other arts (why should
Pascal and Poussin appear at the same time as Corneille and
Racine?). These clusters are collective, that is, social facts, and
they seem to demand a social explanation.[1]

This problem of explaining creativity has interested people
for a long time; the social explanation of the Italian Renaissance goes back to the Renaissance itself. Leonardo Bruni
thought that politics was the key. Like Tacitus, he thought
that the end of the Roman Republic meant the end of Roman
culture:

After the Republic has been subjected to the power of one
man, those brilliant minds vanished, as Cornelius says.[2]

Machiavelli suggested that in general letters flourish in a society after arms; first come the captains, then the philosophers. He did not explain this pattern, he simply described it. Vasari was impressed by the Brunelleschi-Donatello-Masaccio cluster, and commented:

> It is Nature's custom, when she creates a man who really excels in some profession, often not to create him by himself, but to produce another at the same time and in a neighbouring place to compete with him.[3]

Vasari's chief emphasis was on the individual; he chose to organize his art-historical material as 'Lives of the artists'.* His secondary emphasis was on progress in the arts – within a wider cyclical framework. He pictured the Renaissance as a cultural 'take-off' in three stages of increasing perfection, with the proviso that the ancients had been through all this before. But Vasari also addressed himself to the problem of explaining Florence's outsize contribution to the Renaissance, suggesting that in Florence artists had three incentives which were lacking elsewhere:

> The first was the fact that many people were extremely critical, because the air was conducive to freedom of thought, and that men were not satisfied with mediocre works . . . Secondly, that it was necessary to be industrious in order to live, which meant using one's wits and judgement all the time . . . For Florence did not have a large or fertile countryside round about it, so that men could not live cheaply there as they could in richer places. Thirdly . . . was the greed for honour and glory which that air generates in men of every occupation.[4]

The idea that it is the air which generates freedom of thought and greed for glory may seem to us a rather curious one, but this should not prevent the modern reader from seeing that Vasari has suggested explanations of the Florentine achievement in economic terms (challenge and response) and in socio-psychological terms (competitiveness and the need for

---

*But the idea that these artists as well as politicians and soldiers were 'illustrious men' was still a new one.

achievement as a central pattern in Florentine culture).

It was only in the eighteenth century, however, that cultural and social history came of age, in the sense of becoming the subject of systematic study rather than of isolated insights. Voltaire and Herder, who agreed in little else, both tried to displace attention from military history to culture and society. Voltaire declared in his *Age of Louis XIV* (1751) that he would omit the usual 'endless details of wars', because 'not everything that has been done deserves to be written about.' His main criterion of historical importance was cultural, and by this criterion, he suggested, four ages stood supreme. One of them was Italy in the age of the Medici. The others were Athens in the time of Pericles, Rome in that of Caesar and Augustus, and France under Louis XIV. Having said all this, Voltaire went on to describe Louis XIV's wars in considerable detail, but his *Essay on Manners* (1756) has been described as setting up 'the model for modern cultural history'.[5]

The eighteenth century was the age of 'political economy' in which it was natural that men should take an interest in the relation between the arts, politics, trade, and industry. The young Gibbon planned to write 'The history of the Republic of Florence under the house of Medici'. The main theme was to be the loss of liberty – a sort of 'Decline and Fall of the Florentine Republic'. But he went on to say that:

The character and fate of Savanarola (sic) and the revival of arts and letters in Italy will be essentially connected with the elevation of the family and the fall of the Republic.

It was widely believed that commerce encouraged culture; that, as Adam Ferguson put it, 'the progress of fine arts has generally made a part in the history of prosperous nations.' In the Italian case, Voltaire thought that 'prosperity made its contribution', and Adam Smith that, 'The cities in Italy seem to have been the first in Europe which were raised by commerce to any considerable degree of opulence.'[6]

Charles Burney concluded that:

All the arts seem to have been the companions, if not the produce, of successful commerce; and they will, in general, be found to have pursued the same course . . . that is, like commerce, they will be found, upon enquiry, to have appeared first in Italy; then in the Hanseatic towns; next in the Netherlands.

In similar vein John Millar remarked that:

In the twelfth and thirteenth centuries, many of the Italian towns had arrived at great perfection in manufactures . . . The advancement of the common arts of life was naturally succeeded by that of the fine arts and of the sciences, and Florence, which had led the way in the former, was likewise the first that made considerable advances in the latter.

The Scottish Enlightenment was an important stage in the development of sociological thought. It nearly developed a cultural sociology, for Adam Smith planned to write a book about the laws governing customs, arts and sciences but destroyed the manuscripts just before his death. Case-studies in this approach to culture were made by William Roscoe, who wrote about Lorenzo de'Medici and Leo x. Roscoe, who became a banker and an MP for Liverpool, clearly hoped that the Florentine conditions for success were being repeated by Liverpool some three hundred years later.[6]

Adam Smith was called the Newton of the philosophy of society. One might describe the Franco-Scottish model of cultural history as a mechanical model. In the later eighteenth century, a rival organic model was being created in Germany. J. J. Winckelmann took the important step of turning the history of artists, as Vasari had conceived it, into the history of art. As he put it himself, 'We have enough lives of painters. In my opinion it would be better to replace them by a new history of art.' This is just what he did in his *History of Ancient Art* (1764). Goethe called him a 'new Columbus' who 'raised himself above details to the idea of a history of art', and Schlegel wrote of him that, 'He was the first to treat the total world of art of the ancients as one and indivisible, as an organic whole.' The *History of Ancient Art* discussed the relation between art and society and explained the preeminence of Greek art in terms of the climate, the political system, and other extrinsic factors.[7]

A further step in the development of this organic model of culture was taken by J. G. Herder. He shared Voltaire's dislike of 'endless details of wars' and preferred to study literature. He collected folksongs, for example, and wrote that:

> From a study of native literatures we have learned to know ages and peoples more deeply than along the sad and frustrating path of political and military history. In the latter we seldom see more than the manner in which a people was ruled, how it let itself be slaughtered; in the former we learn how it thought, and what it wished and craved for.

Instead of seeing cultural history in terms of an impact of commerce on the arts, he saw art and society as parts of the same whole, expressions of the same time, place, and national character. 'As men live and think, so they build and inhabit.' Europe's unique civilization, he argued, is related to its 'spirit of commerce', its 'peculiar industry in the arts', its 'emulative industry'; in other words, to patterns of culture which modern social psychologists and social anthropologists might describe in terms of competitiveness and the need for achievement. In this context, Herder discussed the economic rise of Venice, Genoa and Florence in his *Ideas about the philosophy of the history of mankind* (part 4, 1791). But a nation, he thought, is united above all by its language; hence the special importance of literature for the historian. By means of literature the historian could imagine or re-experience the thoughts and feelings of another age, a process Herder called 'empathy' (*Einfühlung*). This was possible because literature – the plays of Sophocles and Shakespeare, for example – was related to the beliefs and traditions of the society in which it was created. It grew naturally out of a specific combination of time and place. Thus Herder created the history of literature in the way that Winckelmann created the history of art; but whereas Winckelmann's taste was for the classical, for 'noble simplicity and quiet grandeur', Herder's was for the primitive.[8]

Hegel, unlike Herder, did not find political and military history 'sad and frustrating', but his *Philosophy of History* (lectures given in the 1820s, posthumously published) also assumes the organic unity of a society. A central concept in Hegel is that of 'objective mind' or 'objective spirit' (*Objektive*

Geist). He saw politics, law, religion and the arts as so many 'objectifications' of spirit – the 'spirit of the age'. Discussing the end of the Middle Ages, for example, Hegel presented the flowering of the arts, the discovery of America, and the revival of learning as three related examples of spiritual expansion. Discussing the Greeks, he suggested that the growth of 'real individuality' was a dominant characteristic of their culture, expressing itself in their conceptions of the 'subjective work of art' (that is, the self seen as a work of art) and 'the political work of art'. At much the same time, the Swiss historian Sismondi argued that what caused creative epochs in the arts was republicanism and democracy, and he interpreted the cultural history of fourteenth-century Italy in these terms.

THE SOCIAL HISTORY OF
THE ITALIAN RENAISSANCE

The great nineteenth-century interpretation of Renaissance culture and society was that of Burckhardt. Indeed, it is still influential today. He wrote from a position of personal involvement with Italian culture. When he was in his teens he sometimes signed himself 'Giacomo Burcardo', and his personal discovery of Italy (like Winckelmann's, like Goethe's) was a great experience in his life. He came of an art-loving patrician Basel family; he was something of a 'universal man' himself, who sketched and played the piano, wrote music and poetry. Renaissance Italy was for him something of an idealized version of his own world. No doubt he projected rather too much of himself, and his age, on to Renaissance Italy. Himself 'a good private individual', he saw the Renaissance as an age of individualism. His *Renaissance in Italy* (1860), like Mann's *Buddenbrooks*, also bears the mark of his favourite philosopher, Schopenhauer. It locates the development of self-consciousness and rational planning in time, ascribing it to the Renaissance.

Burckhardt might have said, somewhat like Freud, that the poets and philosophers before him discovered the Renaissance; what he found was the historical method by which it could be studied. The method owes something to Voltaire. As Burckhardt's biographer Kaegi puts it:

It seems to me an overstatement to declare that Voltaire gave Burckhardt the inspiration for the theme of his *The Civilisation of the Renaissance in Italy*, but a hint towards that conception is not to be denied the *Essai* (the *Essay on Manners*). For Voltaire, as for Burckhardt, the matrix of the Renaissance was the wealth and freedom of the towns in medieval Italy.[9]

Burckhardt's method also owes something to Hegel. He rejected Hegel's emphasis on politics and his view of history as progress, and declared proudly that he put forward no philosophy of history – in the sense that he did not see History as marching anywhere. He preferred what he called 'cross-sections' (*Querdurchschnitte*), studies of a society at a particular moment in time, which looked at the typical rather than the individual. But he shared the fascination of the German philosophers with the polarities of inner and outer, subjective and objective, conscious and unconscious. Burckhardt's study of Italy, like Hegel's of Greece, emphasized the growth of individuality and men's awareness of themselves and their states as 'works of art'. Like Herder and Hegel, Burckhardt believed in the unity of an age, writing:

> Every period of culture which presents itself as a completely formed whole expresses itself recognisably not only in political life, religion, art and learning, but also leaves its mark on social life.[10]

But it is characteristic of Burckhardt, with his love of the empirical and his distrust of abstraction, that he should have said that some, rather than all cultural periods formed 'wholes'. On another occasion he expressed graver doubts still:

> As a whole the connexion of art with general culture is only to be understood loosely and lightly. Art has its own life and history.[11]

However, his general approach to cultural history is fairly clear. It is discussed explicitly in his posthumously-published *Reflections on World History*, where he analyses societies in terms of three powers, 'the state', 'religion' and 'culture'. Now:

Nothing wholly unconditioned has ever existed, and nothing that was solely a determinant. At the same time, one element predominates in one aspect of life, and another in another. It is all a question of relative importance, of the dominant at any particular time.

With this introduction Burckhardt goes on to discuss the six possible relationships of the three powers: (1) culture determined by the state, (2) culture determined by religion, (3) the state determined by religion, (4) the state determined by culture, (5) religion determined by the state, (6) religion as determined by culture. It is possible to read this formulation back into the *Renaissance in Italy*, which is divided into six chapters. The central four chapters deal simply with culture, the first relates culture to the state, the last relates culture to religion.[12]

What the *Renaissance in Italy* lacked, as its author admitted, was any serious discussion of Renaissance art. He had been collecting material on popes and other patrons of art, picture prices, and so on, and he went on to write about allegories, confraternities, and other subjects; these papers were found after his death with instructions that they were not to be printed. What were printed were three essays which he wrote between 1893 and 1895, after his retirement; one on the collector, one on the altarpiece, and one on the portrait. In them he discusses types of painting and, in the first essay, varieties of taste (such as the taste for Flemish paintings in Italy) and the place of art in social life.[13]

These essays are interesting, but they are only fragments. Neither they nor the more famous *Renaissance in Italy*, great work though it is, give us that view of the arts in relation to the society of the time which we might have expected from Burckhardt. He discussed social life (*Geselligkeit*), but not society in a deeper sense. He treated both politics and culture without explicitly relating them in the way that his *Reflections* suggest that they should be related. He left economic life out altogether. It seems fair to conclude that he was ambiguous, because ambivalent, about the whole question of the relationship of culture to society. At times he seems as if he is going to do for the Renaissance what Gibbon and Adam Smith only planned. Then he turns away from attempts to interpret the Renaissance in economic, social or political terms. It has been suggested that his retreat is related to his personal turning away from public to private life, from being a newspaper editor to being an academic, from being a citizen to being 'a good private individual'.[14]

Two men might fairly be described as Burckhardt's intellectual heirs: Heinrich Wölfflin and Aby Warburg. Both wrote, and wrote brilliantly, about the Italian Renaissance. Both were interested in the relation between works of art and the cultural world of which they form a part. But neither attempted to realize Burckhardt's larger ambitions.

Wölfflin was a pupil of Burckhardt's; came, like him, from an upper-class Basel family; and succeeded him in the chair of art history at Basel. Wölfflin is often thought of as a supporter of autonomous, even of isolationist art-history, but his approach was more subtle and more ambivalent than that description implies. He was interested in the differences between art-historical periods as well as the differences between individual artists, arguing that not everything is possible at all times, that styles and 'modes of representation' change. But why do these changes occur? This is where Wölfflin's ambivalence came out. He suggested that there are two ways of regarding the problem, and that both are admissible. In the first place, changes in style (the shift from 'linear' to 'painterly' for example) may be seen as the result of an inner development. This is the approach with which Wölfflin's name is more often associated, but he criticized it for implying that man was simply a 'form-producing creature', which he was not. In the second place, he suggested that changes in style could be related to changes outside the world of art.

> To explain a style . . . can mean nothing other than to place it in its general historical context and to verify that it speaks in harmony with the other organs of its age.

In other words he was interested, like Burckhardt, in seeing a period as a whole. He was particularly interested in what we might call the social psychology of the arts. He suggested that the cause of the change from Renaissance to Baroque, from linear to painterly, was a change in men's 'feeling for life' (*Lebensgefühl*), and that this emotional change was reflected in all the arts. The change from Ariosto to Tasso paralleled the change from Raphael to Van Dyck, for example. Of course this approach is dangerous, as Wölfflin was well aware.

> The so-called *kultur-historisch* introductions in textbooks contain a good deal that is ridiculous, summarizing long periods of time under concepts of a very general kind which in turn are made to account for the conditions of public and private, intellectual and spiritual life. They present us with a pale image of the whole, and leave us at a loss to find the threads which are supposed to join these general facts to the style in question.

This point about the 'threads', about the mechanics of the connexion between art and society, is an extremely important one. But Wölfflin did not pursue it. In practice he stuck to explanations of style in intrinsic terms.[15]

Aby Warburg, the eldest son of a Hamburg banker, came of a similar social background to both Burckhardt and Wölfflin. Like them, he was a northerner whose discovery of Italy meant a great deal to him. Like his contemporary Thomas Mann, he was an example of the 'Buddenbrooks effect' himself, the shift from business to culture; in that respect he was perfectly qualified to understand the social history of the Renaissance. He was not a pupil of Burckhardt's, but his work does take off from and continue that of Burckhardt, for example his essays on astrology, on festivals, and on portraits. In 1892 he sent Burckhardt his essay on Botticelli, and the generous comments on this 'fine piece of work' show that Burckhardt thought this study of the social, poetic and humanist milieu of Botticelli did not diverge in essentials from his own. It was a testimony, he wrote, 'of the general deepening and many-sidedness which research on the peak of the Renaissance has reached'. This 'many-sidedness' has a great deal to do with Warburg's inter-disciplinary approach – he thought that the history of art was part of the general history of culture, and disliked any kind of intellectual 'frontier control' (*Grenzwächertum*). To understand paintings better he looked at philosophy and literature; to interpret Botticelli, for example, he looked at Ficino and Poliziano. Like Burckhardt, he saw the age he studied as a whole. His interests extended to economic and social history. He was a friend of Alfred Doren, who wrote on guild organization and the Florentine wool-industry as well as about Fortune in the Renaissance, and in his own work social concepts like 'bourgeois' played a considerable part. However, Warburg came to devote more of his energies to another approach, fascinating but more marginal to the theme of this book, the study of the classical tradition in the visual arts, of iconography, of symbolism. He remained on the fringes of the social history of art.[16]

Historians have often criticized Burckhardt's *Renaissance in Italy* for its comparative neglect of economic life. He was himself aware of what was missing in his approach. In 1874, fourteen years after the book was published, he wrote to a younger friend:

> I believe that your ideas about the early financial development of Italy as the foundation (*Grundlage*) of the Renaissance are extremely important and fruitful. That was what my research always lacked.[17]

If Burckhardt neglected the economic factor, a contemporary of his amply repaired the omission. Like Burckhardt, Karl Marx was born in 1818 and, like him, he studied at Berlin University, the great centre of Hegelianism. But Marx reacted in just the opposite way to Hegel. Burckhardt accepted Hegel's suggestion that all history is fundamentally the history of ideas, the objectification of mind, but rejected the view that history is the story of progress. Marx did exactly the reverse. He agreed with Hegel that history moves towards a goal but did not accept Hegel's stress on consciousness. Marx's famous criticism of the Hegelians could equally well be applied to Burckhardt.

> We do not set out from what men say, imagine, conceive . . . in order to arrive at men in the flesh. We set out from real active men . . . life is not determined by consciousness, but consciousness by life.

Of course historians have in fact to set out from the evidence, from documents. But Burckhardt ran the danger, because of the kind of sources he used, works of art and literature, of accepting the Renaissance myth of the Renaissance, of accepting their image of themselves at face value. Marx's criticism underlines this danger.[18]

How would Marx have written the *Renaissance in Italy*? If true to form, he would, like Burckhardt, have been interested in describing social types, but, unlike Burckhardt, he would have concentrated on changes (the *Renaissance in Italy* has often been criticized for presenting a static picture of some three hundred years of development) and he would have started from the economy. In fragmentary discussions of the Renaissance he did in fact suggest that the art and literature, the 'superstructure', were related to an economic and social 'infra-structure' or 'base'. Where Burckhardt turned away from the eighteenth-century discussions of commerce and culture, Marx built on them, showing more interest than Voltaire, Ferguson or Smith in the precise relationship between material production and 'spiritual production' (*Geistige Produktion*) as he called it. For example, he suggested that:

> Whether an individual like Raphael succeeds in developing his talent depends wholly on demand, which in turn depends on the division of labour and the conditions of human culture resulting from it.[19]

Marx's ideas on the Renaissance were not followed up in the nineteenth century. Until serious research was undertaken on the economic history of the period, they could not be followed up. The first serious attempt to fill the gap was Alfred Doren's monograph on the Florentine cloth industry of the fourteenth and fifteenth centuries. Doren suggested that 'modern industrial capitalism' was to be found as far back as that. He noted the concentration of capital in the hands of a few families, such as the Medici; the division of labour within the cloth-making process; the existence of some large workshops where men worked for daily wages – in other words, 'factories'; and the dependence of the workers, especially the unskilled workers, on the entrepreneurs. He did not assert that this form of economic organization was typical of the period; his argument was that a new form of organization had emerged which was to become dominant later. Like Max Weber, who was writing on Protestantism and Capitalism at much the same time, Doren was not talking about the average but about the new. Doren was also aware that the Florentine cloth industry of the fourteenth and fifteenth centuries was very different from nineteenth-century industry. It was small in scale; there was no mechanization of the processes of production; a bridge between capital and labour was formed by the small masters. But his followers and his critics both tended to forget that these qualifications had been made.

Doren's material was built into a Marxist interpretation of the Renaissance by Alfred von Martin and Frederick Antal. Alfred von Martin published his *Sociology of the Renaissance* in 1932. He does not cite Marx in it, but his book reads like a mixture of Marx and Burckhardt. He was concerned with the Burckhardtian themes of the origin of the modern and of individualism, but, unlike Burckhardt, he emphasized the 'curve of development', as he called it, and the economic basis of the Renaissance. Von Martin's Renaissance is a 'bourgeois revolution'. Its individualism, its stress on rationality and calculation, and above all its modernity, all spring from this.[20]

In the first part of his book, 'the new dynamic', von Martin relates changes in world-view to changes in the social structure. His central theme is the rise of the capitalist, who replaces the noble and the cleric as leader of society. Where nobleman and cleric have a vested interest in continuity, the capitalist has a vested interest in change. Nobles and clergy did not disappear but assimilated themselves to the capitalist; the nobles took up commerce, the clergy became more secular in outlook. There was a general rise of rational and detached calculation. The world was seen as amenable to manipulation. In parts Two and Three, von Martin concentrates on the changing style of life and psychology of the bourgeois. He turned conservative, turned timid. He adjusted himself to the nobility and clergy instead of the other way round. The merchant invested in land, and his sons fought in tournaments. The humanist retreated from the world. The conformist ideal of the courtier replaced the individualist ideal of the entrepreneur.

Even in this brief summary the intellectual elegance and force of the book should be clear. But it is important not to misunderstand the author's aims. He was not writing social history but sociology. He was interested in Renaissance Italy as a typical example of a bourgeois civilization. He studied its development to discover typical stages or 'rhythms'. Hence the parallels, which may make the historian wince, between Machiavelli and Spengler, between fifteenth-century humanists and twentieth-century intellectuals (the book was dedicated to Karl Mannheim). As he acknowledges in the preface, von Martin's whole approach would have been impossible without 'the concept of ideal type which was evolved by Max Weber', although this concept simply makes more self-conscious the interest in 'the typical' shown by Burckhardt. Von Martin's types, or models, include 'Renaissance man' and 'medieval man'; at a more specific level, 'Renaissance noble' or 'Renaissance bourgeois'; at a more specific level still, 'early Renaissance upper bourgeois'. These types are not averages. To construct a model of the Renaissance noble following Weber's method, one pictures the behaviour of individual nobles; but then alters the picture to emphasize the difference between *Renaissance* nobles and nobles at other periods, between Renaissance *nobles* and members of other social groups.[21]

From the standpoint of his own aims, it is still possible to criticize von Martin's method. The central concept of his book is that of the bourgeois. But 'bourgeois' is not an easy term to define in opposition to 'noble' and 'cleric', for a society where some nobles trade and some professional men are churchmen. There is a danger of circular argument, of saying that wherever a rational calculating approach is found, the man in question (Alberti, let us say) is a bourgeois, and then of concluding that the bourgeoisie were more rational and calculating than other social groups, and that their social rise caused the rise of a rational calculating world-view. This criticism does not destroy von Martin's approach; it simply points to a danger. There are non-circular ways of defining 'bourgeois' (in terms of occupation, for example). To make his case, von Martin would not have to show that all occupationally-defined bourgeoisie have a 'bourgeois' world-view, and that no one else does; he was talking only about types. But he does have to show that significantly more merchants and lawyers (say) have a rational calculating view than others. This he does not do. In a book of that size one could not expect a full demonstration. But the case depends on it.

Again, questions are begged when von Martin describes the style of Giotto and Masaccio as that of 'democratic realism'. He suggests that the rise of the naked figure and the rise of the

bourgeoisie are related, that nakedness is egalitarian, democratic. But this approach to art is developed much further by
Frederick Antal. Antal (a pupil of Wölfflin's, incidentally) wrote
his book on *Florentine painting and its social background*
in the 1930s, though it was not published till 1948. It starts
with a vivid contrast between two Madonnas, then hanging
together in the National Gallery, both painted between 1425
and 1426, one by Masaccio, one by Gentile da Fabriano.
Masaccio's is 'matter-of-fact, sober and clear-cut' while Gentile's is 'ornate', 'decorative' and 'hieratic'. Antal goes on to
explain the differences by the fact that the works were
intended for 'different sections of the public'. These different
sections were social classes, with different world-views or
ideologies, which affected their taste. For example, in Florence
in the early fifteenth-century there was an 'upper middle class'
of wealthy families from the greater guilds. Their world-view
was rational, sober and 'progressive', which explains their
preference for pictures in a new style which was simple and
clear. Gentile's pictures, in a more traditional style, are related
to a more traditional and hieratic world-view, the 'feudal' one.
The conclusion is that Masaccio's appearance on the Florentine
scene reflected the rise of the upper middle class, and that his
style lacked successors because their class became assimilated
to the aristocracy.[22]

It is difficult not to admire this brilliant application of
Marxism to art history. With great intellectual economy, a
few central ideas of Marx provide hypotheses which interpret
both art and society both on a level of detail and on a level
of extreme generality. However, his method can be criticized
on two serious counts. The first charge is that of anachronism,
of projecting on to the Renaissance attitudes appropriate only
to a much later period. Is it meaningful to talk of 'progressive'
attitudes in the fifteenth century, or even of 'classes'? The
second charge concerns Antal's handling of evidence. Like
von Martin, Antal associates a particular world-view with a
particular social group, and, like him, runs the risk of circularity in so doing. As Antal knows, Palla Strozzi, a patron of
Gentile da Fabriano, was father-in-law of Felice Brancacci,
patron of Masaccio. Do they belong to different classes? Antal
qualifies his thesis by arguing that there was a less progressive
section of the upper middle class which borrowed a feudal

ideology from the aristocracy. But how do we tell the progressive section of the upper middle class from the rest – apart
from looking at the paintings they commissioned? Circularity
is not inevitable. There may be correlations between social,
political and aesthetic attitudes in fifteenth-century Florence,
but these have yet to be demonstrated. Similar criticisms apply
to Arnold Hauser's work in his *Social History of Art*.[23]

It has, of course, been argued that the Marxian approach is
totally on the wrong lines. In a review of Hauser's book,
Professor E. H. Gombrich distinguished two senses of the term
'social history of art'. It can mean 'an account of the changing
material conditions under which art was commissioned and
created'; the study of 'art as an institution'. It can also mean
social history as reflected in art, and this approach Gombrich
dismisses as irrelevant. The first sense corresponds to what has
been called the 'micro-sociological' approach, the second to the
'macro-sociological'. Von Martin, Hauser, and to a lesser extent
Antal, concentrate on the macro-sociological. Another group
of historians have concentrated on art as an institution. Martin
Wackernagel, for example, wrote a book about the Florentine
Renaissance which concentrated on the organization of the
arts; the workshop, patronage and the art market. That is,
he concentrated on the artist's milieu, his *Lebensraum* (an
unhappy choice of term in a book published in 1938), defined
as, 'the whole complex of economic-material as well as social-
cultural circumstances and conditions'. Gombrich's work on
Medici patronage and Professor Rudolf Whittkower's work on
Italian Renaissance artists might be described as being in the
Wackernagel tradition, which anyway differs only in its
economic-social emphasis from the study of the artist's milieu
practised by Burckhardt and Warburg.[24]

This kind of approach has only recently been applied to
humanism. The Wackernagel of humanism is Professor Lauro
Martines, and his 'Lebensraum' is *The social world of the
Florentine humanists* (1963). Von Martin – as one might have
expected from someone in Mannheim's circle – was extremely
interested in the history of the intelligentsia and in their
world-view. But, following the lead of the sociologist Georg
Simmel, he concentrated on similarities and connexions
between money and intellect. He was concerned to show that
a rationalistic world-view depends on a money economy,

because the use of money facilitates abstraction, objectivity, quantification, precision. Martines, however, concentrates on the social origins and status of the humanists themselves, arguing that the men associated with the humanist movement in Florence tended to be either professional men (lawyers, for example) or businessmen, and that humanism reflects the values of its 'social world'. A similar approach to music can be found in Mme Nanie Bridgman's book *La vie musicale au quattrocento* (1964), which is a study of the status and role of musicians, the kinds of patronage available at court, in the Church, and in towns, and the social functions of music. What is still lacking for Italy is a microsocial approach to literature, on the model, say, of Raymond Williams's studies of the social history of English writers and the growth of the reading public.[25]

This 'art as an institution' approach is fascinating and valuable – as far as it goes. Where it is unlikely to satisfy the ordinary historian is in its explanations, for it does not carry them very far. Art is related to the patronage system, but the patronage system is not related to anything else in that society. The choice seems to be between a method which jumps to its conclusions and a method whose only risk is that of not reaching conclusions at all. It is natural to ask at this point whether a synthesis of the two approaches is possible. But before discussing this, something should be said about some recent alternative macrosocial approaches, two in particular. One is essentially economic and the other essentially political, and they are associated respectively with Professor Robert Lopez and Professor Hans Baron.

In an essay published in 1953, Lopez started by making the point that the fourteenth and fifteenth centuries were a period of economic recession in Europe as a whole, and that Italy felt the impact of that recession most. He then went on to discuss the possible relation of this recession to the culture of the Renaissance. The recession theory is obviously fatal for the conventional view of the social conditions of the Renaissance, as expressed by Voltaire, Marx and others. The base and the super-structure seem to be out of phase. One could in fact save the conventional view by introducing a refinement, an 'epicycle', the concept of 'cultural lag'. This idea Lopez firmly rejects.

Cultural lags, as everybody knows, are ingenious elastic devices to link together events which cannot be linked by any other means . . . Personally, I doubt the paternity of children who were born two hundred years after the death of their fathers . . . the Renaissance . . . was conditioned by its own economy and not by the economy of the past.

Instead he produces an alternative theory, that of 'hard times and investment in culture', which turns the conventional view upside-down. Lopez had been struck by the fact that medieval Italy had a booming economy and small churches, while medieval France had great cathedrals and a less successful economy. Why? It could be that the cathedrals ate up capital and labour which could have gone into economic growth. Conversely, Renaissance merchants perhaps spared more time for culture than their predecessors because they were less busy. The value of culture 'rose at the very moment that the value of land fell. Its returns mounted when commercial interest rates declined.' It is not clear from the essay how seriously we are to take the term 'investment' (see p. 107 below). Lopez is interested in correlations on the grand scale, not in the details of merchants' motivation. But the prosperity theory of culture now has a serious competitor.[26]

The political approach to the Renaissance is that of Professor Hans Baron, and received its fullest statement in his *Crisis of the early Italian Renaissance* (1955). Baron dedicated the book to his master Walter Goetz, who 'taught me that history should be a study of both politics and culture'. He starts from two assumptions. In the first place, that the Renaissance was fundamentally a turning-point in the history of thought. Changes in art can be related to new ideas and new ideals. In the second place, the explanation of cultural changes has to be sought in society as a whole. Like Lopez, Baron is concerned with the fact that the dates do not fit von Martin's explanations. The years around 1400 are important in the history of Italian thought, but 'By then, the civic society of the Italian city-states had been in existence for many generations and was perhaps already past its prime.' If society does not change at the same time as culture, perhaps politics does. Baron takes up the suggestion made at the time by Bruni, and followed four hundred years later by Sismondi, that an important condition of the Florentine Renaissance was Florentine liberty, but puts a greater emphasis on self-consciousness. His argument is that about 1400 Florentines suddenly became aware of their collective identity, of the unique characteristics of their society. This awareness led them to identify with antiquity, with Athens and Rome, the great republics of the past, and this identification led to changes in historical and political thought and in the arts. This awareness Baron goes on to explain in political terms, as a response to the threat to Florentine liberty from Giangaleazzo Visconti of Milan, whose imperialistic aims in North Italy were resisted by the Florentines from 1390 to 1402, when Giangaleazzo suddenly died of plague. To become aware of one's ideals, there is nothing like fighting for them.[27]

The value of both Lopez and Baron lies in adding something to a common store, rather than in sweeping away all previous explanations of the Renaissance. For example, Baron's emphasis on political events does not make full sense without some consideration of social pre-conditions. To ask why Florence resisted Milan when other city-states did not forces one to move from the events to underlying structures.

The same criticism, that of incompleteness, might be made of both the microsocial and macrosocial approaches in general. The macrosocial approach, Marxian or not, runs the danger of what the late C. Wright Mills called 'Grand Theory'; too much interpretation to too few facts, too rigid a framework, and consequently the danger of circularity. This approach tends to create the impression that society acts on culture in a crude, direct way, that artists are no more than the expressions of social forces, social forces which tend to become hypostatized. But then there are dangers for microsocial historians too, above all the danger of what Mills called 'Abstracted Empiricism'. Here there are too many facts and too little interpretation, not circularity but incoherence.[28]

There seems to be a strong case for a pluralistic approach which draws recent research into a general synthesis and on the way tests the broader theories, new and not so new. I have tried to employ such a method in the remaining chapters, each of which will illustrate and try to test a different approach to cultural history.

The next chapter is descriptive; an attempt to sketch the profile of Italian culture in the period, to discuss whether

trends in painting, for example, have anything to do with trends
in poetry or music. There is also a chapter on iconography.
Microsociological approaches are illustrated by a chapter on
artists and writers, their recruitment, training and status; a
chapter on patrons and clients, the kind of men they were and
their relationship with artists and writers; and a chapter on
'taste', which attempts on the basis of literary evidence to
establish what men were looking for in works of art at this
time, and consequently what they saw in them. Macrosocio-
logical approaches are illustrated by a chapter on the functions
of works of art; by another on world-views, the whole complex
of attitudes of which 'taste' is only a part; and by a chapter
on the economic, political and social structure of Italy in the
period, including a section on the Church. The last two
chapters attempt to tie the threads of these different approaches
together by considering the major changes within the period
and by making comparisons with similar cultural syndromes
in the Netherlands and in Japan.

It will be clear that one well-known nineteenth-century
approach to the study of creative epochs has been omitted:
the genetic. Not long after Darwin had published the *Origin of
Species*, Hippolyte Taine put forward his theory that creativity
could be explained by three factors: *race, milieu* and *moment*.
Later on, Taine even wrote about 'natural selection' in the arts.
Soon after Taine, Francis Galton took up the problem of
genetics and creativity in his book *Hereditary Genius* (1869),
which includes a discussion of eminent painters in Italy and
the Netherlands between 1400 and 1600 in which he noted that
art often ran in families, quoting, among others, the examples
of the Bellini and Caracci families and the artist relatives of
Raphael, Titian and others. He concluded that, 'Lads follow
painting as a profession usually because they are instinctively
drawn to it, and not as a career in which they were placed by
accidental circumstances.'

It is important to distinguish two different points here.
There is the argument that there is a genetic explanation for
the creativity of a given individual, which has no bearing on
the question of creative epochs or cities. More relevant to the
social history of art, but less firmly based, is Taine's point
about the importance of race; the argument that the creativity
of social groups can be explained in terms of genetic differ-

ences. Thus Emile Münz, at the end of the nineteenth century,
offered three explanations for Florentine pre-eminence in the
arts during the fifteenth century. One explanation was the
existence of an artistic tradition; a second was in terms of
Florentine 'public spirit'; and the third was the intelligence
of the 'Florentine race'. In other words, Taine and Münz
would argue that the Florentines have a collective hereditary
genius for painting, that they are a Bellini family writ large,
as it were. (It is curious that the best Italian examples of
painter-families are not Florentine.) But if the Florentines have
this genius, why did Florentine art flourish only for a few
centuries? Taine might reasonably answer that the *milieu* and
the *moment* are also necessary conditions for creativity, and
that they had changed. But this would be to expose his throat
to the menace of Ockham's razor. *Milieu* and *moment* are
concepts which between them account for differences in
creativity in space and time, rendering any third concept
superfluous. The interpretation of Italian cultural history put
forward here will be in terms of these two concepts alone; or
as contemporary French historians put it, in terms of *structure*
and *conjoncture*, the long-term and the short-term.[29]

The aim of this book is to make a contribution to Italian
history but also to the sociology of art and literature. This
double aim necessitates a few remarks on its intended scope
and actual limitations. It is not concerned with the extremely
general, as a book on the sociology of art would be, nor, like
a historical monograph, is it concerned with the extremely
particular.[30] It is essentially about typical ideas, habits and
structures in a particular society. Regional variation remains
in the background. I have tried not to give the Florentines more
attention than they deserve. The Venetian achievement has had
considerably less than its due, partly for accidental reasons. In
the sixteenth century, a Venetian, Michiel, was collecting
material for lives of Italian painters, but hearing about Vasari's
enterprise, he stopped, robbing posterity of information necessary to counter Vasari's Tuscan bias. More recently, whereas
Wackernagel successfully completed his book on Florentine
art and society, Thode died with his similar work on Venice
unpublished and incomplete. It is to be hoped that someone
will fill this gap, but this book does not attempt to do so.
Important as the study of regional variation is, it only makes

sense when one has an image of the typical, the standard from which regions vary. Similarly, the book is not primarily concerned with changes within the period. They are important and they have a chapter devoted to them, but they are much less important than the differences between the fifteenth century and the twentieth. In other words, pluralistic as it is, this book would not claim to offer the only possible social approaches to the arts. And the social approach to the arts is itself not the only one. Art, literature and music reflect three levels of experience and response: the individual level, the group level and that of mankind in general. Only the second level is studied here, but this is due to the limitations of social history, not the limitations of the arts.

A Profile of Italian Culture

The purpose of this chapter is to describe, with great brevity, what the rest of the book will attempt to explain: the main characteristics and trends of Italian culture between 1420 and 1540. It will, in however sketchy a way, try to test for this area and period the general hypothesis of the cultural unity of an age. The stress will be on the period taken as a whole, not on trends within the period; on Italian culture as posterity sees it, rather than as contemporaries saw it; and on characteristics which seem to cut across several arts, rather than on those which are peculiar to just one.[1]

I started this book with a fairly clear picture of the pattern of achievement in the arts at this time. They flourished; they were the origins of the modern; and they exemplified certain major trends, notably realism, secularization, and individualism. All these certainties tended to dissolve as the book proceeded. If they can be saved, it is only at the price of marked reformulations.

To say that the arts 'flourished' in a particular society is to say, surely, that better work was produced than in many other societies, which leads one straight out of the realm of the empirically verifiable. Of course, there is always the argument from consensus. Educated men have tended to agree from the early sixteenth century to the present that Raphael was a great artist and Ariosto a great writer, but there has been no such consensus about Masaccio, Josquin des Prés or Michelangelo. About the greatness of the period there has been less disagreement, and few would quarrel with the suggestion that Italy in this period was a place where cultural achievements 'clustered' thickly.[2] The clusters are most spectacular in painting, from Masaccio to Titian; in sculpture, from Donatello to Michelangelo; and in architecture, from Brunelleschi to Palladio. The period 1375–1475 has been called a 'century without poetry', but 1475–1540, from Poliziano to Berni, is full of achievement. Italian prose too, with Aretino, Bandello and many others, is much more important in the second half of the period than in the first. In the realm of ideas there are many outstanding figures. In historical and political thought, there are Bruni, Alberti, Machiavelli, Guicciardini. In philosophy, Valla and Ficino. In physics, Paul of Venice and Leonardo. In medicine, Fracastoro. The great gaps are in music and mathematics. Much fine music was written in Italy at this time, but most of it by Netherlanders; it is only at the end of the period that outstanding Italian composers appear, Festa and Andrea Gabrieli among them. In mathematics, the famous Bologna school comes just after 1540.

The fifteenth and sixteenth centuries were a period of innovation in the arts; new genres, new styles, new techniques. The period is full of 'firsts'. On the technical side, there was the first oil-painting, the first wood-cut, the first copper-plate and the first printed book – though all these innovations came to Italy from Germany or the Netherlands. In the case of genres, the line dividing the new from the old is more difficult to draw, but the changes are obvious. In painting there is the rise of the portrait, the landscape, the still-life, though the last two genres were only becoming independent at the end of the period. In sculpture, the rise of the portrait-bust, the equestrian statue, the free-standing statue itself. In music, the emergence of the *frottola* and of the madrigal. In literature, the first secular play in Italian, the rise of the comedy, the tragedy, the pastoral; the development of art theory, literary theory, music theory, and political theory.

Innovation was conscious, though sometimes seen as revival. The classic statement of innovation and progress in the visual arts is that of Vasari, with his theory of the three stages of progress. Less formally, the same pride in innovation can be felt in his description of his work at Naples, 'the first frescoes at Naples painted in the modern manner (*lavorati modernamente*)'. Musicians also thought that great innovations had been made in the fifteenth century. Tinctoris, a Netherlander living in Italy, writing in the 1470s, dated the rise of the *moderni*, the modern composers, to the 1430s and added,

Although it seems beyond belief, there does not exist a single piece of music, not composed within the last forty years, that is regarded by the learned as worth hearing.

This repudiation of tradition was a cultural fact of enormous significance. It is paralleled in the visual arts by Filarete's and Vasari's criticisms of what they call the 'Greek' or 'German' style; in other words 'Gothic'. Filarete did in fact suggest that the barbarians had brought this style into Italy. This disrespectful attitude to the past suggests that one reason for the central place of Italy in the cultural changes of the fifteenth century was the fact that Italy had been less involved in Gothic than such regions as France, Germany, and England had been. There may be something in a 'cultural vacuum' theory, suggesting that innovations in the arts take place in areas where the previous tradition has penetrated less deeply than elsewhere. Germany was less deeply affected by the Enlightenment than France, and this made the German transition to Romanticism an easier one. Similarly, it was easier to innovate in fifteenth-century Florence than in fifteenth-century Milan.[8]

Yet Renaissance Italians were unable to do without tradition altogether. Having rejected their own, they needed a substitute, and found it in antiquity. Admiration for antiquity allowed them to attack their own tradition as itself a break with tradition. When Filarete refers to 'modern' architecture, he means the Gothic style which he is rejecting. This position was much like that of most rebels, revolutionaries and reformers in Early Modern Europe, who claimed to be the real conservatives, since they were trying to go back to the 'good old days'. And so a common characteristic of a number of the arts at this time is their imitation of antiquity, Greek and Roman. In architecture, this imitation is especially clear. Vitruvius was studied, ancient buildings measured and the whole vocabulary of classical form taken up: egg-and-dart mouldings, Doric, Ionic and Corinthian columns, pediments, and so on. In sculpture, the portrait-bust and the equestrian statue were classical genres revived. Comedies imitated Plautus and Terence; tragedies, Seneca. In narrative poetry there was a move from romance to epic, from the Chrétien de Troyes model to the Virgil model. Imitation of antiquity was most difficult in painting and music because classical examples were not available – the examples known to us have been discovered since the

Renaissance. But it took more than this to stop the imitators; there were always literary sources. Botticelli's 'Calumny' and 'Birth of Venus' are attempts to reconstruct lost paintings by Apelles. The literary criticism of the ancients was pressed into service to provide criteria for good paintings on the principle 'as is poetry so is painting'. In music, arguments about what Greek music *must* have been like occur late in the sixteenth century – a delay which suggests that music was 'out of phase' with the other arts.[4]

Contemporaries cannot be trusted to describe their own achievements accurately. They said that they were imitating the ancients and breaking with their own past. In practice, they borrowed from both traditions and followed neither. As is so often the case with cultural change, the new was added to the old rather than substituted for it. Humanism did not destroy interest in scholastic philosophy. Lorenzo de'Medici can be found writing to Giovanni Bentivoglio to search the Bologna bookshops for a copy of Buridan's commentary on Aristotle's *Ethics*. Ficino owed a great deal to the tradition of Scholasticism. Venus came in, but the Virgin Mary did not go out; the two figures, and the two traditions, coexisted and interacted. Hybrids can be found; Botticelli's Venuses are difficult to tell from his Madonnas. Michelangelo created an Apollo-Christ. A Renaissance prince would be as likely to read, or listen to, the story of Tristan as that of Aeneas. One fifteenth-century poem compares Aeneas's love for Dido to Tristan's love for Iseult, and Ariosto's *Orlando Furioso* is a hybrid epic-romance. Again, the composition of Botticelli's 'Birth of Venus' derives from the conventional 'Baptism of Christ' scheme, and Poliziano's *Orfeo* begins with the entry of Mercury, who takes over the place and function of the introductory angel in Italian mystery-plays, and perhaps his property wings as well . . .[5]

The other substitute for tradition in the arts was 'realism' or 'naturalism', to use terms which Burckhardt applied to the sculpture of Donatello, for example. The trouble with the term 'realism' in this context is that it has anachronistic overtones (it was coined in the nineteenth century to refer to literature, and applied to paintings, such as Courbet's, in the 1850s) and also that it has too many meanings, which need discrimination. In the first place, 'realism' can refer to subject-matter; to the choice of the low-status, the ordinary, the everyday as a subject for painting and literature, as opposed to the selection of privileged moments or privileged people. Courbet's stone-breakers, Pieter de Hooch's scenes from everyday Dutch life are examples of this kind of realism, which I propose to call 'domestic realism'. In the second place, 'realism' can refer to style, for example to paintings which produce the illusion that they are not paintings. One might call this kind of realism 'deceptive realism'. A third kind of realism might be called 'psychological realism'; it involves the distortion of outward reality the better to express what is within, as in the case of a portrait where the face is altered in order to express character better, or a scene (like Leonardo's 'Last Supper') where the natural gesture is sacrificed to a more expressive one.[6]

To take domestic realism first. What often strikes the modern spectator as most memorable in Italian Renaissance paintings is their backgrounds, whether of landscape or figures. Cri-velli's 'Annunciation' lingers lovingly on carpets, embroidered cushions, plates, books, and the rest of the interior decoration of the Virgin's room. Ghirlandaio's 'Adoration of the Shepherds' includes (as Wölfflin noticed) 'the family luggage – a shabby old saddle lying on the ground with a small cask of wine beside it.'[7] It is important to remember both that these details are there and that they are merely in the background. *We* often see the details as genre paintings in miniature, and reproduce them as such; *they* did not have the concept of genre-picture, and probably saw the details either as symbolic or as ornaments to fill up a blank space. In literature one can find equivalents to the Crivelli and the Ghirlandaio in the mystery plays of the time, the *rappresentazioni sacre*. For example, an anonymous play of about 1500 deals with the birth of Christ. The shepherds, Nencio, Bobi, Randello, and others, do not forget to take food with them when they go to adore Christ, and they eat it on stage. But in literature, unlike painting, there were genres in which domestic realism filled the foreground. There was the *novella*, for example those of Masuccio Salernitano; the comedy, which may be about peasant life, as some of Ruz-zante's are – and in Paduan dialect too; and poems of everyday life such as Lorenzo de'Medici's 'partridge hunt'. There is even music written round hunting and market scenes. Lorenzo and Poliziano wrote poems about violets, just as Leonardo made a drawing of violets. A similar interest in nature is reflected by a bronze crab and a bronze toad, made in Padua about 1500.

The question of deceptive realism is a more difficult one. From Vasari to Ruskin, it was argued that an important feature of the Renaissance was the artist's skill in making progressively more accurate representations of reality. At the end of the nineteenth century, about the time of the rise of abstract art (surely no coincidence), art-historians lost faith in the idea of the imitation of nature. Wölfflin wrote that, 'it is a mistake for art history to work with the clumsy notion of the imitation of nature, as though it were merely a homogeneous process of increasing perfection,' and Riegl, more dramatically still, that, 'Every style aims at a faithful rendering of nature and nothing else, but each has its own conception of nature.' What about the discovery of the laws of perspective? According to the French art-historian Pierre Francastel, this is no counter-example: 'Linear perspective does not correspond to an absolute progress on the part of humanity towards an increasingly adequate representation of the outer world on a two-dimensional surface, but it is a set of conventions, like any other.'[8]

If Riegl and Francastel are right, to talk about 'Renaissance realism' is to talk nonsense. But Riegl's arresting formulation is in danger of unfalsifiability, of circularity; the best evidence of the conception of nature of a particular artist comes from his paintings, which are then interpreted in terms of that same conception. It seems best to start from the empirical fact that some societies, like some individuals, take more interest in the visible world than others. Renaissance Italians took a great interest in it. Wax images, often life-size and dressed in the clothes of the person they represented, were placed in churches; life-masks and death-masks were made; and some artists dissected corpses in order to understand the structure of the human body. Deceptive realism was not the only aim of artists; Paolo Uccello coloured his horses according to quite different criteria. But Vasari criticized Uccello for precisely this lack of verisimilitude. New means for achieving illusionistic effects were developed, such as linear and aerial perspective and chiaroscuro. All art expresses a view of the world, but some world-views are closer to the surface of reality than others.[9]

Within deceptive realism there is another important distinction to be made. Artists and writers can use different methods to give their spectators and audience the sense that they are seeing or hearing a work of nature rather than a work of art, and these means may even be inconsistent with one another. There is a realism of detail and a realism of structure. Realism of detail includes the Holy Family's luggage in the Ghirlandaio, the numerous delineations of flowers, and birds, trees and hills in foregrounds and backgrounds; or in literature, giving a peasant character appropriate turns of phrase, as Ruzzante does, or describing individual places with precision, as Ariosto does. An example of structural realism, on the other hand, is Masaccio's 'Tribute Money' where it is the sacrifice of detail which gives the illusion of three-dimensional space. Structural realism in literature might involve not only giving each character plausible motives, but constructing a plot such that one could believe the events really happened. A parallel to Masaccio in literature might be Leonardo Bruni's history of Florence, which lacks the vivid detail of his predecessor Villani, but contains an account of the war between Florence and Milan which shows clearly how and why things happened as they did.[10]

Another characteristic of Italian culture in this period was that it was, relative to the Middle Ages, secular. This was one of the most distinctive features of the Renaissance, but all the same the pace of change has often been exaggerated. A sample-study suggests that the proportion of Italian paintings which were secular in subject rose from about 5 per cent in the 1420s to about 20 per cent in the 1530s. 'Secularization' here means no more than that the minority of secular pictures grew somewhat larger. In sculpture, literature and music it is more difficult to apply a quantitative method, but an impression of secularization remains. It can be illustrated by the fact that a number of the new genres were secular ones (the equestrian statue, the comedy, the madrigal are examples), or by juxtaposing medieval and Renaissance works, like Innocent III and Gianozzo Manetti on the world and on man, or Aquinas and Machiavelli on politics.[11]

There is also a trend, most obvious in painting, which might be called 'crypto-secularization'. Pictures which are officially about St George or St Jerome seem progressively in the fifteenth and sixteenth centuries to devote less attention to the doings of the saint, and more to the landscape background; the saints become smaller, for example. This suggests a tension between what people, artists or patrons really wanted and what they considered legitimate. But they did not make any sharp distinction between the two areas, and were continually profaning the sacred, sanctifying the profane. Ficino called himself 'priest of the Muses'. There was a 'chapel of the muses', at Urbino. God and the pope were addressed by titles such as 'Jupiter' and 'Apollo'. Masses were based on the tunes of popular songs. It was only in the mid-sixteenth century that practices like these were generally considered shocking.[12]

Another general trend was that towards the autonomy of the arts. They were becoming more independent of practical functions, and more independent of one another too. Music, for example, was ceasing to need words, and sculpture to need architecture. Instrumental pieces grew longer and more important; the organ compositions of A. Gabrieli and M. A. Cavazzoni at the end of the period are examples. The statue was emancipated from the niche at the beginning of the period. There are sculptures which have no subject in the sense that they do not illustrate a story, and a few paintings which have also been emancipated from religious, philosophical and literary meanings.

It is interesting to find the term *fantasia* used of both paintings and pieces of music in this period, to mean a work which the painter or composer has created 'out of his head' (his imagination, his fantasy) and which does not illustrate anything. In literature, the closest parallel to *fantasia* is perhaps the nonsense-verse of Burchiello; though one Burchiello does not make a trend. One does not expect to find such an emancipation-movement in literature; for it was above all from literature that the other arts were freeing themselves. The autonomy of the aesthetic is perhaps linked to the autonomy of the political. Croce emphasized the importance of both at the Renaissance, suggested that Machiavelli:

discovered the necessity and the autonomy of politics, politics which is beyond good and bad morals, which has its own laws against which it is futile to rebel, which cannot be exorcised and banished from the world with holy water.

Political theory, like art theory, freed itself from philosophy in this period. Alberti wrote some of each.[13]

Another kind of autonomy associated with this period is that of the creator; 'individualism' in the arts. Like 'realism', 'individualism' is a term which has come to bear too many meanings. Here I use it to refer to the fact that works of art in this period (unlike earlier periods) are made in a deliberately personal style, as well as in a period and regional style. But is this really a 'fact'? To the twentieth-century observer, Renaissance paintings tend to look more like the work of individuals than medieval paintings do. Is he falling into the trap of 'all Chinese look alike' (to the non-Chinese)? The testimony of contemporaries suggests that he is treading on fairly firm ground. In the fifteenth and sixteenth centuries, there are a number of references to personal styles, or to a plurality of styles. Cennini advises painters 'to find your own style,' *pigliare buna maniera propia per te*. Castiglione suggests that Mantegna, Leonardo, Raphael, Michelangelo and Giorgione are each perfect 'in his own style', *nel suo stilo*. Francisco de Hollanda makes a similar point about Leonardo, Raphael and Titian; 'each one paints in his own style', *cada um pinta por sua maneira*. In literature, Poliziano attacked the ideal of writing like Cicero, and suggested self-expression instead; 'it is myself that I express, or so I think'; *me tamen, ut opinor, exprimo*. All this is not to say that there was not a great deal of imitation of other artists and writers. Such imitation was probably the norm. The point about deliberate individualism, like secularization and autonomy, is not that it was dominant but that it was new, and marks the period off from earlier times.[14]

It seems that all the apparently obvious characteristics of Italian culture 1420–1540 – the flourishing of the arts, the origins of the modern, realism, secularization, individualism – are not absolute characteristics, but that they can be saved, at the price of qualification. Some other cultural trends across the arts may also be worth mentioning.

The split between art for an educated élite and popular art was not great, but it was widening. This split was probably the result of the acceleration of innovation. The new styles took time to spread, geographically and also socially. Of course this had been true of new styles in the past, but the more radically new the style, the greater the split between élite art and popular art is likely to be. It is unfortunate that we know so little about which social groups enjoyed the innovations, but of one thing we can be sure; that they were a minority. And so, in fifteenth-century Italy, 'the court dance and the popular dance separated.' In the theatre, the rise of the 'learned drama' based on classical models left the mystery plays for the unlearned. In narrative poetry, Boiardo and Ariosto moved away from the traditional recitations about Charlemagne, Roland and Ganelon. Tuscan was the language of élite literature, and Tuscan was gaining at the double expense of Latin and other Italian vernaculars. In the early fifteenth century a Venetian aristocrat, Leonardo Giustinian, had written poems in Venetian which passed into popular tradition. In the late fifteenth century Lorenzo de'Medici and Poliziano were fond of popular poetry and were sometimes inspired by it; but what they wrote themselves was becoming more and more different from that tradition. In painting, too, there was a split between élite art and popular art. The new secular themes would have been unintelligible to anyone without a classical education, as modern students of the Renaissance have good occasion to realize. The unlearned were not likely even to see secular paintings, which were usually made for private houses. The 'Birth of Venus' and the 'Primavera', for example, were not on public display – but hung in a villa.[15]

At the same time as this split was widening, a record of popular culture was being made. By the early sixteenth century, the cost of printing was low enough to make the publishing of broadsheets and chap-books a commercial venture. The Bindoni family, Venetian printers, specialized in this kind of literature. It is usually anonymous, often in dialect. The 'debate' (*contrasto*) is a favourite genre. There are debates between angel and devil, blonde and brunette, Florentine and Bergamask, living and dead, water and wine. There are poems about the passion of Christ, the treachery of Ganelon, about 'Captain Death'. It would be fascinating to know who bought them. The odds are that these items appealed to an artisan and shop-keeper public, who were more likely to be literate than peasants were; there are poems about the 'malice of peasants' (*villani*). It would be interesting to know how far these broadsheets were simply printings of what had long been current orally, and how far popular culture had changed between the 1420s and the 1520s, but it is difficult to find out much about the earlier period, apart from casual references to stories like those of the '30 old women' (*Trenta Vecchie*) with which Florentine mothers used to frighten their children.[16]

The split between élite and popular culture may well have been heightened by the rise of the heroic, of the 'grand style' (*maniera grande*). This grand style was characteristic of the later part of the period in particular and ran counter to some of the trends already discussed, such as deceptive and domestic realism. Homely details disappear from the backgrounds of narrative pictures in this style, and illusionism is often sacrificed to idealization. If the sitter does not look suitably heroic, he has to be altered to fit the ideal, as Michelangelo altered Lorenzo and Giuliano de'Medici in the Medici chapel. Bembo's Ciceronianism is a literary example of the grand style.

There were other counter-trends or cross-currents in the early sixteenth century. In the painting and architecture of the 1520s, a number of artists, such as Michelangelo, Giulio Romano, Parmigianino, Pontormo and Rosso, deliberately broke the rules of decorum, proportion and perspective, to produce asymmetrical, centrifugal works of art which the spectator may find disturbing to the point of nausea, or works of an aloof elegance which communicate a sense of tension or constraint.[17]

Another general characteristic of Italian culture at this time was the breakdown of compartments, the cross-fertilization of disciplines. The gap between theory and practice in a number of arts and sciences narrowed, and this was a cause, or consequence, of a number of famous innovations. For example, Brunelleschi's panel which dramatized his discovery of the laws of perspective was a contribution to both theory and practice; to optics (which is what the term 'perspective' meant in his day) and to the craft of painting. Alberti was a man of theory (a humanist, a mathematician) and a man of practice (an architect) and each helped the other. He argued that scholars could learn from observing craftsmen at work, and his mathematical studies were put to use in his architecture, which was built on a system of mathematical proportions. Leonardo's studies of optics and anatomy affected his painting. In music, some writers, like Pietro Aron, bridged the old gap between

the theorist of music and the player-composer. In the history
of political thought Machiavelli, a sometime professional civil
servant, bridged the gap between the academic way of thinking
about politics, exemplified in treatises about the good prince,
and the practical way, which can be illustrated before his time
in the dispatches of ambassadors.[18]

Another gap that was closing was that between the arts of
different parts of Italy, because in the visual arts, as in literature, Tuscan achievements became the model for the rest.
Tuscan visitors played an important part in the cultural transformation of the rest of Italy, the export of the Renaissance;
Masolino at Castiglione Olona in Lombardy, Donatello at Padua
and in Naples, Leonardo in Milan, and so on. Important regional
variations still continued to exist. Venetian art exhibited the
sharpest contrasts to the Tuscans, with its emphasis on colour
rather on design in painting and its richly decorated architecture. In Lombardy there was a similar taste for ornament, as
in the Colleoni Chapel at Bergamo, and some of the leading
sculptors and architects in Venice were in fact Lombards.
Insofar as Liguria and Piedmont participated in the Renaissance
in this period, it was the Lombard, not the Tuscan Renaissance
in which they shared. In the South there developed an eclectic
style in painting, part Flemish, part Catalan, part Lombard,
but not Tuscan. However, the minor art centres were being
pulled stylistically towards the greater ones. Sienese art was
becoming more like that of Florence. Umbria and the Marches
were also strongly influenced by Florence, and in the sixteenth
century ceased to be independent schools. Emilia was pulled
towards both Lombardy and Tuscany. The rise of Rome, a
city with a weak local tradition, as a great cultural centre in
the sixteenth century encouraged an inter-regional Italian art.
In general, it can be said of the visual arts, as of literature, that
they were much more Italian in 1540 than they had been in
1420.[19]

To return to the question with which this chapter began.
Can it be said that the age is a cultural unity? Several obvious
points can be made against this hypothesis. There is the survival
of the traditional; the Middle Ages did not end in the arts
when the Renaissance began. There is regional variation,
important even if decreasing. There are developments within
the period. There is élite art and popular art. At the same time

there do seem to be a number of important trends which cut across two or more arts; in that sense the age is unified. This unity needs explanation. It need not be explained in terms of a mechanically-conceived social determination, nor in terms of a 'spirit of the age' seen as a separate entity, which then becomes vulnerable to Ockham's razor. Two other explanatory approaches may be fruitful. The first is to account for the apparent cultural unity in terms of the interpenetration of the arts, itself related to the fact that, in spite of their growing autonomy, the arts were often associated in performance. A *frottola* or a madrigal was a poem set to music. Isaak set poems by his patron Lorenzo de'Medici; Tromboncino set poems by Petrarch; Arcadelt set poems by Michelangelo. The theatre, both religious and secular, associated painting and music with literature. Baldassare Peruzzi designed the scenery for Bibbiena's *Calandria*. Most plays were 'musicals' and some of the music was by famous composers. Della Viola and De Rore wrote the music for Giraldi's plays. The court festival also brought the arts together; the festivals planned by Leonardo for the Sforzas at Milan can be seen as a total work of art, a *Gesamtkunstwerk*. Given these associations it is not surprising that there was conscious borrowing of ideals. Painters tried to be more like poets, for example; Titian even called some of his paintings 'poems'. The second explanatory approach is to point out that men, especially creative individuals, often do not compartmentalize their experiences. Painters, musicians, poets living in the same society shared common experiences, so it is not surprising that these common experiences should sometimes have led to similar creations, to the expression of the same moods. This second approach is in any case a major theme of the rest of this book.

3

Artists and Writers

Let us begin by assuming that artistic and other creative abilities are randomly distributed among the population. In conditions of perfect opportunity, a cultural élite, that is, the people whose creative abilities are recognized, would in all other respects represent a random sample of the population. In practice this never happens. Societies always set obstacles in the way of some of their groups, and Renaissance Italy was no exception. The 600 painters, sculptors, architects, composers, humanists, scientists and writers studied in this chapter were in many ways untypical of the Italian population.*

To begin with the most spectacular example of bias. One 'variable' in the survey of artists and writers appears to be almost invariable: their sex. Only three out of the 600 are women: Vittoria Colonna, Veronica Gambara and Tullia d'Aragona. All are poets, and all come at the end of the period. Of course this bias is not uniquely Italian or Renaissance, whether it is to be explained psychologically (male creativity as a substitute for inability to bear children) or sociologically (women's abilities being suppressed in a male-dominated society). When the obstacles are a little less than usual, women artists and writers appear. For example, the daughters of artists sometimes paint. For example, Tintoretto's daughter Marietta painted portraits (nothing which is certainly by her has sur-

* For the composition of this group, hereinafter referred to as 'the élite' or 'artists and writers', see p. 349 below. Of the seven sub-divisions, 'pittore' and 'scultore' are regularly used in the period; 'architetto' and 'compositore' can be found, but coexist with terms more like 'mason' and 'musician'; 'umanista' was student slang for a university teacher of grammar, rhetoric, history, poetry and ethics; 'scientist' is a convenient anachronism to avoid the circumlocution 'writer on physics, medicine, etc.'.

vived); Vasari says that Uccello had a daughter who 'knew how to draw', and became a Carmelite nun. Nuns sometimes worked as miniaturists; S. Caterina da Bologna, for example, falls inside this period. There is also a sculptress from Bologna, Properzia de'Rossi, whose life was written by Vasari, with appropriate references to such gifted women of antiquity as Camilla and Sappho. In the case of women writers, one can add to Vittoria and Veronica the names of Gaspara Stampa, Laura Terracina and Laura Battiferri. They all flourish just before the middle of the sixteenth century. It has been suggested that the emergence of women writers is to be explained by the opening of literary society which had been closed and restrictive; that it can be related to the shift in the balance between vernacular and Latin in favour of the vernacular, the rise of the professional writer (e.g. Aretino) and of artist-writers (Vasari, Cellini).

Even among adult males, however, the creative élite is not a random sample. It is affected by geographical and social origin. Dividing Italy into seven regions, it is distributed as follows: 26 per cent of the élite come from Tuscany; 23 per cent from the Veneto; 18 per cent from the States of the Church; 11 per cent from Lombardy; 7 per cent from South Italy; 1·5 per cent from Piedmont; 1 per cent from Liguria. Another 7 per cent came from outside Italy altogether, the remaining 5.5 per cent being of unknown origin.

The significance of these percentages should become apparent by juxtaposing them with the total populations of those areas (below p. 301). We can divide regions into those which produce more élite than their share, and those which produce less. *a.* Tuscany (10 per cent population, 26 per cent élite); Veneto (20 per cent population, 23 per cent élite); States of the Church (15 per cent population, 18 per cent élite); Lombardy (10 per cent population, 11 per cent élite); *b.* South Italy (30 per cent population, 7 per cent élite); Piedmont (10 per cent population, 1·5 per cent élite); Liguria (5 per cent population, 1 per cent élite). In other words, the Italian Renaissance is created by four regions, with just over half the population of Italy; the other half, from Piedmont to Sicily (a contrast to modern Italian history, this juxtaposition) is culturally underdeveloped. The total population figures also make it clear that the Tuscan contribution (I suppose one has to call this 'creativity per capita'!) is much more spectacular than the Venetian, though the absolute figures are much the same.

Another striking regional variation is between regions where more of the élite practise the visual arts, compared to the rest. In Tuscany, the figures are 95 visual; 62 non-visual (60 per cent visual). In the Veneto, it is 75 visual to 62 non-visual (55 per cent visual). In Lombardy, 45 visual, 19 non-visual (70 per cent visual). The States of the Church are 54 visual to 54 non-visual, breaking exactly even. But in South Italy, it is 24 non-visual to 17 visual (58 per cent non-visual). Genoa has 4 humanists to 1 artist.

In other words, the region he is born in appears to affect the chances of any individual entering the creative élite, and also which part of it he enters. The size of the town a man is born in has a similar effect on his chances of entering the élite (though not, apparently, on which part). Let us divide towns into three categories. A large town, which has a population of 60,000 or more (there are seven of them: Florence, Venice, Milan, Bologna, Genoa, Naples, Palermo). A medium town goes from 10,000 to 55,000 (figures are to the nearest 5,000). A small town or village has a population of 5,000 or below. The élite are evenly distributed between these three categories; about 30 per cent from each, the remaining 10 per cent being unknown. However, something like 6 per cent of the population at most lived in large towns, and 7 per cent in medium towns. In other words, some 13 per cent of the population, living in towns of 10,000 or more people, form the reservoir from which 60 per cent of the élite is drawn.

Rome's poor contribution deserves emphasis. Only four artists and writers in the élite were born in Rome: a humanist, Lorenzo Valla; an architect-painter, Giulio Romano; a sculptor, Gian Cristoforo Romano; and a painter, Antoniazzo Romano. Of course, Rome was no more than the eighth city in Italy at this period, with a population rising to something like 55,000 before the sack of 1527; but 15 members of the élite were born in Ferrara, which was smaller (about 40,000); and seven in tiny Urbino, with a population of less than 5,000!*

---

* Raphael is the best known, but there is also the historian Polidore Virgil, the mathematician Commandino, the composers M. A. Cavazzoni and his son Girolamo, the painters G. Genga and G. Santi (Raphael's father). Bramante was born nearby.

Sculptors and architects tended to be born in regions where the stone was good for carving and building. In Tuscany, Isaia da Pisa came from Pisa, near the white marble on the west coast; Desiderio da Settignano, Antonio and Bernardo Rossellino, and Bartolomeo Ammanati all came from Settignano, a village just outside Florence where there were stone-quarries. Michelangelo was put out to nurse there with a stonecutter's wife – hence his joke, about sucking in his love of sculpture with his nurse's milk. Lombardy, with 10 per cent of the total élite, had 22 per cent of the sculptors and 25 per cent of the architects, again because it contained regions of good stone. Domenico Gaggini and Pietro Lombardo, founders of dynasties of sculptors and architects, both came from the Lake Lugano area; Domenico from Bissone, and Pietro from Carona. After Tuscany and Lombardy, a third region where sculptors and architects were 'produced' was Dalmatia, another region of good stone, outside Italy but close to it and linked to Venice in particular by economic ties. Luciano Laurana the architect and Francesco Laurana the sculptor both came, in all probability, from La Vrana in Dalmatia. The famous sculptor Ivan Duknovic (known to Italians as 'Giovanni Dalmata') came from Trogir in Dalmatia. The architect-sculptor Juraj Dalmatinac (called 'Giorgio da Sebenico' by Italians) came from Sibenik, also in Dalmatia.

These Dalmatian sculptors and architects are a reminder of the existence of artists and writers who worked in Italy but were born outside it. There are 41 of them in the élite. They are predominantly non-visual (31 to 10) as one might have expected in an age of great Italian achievement in the visual arts; the ten include (besides the sculptors and architects mentioned in the last paragraph) the painter Jacomart Baçó from Valencia, and the painter Giorgio Schiavone from Dalmatia. Twenty-one out of the 31 foreigners are musicians (compared to 28 Italian musicians in the élite); mostly Flemings like Dufay, Josquin, Isaak, Willaert, though Ramos de Pareja came from Spain and John Hothby (the Italians called him 'Ottobi') from England. There are some humanists, especially Greeks, such as Janos Argyropoulos, Cardinal Bessarion, Georgios Gemistos Plethon. There is a poet from Barcelona, Benedetto Gareth 'il Chariteo' (writing in Italian rather than Catalan).

These 41 foreign members of the élite are far from being the only artists and writers working in Italy at this time. At the court of Milan, nearly all the 40 singers named in the register of 1474 came from Flanders or Picardy. The court painter at Ferrara in the middle of the fifteenth century was one 'Michael the Hungarian' – this at much the same time that Masolino was working in Hungary. In the early sixteenth century, Greek icon painters, like Janos Platypodis and Markos Cauzo, both from Crete, can be found in Venice. Then there are relatively short visits by distinguished northern painters. Jean Fouquet worked in Italy in the 1440s; Petrus Christus was on the payroll of the duke of Milan in 1456; Justus of Ghent worked for Federico of Urbino.

In another sense of 'foreigner' some of the most distinguished artists and writers in Florence were foreign, i.e. they were born outside the city with which they were primarily associated. Leonardo Bruni came from Arezzo; Ficino from Figline in the Valdarno; Leonardo from Vinci; Masaccio from Castello S. Giovanni in the Valdarno; Poggio from Terranova in the Valdarno; Poliziano from Montepulciano, near Siena. Nor did Giorgione or Titian come from Venice. Giorgione was born in Castelfranco, Titian in Piero di Cadore. Being outsiders did they find it easier to innovate?

A key question in modern sociological research is that of social class, defined in terms of father's occupation. Whether or not 'classes' in the modern sense existed in Renaissance Italy (see p. 294), it may be interesting to inquire whether members of the élite were typical or untypical of the rest of the population in terms of social origin. It is disappointing to find that the 'not known' answer to this question is as high as 340 out of 600, or 57 per cent. However, while disastrously little is known (for example) about the social origin of the musicians, or the members of the élite born in the States of the Church, we do know something like half of the social origins of artists and writers in Tuscany and the Veneto. Another problem is that we cannot assume that the unknowns follow the same pattern as the knowns; the cases where we do know are more likely to be cases where the social origin is a high one, both because men may conceal a humble origin (as Aretino tried to conceal the fact that he was a shoemaker's son) and because there is more chance of men of high origin leaving some record whereby that origin can be known. A third problem is one of definition. Suppose we divide the population into five social groups: cleric; noble; merchant and professional; artisan and shopkeeper; peasant. (For problems raised by this classification, see p. 295 below.) Clerics can be omitted; they are known to have fathered only two of the élite, Filippino Lippi and Tullia d'Aragona, who can also be classified as the son of a painter and the daughter of a nobleman. The social origins of the élite are as follows: 114 are children of artisans/shopkeepers; 84 are children of nobles; 48 are children of merchants and professional men; 7 are children of peasants; 345 are of unknown origin; total 600. 'Peasants' include one miller (Scala's father) and one vine-grower (Taccola's father). The merchant/professional group is overwhelmingly professional, including 10 notaries (Brunelleschi's father among them); 9 lawyers (Machiavelli's father); 9 university professors (Flaminio's father); 7 doctors (Ficino's father), 35 professional men altogether. Nobles include Florentine and Venetian patricians who engaged in trade, which helps explain why only 13 fathers are classified as simple merchants. The artisan/shopkeeper group include 9 miscellaneous service occupations such as barber (Uccello's father); carrier; boatman; soldier. It also includes 6 shopkeepers who were not craftsmen, 4 poultry-sellers and 2 butchers. The other 99 fathers are all craftsmen of some kind. There are 24 painters, 13 goldsmiths, 9 masons, 7 architects, 7 sculptors, 7 carpenters. Sixteen of them are textile workers – 6 tailors, 5 weavers, 1 wool-comber, 1 cloth-shearer, 1 bleacher, 1 dyer and 1 tapestry-worker. There are 3 shoemakers, 2 saddlers, 2 tanners, 2 smiths and 2 glassmakers.

One general conclusion emerges from considering this motley collection of occupations. Omitting musicians from lack of data, one finds that the social origins of painters/sculptors/architects were very different from that of writers/scientists/humanists. The known fathers of painters/sculptors/architects include 96 artisans/shopkeepers, compared to 40 nobles/merchants/professionals. The fathers of writers/scientists/humanists include 95 nobles/merchants/professionals, compared to 7 artisans/shopkeepers. The contrast is a dramatic one.

Since the artisan/shopkeeper group is a large one, it may be useful to divide it into three: 1, artists; 2, artisans with some connexion with the arts, such as carpenter, mason, goldsmith;

3, artisans and shopkeepers unconnected with the arts, such as tailor or poultry-seller. The 96 artisan/shopkeeper fathers of artists break down into 36 artists; 34 artisans connected with the arts; 26 unconnected. There are no figures for the total number of artisans in Italy in each of these groups, so percentages cannot be worked out; however, it looks as if the nearer a craft is to painting or sculpture, the higher the chance of the craftsman's son becoming a painter or sculptor, It is also clear that the arts run in families. Thirty-eight per cent of the élite have 1 or more known relatives in one or another of the seven fields, usually a related one; 10 per cent have 3 or more relatives in such fields. Some examples are extremely well known; that Raphael was the son of an artist, for example. Or the existence of the Bellini family; the father Jacopo, the sons Gentile and Giovanni, the son-in-law Mantegna. Or the brothers Pollaiuolo. Or the great sculptor-architect dynasties; that founded by the architect and sculptor Pietro Lombardo, for example – his sons Tullio I and Antonio I, and their descendants; or the Gagginis; or the Sangallos; or the Solaris, of whom four are members of the élite (Andrea, Cristoforo, Guiniforte, Pietro Antonio) – but the artists in the family ran into five generations at least. What I would like to emphasize is how common these dynasties were. Think of an artist of the Italian Renaissance; the odds are 50–50 that he has known artist relatives. Masaccio, for example. His brother Giovanni was also a painter; and Giovanni had two sons, one grandson and one great-grandson who were painters. They do not occur in histories of art; perhaps they do not deserve to do so; but they existed. They are, as Durkheim would say, a social fact. Similarly, Titian had a brother and a son who were artists; Tintoretto had two sons and a daughter who were artists. And one should not let the dissimilarity of names hide the fact that Gian Cristoforo Romano the sculptor was the son of another sculptor, Isaia da Pisa.

What is the significance of these artist-dynasties? Galton (above, p. 34) appealed to them as evidence of the importance of 'hereditary genius'. But a sociological explanation may be as relevant as a biological one. As in traditional Dahomey or Polynesia or other traditional societies, in the Italy of the period painting and sculpting were (like other crafts) family businesses. Children were encouraged to become painters and sculptors like their fathers. Occasionally there is evidence that parents thought in this way. The painter Sodoma called his son, hopefully, 'Apelles', but the boy died young. The architect Vincenzo Seregni called his son 'Vitruvio'; he survived and became an architect like his father. Guild regulations worked in the same direction by allowing cheap rates for the sons of masters. The fifteenth-century statutes of the painters' guild at Padua laid down that an apprentice joining the guild should pay 2-lire entry fee, but if he were a son, brother, nephew or grandson of a master already matriculated, then he paid only 20 small soldi – in other words, half-price. A master was allowed to take a relative as apprentice without charging him. Another point in favour of the sociological as against the biological explanation of artist dynasties is a statistical one. In the case of the visual arts, 48 per cent of the élite had known artist relatives. In the case of the other arts, the proportion sinks to 27 per cent. But the literary arts were not organized on family lines; hence the difference between the two percentages must be the work of social forces.

All this information about the geographical and social origins of artists and writers can be related to a general theory of why the Renaissance happened in Italy. Let us assume that social forces cannot produce great artists but can frustrate them. Art and literature flourish in the places and times in which abilities are frustrated least. In early modern Europe there were two major kinds of frustration, operating at the opposite ends of the social scale, discriminating against the able sons of nobles and of peasants. Italy was no exception here.

In the first place, a talented but well-born child might be unable to become a painter or sculptor because these occupations were considered beneath him. Vasari tells several stories about parental opposition. He says that when Brunelleschi's father found that his son Filippo (see Pl. 1) had artistic inclinations, he was 'greatly displeased' because he had wanted Filippo to become a notary like himself or a physician like his great-grandfather.* Baldovinetti's family had long been merchants and young Alessandro became interested in art 'more

* But the anonymous life of Brunelleschi, some sixty years nearer the events, records that his father made no objection, 'as he was a man of discernment'.

or less against the will of his father, who would have liked him to have gone into business'. In the case of Michelangelo, the son of a magistrate, Vasari comments that his father 'probably' thought Michelangelo's interest in art unworthy of their old family; another pupil of Michelangelo's, Condivi, records that Michelangelo's father and uncles hated art and thought it shameful that their boy should practise it. Anyhow the figures speak for themselves. The known fathers of 320 painters/sculptors/architects include 40 nobles/merchants and professional men; the known fathers of 231 writers/scientists/ humanists include 95 nobles/merchants and professional men.[1]

At the other end of the social scale, it was difficult for the sons of peasants to become artists and writers because they would not know about these occupations, or could not easily acquire the necessary training. Ghiberti and Vasari have a story (which sounds like a myth) about the boy Giotto, who was a peasant's son, being set to mind the sheep and being discovered by Cimabue, who just happened to be passing, drawing on a rock with a piece of stone. Such a run of luck was virtually necessary for a peasant's son to become an artist; though Giotto had the advantage that his village was just 14 miles from Florence. Seven members of the élite are known to have been the sons of peasants. Scala the humanist was the son of a miller, who was probably well off; millers proverbially were. Taccola the engineer was the son of a vine-grower; how he got his opportunity is not known. Fra Angelico and the humanist Campano, who became a bishop, climbed the traditional ladder for poor men's sons, the ecclesiastical one. The remaining three are Castagno, Beccafumi, and Andrea Sansovino, and in each case stories about their 'discovery' have survived. Of Castagno the book of Antonio Billi says, 'he was taken from keeping animals by a Florentine citizen who found him drawing a sheep on a rock, and brought him to Florence.' This story sounds all too like the childhood of Giotto; Vasari tells a similar story, with additions. He says that Castagno came from Castagno, a village in the Mugello near Florence, and that, on the death of Castagno's father, his uncle put him to looking after cattle, but the boy saw a painter at work, and so began to draw on a wall with a piece of coal. This came to the notice of a certain Bernadetto de'Medici, who had property at Castagno, who gave him the opportunity to become an artist. Unfortunately, one of the few documented facts about Castagno's private life is that his father outlived him. Of course, because Vasari is wrong on a detail like that (just as both Antonio Billi and he say that Castagno murdered Domenico Veneziano, whereas Castagno died four years before Domenico), it does not mean that he is wrong about the discovery; the trouble is that the discovery of talent *is* a stereotype, and also that Vasari in general writes to glorify the Medici, and here is a Medici as fairy-godmother. In the cases of Beccafumi and Sansovino, we have only Vasari's word for the discovery. Beccafumi, the son of an agricultural labourer (Giacomo di Pace), came from the Sienese countryside near Montaperti. He was noticed by the landowner, a Sienese citizen called Lorenzo Beccafumi; was taken to Siena; and took his benefactor's name. This time it was the sand which the boy was drawing on : 'One day Lorenzo saw him drawing with a pointed stick in the sand of a little stream as he was keeping his sheep.' Andrea Contucci came from Monte San Savino near Arezzo, the son of a poor labourer : 'He kept cattle like Giotto, drawing in the sand and on the ground the beasts which he was watching.' He was found by the local podestà, Simone Vespucci, and taken to Florence for training.[2]

Whatever one thinks of the details of these stories, something nearly as dramatic must have happened for these artists to get the opportunity to be trained at all. In the case of Polidoro da Caravaggio, whose social origin we do not know, it is said that he discovered his vocation as a painter while working as a mason in the Vatican; one may suspect that if he had not discovered it before, it was because he came from a poor and rural family. But the best-authenticated discovery of talent is the case of Palladio. His father, a poor man, apprenticed his son to a stone-carver at Padua. The boy ran away after two years, to Vicenza, where he became a stone-carver's apprentice again. His gifts were noticed by the humanist nobleman G. G. Trissino, on whose house the young man was working, and Trissino had him educated.

Unlike the sons of nobles and peasants, the sons of artisans would not be discouraged or frustrated in these ways; and many of them would be used to thinking in a plastic manner from childhood, from having watched their fathers at work. The conclusion seems inescapable that for the visual arts to flourish in this period, a concentration of artisans was necessary, which meant large towns, numerous towns, or both. In the fifteenth and sixteenth centuries, the most highly urbanized regions in Europe were in Italy and the Netherlands; these are the regions where the greatest contributions to the visual arts were made. To produce the necessary concentration of artisans, towns had to be oriented towards craft-industrial production, rather than towards commerce or services. Within Italy, the city most oriented towards industry, Florence, made the greatest contribution to the arts; the cities least oriented in this direction, Rome and Naples, were the birthplaces of very few artists. If the preponderance of artisans within a city was a necessary condition of creativity in the visual arts, it was not a sufficient condition. Milan was as oriented towards industry as Florence (below p. 304) but only 15 of the élite were born there, compared with 91 in Florence. But it is curious to observe that *c.* 1500 Venice turned from trade to industry, and Venetian art began to overtake Florentine.

It should not be too difficult to explain why in literature, science and humanism, the sons of nobles and professional men predominate, with a few sons of apothecaries (Caro, Palmieri, Poggio) or rich merchants (Alciati, Niccoli). A university education was much more expensive than an apprenticeship. Social prejudice also discouraged other men's sons from making careers of this kind. It seems to have been as difficult for the son of an artisan to become a writer, humanist or scientist as for a peasant's son to become an artist. There are five definite cases in the élite. Aretino was a shoemaker's son; Burchiello, a carpenter's son; Doni, son of a scissors-maker; Guarino of Verona, son of a smith; Michele Savonarola, the son of a weaver. In social terms the creative élite was not one group but two, a visual group recruited from artisans and a literary group recruited from the upper classes. The composers, about whom we know much less, were usually foreigners. But there is one important qualification to make to this conclusion. The great innovators in the visual arts were not typical of the group in their social origin. They were not the sons of craftsmen. Brunelleschi, Masaccio and Leonardo were all the sons of notaries, and Michelangelo the son of a magistrate. Donatello was the son of a wool-comber, but his family was expatrician – a branch of the Bardi fallen on hard times.

Socially as well as geographically it was the outsiders, who were not brought up in the craft-tradition, who tended to be the innovators.

TRAINING

There were three main types of school in Italy at this time. The most numerous taught reading and writing. For arithmetic, children were sent to a special kind of school, the 'abacus school'; for example, that kept in late fifteenth-century Florence by Benedetto 'dell'Abbaco', which Leonardo may possibly have attended. To learn Latin, children were sent to a 'master of grammar', as the seven-year-old Niccolò Machiavelli was sent by his father in 1476. There they studied the 'Donatello', the late-classical textbook of Donatus. Two famous grammar-schools were kept by Guarino da Verona and Vittorino da Feltre. Some children were educated by private tutor, as the future Leo X (see Pl. 13) was educated by Poliziano; and others picked up their education as pages. The poet Serafino d'Aquila was a page of the count of Potenza, and the painter Giulio Campagnola was a page at the court of Ferrara.

Training, like recruitment, shows that artists and writers were in fact two cultures. Painters and sculptors were trained, like other craftsmen, by apprenticeship. Only one of them is likely to have been to university; the painter Carlo da Milano, described once as *artium doctor et pictor*. But scientists, humanists, and (to a lesser extent) writers tended to go to university. At least 45 per cent of them went; 32 out of 53 scientists, 46 out of 103 humanists, 25 out of 75 writers. Architects and composers do not quite belong to either culture and their training will be discussed separately after an account of apprenticeship and of universities has been given.

The process of training in a painter's workshop (see Pl. 16) was described at the beginning of the period by Cennini. He suggested that it should take thirteen years and that the apprentice needed:

To begin as a shop-boy studying for one year, to get practice in drawing on the little panel; next, to serve in the shop under some master, to learn how to work at all the branches which pertain to our profession; and to stay and begin the working up of colours; and to learn to boil the sizes, and grind the gessos; and to get experience in gessoing anconas, and modelling and scraping them; gilding and stamping; for the space of a good six years. Then to get experience in painting, embellishing with mordants, making cloths of gold, getting practice in working on the wall, for six more years, drawing all the time, never leaving off, either on holidays or on workdays.

Thirteen years' training is a long time; it should be related to the variety of tasks which a painter might be called on to perform at the beginning of the fifteenth century. Cennini expects painters to be asked to work on parchment, cloth, panel, silk, walls, glass, and iron; and to make devices out of gilded paper (for tournaments) into the bargain. All the same, thirteen years was probably a counsel of perfection. The thirteenth-century statutes of the painters' guild in Venice (which remained in force during the fifteenth and sixteenth centuries) laid down that a craftsman had to be an apprentice (*garzone*) for five to seven years, and a journeyman (*lavorante*) for two to three years, before being allowed to 'graduate', to make a 'masterpiece' and become a master (*maestro*), with the right to open his own shop. In other words, a maximum of ten years' training and a minimum of seven. These rules may also have been more ideal than reality.[4]

All the same, it is not surprising to find that painters often started young. Andrea del Sarto was seven (says Vasari) when he was apprenticed to a goldsmith. Titian was nine (says Dolce) when he was sent to work in the studio of Sebastiano Zuccato at Venice. Mantegna was ten when he entered Squarcione's shop, and Sodoma was ten when he was apprenticed to the Piedmontese painter Spanzotti. Uccello was already one of Ghiberti's shop-boys when he was eleven. Michelangelo was thirteen when he was apprenticed to Ghirlandaio, and Palladio was apprenticed to a stone-carver at thirteen. It looks as if Botticelli and Leonardo left things a little late, for Botticelli was still at school when he was thirteen, and Leonardo was about fourteen or fifteen when he was apprenticed to Verrocchio. Thus artists did not usually have time for many years at school, though it is likely that some went to abacus-school, as Brunelleschi, Luco della Robbia, Bramante and Leonardo almost certainly did.

In general, apprentices would form part of the extended family of their master, living in his house, getting their food and clothes from him. Sometimes the master was paid for his instruction. When Sodoma's father placed him with Spanzotti, he gave the painter 50 ducats to cover board, lodging, clothes and education for seven years. In 1467 a certain Giovanni di Uguccione agreed to pay Squarcione half a ducat a month plus the 'usual gifts' in return for training. On other occasions, the master paid the apprentice for his help. When Timoteo Viti entered the studio of Francia, he undertook to work for nothing the first year; for sixteen florins a quarter the second year; after this, to be paid piecework rates and to be able to leave when he pleased. Similarly, Michelangelo's contract with the Ghirlandaio workshop laid down that he was to receive 24 florins over three years: six in the first year, eight in the second, and ten in the third.

The fact that apprentices sometimes took their master's name, as in eighteenth-century Japan, is a reminder of the importance of the master by whom an artist was trained. Jacopo Sansovino was not the son but the pupil of Andrea Sansovino; Domenico Campagnola not the son but the pupil of Giulio Campagnola. Piero di Cosimo was so-called after his master Cosimo Rosselli. It is possible to identify whole chains of artists, each the pupil of the one before. Bicci di Lorenzo taught his son Neri di Bicci, who taught Cosimo Rosselli, who taught Piero di Cosimo, who taught Andrea del Sarto, who taught Pontormo, who taught Bronzino. The differences in style of each generation in this example shows that the system did not necessarily produce a conservative art. Again, Gentile da Fabriano taught Jacopo Bellini, who taught his sons Gentile (named after Jacopo's master) and Giovanni. Giovanni had a host of pupils, traditionally said to have included Giorgione and Titian. A few workshops seem to have been of central importance in art history; for example, Ghiberti's, Verrocchio's, and Raphael's. In Ghiberti's workshop were trained Donatello, Michelozzo, Uccello, Antonio Pollaiuolo, and possibly Masolino. In Verrocchio's, besides Leonardo, there were trained Botticini, Domenico Ghirlandaio, Lorenzo di Credi, and Perugino. Raphael's workshop (linked to Verroc-

chio's via Perugino) included Giulio Romano, Gianfrancesco
Penni, Giovanni da Udine, Polidoro da Caravaggio, Perino del
Vaga, and Lorenzo Lotti.

In the case of painters, an important part of the training was
the study and copying of the workshop collection of drawings,
which served to unify the shop style and maintain its traditions. A humanist described the process in the early fifteenth
century: 'When the apprentices are to be instructed by their
master . . . the painters follow the practice of giving them a
number of fine drawings and pictures as models of their art.'
Such drawings were an important part of a painter's capital,
and might be mentioned specially in wills, as they are in
Tura's will in 1471. It is possible that as deliberate individualism
in style came to be more highly prized (above, p. 45) these
drawings became less important. Vasari, describing the training
of Beccafumi at Siena, says that his master taught him 'with
the designs of some great painters which he had for his own
use, as is the practice of some masters unskilful in design . . .'
a comment suggesting that the practice was dying out.

Workshop drawings, for example of machines, might be
lettered in code to keep them secret. Leonardo's habit of writing
backwards is well known. A more recent discovery is a note-
book from the Ghiberti workshop written in a code which
replaces each letter by the preceding letter of the alphabet.[5]

For humanists and scientists (and to a lesser extent, writers,
for 'writer' was an amateur role) the equivalent of apprenticeship was a university education, as it was for lawyers. To join
the guild of judges and notaries in fifteenth-century Florence,
it was necessary to prove that one had studied law at university
for five years or more.

In 1420, there were about 13 universities in Italy (see Pl. 6):
Salerno, Bologna, Ferrara, Florence, Naples, Padua, Pavia,
Perugia, Piacenza, Pisa, the Roman court, Siena and Turin.
During the period, Pope Eugenius IV revived the City Univer-
sity of Rome (but Leo X merged it with that of the court).
Alfonso of Aragon founded a university at Catania, and
Lodovico Sforza revived the university at Milan, but the
Florentine *studio* was dissolved to the benefit of Pisa. Of these
universities, the most important by far was Padua. Fifty-two
members of the élite were educated at Padua, which was
particularly popular at the end of the period (17 of the élite

studied there between 1500 and 1520). The growth of Padua was encouraged by the Venetian government, in whose territory the university lay. They increased the salaries of the professors, forbade Venetians to study elsewhere, and made a period of study there a prerequisite for office. It was convenient to have a university outside the capital. Lodgings were cheap, and the prosperity which the university brought helped to secure the loyalty of a subject-town. It was not only Venetian subjects who went to Padua. Of the 52 élite who went there, about half were born in the Veneto. It attracted students of scientific subjects (natural philosophy and medicine) in particular; of the 53 'scientists' in the élite, at least 18 studied there. The next most popular university among the creative élite was Bologna, where 26 of them are known to have studied. The senior university of Italy, Bologna had been through a decline, but was reviving during the fifteenth century. Next came Ferrara, which catered for 12 of the élite. It had an international reputation for cheapness: a sixteenth-century German student wrote that it was commonly known as 'the poor man's standby' (*miserorum refugium*). Pavia (which serviced the state of Milan), Pisa (which serviced Florence), Siena, Perugia and Rome each accounted for about half-a-dozen of the élite. It is a pleasure to add that two of them were Oxford men, John Hothby and Paul of Venice. Their colleges are not known.

Students tended to go to university younger than they do now. Guicciardini went up to Ferrara when he was sixteen, going on later to Padua and Pisa. They began by studying 'arts', by which was meant the seven liberal arts, divided into the more elementary, grammar, logic and rhetoric (the *trivium*) and the more advanced, arithmetic, geometry, music and astronomy (the *quadrivium*). In the early fifteenth century, incidentally, the term *artista* meant not a painter or sculptor but a university student of the seven liberal arts; for example, the Greek humanist Janos Argyropoulos was styled *rector artistarum* at the university of Padua. The curriculum was the traditional medieval one, and formally nothing changed during this period. However, what is actually taught in a university (let alone what is studied) does not always correspond to what is officially on the curriculum. Recent research on British universities in the sixteenth and seventeenth centuries, based on the study of student notebooks, shows that a number of unofficial new subjects, such as history, had been introduced. No equivalent study of Italian universities has been made, but one may suspect that history, poetry and ethics, three of the 'humanities' which were not among the seven liberal arts, were studied at least as much as anything in the *quadrivium*. After arts, it was possible to go on and take one of three higher degrees: theology, law, or medicine.

In some ways going to university was like being apprenticed. The disputation by means of which a man became 'master of arts' was the equivalent of the 'masterpiece'. A master of arts had the right of teaching his subject, in other words he was a member of the guild with the right to set up shop on his own. But there was one great difference between students and apprentices. At university, teaching and learning were in Latin, the symbol of a learned and separate culture. Spies or 'wolves' (*lupi*) ensured that Latin was spoken among the students, and those who broke the rule were fined. Another obvious difference between apprentices and students was the expense of university training. It has been calculated that in Tuscany c. 1400, it cost about 20 florins a year to keep a boy at university away from home, which was the price of keeping two servants for the same period. In addition, a new recruit to the doctorate would be expected to lay on expensive banquets for his colleagues. Guicciardini's doctorate of civil law at Pisa cost him 26 florins in 1505. Even Ferrara, the poor man's standby, was really the standby of the not so very well off.[6]

Architects and composers need to be considered apart from the rest. Architecture was not recognized as a separate craft, so there was no guild of architects and no apprenticeship system. Consequently, the men who designed buildings during this period had one thing in common: that they were formally trained in something else. Brunelleschi was trained as a goldsmith; Alberti was a university man, and a humanist; Michelozzo was trained as a sculptor; Antonio di Sangallo the elder was trained as a carpenter. It is likely but not certain that Coducci (whose brother was a stonemason) and Pietro Lombardo (who joined the mason's guild at Venice) were trained in that craft, from which most of the designers of Gothic cathedrals had come. Palladio was apprenticed to a stone-carver.

The fact that there was no formal training in the study of Roman architecture does not mean that all the architects in the élite had to start from scratch, though Brunelleschi perhaps did. The analogy with universities holds; there were opportunities for informal training. Bramante's workshop in Rome was the place where Antonio da Sangallo, the younger Giulio Romano, Peruzzi and Raphael learned how to build; its importance in the history of architecture is something like that of Ghiberti's workshop in Florence for sculpture a hundred years before. Other famous architects were trained by men who, whether they called themselves sculptors or masons, designed buildings in Renaissance style. Bartolomeo Bon was trained by Coducci; Jacopo Sansovino by Andrea Sansovino; Antonio and Tullio Lombardo by their father Pietro; and Sammicheli was the son and nephew of architects.[7]

Composers were not distinguished from performers, but performers had to be taught how to sing and play. A number of composers went to choirschool in the Netherlands; Josquin des Près was a choirboy at St Quentin. Hothby taught grammar, arithmetic and music at a school attached to Lucca cathedral, presumably for the choirboys. Theory of music was part of the *quadrivium* at university, and several composers in the élite had degrees. Tinctoris was a doctor of law and theology, and Dufay was a bachelor of canon law. Formally there was no training in composition, but informally the circle of Okeghem, in the Netherlands, was the equivalent of the workshop of Ghiberti and Bramante; his pupils (to mention only members of the élite, composers who worked in Italy) included Alexander Agricola, Antoine Brumel, Loyset Compère, Gasper van Weerbecke, and, probably, Josquin des Près. From Josquin there is a kind of apostolic succession of master-pupil relationships linking the great Netherlanders to Italian composers and them to seventeenth-century Germany. Josquin taught Mouton, who taught Willaert, who taught Andrea Gabrieli, who (at the limit of our period) taught Giovanni Gabrieli, who taught Schütz.

To sum up: in Italy at this time there were two cultures, two systems of training, apprenticeship and university, manual and intellectual, Italian and Latin. Even in architecture and music it is easy to pick out which ladder an individual has climbed. The existence of this double system raises certain problems for the cultural historian. If artists were such 'early leavers', how did they acquire the familiarity with antiquity which is shown by paintings, sculptures and buildings? What about the famous 'universal man' of the Renaissance? Has he any existence outside the imagination of nineteenth-century historians?

Writers on art in the period were well aware of the relevance of higher education for artists. Ghiberti wanted painters and sculptors to study grammar, geometry, arithmetic, astronomy, philosophy, history, medicine, anatomy, perspective and 'theoretical design'. Alberti wanted painters to study the liberal arts, especially geometry, and the humanities, rhetoric, poetry and history. He wanted architects to study painting and mathematics and acquire a 'tincture' of all the liberal arts. Filarete wanted the architect to know about music and astrology:

> For when he orders and builds a thing, he should see that it is begun under a good planet and constellation. He also needs music so that he will know how to harmonize the members with the parts of a building.

The ideal sculptor for Gauricus would be 'well-read' (*litteratus*) and skilled in arithmetic, music and geometry.[8]

The problem for the historian is to discover whether it was in fact possible to acquire this knowledge at school, by the age of about twelve, or in the workshop, as well as at university. For it is unlikely that any 'academies' for the training of artists existed before the very end of the period at the earliest. The most famous description of such an academy, that of the sculpture garden in S. Marco in the time of Lorenzo de'Medici, given by Vasari in his *Lives*, has turned out to be extremely suspect. The existence of the academies associated with Leonardo and Bandinelli is also doubtful.[9]

One important piece of evidence for the intellectual horizons of fifteenth-century artists comes from the inventory of the goods of Giuliano and Benedetto da Maiano, made in 1498. Between them they owned 29 books. More than half of the books were religious; a Bible, a life of St Jerome, a book of the miracles of Our Lady were among them. Among the secular books there were the two Florentine favourites, Dante and Boccaccio; and a history of Florence, whose author is not named. Classical antiquity is represented by a life of Alexander, and three decades of Livy. This kind of mixture, predominantly traditional in orientation but with some tincture of the new learning, is rather similar to the intellectual interests of Florentine merchants in the early fifteenth century, as shown in their libraries. Artists with these kinds of book in their possession were clearly interested in the classical past, and not only in its style – though that kind of interest can be documented from inventories too. At the time of his death, Neroccio de'Landi owned several pieces of antique marble sculpture, and 43 plaster casts of fragments. The most conspicuous absence from the da Maiano library is of anything concerned with classical mythology; an Ovid's *Metamorphoses* or a Boccaccio's *Genealogy of the Gods*. Artists with such a library would have been more at home with religious paintings and sculptures than with scenes from the lives of the Greek and Roman gods. One wonders whether Botticelli, who was of the same generation, city and social origin as the da Maianos, had a collection of books very different from theirs. If not, then the role of a patron or his adviser must have been crucial in the creation of mythologies like the *Birth of Venus*, and conversations with the patron are likely to have been an important part of an artist's education.

That modest collection of 29 books needs to be set in time. In 1498, printing had been established in Italy for thirty years. It is unlikely that artists early in the fifteenth century could have amassed so many books. But there is quite an amount of sixteenth-century evidence suggesting that some artists, at least, were well educated. A recently-discovered list reveals that Leonardo had 116 books in his possession *c.* 1503; books in Latin and Italian, including three Latin grammars, some modern Italian literature (Burchiello, Masuccio Salernitano, Pulci), some of the Fathers (Augustine, Ambrose) and books on anatomy, astrology, cosmography and mathematics. It would be foolish to take Leonardo as typical of anything, but there is a fair amount of sixteenth-century evidence besides this. Bramante, Bronzino, Raphael (and of course Michelangelo) all wrote poetry. Giulio Campagnola and Giovanni Giocondo both knew Greek as well as Latin. Vasari was tutored by the humanist Piero Valeriano. A few artists are known to have gone to grammar school; Michelangelo, who insisted on leaving to become apprenticed; Paris Bordone; and Pontormo. Some clues to the education of artists may be obtained from the study of their handwriting. In the fifteenth century, artists tended to write *alla mercantesca*, in the style of merchants and artisans, a kind of handwriting which was probably taught in the abacus school. In the sixteenth century, a number of artists, including Raphael and Michelangelo, wrote in the new italic style. In other words, it is likely that the education as well as the status of the artist rose during the period.[10]

The second problem raised by the coexistence in the period of two separate systems of training is that of the universal man, fact or fiction. The idea of the universal man certainly existed in this period. One character in Palmieri's dialogue *On civil life* (c. 1435) remarks how 'A man can learn many things, and make himself universal in many excellent arts (*farsi universale di più arti excellenti*).' The most famous exposition of the idea is, of course, Castiglione's *Courtier* (published 1528), in which the speakers expect the perfect courtier to be able to fight and dance, paint and sing, write poems and advise his prince. But this is all theory. Alberti, Leonardo and Michelangelo all produced spectacular achievements in several arts; but were there any others? Eighteen of the creative élite can be classified as having practised three arts or more.* They are as follows: Leon Battista Alberti, architect, humanist and writer, possibly medallist and painter; Silvestro Aquilano, sculptor, painter and architect; Donato Bramante, architect, engineer, painter and poet; Filippo Brunelleschi, architect, engineer, sculptor, painter; Antonio Filarete, architect, sculptor and writer; Lorenzo Ghiberti, sculptor, painter, architect and writer; Giovanni Giocondo, architect, engineer and humanist; Francesco di Giorgio, architect, engineer, painter and sculptor; Leonardo da Vinci, painter, sculptor, architect, scientist; Piero Ligorio, architect, painter, humanist; Guido Mazzoni, sculptor, painter and theatrical producer; Michelangelo, painter, sculptor, architect and writer; Alessandro Piccolomini, writer, humanist, scientist; Sebastiano Serlio, architect, painter, writer; Antonio

* Counting only seven arts: painter, sculptor, architect, writer, humanist, scientist, composer. Engineers count as scientists; makers of woodcuts as painters; woodcarvers as sculptors. Such a classifica-tion tends to play down the many-sidedness of the creative élite rather than exaggerate it.

Tebaldeo, writer, humanist and composer; Giorgio Vasari, painter, writer, sculptor, architect; Lorenzo Vecchietta, painter, sculptor and architect; Bernardo Zenale, painter, architect and writer.

About half of these eighteen universal men were Tuscans; about half were the sons of upper-class fathers (nobles, merchants and professional men); no less than fifteen of them were, among other things, architects. Either architecture attracted universal men, or it created them. This is not surprising since architecture was the bridge between science (since the architect needed to know mechanics), sculpture (since he worked with stone), and humanism (since he needed to know the classical vocabulary of Renaissance architecture). A look at this list suggests that it is probably more correct to explain many-sidedness in terms of the tradition of the non-specialist crafts-man, than in terms of the gifted amateur. The theory and the practice of the universal man coexisted without much contact. Of all the eighteen, only one, Alberti, fits easily into the gifted amateur category. The greatest of all, Michelangelo, did not believe in universality. For example, he complained to his father in 1509 that painting was not his job – *non esser mia professione*. He created masterpieces in painting, architecture and poetry, while continuing to protest that he was just a sculptor.

THE ORGANIZATION OF THE ARTS

For painters and sculptors the fundamental unit was the work-shop, the *bottega*; a small group of men producing a wide variety of objects in collaboration, a great contrast to the specialist, individualist artist of later times. Although a distinc-tion had been drawn by the fourteenth century between painters of panels and frescoes, on the one hand, and painters of furniture on the other, during the fifteenth century one can still find Botticelli painting banners and *cassoni*; Tura painting horse trappings and furniture; Catena painting cabinets and bedsteads. Even in the sixteenth century, Bronzino painted a harpsichord cover for the duke of Urbino. To produce all these objects, masters often used to employ assistants, particularly popular masters or those who tended to paint large subjects.

Ghirlandaio, Perugino, the Bellinis, Fra Bartolomeo, and Raphael are all known to have had assistants (see Fig. 16). In his long working life it is reasonably certain that Giovanni Bellini employed 16 assistants, and he may have employed many more. Sometimes these 'boys' (*garzoni*) as they were called, irrespective of age, worked permanently in the shop; others were taken on for a particular job, and the patron might guarantee to pay their keep, as the duke of Ferrara promised Cosimo Tura in the contract for the painting of a chapel in 1469.

The workshop was often a family affair. A father, like Jacopo Bellini, would train his sons in the craft; he might take on other *garzoni*, but they would be treated (as apprentices in the fifteenth century usually were) as members of the extended family. They might marry the daughter of their master, as Mantegna married Jacopo Bellini's daughter, or as Battista Angolo married Torbido's daughter. When Jacopo Bellini died, he left Gentile as the head of the workshop, bequeathing him the sketchbooks and the unfinished commissions. Giovanni succeeded his brother Gentile; and Giovanni's nephew Vittore Belliniano succeeded him. When a painting is signed by the head of a workshop, it probably means, not that he painted it with his own hand, but that he took responsibility for it as being up to the standards of the shop. It is surely this form of organization which explains the high proportion of Renaissance artists whose relatives also practised the arts.[11]

Not all artists could afford to set up a workshop, with all its expenses for rent and equipment. Sometimes artists, like other small masters, dyers for example, joined together to do so. Usually, though not always, they acted like a trading company and pooled expenses and receipts. In 1431 Pesello and six other Florentine artists were members of the same 'company' (*compagnia*), as it was called. Other examples of business partnerships between painters are that between Baccio della Porta and Mariotto Albertinelli; and that between Giorgione and Catena. Such an association offered its members several advantages; not only the obvious sharing of expenses but also insurance against illness or defaulting clients. There may have been division of labour inside the shop. When there were shields and banners and beds to be painted as well as panels, it might be the case that some artists specialized in one kind of work.[12]

These habits of collaboration make it easier to understand how well-known artists could work on the same paintings. In Rome, Pisanello once finished a picture, of St John the Baptist, which Gentile da Fabriano had begun. In the Ovetari Chapel at Padua, four artists worked on the frescoes in pairs: Pizzolo and Mantegna, Antonio da Murano and Giovanni d'Allemagna. This practice continued till the end of the period. Pontormo made two paintings from cartoons by Michelangelo at a client's request. Michelangelo agreed to finish Torrigiani's statue of St Francis. This system of collaboration was clearly a force acting against deliberate individualism of style, and helps explain why it did not emerge earlier.

The organization of the workshops of sculptors was similar. Assistants were all the more necessary, since sculptures take longer to make and because the head of the shop might have more administrative duties than a painter. He might have to arrange for marble to be quarried in order to execute a particular commission, with the problem that if it turned out badly (as Michelangelo complains in his letters) hundreds of ducats might be wasted and it might be difficult to prove to the customer that the expenditure was necessary or even that it had taken place. As in the case of painting, there are well-known examples of the family business, such as the Gaggini and Solari families, and of the partnership, for example, between Donatello and Michelozzo.[13]

Architecture was, naturally, organized on a larger scale and with more division of labour than painting or sculpture. A relatively small palace like the Ca d'Oro in Venice had 27 craftsmen working on it in 1427. There would be masons (with two main subdivisions, hewing and laying); carpenters; unskilled workmen, to carry materials; and perhaps foremen. Co-ordination therefore became a problem. As Filarete put it, a building project is like a dance; everyone must work together in time (see Pl. 5). The man who ensured this was sometimes called the *architetto* in this period, and sometimes the *proto-maestro*, the chief of the master-masons. It is likely that the two names reflect two different conceptions of the architect's role: the designer, or the senior craftsman on the job.

Co-ordination involved considerable administrative work. Some-one had to arrange for all the supplies necessary for the work: lime, sand, brick, stone, wood, ropes, and so on; to appoint and pay the masters and other workmen; and, of course, to design the building. All this work could be organized in a number of different ways. In Venice, building firms, the equivalents of the painters' and sculptors' workshops, were usually small, because master-masons were not allowed to take more than three apprentices each. When a large building was needed, it was common for an entrepreneur, or *padrone*, to contract for the whole work and then subcontract with different workshops. At St Peter's in the 1520s and 1530s, there was one large shop with a whole staff of office workers: a *curatore*, a *computista*, two *mensuratori*, two *depositari*, a *segretario*, and others. But the scale of this enterprise must have made the whole organization untypical. Filarete recommends that there should be an architect, craftsmen, and one middleman between them, an agent or *commissario*. Alberti seems to have followed this system, employing Matteo de'Pasti as his agent in Rimini, Bernardo Rossellino as his agent in Rome, and Luca Fancelli as his agent in Mantua and in Florence.[14]

This division of labour has created problems for art-historians as well as the agents. It is difficult enough to assign respon-sibility to individuals for particular pieces of painting and sculpture, and much more difficult in the case of a building to know whether patron, architect, agent, master-mason or mason was responsible for a given detail. This difficulty is increased by the fact that it was not customary in this period for the architect to give his men measured drawings to work from. Many of his instructions were, as the life of Brunelleschi says, given *a bocca*, by word of mouth. We are lucky that Alberti did not stay at Rimini while S. Francesco was being built, but designed it by correspondence, some of which has survived. The agent, Matteo de'Pasti, was apparently thinking of altering the proportions of some pilasters, and Alberti wrote to stop him. There is a letter from de'Pasti to the client, Sigismondo Malatesta, saying that a drawing of the façade and of a capital had arrived from Alberti, and that he had shown it to 'all the masters and engineers'. Unfortunately there was one snag: in certain respects the drawing conflicted with a wooden model of the building which Alberti had previously provided. 'I hope to God that your lordship will come in time, and see the thing with your own eyes.' Later another craftsman working on S. Francesco wrote to Sigismondo asking permission to go to Rome and talk to Alberti about the vaulting.

The fact that architecture was such a co-operative enterprise must have acted as a brake on innovation. Since craftsmen were trained by older craftsmen, they learned tradition as well as techniques. When executing a design which was strange to them, if they were not closely supervised, they would be likely to normalize it. Michelozzo's design for the Medici Bank in Milan was executed by Lombard craftsmen in a local style. A detail, but a significant one, is the difference in proportions between capitals made for Brunelleschi in Florence while he was at hand, and one made in 1430 while he was away.[15]

Of the creative élite, 116 men practised two arts. Forty-one practised architecture and sculpture, 20 practised painting and sculpture, and 8 practised architecture and painting. This versatility of architects can be explained in terms of the organization of the arts. Building was a seasonal occupation, which stopped in winter. Since the role of the architect was a directing role, it could be taken up by men without any training as masons, who knew about the proportions of classical architecture but not about construction. Alberti is the obvious example of the amateur as architect, but Bramante, too, was no expert on construction, as the collapse of part of the Vatican illustrated.

Changes in the design of buildings are related to the appearance of a new kind of designer, the architect who had not been a mason. There was a similar development in shipbuilding at Venice. A group of senior ship carpenters were the men who usually designed the ships in the fifteenth century. In the sixteenth century, they were challenged by an amateur. The role of Alberti was played by the humanist Vettor Fausto, who proposed to the Senate the revival of the ancient quinquereme. He designed it, and it was launched in 1529.

The larger unit of organization for painters, sculptors and masons, but not architects, was the guild. Guilds had several functions. They regulated relations between employers, masters, journeymen and apprentices. They regulated standards of quality. They lent or gave money to members who needed it, collecting the money from subscriptions and bequests. They also organized religious services in honour of the patron of the guild. A favourite patron for guilds of painters was St Luke, because he was supposed to have painted the Virgin's portrait. Sometimes painters had a guild of their own, as at Padua or Venice. In other places painters formed part of a larger guild. In Florence they were part of the 'doctors and apothecaries' (*Medici e speziali*), though they had a social guild of their own, the Company of St Luke. In Bologna, they belonged to the guild of paper-makers. Florentine sculptors usually joined the guild of stone-workers, and Venetian sculptors the guild of the masons.

To gain a more vivid impression of the activities of a guild, it may be useful to look in more detail at the statutes of one of them, the painters of Padua, whose statutes were drawn up in the mid-fifteenth century.[16] The officers of the guild were a bursar, two stewards, a notary and a dean. On certain days they went in procession with 'our gonfalon', and members were fined for non-attendance. There was a rota to visit sick members, and encourage them to confession and communion; and there were fines for not attending funerals of members. Alms were given to the poor and to lepers through the guild. All this represented the religious side of the guild's activities. Then there were regulations about the training of apprentices. The master had to keep them for three years at least; and there was to be no poaching of apprentices 'by gifts or blandishments' (*donis vel blandimentis*). Then there was the insurance or poor-relief function; a poor master of the guild could sell a piece of work to the guild, which the bursar would try to sell 'as best he could' (*ut melius poterit*). Other guilds lent money; Botticelli, for example, was in debt to the Company of St Luke of Florence between 1503 and 1505. Vincenzo Catena left 200 ducats to the Venetian painters' guild for charitable purposes. Then there was the maintenance of standards; houses were inspected to see if work was being 'falsified' (*si falsificetur aliquod laborerium nostre artis*). This went with the usual examination of the candidates for masters; standards and fair prices were also maintained by the common practice of calling in artists to value the work of another – artistic judgement by one's peers – when there was a dispute between artist and patron. For example, in 1508, Bastiani, Carpaccio and Belliniano were called in to value Giorgione's frescoes for the Fondaco dei Tedeschi at Venice. Finally, there was the restrictive side of the guild's activities. The Padua statutes forbade members to give or sell anything pertaining to the craft to non-members; they laid down that no work was to be brought from another district to Padua to sell, and three days only were allowed for the transit of such 'alien' work through the guild territories. Similarly, the Venetian *scuole* became more restrictive in the fifteenth century, laying down in 1436 that to be accepted into the guild one had to be an inhabitant of Venice. It has been suggested that when the Tuscan Castagno was working in S. Marco at Venice, he had to be supervised by Giambono because Giambono was a Venetian. When Dürer was in Venice in 1506, he commented on the unfriendliness of the painters: 'They have summoned me three times before the magistrates, and I have had to pay four florins to their guild.' In Florence, however, the guild did not have such power; the Florentine government would not allow it to force all craftsmen to join; hence 'foreigners' could come and work in Florence, and some artists, like Botticelli, only entered a guild at the end of their careers. This more liberal policy, allowing the fertilization of local tradition from outside, may have had something to do with Florence's cultural lead.[17]

Writers, humanists, scientists and musicians had no guilds and no workshops. The nearest analogy to the guild in their world was the university, a term which meant 'association' and was sometimes applied to painters' guilds in the period. But the analogy between students and apprentices, tempting as it is, breaks down in some respects. Most of the students did not go to university to learn how to be professors, but looked forward to careers in Church and State. The students had more power in Italian universities than apprentices did in guilds. Bernardo Torni, who taught philosophy and medicine at the university of Pisa, had his salary raised as a result of a petition from the students. The university was not geared to the production of books by the dons. Their job was lecturing, and their books were something of a hobby.

Humanists and scientists had universities to work in, but writers had no form of organization at all. Writing was something a man did, whereas what he really *was* was a soldier, a diplomat, or a bishop.

Among the few exceptions to this rule were the singers of tales, or *cantastorie*, improvisers of epic poetry, the survivals in Renaissance Italy of a form of culture we tend to associate with 'heroic ages' like Homeric Greece or the England of the age of Beowulf. And so, in this period, the writing of literature cannot be usefully regarded, like painting and sculpture (or like writing in the nineteenth century), as an industry. However, the reproduction of literature – the making of books – certainly can. Of course, some men who needed books simply copied them by hand, and others asked someone else to do the copying for them (as Coluccio Salutati asked Poggio), and as far as this was the case no 'organization of production' was needed. But in fifteenth-century Italy the production of manuscripts had become more industrialized than this. It was in the hands of *stationarii*, a word from which the modern English word 'stationer' is derived, and which then meant both 'bookseller' and 'organizer of a *scriptorium*', which one might perhaps define as a workshop for producing manuscripts. The term *stationarius* had both meanings because one man tended to perform both functions; that is, fifteenth-century booksellers, unlike modern ones, were responsible for making the books which they sold. *Stationarii* were members of guilds; in Florence, for example, they were, like painters, members of the Doctors and Apothecaries. The most famous Renaissance bookseller was the Florentine Vespasiano da Bisticci, who immortalized himself by writing the lives of his customers. From this book one gains the impression of a highly-organized manuscript-copying system, reminiscent in this respect of the Rome of Cicero and Atticus.

For example, in his life of Cosimo de'Medici, Vespasiano says that he built up Cosimo's library, and that to do this he engaged 45 scribes, who were able to complete 200 volumes in 22 months. This would average out at one scribe taking five months to write one volume; but what is impressive is not the speed of the individual copyist (who seems rather slow, but perhaps it was a special order, or the volumes were big ones) as the fact that a man could go to a bookseller and have 200 volumes written for him in less than two years. One wonders how the actual writing was organized; whether popular works were ever copied by 10 or 20 scribes writing from dictation, or whether the whole industry was organized on a 'putting-out' basis, with each scribe turning up at the bookseller's every few months to collect a volume to be copied and supplies of vellum, and then going back to his house to write. This latter method seems likely in view of the fact that scribe was often a part-time occupation, usually paid by the quintern. Vespasiano da Bisticci employed as scribes men who were notaries (Ser Giovanni da Stia, Ser Niçcolò di Berto Martini) and priests (Piero Strozzi).[18]

From the mid-fifteenth century on, this copying system had to compete with another: with books which were 'written' mechanically, as early printed books sometimes describe themselves. In 1465, two German clerics called Sweynheym and Pannartz arrived at the Benedictine monastery of Subiaco, a few miles east of Rome, and set up a press there, the first in Italy. Two years later they moved to Rome itself. It has been estimated that in five years they produced 12,000 volumes, a number which Vespasiano would have had to find 1,000 scribes to equal in the time. It is clear that the new machine was a formidable competitor; and by the end of the century, some 150 presses had been founded in Italy. It is not surprising that Vespasiano, who had for the new method something of the contempt a skilled wheelwright might have felt for the horseless carriage, gave up bookselling in disgust and retired to his country estate to relive the past.

Other scribes were more adaptable; some became printers themselves, like Dominico de'Lapi and Taddeo Crivelli, who produced the famous Bologna Ptolemy in 1477. Just as early printed books often look rather like manuscripts (and have illuminated initials in some cases) so the printers, a new occupation, stepped into the shoes of the *stationarii*. Like them they tended to unite roles which in the twentieth century we tend to think of as distinct: that of producing books and that of selling them. They soon added a third, that of 'publisher', that is, that of a man who issues under his imprint, or takes responsibility for, books which were in fact printed by someone else. In Venice c. 1500, Lucantonio Giunta is an example of a publisher rather than a printer. For example, the colophon of the 1497 edition of Ovid's *Metamorphoses* declares that it was printed by 'Zoare Rosso' at the instance of (*ad instantio del*) Giunta. Printers sometimes added a fourth role: that of merchants in commodities other than books.

The effects of the invention of printing on the organization of literature were enormous. In the first place, it was a disaster to scribes and *stationarii* who were not prepared to adapt themselves and begin their careers again. In the second place, the expansion of the production of books meant the creation of new roles into which the creative writer might fit. Libraries became bigger; librarians were needed. Several members of the creative élite were occupied as librarians; the philosopher Agostino Steuco, for example, was librarian to cardinals Marino and Domenico Grimani. The Venetian poet and historian Andrea Navagero was librarian of the Marciana. The grammarian Giovanni Tortelli was the first Vatican librarian (to Pope Nicholas v); the humanist Bartolomeo Platina was librarian to Cardinal Bessarion, and also Vatican librarian. Again, the rise of printing created the role of corrector for the press, a useful part-time occupation for a writer. Platina was a corrector for Sweynheym and Pannartz at Rome; the humanist Giorgio Merula was corrector for the Speyers, the first press to be established in Venice; the humanist Giovanni Antonio Campano was corrector for the press at Rome. By the sixteenth century, publishers had begun to ask writers to translate books, or even to write them; a new form of literary patronage which was to lead to the rise of the professional writer. In fact, in the mid-sixteenth century, especially at Venice, there are writers who can be described as professional (*poligrafi*, they were called). Aretino is the most famous of them, but there is a group of some half-a-dozen or so, most of whom moved in his orbit: his secretary Niccolò Franco; his sometime friend and sometime enemy Anton Francesco Doni; Lodovico Dolce; Giuseppe Betussi; Girolamo Ruscelli; Francesco Sansovino. The firm of Giolito at Venice, which concentrated on books which were popular rather than scholarly at a time when this was still unusual, seems to have been a pioneer in its use of professional writers; Betussi and Dolce were both in Giolito service, editing, translating and writing. In spite of this handful of examples at the end of the period, one can still say that, in general, writing, unlike painting and sculpting, was an amateur and not a professional role.

Music was like literature in that reproduction was organized but production was not. Churches had their choirs, towns their drummers and pipers, and courts had both, but the role of composer, like the role of writer, was scarcely recognized. Although the word *compositore* is sometimes used, the more common term is the more general *musico*, which makes no distinction between the man who invents a tune and the man who plays it. In their own day, all the 49 composers in the creative élite were thought of as writers on the theory of music, or as singers, or as players of instruments, as some of their names, like Alfonso della Viola and Antonio degli Organi, may remind us.

Some 25 per cent of the élite travelled a great deal. Some travelled because they were unsuccessful wherever they settled, like Lorenzo Lotto, who worked in Venice, Treviso, Bergamo, Rome, Ancona and Loreto. Others travelled because they were successful, and received invitations from abroad, like Jacopo de'Barbari, who worked in Nuremberg, Naumburg, Wittenberg, Weimar, Frankfurt-on-Oder and Malines.

That architects were hardly ever sedentary is no surprise. Humanists and composers tended to be more mobile than painters and sculptors, perhaps because it was their personal services which were needed, while painters and sculptors could always send their work off but stay at home themselves. One example of the mobile humanist is Pomponio Leto, whose career took him to Salerno, Rome, Venice, Germany and Muscovy; but he is easily beaten by Francesco Filelfo, who visited Germany, Hungary, Poland and Constantinople, and in Italy worked in Padua, Venice, Vicenza, Bologna, Siena, Milan, Pavia, Florence and Rome. From Burckhardt to the present, the theme of the wandering humanist has received much emphasis. One historian working on humanism has recently expressed scepticism about its importance, and wondered whether the stay-at-home humanists were just as numerous and important. Of the 103 humanists in the élite, 14 were extremely sedentary; 29 were fairly sedentary; 12 were fairly mobile; 46 were extremely mobile. The remaining two were unclassifiable. Thus the balance tips in favour of the wanderers. Printers also sometimes travelled widely; between 1506 and 1515 the printer Simon Bevilaqua worked in Venice, Saluzzo, Cuneo, Novi Ligure, Savona and Lyons. If humanists and printers were on the road from year to year, other men connected with the arts travelled from day to day: actors, singers of tales and pedlars of books, not to mention students in vacation. There may have been some artists in this class too: the fifteenth-century painter Dario da Udine is described in a document as *pictor vagabundus*.[19]

One important aspect of the organization of the arts is the extent to which they were full-time or part-time, amateur or professional occupations. It has already been suggested that painting, sculpture and music were usually professional and full-time occupations, that writing was usually amateur and part-time, and that architects usually practised another art besides architecture. There are a number of points to add to this. Humanists were usually professional, but amateurs like Lorenzo de'Medici or Cyriac of Ancona also existed. A scientist was an amateur whose professional description was usually 'doctor', 'university teacher' or 'cleric'. The role of the clergy in the creative élite needs clarification. At least 78 out of the 600 were clerics, and there may have been a few more, because it is not always easy to tell whether a man was in orders or not. These 78 include 22 writers, 22 humanists, 20 composers, 7 scientists (Paul of Venice, for example), 6 painters, of whom Fra Angelico and Fra Bartolomeo are the most famous, and 1 architect, Fra Giovanni Giocondo. Only 15 of out these 78 were born in large towns, such a surprisingly small proportion as to suggest that the Church still performed an important function in providing cultural opportunities for boys who would otherwise have missed them.[20]

An obvious part-time occupation for the needy writer or humanist was teaching. At least 45 out of the 178 writers and humanists in the élite taught at schools or universities or were engaged as private tutors; Poliziano was tutor to Piero de'Medici, and Matteo Bandello was tutor to Lucrezia Gonzaga. For some humanists, like Vittorino da Feltre and Guarino of Verona, teaching was a vocation. For others it was a fate to be cursed; as one humanist wrote to Poliziano in 1480, 'I, who until recently enjoyed the friendship of princes, have now, because of my evil star, opened a school.'[21]

Another common part-time employment for writers and humanists was that of secretary, because of their skill in rhetoric and so in letter-writing. Sometimes the office was a public one: Bruni and Poggio were chancellors of Florence. Chariteo and Pontano were secretaries of state at Naples. Sometimes the job was more like what we would call 'private secretary', as the poet Annibale Caro was secretary to various members of the Farnese family, or the novelist Masuccio Salernitano to prince Roberto Sanseverino. A number of writers followed military or political careers, but this was rather because they were noblemen than because they were writers, and not a way to earn a living: among poets, for example, Boiardo was governor of Reggio, Leonardo Giustinian was one of the council of ten at Venice, and Lorenzo de'Medici governed Florence. In the case of scientists, a number were, like humanists, teachers, especially at university; doctor was another part-time occupation for them, in 22 cases out of the 53, including men more distinguished for physics than physic, like Giovanni Marliani, who wrote on mechanics. 'Doctor' was a recognized social role, whereas 'scientist' was not.

In a few cases, artists' and writers' other occupations are surprising, not to say bizarre. Mariotto Albertinelli was at one time an innkeeper; Niccolò dell'Abbate, Platina and Calcagnini were all soldiers. Giorgio Schiavone sold salt and cheese. Catena possibly sold drugs and spices, and Caroto kept an apothecaries' shop; this combination of art and drugs may be explained by the fact that apothecaries sold some artists' materials, hence the Florentine painters were matriculated in the guild of the Doctors and Apothecaries. The Fogolino brothers combined their work as painters with that of spies, for the Venetians in Trento. Squarcialupi combined playing the organ with keeping a butcher's shop. Burchiello was a barber and a poet. Taccola was a sculptor, an engineer and a notary. Cecchi and Grazzini, besides being dramatists, were a wool-merchant and an apothecary respectively. Many of these part-time occupations are a useful reminder to the modern reader not to attribute too high a status to the artists and writers of the period.

THE STATUS OF THE ARTS

Unlike writer and scientist, the roles of painter, sculptor, architect, humanist and composer were usually professional ones. The problem of the status to be given these roles was a special case of the problem of accommodating in the social structure, as the division of labour progressed, all roles other than those of priest, knight and peasant – those who prayed, fought and

worked – which were the only roles recognized in the earlier
Middle Ages. If the status of an artist was ambiguous, so was
that of a merchant. And just as Italian society (in some regions)
had gone further towards the social acceptance of the merchant
than most of Europe had, so it was in Italy that the status of
the artist seems to rise furthest. Just how far this trend had
gone in the period must now be discussed. Status of course is
something intangible, let alone measurable, but the attempt
must be made.[22]

Artists in the Renaissance regularly declared that they had,
or ought to have had, a high status. Cennini at the beginning
of the period and Leonardo towards its end made similar points.
They compared the painter with the poet; both the painter
and the poet use their imagination, their *fantasia*, for their
creations. Another point in favour of the high status of painting
(a revealing one for the way in which Renaissance men thought)
was that the painter could wear fine clothes or listen to music
while he painted. As Cennini put it, 'know that painting on
panel is a gentleman's job, for you can do what you want with
velvet on your back.' And Leonardo: 'The painter sits at his
ease in front of his work, dressed as he pleases, and moves his
light brush with the beautiful colours . . . often accompanied
by musicians or readers of various beautiful works.' Alberti, in
his treatise on painting, offered several other arguments which
remained popular throughout the period. There was the argument from the example of antiquity: Alexander the Great
prized Apelles, distinguished Roman citizens had their sons
taught to paint, and works of art fetched high prices. There
was the argument from training; painters need to study such
high-status subjects as geometry and rhetoric.

Some people who were not painters seem to have accepted
the claim that painters were not ordinary craftsmen. Guarino
of Verona wrote a poem in praise of Pisanello, and the court
poet of Ferrara dedicated a Latin elegy to Cosimo Tura.
St Antonino, archbishop of Florence, noted in his *Summa* that
whereas in most occupations the just price for a piece of work
depended essentially on the time and materials employed:

Painters claim, more or less reasonably, to be paid the salary
of their art not only by the amount of work, but more in

proportion to their application and greater expertness in their trade.

In Castiglione's *Courtier* one of the speakers, Count Lodovico, declares that the ideal courtier must know how to draw and paint. A few Venetian patricians of the early sixteenth century actually did. When Federico of Mantua gave Giulio Romano (see Pl. 3) a house, the deed of gift opened with a brave statement of the honour due to painting:

Among the famous arts of mortal men it has always seemed to us that the most glorious (*praeclarissimus*) is painting . . . we have noticed that Alexander of Macedon thought it of no small dignity, since he wished to be painted by a certain Apelles.[23]

A few painters were undoubtedly of high status, according to the criteria of the time. Several were knighted or ennobled by their patrons. The best-known example is that of Titian who was made a count (*Pfalzgraf*) by Charles V in 1533. Mantegna was made a count by Pope Innocent VIII, and Gentile Bellini by the Emperor Frederick III. Crivelli was knighted by Ferdinand prince of Capua; Sodoma, by Leo X; Pordenone, by the King of Hungary; and Dello, by the King of Spain. For the patron it was a cheap way of rewarding service, but for the artist the honour was real enough. Some painters held offices which conferred status as well as income. Giulio Romano held office at the court of Mantua; Giovanni da Udine and Sebastiano del Piombo held office in the Church. Sebastiano's nickname, 'The Lead', was in fact a reference to his office of Keeper of the Seal. Other painters held civic office. Signorelli was one of the priors of Cortona; Perugino, one of the priors of Perugia; Caporali was 'Captain of the People' at Perugia; Jacopo Bassano, consul of Bassano; Piero della Francesca and Giovanni da Udine were town councillors of Borgo S. Sepolcro and Udine respectively.

Again, a few painters are known to have become rich. Pisanello inherited wealth, but Tura, Zenale, Perugino, Mantegna, Catena, Raphael and Titian all seem to have become rich by their painting. Wealth gave them status, and the prices they commanded show that painting was not held cheap. There is also the testimony of a visiting foreigner, Dürer, who wrote from Venice to his friend Pirckheimer: 'Here I am a gentleman, at home a sponger' (*Hie bin ich ein Herr, doheim ein Schmarotzer*).[23]

Similar evidence can be collected for the status of the sculptor and the architect. Ghiberti's programme of studies for sculptors, and Alberti's for architects, imply that these arts were among the liberal arts. A patent of Federico of Urbino pointed out that architecture is founded on arithmetic and geometry, which are among the most important of the seven liberal arts. Alberti suggested that architects should work only for men of quality, 'because your work loses its dignity by being done for mean persons'. The papal *motuproprio* of 1540, freeing sculptors from the need to belong to the guilds of 'mechanical craftsmen', remarked that sculptors 'were prized highly by the ancients' and called them 'men of learning and science' (*viri studiosi et scientifici*). Some sculptors, Antonio Rizzo for example, had poems addressed to them. Some sculptors were ennobled. King Mátyás (Matthias Corvinus) of Hungary ennobled the sculptor Ivan Duknovic (Giovanni Dalmata, who worked also in Rome) and even gave him a castle. Charles VIII of France ennobled Guido Mazzoni. Charles V made Leone Leoni a knight of Santiago. Bandinelli was made a knight of Santiago by Charles V and a knight of St Peter by Clement VII. Some sculptors and architects are known to have become rich by practising their arts. Ghiberti bought an estate, complete with manor-house, tower, moat and drawbridge. Amadeo, Bambaja, Brunelleschi, Cronaca, the brothers da Maiano and Bernardo Rossellino were also prosperous.[24]

Composers of the period, like artists, sometimes compared themselves to poets: a way of drawing attention to their existence, since they were in danger of being squeezed out between theorists of music on one side and skilled performers on the other. Tinctoris, who was a composer and a theorist, dedicated his treatise on modes to two composers, Ockeghem and Busnois, a revolutionary thing to do since the traditional view was that theory was the master, and practice (that is, composition as well as playing) was only the servant. A number of composers were treated with honour in Italy at this time, but it is not easy to decide whether this was a tribute to their

compositions or their performances – probably the latter. The
humanists Guarino and Beroaldo wrote epigrams in praise of
the lutenist Piero Bono, and medals were struck in his honour.
When Squarcialupi died, Ficino and Poliziano wrote elegies,
Lorenzo de'Medici put up a bust of him in the cathedral, and
composed the epitaph. Lorenzo's son Pope Leo x made the
lutenist Gian Maria Giudeo a count, and Philip the Handsome
of Burgundy did the same for the singer-composer Marbriano
da Orto. Duke Ercole of Ferrara treated Obrecht with respect,
as the preparations made for his arrival at Ferrara testify. At
the court of Mantua in Isabella's time, Cara and Tromboncino
were honoured members of a musical circle. In Venice, Willaert
(see Pl. 14), master of St Mark's chapel, died rich, and Zarlino,
also a master of St Mark's, had medals struck in his honour
by the Republic and ended his days as a bishop.[25]

The social status of Florentine humanists between 1390 and
1460 is the subject of a recent study by Martines. He argues
that humanists belonged to the top 10 per cent of Florentine
families. As indicators of status, Martines takes wealth, public
office, family and marriage, and the Florentine attitude towards
the humanist. He notes that Bruni, Poggio, Marsuppini, Manetti
and Palmieri were all wealthy; as for office, Bruni, Poggio and
Marsuppini were all chancellors of Florence; Manetti had a
distinguished career as a diplomat and administrator – for
example he was capitano of Pistoia; and Palmieri 'took office
at least 63 times'. Marsuppini, Manetti and Palmieri were born
into the upper class; Bruni (the son of a grain dealer) and
Poggio (the son of a poor apothecary) entered it through their
own efforts. All five made high-status marriages. The identity
of Bruni's wife's family is unknown, but he made a good
marriage for his son, into the Castellani family; Poggio married
into the Buondelmonti, Manetti into the Tobalducci, Marsuppini into the Corsini, and Palmieri into the Serragli. Finally,
Bruni, Marsuppini and Palmieri were all given grand state
funerals.[26]

This refreshingly precise and empirical study of the status
of humanists is a valuable corrective to a traditional image
which stressed their humble origins and later poverty. Of
course, it applies only to one city and two generations, and
other regional studies are needed to complete the picture.
Until they appear, a brief account of 32 non-Tuscan humanists

who flourished between 1420 and 1540 may be of some use.*

Of these 32 humanists, eight were the sons of noblemen; Pico, Francesco Barbaro, Andrea Navagero and Pius II are among them. One, Alciati, was the son of a wealthy merchant who held political office. Six were the sons of professional men: lawyers, doctors and other humanists. In five cases it is known that their fathers were from one of the lower classes; Guarino of Verona, for example, was the son of a smith. In 12 cases the status of the humanist's father does not seem to be known. So at least 15 out of the 32, nearly 50 per cent, had fairly high-status fathers. Four of them, as foreigners, were marginal to the Italian social structure anyway (Argyropoulos, Bessarion and Gemistos Pletho were all Greeks, and Leone Ebreo was a Portuguese Jew). Turning to their own careers, we find that three were ennobled: Bonfini by Lajos II of Hungary, Nifo by both Leo X and Charles V, Filelfo by Alfonso of Aragon. Twelve had distinguished careers as ambassadors or councillors to princes. One became a pope, two became cardinals and one a royal chaplain. Eleven were university teachers. In short, 26 out of 32 seem to have had successful careers by worldly standards.

It is tempting to conclude that artists and writers enjoyed an unusually high status in Italy at this time, and that this fact is related to the spectacular cultural achievements of the period. This may well be true, but the picture so far presented is too simple and certain qualifications need to be sketched in. Not everyone respected artists, composers and humanists. Not every member of the creative élite whose achievement is recognized now had an easy time of it in his own age.

To take the visual arts first. There were three social prejudices against artists which were still powerful. Artists might be thought of as ignoble because their work involved manual labour; because it involved retail trade; and because they were uneducated.

Painting, sculpture and architecture were not 'liberal' but 'mechanical' arts, to use a twelfth-century classification still

---

* Their names are marked with an asterisk in the list of the creative élite printed in the Appendix. Thirty-two were chosen because 32 of the Florentines studied by Martines fall within the period 1420–1540.

current in the period. As Vergerio put it, *designativa . . . non est pro liberali*. They were also dirty; a nobleman would not like to get his hands dirty using paints. The argument from antiquity, which Alberti used in defence of artists, was double-edged. Men remembered that Aristotle had excluded craftsmen from citizenship because their work was 'mechanical'; that Plutarch had suggested that no man of good family would want to become a Phidias. Leonardo's protest against this prejudice has become a classic:

> You have set painting among the mechanical arts! . . . If you call it mechanical because it is by manual work that the hands represent what the imagination creates, your writers are setting down with the pen by manual work what originates in the mind.

But even Leonardo shared the prejudice where sculptors were involved:

> The sculptor produces his work by . . . the labour of a mechanic, often accompanied by sweating which mixes with the dust and turns into mud, so that his face becomes white and he looks like a baker.

The argument against the manual labour of the artist is not a very good one. Leonardo might have added that fighting with a sword in one's right hand was as much manual labour as sculpture. The argument is best regarded as a rationalization on the part of established élites, military and clerical, to prevent their position being challenged by others. However, for the social historian the point is not whether the argument is logically defensible, but whether men held it. Some certainly did, though it is not possible to determine how widespread it was.[27]

The second point commonly made against artists was the argument from retail trade. Painters kept shops and sold their works for money; so they must have the same status as cobblers and grocers. Nobles would be ashamed to work for money. Boltraffio, a Lombard nobleman, usually painted small works, perhaps because they were intended only as gifts for his friends. His epitaph emphasized that although a painter, he was an amateur not a professional. Leonardo threw this accusation back into the faces of the humanists:

> If you call it mechanical because it is done for money, who fall into this error . . . more than you yourselves? If you lecture for the schools, do you not go to whoever pays you the most?

In practice a distinction was often made between keeping a shop and being on the payroll of a prince, which could happen to the best people. Michelangelo insisted vigorously on this distinction:

> I was never a painter or a sculptor like those who set up shop for that purpose. I always refrained from doing so out of respect for my father and brothers.

Vasari, after years in the service of princes, was able to refer with contempt to a minor painter as, 'One of those who keep an open shop and stand there in public, working at all sorts of mechanical tasks.'[28]

The third prejudice against the visual arts was that artists were ignorant, that is, that they lacked a certain kind of training, in the classics or in theology, which had a higher esteem than the training which they had received and others had not. When Cardinal Soderini was trying to excuse Michelangelo's flight from Rome, he said to the pope, 'He has erred through ignorance. Painters are all like this, both in their art and out of it.' It is a pleasure to record that Julius did not share this prejudice. He shouted at the cardinal, 'You are the ignorant one, not him!'[29]

Although a few artists became rich by means of their art, many remained poor. This was no doubt partly the result and partly the cause of the prejudices against the arts. The Sienese painter Benvenuto di Giovanni declared in 1488, 'The gains in our profession are slight and limited, because little is produced and less earned.' Vasari agreed, 'The artist today struggles to ward off famine rather than to win fame, and this crushes and buries his talent and obscures his name.' Vasari's comment might be dismissed as empty rhetoric, inconsistent with what he says elsewhere and with his own profits from the arts, and Benvenuto's remarks come from his tax-return. But there is evidence that distinguished artists were in poverty at some points in their careers. Verrocchio remarked in his tax-return for 1457 that he was not earning enough to keep his firm in hose (*non guadagniamo le chalze*); Botticelli and Neroccio de'Landi went into debt; Lotto was once reduced to trying to raffle 30 pictures, and even then he could dispose of only seven of them.[30]

Humanists too were not always rich and not always respected. To return to the 32 humanists who were not Tuscans, they were not uniformly successful. Janos Argyropoulos is said to have been so poor at one time that he was forced to sell his books to buy bread. Fazio had an up-and-down career, at one time a schoolteacher in Venice and Genoa, at another a notary in Lucca, before landing a safe and well-paid post as secretary to Alfonso of Aragon. Platina did a number of odd jobs – soldier, private tutor, press-corrector, secretary – before becoming Vatican librarian. Decembrio was at one time a schoolmaster in Milan, Leto in Venice, and Filelfo in several different towns; and Guarino of Verona and Vittorino da Feltre were never more than schoolmasters, though it has to be added that they chose this career deliberately and that their schools were attached to courts. Aconcio was at one time a notary, at another secretary to the governor of Milan, at another trying his luck in England. Giorgio Valla seems not to have risen above schoolmaster or tutor. And these humanists are the distinguished ones. To calculate the status of the group as a whole, we need to study the less important ones, to calculate the material prospects of an Italian student who decided to devote his career to the 'humanities'. Only a study of the careers of all the graduates of the period (which gaps in the evidence may well prevent) would answer this question accurately. I would guess that there was a considerable status gap between the few successful humanists, chancellors of republics or secretaries to princes, and the many unsuccessful, teaching in a small town, or correcting for the press, even if the poor humanist, as an educated man, might enjoy a status higher than that of the successful but 'ignorant' artist. Similarly with musicians, whose low status Alberti lamented; for every lutenist who was richly rewarded by a patron as generous as

Leo x, there must have been many who were poor, simply because there were not many courts in Italy, and no honourable position available elsewhere.

To conclude: there is evidence both for and against the high status of artists and writers at this time. It is tempting to take the easy way out and to close on a note of 'on the one hand . . . on the other'. But a few more precise points can also be made. In status terms there were 'two cultures', with literature, humanism and science enjoying a higher status than the visual arts and music. But to choose the career of professional humanist was to take a considerable risk. Many were trained but few were chosen. In the second place, artists were a case of what sociologists call 'status dissonance'. Some enjoyed high status, others did not; in general, artists were high-status according to some criteria, low according to others; they were respected by some of the noble and powerful but despised by others. The status insecurity resulting from this situation may well explain the touchiness of some artists, such as Michelangelo and Cellini. Lastly, the status of both artists and writers was probably higher in Italy than elsewhere in Europe; higher in Florence than in the rest of Italy; and higher in 1540 than it had been in 1420. The social rise of the artist is symbolized if not confirmed by the appearance of the term 'artist' in its modern meaning. In the fifteenth century, *artista* had meant a university student of the liberal arts; in the sixteenth century, as in Michelangelo's poem *non ha l'ottimo artista* . . . it means painter or sculptor. It may be argued that a society gets the artists it deserves; great artists appear when society respects them most because talent is less likely to be frustrated. Conversely, it is plausible to suggest that it was the genius of Italian artists which won them their (partial) emancipation from the status of craftsman. It was implausible to call sculptors 'mechanics' in the lifetime of Michelangelo.

ARTISTS AS SOCIAL DEVIANTS

If the artist was not an ordinary craftsman, what was he? He could if he wanted take up the style of life of a gentleman, a model suitable for those endowed with money and self-confidence and the capacity to behave like something out of

Castiglione's *Courtier*. A number of artists, mainly sixteenth-century ones, are described by Vasari in these terms. Giorgione and Raphael, who was a friend of Castiglione, are obvious examples. There was Cristoforo Romano the sculptor, a character in the *Courtier*; Vasari's kinsman Signorelli; Filippino Lippi, described as 'courteous, affable and a gentleman'; and a small number of others. But the artist who did adopt this model of behaviour still ran up against the fact that many contemporaries would not have regarded him as a gentleman because he worked with his hands, a prejudice which was if anything becoming stronger in sixteenth-century Italy. For other artists, the craftsman style of life seemed a good enough model. For those who were no longer content to be ordinary craftsmen and lacked the education and poise necessary for becoming gentlemen, a third model was developed in this period; that of the eccentric, the social deviant.

A number of stories have been recorded about Italian artists of the period who killed men or wounded them in brawls (Cellini, Leoni, Torbido); who committed suicide (Rosso, Torrigiani); who were homosexuals (Donatello, Leonardo, Michelangelo). The significance of these stories is difficult to determine. The evidence is not good enough to be sure that these artists were what they were described to be, and, even if it were, we have no reason to conclude from these few cases that artists were more likely to kill others or themselves or to be homosexual than members of other professions.[32]

There is a much richer vein of contemporary comment about another kind of eccentricity associated with artists: about their working habits. For example, they did not always work according to a regular rhythm. Bandello has a well-known account of Leonardo's working habits, which stressed the element in them of caprice and whim (*capriccio, ghiribizzo*). Vasari makes similar comments about Leonardo, and has him justifying his long pauses to the Duke of Milan with the argument that 'Men of genius sometimes accomplish most when they work the least; for they are thinking out *inventioni*.' The key concept here is 'genius', a term which turned the eccentricity of artists from a liability into an asset. Patrons had to learn to put up with it. The marquis of Mantua, presumably thinking of Mantegna in particular, made the resigned remark that 'these excellent masters are commonly a bit fantastical' (*hanno del fantasticho*). Other customers were less tolerant. Vasari remarked of Pontormo that, 'What most annoyed other men about him was that he would not work save when and for whom he pleased and after his own fancy.' When Duke Ercole d'Este wanted to hire a musician, he sent one of his agents to look at both Isaak and Josquin des Près. A letter from the agent survives informing Ercole that, 'It is true that Josquin composes better, but he does it when he feels like it, not when he is asked to.' It was Isaak who was hired. (Below p. 127.)

In the case of other artists, their eccentric working habits took the form of doing too much rather than too little, neglecting all that was not to do with their art. Vasari's accounts of Masaccio and Uccello emphasize such a neglect.* Masaccio was 'absent-minded' (*persona astrattissima*), and that

> Having fixed his mind and will wholly on matters of art, he cared little about himself and still less about others . . . he would never under any circumstances give a thought to the cares and concerns of this world, nor even to his clothes, and was not in the habit of recovering his money from debtors.

Uccello was so fascinated by his 'sweet' perspective that

> He remained secluded in his house, almost like a hermit, for weeks and months, without knowing much of what went on in the world and without showing himself.

Vasari also has an account of the 'strangeness' of Piero di Cosimo, who was absent-minded, loved solitude, would not have his room swept, and could not bear children crying, men coughing, bells ringing, or friars chanting. This looks like an attempt to preserve himself and his work from distractions; all that is surprising in this account is Vasari's own surprise.

That Masaccio, in the middle of fifteenth-century Florence,

---

* Masaccio died in 1428, Uccello in 1475. Vasari could have learned about them from the oral traditions of Florentine artists; but he was not born till 1511. The reader can make his own calculations about the reliability of information transmitted in these circumstances.

was not interested in money, is a trait worth emphasis. A still greater 'conspicuous contempt' for money was shown by Donatello, in a story told not only by Vasari but also by Gauricus at the beginning of the century:

> It is said by those who knew him that he kept all his money in a basket, suspended from the ceiling of his workshop, so that everyone could take what he wanted whenever he wanted.

This sounds like a conscious rejection of the fundamental values of Florentine society; calculating and bourgeois. Why Donatello should have rejected conventional Florentine values emerges from another story of Vasari's, about the bust Donatello made for a Genoese merchant, who claimed that he was overcharged because the sculptor had worked on it for only a month, so that the price worked out at more than half a florin a day:

> Donatello considered himself grossly insulted by this remark, turned on the merchant in a rage, and told him that he was the kind of man who could ruin the fruits of a year's toil in the hundredth part of an hour; and with that he suddenly threw the bust down into the street where it shattered into pieces, and added that the merchant had shown he was more used to bargaining for beans than for bronzes.

In other words, works of art are not ordinary commodities, and artists not ordinary craftsmen, to be paid by the day. One is reminded of what the Attorney-General said to Whistler about his *Nocturne*, and Whistler's reply:

> The labour of two days then is that for which you ask 200 guineas? No: I ask it for the knowledge of a lifetime.

In Italy in the fifteenth and sixteenth centuries, the same question was being discussed. St Antonino (above p. 84) recognized that artists claimed with some justification to be different from ordinary craftsmen. Francisco de Hollanda made the same point more forcefully in the mid-sixteenth century:

Works of art are not to be judged by the amount of useless labour spent on them but by the worth of the skill and mastery of their creator (*lo merecimento do saber e da mao que as faz*).

The same idea, that the artist is not an ordinary craftsman, may well underlie the behaviour of Pontormo (again according to Vasari) who would reject a good commission and then do something 'for a miserable price'. He was showing the client that he was a free man.[38]

4

Patrons and Clients

Why do you think that there was such a great
number of capable men in the past, if not because
they were well treated and honoured by princes?
Filarete

I cannot live under pressures from patrons, let
alone paint. *Michelangelo*

Systems of patronage differ. It may be useful to distinguish
five main types. First, the household system; a rich man takes
the artist or writer into his house for some years, gives him
board, lodging and presents, and expects to have his artistic
and literary needs attended to. Second, the made-to-measure
system, again a personal relationship between the artist or
writer and his client, but a temporary one, lasting only until
the painting or poem is delivered. Third, the market system,
in which the artist or writer produces something 'ready-made'
and seeks to sell it, either directly to the public or through a
dealer. Fourth, the academy system; government control of the
arts by means of an organization staffed by reliable artists and
writers. Fifth, the subvention system, in which a university or
foundation pays an artist or writer while he is working but
makes no claim on the finished product. In Italy in this period,
the dominant types of patronage for all the arts were the
household and the made-to-measure systems, although a market
in the arts was coming into existence.[1]

Frederick Antal (above p. 29) once contrasted Masaccio,
working in a 'rational' and 'realistic' style for the 'upper
bourgeoisie', with Gentile da Fabriano, working in the Gothic
style for traditional noble families. This is to put forward two
important and controversial theses: one about the sociology
of taste (below, p. 174) and one about the importance of the

patron's influence on the work of art. The key problem for discussion in this chapter will be the extent to which it was the patron or client, and not the artist, writer or composer, who determined the content and form of works of art. A second important problem is that of discovering what sorts of people gave artists commissions, and why they did so. A final question, to which the epigraphs allude, is whether one should see the patronage system of the time as encouraging or discouraging to artists; did the Renaissance happen in Italy because of its patronage system or in spite of it?

WHO ARE THE PATRONS?

One can classify patrons of paintings, sculpture and buildings in various ways. Some were lay, others churchmen; some were corporate, others individual; some rich, others relatively poor; some temporary, others permanent. If we only had enough data which could be treated quantitatively, so that we could say where and when in Italy and in which art or genre different kinds of patron were dominant, we should be much closer to explaining why Italian culture took the forms it did. But evidence is fragmentary, as usual.

Some patrons are ecclesiastical, others lay. At first sight a simple and useful dichotomy, between, for example, Perugino painting an altarpiece of the Ascension for the monks of S. Pietro at Perugia, and Botticelli painting the *Primavera* for Lorenzo de'Pierfrancesco de'Medici. The Church was *the* traditional patron of art, and the predominance of religious pictures in Europe over a long period, perhaps from the fourth to the seventeenth century, is surely related to this. In Renaissance Italy, however, it is likely that most religious pictures were commissioned by laymen, although abbots and parish priests might ask artists for altarpieces or buy illuminated missals. In the first place, a layman might commission a religious painting for a church, especially for his family chapel if he had one. Palla Strozzi asked Gentile da Fabriano to paint his *Adoration of the Magi* for the Strozzi Chapel in the church of S. Trinità in Florence. Giovanni Tornabuoni asked Ghirlandaio to paint frescoes in his chapel in S. Maria Novella : the contract describes Tornabuoni as the *patronus* of the chapel.

There are many such examples.

In the second place, a layman might commission a religious painting for his house. Alfonso of Aragon kept religious paintings by Jan van Eyck and Roger van der Weyden in his private rooms: an *Annunciation*, a *Deposition*, a *Passion*. The Medici did the same thing. It might also happen (surely no surprise to anyone with the conventional picture of Renaissance prelates) that churchmen might commission works of art quite secular in subject-matter. Portraits of themselves, for example. Or again, the *Parnassus* that Raphael painted for Julius II in the Vatican. It may still be true, of course, that laymen were more likely to commission secular works: here is a point where quantifiable evidence would be welcome, but is lacking.

A second division of patrons is into corporate and individual, or public and private. There are some famous examples of corporate patronage in Florence in the early fifteenth century. The wool-guild, the *Arte della Lana*, was responsible for the cathedral in Florence – thus a lay guild gave out many important commissions of religious subjects. For example, they commissioned Donatello to make a statue of the prophet Jeremiah for the Campanile of the Cathedral. The body which acted as patron was known as the Board of Works of the Cathedral, the *Operai del Duomo*; the consuls of the wool-guild are sometimes mentioned in contracts too. Similarly, the cloth-guild, the *Calimala*, was responsible for the Florentine Baptistery; hence it was this guild which commissioned Ghiberti to make the famous doors. The lesser guilds as well as the greater commissioned statues for the façade of the church of Orsanmichele: Donatello's *St George* was commissioned by the guild of armourers. These early fifteenth-century Florentine guild commissions were above all for sculpture, but not exclusively. In 1433 the *Linaiuoli*, the linen-guild, commissioned Fra Angelico to paint a Madonna for their guildhall.[2]

Another kind of corporate patron, perhaps still more important, if one takes the whole of Italy and the whole period into account, was the religious confraternity (p. 259 below). This was a religious and social club, usually attached to a particular church, which might perform works of charity and might act as a bank. It might, but need not, appeal to a particular group. The Venetians called their guilds *scuole*. For example, there was the *Scuola* of St Ursula, for whom Vittore Carpaccio painted his *St Ursula* pictures in the 1490s. Its members marched together in processions; there was a monthly mass in the Chapel of St Ursula; when one member died, the others went to the funeral. This confraternity had a mixed membership: men and women, nobles (the Loredano family, for example) and commoners. Another Venetian confraternity was the *Scuola* of S. Giorgio, which was founded by Dalmatians living in Venice and was pledged to help Rhodes against the Turks; it too commissioned Carpaccio. Another was S. Rocco, founded during a plague (it gave a famous commission to Tintoretto after 1540). Another, and a rich one, was the confraternity of St John the Evangelist, for whom Diana painted a picture of alms-giving and for whom Gentile Bellini painted a number of pictures, including that of the Procession of the reliquary of the Cross. These confraternities were not peculiar to Venice, though they seem most numerous there: for example, it was the Confraternity of the Conception of the Virgin at the church of S. Francesco at Milan which commissioned Leonardo (and the de Predis brothers) to paint the *Virgin of the Rocks*. It was the Confraternity of Corpus Christi at Urbino which commissioned Justus of Ghent's *Institution of the Eucharist*, and Uccello's *Profanation of the Host*. The advantage for art of these confraternities was that they made possible patronage by people who did not have the money to commission an artist by themselves. People might club together privately to order a picture: in 1473 Bartolomeo Vivarini painted an altarpiece for the Church of S. Maria Formosa in Venice; it was paid for by five people, four women and a man. But clearly this was more likely to happen when the process was institutionalized in a confraternity. What one would like to know is something about the problems of collective patronage; the discussions that went on before a particular artist or subject was chosen. Is a group likely to be a more conservative patron than an individual in the Renaissance, or is this way of looking at the problem anachronistic? It is intriguing to find that in 1433 the Florentine *Operai del Duomo* delegated their authority to one man, Neri Capponi, to work out the details of the commission to Donatello of sculptures for the singing gallery in the cathedral.[3]

A third kind of corporate patron was the state. The Florentine government, for example, commissioned Michelangelo to make his bronze David (the marble one was for the *Operai del Duomo*) and to paint the *Battle of Cascina*; when the republic was restored, it was the government, the Signoria, which commissioned *Hercules and Cacus* from Michelangelo. He was also in charge of the Florentine defences during the siege. In Venice, state patronage was even more important. The most celebrated instance of it was the appointment of Giovanni Bellini as painter to the Republic of Venice, in 1483. Dürer was offered a similar position. A number of architects were in the service of the Venetian government: Bartolomeo Bon; Michele Sammicheli; and Antonio Rizzo, who defended Scutari against the Turks (1474–7) and also worked on the doge's palace.

Venetian state patronage included official portraits of doges, painted, for example, by Bellini and Titian, and historical paintings of scenes showing Venetian triumphs. In the 1420s, Gentile da Fabriano and Pisanello were painting the Hall of the Great Council in the doge's palace with battle-scenes. In the 1470s, Giovanni Bellini was commissioned to replace these frescoes by canvases. It was an enormous job. By 1495 there were nine painters, including Bellini and Alvise Vivarini, working on the decoration of the Hall; their joint salaries amounted to 306 ducats a year. Titian painted a battle scene in the same place.

The problems of patronage by committee, which was the system of the Venetian state, emerge clearly in the surviving documents referring to Titian's battle scene. He petitioned the Council of Ten to be allowed to paint it in 1513. He asked for a broker's patent for himself (that is, a sinecure worth 100 ducats a year plus tax exemption) and for two assistants, to be paid by the salt office. (It was customary in the sixteenth century for specific expenditures to be assigned to specific sources of income, like the salt tax). A resolution accepting Titian's offer was carried (10 votes to 6); Bellini protested. In March 1514 the decree was revoked (14 votes to 1) and Titian's assistants were struck off the payroll; Titian protested. In November the revocation was revoked (9 votes to 4) and the assistants reappeared on the payroll. It was then reported that three times as much money had been spent as need have been, and all arrangements were cancelled. Titian made a new offer, which was accepted in January 1516: he was to have only one assistant. The battle-scene was still unfinished in 1537.[4]

When a state was ruled by a prince, it is more difficult to decide whether one is dealing with state patronage or with private patronage; this distinction between private and public roles was one that was not made by princes at the time. Another problem for the historian of princely patronage is one of evidence. One cannot be sure that a prince is really the patron of every work of art executed at his court, except in a vacuous definitional sense. One may well read in a chronicle or list of payments that a particular work was made 'for' the prince – but what does that mean? There is a kind of shorthand used here, similar to the shorthand of politics where Charles v, say, is said (by contemporaries, by historians) to have made a decision, whereas in fact a group of councillors acted in his name, and their differences of opinion have not been recorded. Princely patronage gave the artist higher status. The fact that an individual, not a committee, was at the top and might take a personal interest in what was done sometimes eliminated delays; haste, not delays, might be what the artist had to complain about:

> We want you to work on some paintings which we wish to have made, and we wish you, as soon as you have received this, to leave everything, jump on your horse and come here to us.

Thus the duke of Milan, G. M. Sforza, wrote to Foppa in 1475. G. M. Sforza commanded painters to work night and day on the Castello Sforzesca – Corio has a story of a room painted in a single night.[5]

Federico Gonzaga of Mantua was another impatient patron. He wrote to Titian in 1531 asking for a picture of the Magdalen, 'and above all, let me have it quickly.' Titian sent it in less than a month, with a letter saying that he had dropped everything in order to oblige the prince. In August 1536, Federico wrote to Titian asking for a painting of Christ for September. There is a similar impatience to be seen in his dealings with Giulio Romano, whose assistants were not decorating the Palazzo del Te quickly enough. This letter, for example:

We are not amused that you should again have missed so many dates by which you had undertaken to finish . . . if you wish to finish on the promised date you must make them work diligently; if you do not wish to do this we will provide other painters who will finish.

Giulio replied obsequiously.

The greatest pain I can receive is when Your Excellency is angry . . . if it is pleasing to you, have me locked up in that room until it is done.

This seems a far cry from Federico's comparison of his painter with Apelles (above p. 85); but perhaps Alexander really treated Apelles the same way.

Alfonso d'Este of Ferrara was a man of the same stamp. When Titian did not produce a painting on time in 1519, Alfonso instructed his agent:

To tell him instantly, that we are surprised that he should not have finished our picture; that he must finish it under all circumstances or incur our great displeasure; and that he may be made to feel that he is doing an ill turn to one who can resent it.[6]

Another important distinction was between permanent patrons, who took artists into their service, and temporary ones, who merely commissioned a single work. Let us call the first group 'patrons' and the second 'clients'. The distinction is blurred, of course, by the existence of large single commissions which might take years to execute. Florence and Venice were the homes of clientage, while patronage was dominant elsewhere. It is princes who were most likely to take artists into permanent service; Tura was court painter at Ferrara, Mantegna at Mantua, Spanzotti in Savoy, Leonardo at Milan.

From the artist's point of view each system had advantages and disadvantages. Permanent service at court meant relative economic security, board and lodging and presents of clothes and money and land; it also meant relatively high status without the social taint of shop-keeping. Michelangelo (above p. 90) refused to 'set up shop' for this reason. Security was only relative, however. When princely patrons died, their successors did not inherit their taste along with their wealth, and artists might be dismissed. Vasari was in the service of Alessandro de'Medici, duke of Florence, till the duke was murdered in 1537 – Vasari wrote to his uncle that his hopes had been 'blown away by a puff of wind'. The advantages of permanent service did not include freedom. It was not possible to evade the demands of patrons as easily as those of clients. At the court of Mantua, Mantegna had to ask permission to travel or accept outside commissions. The great danger for a court artist, from posterity's point of view, at least, was turning into a glorified odd-job man.

To take some examples. Alfonso of Aragon made the Lombard Leonardo Molinari da Besozzo his court painter, and employed him on painting decorations for the Castel Nuovo, banners and shields. Cosimo Tura entered the permanent service of Borso d'Este at Ferrara; he had a regular salary from 1452 onwards. He did not simply paint pictures; he painted furniture, gilded caskets, tournament costumes and horse trappings, designed chair-backs, door curtains, bed-quilts, a table-service and so on. Leonardo da Vinci at the court of Lodovico Sforza at Milan was similarly occupied in miscellaneous projects. He painted the portrait of the duke's mistress, Cecilia Gallerani; he decorated the *Sala delle asse* in the Castello Sforzesco; he worked on 'the horse', an equestrian monument to the duke's father; he also designed costumes and stages for court festivals, and was employed on military projects. One might say that at least he went to court with his eyes open; his draft letter asking Lodovico to take him into his service still exists, with its list of what he can do in the way of bridges, mortars and chariots, ending 'in the 10th place' that he could also paint and sculpt. But it is surely a judgement on the court milieu that we remember Leonardo at Milan for two works, *The Last Supper* and the Louvre *Virgin of the Rocks*. Neither of these was for Lodovico (though he may have arranged the first of these commissions); one was for a monastery, the other for a confraternity.

One should not exaggerate the disadvantages of courts. Republics too wanted festival decorations sometimes. Mantegna, court artist to the Gonzagas at Mantua, seems to have been employed mostly on painting. Still, one has the impression of court artists as somewhat less free, more likely to dissipate their energies on the transient and the trivial than others, like court mathematicians in seventeenth-century Versailles, concerned with the hydraulics of fountains or with working out the mathematics of probability for royal games of cards.

When an artist kept an open shop, he had less economic security and a lower social status. On the other hand, it was easier for him, as will be seen, to evade the commission he did not want. Of course, clients too might offer artists a variety of odd jobs, from painting house-fronts and *cassoni* (chests for the bride's trousseau) to portraits and mythologies. Verrocchio's studio is remembered for the variety of work done there when Leonardo was an apprentice. But artists in open shops could specialize, if they wanted, by combining with others. Some companies of painters were so organized that different members executed different kinds of commission. One wonders how important this freedom was to artists. When Mantegna was appointed court painter in Mantua in 1459 he lingered on in Padua, as if the decision was a difficult one to take. Here may be part of the explanation for the fact that the great innovations of the period happened not at courts but in republics of shop-keepers, Florence and Venice.[7]

Another distinction between patrons is that between rich and poor, high-status and low-status. What sort of people would think – could afford to think – of buying a painting? Architecture and sculpture were obviously expensive to patronize, but the question of the clients for paintings is harder to answer. There are the usual gaps in the evidence. If, for example, one tries to list all the private commissions for paintings known to have been made in Florence between 1420 and 1439 (say) one produces a list dominated by the great families: the Alessandri (who commissioned Lippo Lippi); the Brancacci (Masaccio and Masolino); the Medici (Fra Angelico); the Bardi (Bicci di Lorenzo); the Compagni (Bicci di Lorenzo); the Strozzi (Gentile da Fabriano); the Quaratesi (Gentile da Fabriano); the Marsuppini (Lippo Lippi); the Cardoni (Masaccio) and so on. These families are old patrician families; except for Felice Brancacci and Carlo Marsuppini, new men but prominent as businessman and a professional man respectively. But this is only a small proportion of the total commissions; those of which record has survived.

Documentary evidence for important commissions, especially frescoes, is more likely to survive than evidence for small commissions; and if it does survive for a small commission, it may be difficult to find out anything about the client, except his name. Wackernagel suggested that in fifteenth-century Florence, patrons came from 'all social groups from the petty-bourgeois artisans upwards'. It is indeed possible to find examples of artisans and shopkeepers commissioning works of art. Vasari says that Andrea del Sarto painted Madonnas for a mercer and a joiner, and Pontormo's first work was painted for a tailor. What we do not know is whether this situation was at all common.[8]

It may be useful to distinguish three main motives for the patronage of paintings and sculpture: piety, prestige and pleasure. In the first place, piety, whether focused on the glory of God or on the salvation of the client's soul. Pious commissions are likely to be for churches; a large city full of churches as Florence was would be a magnet for commissions for frescoes and altarpieces. This motive sometimes finds its way into the contract. That for the Ghirlandaio frescoes in S. Maria Novella, commissioned by Tornabuoni, refers to the 'piety' and the 'love of God' of the donor, though the historian need not assume that the love of God was Tornabuoni's only motive, or even his main one.

In the second place, the prestige motive; the glory of the client, or his family, or his city. The Hawkwood monument in Florence cathedral was commissioned 'for the honour of the said commune' rather than for that of the late *condottiere*, according to the contract. When the *Operai del Duomo* at Florence commissioned twelve apostles from Michelangelo, they made reference to the 'fame of the whole city' and its 'honour and glory'. Coats of arms and portraits of donors occur so frequently in religious pictures that it is difficult to disentangle the motives of prestige and piety. The Ricci family are said to have restored S. Maria Novella only when they secured a promise that their arms would be displayed prominently there. In the Tornabuoni contract for frescoes for the same church, the painters promised to paint the Tornabuoni coat of arms as often as Giovanni wanted, and in whatever parts of the fresco he wanted. The most extraordinary example of the mixture of piety and prestige is surely the tabernacle commissioned by Piero de'Medici which is inscribed, 'the marble alone cost 4,000 florins' (*Costó fior. 4 mila el marmo solo*). This is such a classic piece of nouveau-riche exhibitionism as to make one wonder whether new families were more active patrons than old ones, seeing in patronage a way of showing the world that one had reached the top, and having to commission something grand to make this absolutely clear.

The prestige acquired by patronage might be of political value to a prince. Filarete, who of course had an axe to grind (or rather, a palace to build), argued this case, and tried to demolish the economic argument against building:

> Magnanimous and great princes, and republics as well, should not hold back from building great and beautiful buildings because of the expense. No country was ever impoverished nor did anyone ever die because of the construction of buildings . . . In the end when a large building is completed there is neither more nor less money in the country, but the building does remain in the country or city together with its reputation or honour.

Machiavelli saw patronage as politic, suggesting that 'a prince ought to show himself a lover of ability, giving employment to able men and honouring those who excel in a particular field.' Great building projects and splendid festivals were the obvious artistic ways of increasing the reputation of princes.

The third main motive for patronage was 'pleasure', a delight in works of art which might be discriminating or not, and includes the patron who thought of pictures as interior decoration as well as the man who saw them as objects in their own right. It is likely that this motive was more important and more self-conscious in Italy at this time than it had been anywhere in Europe for a thousand years, but this quantitative point is, as usual, incapable of being established on a quantitative basis. One can simply quote examples. Filarete stressed the pleasure in building for its own sake, 'a voluptuous pleasure as when a man is in love'. The more the patron sees the building, the more he wants to see it; he loves to talk to everyone about it – typical lovers' behaviour. The names of some villas of the period suggest that they were playthings: *Schifanoia* (avoid boredom) at Ferrara; *Casa Zoiosa* (happy house) at Mantua. According to the bookseller Vespasiano da Bisticci, who did not go out of his way to praise the visual arts, two of his prominent clients, Federico of Urbino and Cosimo de'Medici, took a great pleasure in sculpture and architecture. To hear Federico talk to a sculptor, 'one would have thought it his trade'. Cosimo de'Medici was so interested in architecture that people who intended to build went to him for advice. Two Venetian nobles were said in 1510 to have commissioned paintings from Giorgione 'for their own enjoyment' (below p. 134). Again, the correspondence of Isabella d'Este leaves the reader with the impression that the reason she commissioned paintings was simply to have them.[9]

A fourth possible motive has recently been suggested – investment. If investment in works of art means buying them (as happens now) on the assumption that they will be worth more in the future, then I can find no evidence of this motive in the period. One does find merchants buying works of art for resale (see below p. 135) but the resale was almost immediate.

The desire to acquire works of art for their own sake is the most interesting of these motives, because the newest. The families which seem to show it mostly clearly have something important in common: humanist education. After Gianfrancesco Gonzaga brought Vittorino da Feltre to Mantua to teach his children, they grew up to be patrons of the arts. Federico of Urbino also studied under Vittorino. Guarino of Verona went to Ferrara to tutor the d'Este children, and they grew up to be important patrons. Lorenzo de'Medici was educated by Ficino and Landino. Though, as we have seen, humanists did not always respect artists, the study of the humanities seems to have encouraged a taste for pictures and statues.

PATRONS AND ARTISTS

The crucial question here is the extent to which it was the patron rather than the artist who determined what the painting, sculpture or building would actually be like. I shall also discuss how artists acquired patrons, and patrons or clients acquired artists; what the patrons tended to expect from artists; and the problem of the humanist adviser.

When artists heard of important commissions going, they might approach the patron, directly or through an intermediary. Domenico Veneziano wrote to Piero de'Medici in 1438:

> I have heard that Cosimo has decided to have an altarpiece painted, and wants a magnificent work. This pleases me a great deal, and it would please me still more if it were possible for me to paint it, through your mediation (*per vostra megianità*).

In 1474 there was news that the duke of Milan wanted a chapel painted at Pavia. The duke's agent complained to him that, 'all the painters of Milan, good and bad, asked to paint it, and trouble me greatly about it.'

Again, in 1488 Alvise Vivarini petitioned the doge and signoria to let him paint in the *Sala di Gran Consiglio* in Venice as the Bellinis were doing, and this was agreed. In 1515 Titian made a similar request, adding that he would do the work for half what Perugino had been given. In these requests (as in many other matters in Renaissance Italy), friendships and relationships helped a great deal. This may be illustrated from the careers of Vasari and Bandinelli. Vasari came to work for the Medici because his father was a distant relative of Cardinal Silvio Passerini, who was the guardian of Alessandro and Ippolito de'Medici; thus he met them. First he worked for Ippolito, and then Ippolito passed him on to Pope Clement VII, another Medici, and Pope Clement passed him on to Alessandro. He also executed commissions for Ottaviano de'Medici, and later entered the permanent service of Cosimo de'Medici, duke of Tuscany. Bandinelli also had a family connexion with the Medici in that his father had worked for them before their expulsion in 1494. After their restoration in 1513, he took a wax St Jerome to Cardinal Giovanni de'Medici (soon to become Leo X), and his brother Giuliano, and introduced himself. Giuliano arranged for the Cathedral *Operai* to commission a marble St Peter from him. For Giulio de'Medici, who became Clement VII, Bandinelli made statues of Orpheus and Laocöon, and painted the martyrdom of Saints Cosmas, Damian and Laurence (an obvious reference to the traditional Medici names 'Cosimo' and 'Lorenzo') for the church of S. Lorenzo in Florence. He also expected to get the commission to make the tombs of Popes Leo and Clement, and went to see Cardinal Salviati to arrange this so often that he was mistaken for a spy of Alessandro de'Medici's and nearly assassinated.[10]

It is sometimes possible to discover the other half of the story; how would-be patrons or clients found particular artists. Vespasiano's life of Cosimo de'Medici mentioned people who wanted advice on architectural projects coming to him. There is evidence of his grandson Lorenzo doing the same sort of thing. For example, when Alfonso of Calabria wanted an architect, Lorenzo arranged for Giuliano da Maiano to go to Naples. When Giuliano died, Lorenzo looked for a successor, first in Florence and then outside. Even in Florence, a would-be client might ask the advice of his friends. Ludovico Capponi, for example, wanted his chapel at S. Felicità decorated, and asked his friend Niccolò Vespucci. Vespucci recommended Pontormo, and Pontormo did go and work for Capponi. This is the kind of incident which one can imagine often happening and rarely being recorded. For the better commissions, choosing must have been the only problem, whether this was done on artistic or on financial grounds. Different painters went to see the duke of Milan in 1474: some said they would paint the chapel for 200 ducats, others for 150, others for 100. The duke told his agent to summon them all and then decide. In the event, the agent chose the 150 ducat men because the painters all denied having spoken about 100 ducats.

In this case we see an informal system of competitive tenders in operation. More formalized competitions for commissions can also be found. They seem to be most common in Florence and Venice, which one might have expected, since merchants were important there and since the political system in republics was more competitive (and so achievement-oriented) than that of principalities. The most famous competition in Florence was that for the Baptistery doors commission in 1400; Brunelleschi and Ghiberti competed, and Ghiberti won. Ghiberti won another competition in 1432, for a reliquary for the head of St Zenobius, a patron saint of Florence. Another example is the competition between Piero Pollaiuolo and Verrocchio for the commission for the Forteguerri tomb in Pistoia, which Verrocchio won (1477); and another, the competition for a design for the façade of Florence cathedral (1491). In Venice, where even the organists at S. Marco were appointed after competition, there are a number of examples from the visual arts too. Gentile Bellini defeated Squarcione in an attempt to get the commission for two pictures for the *Scuola di S. Marco* (1466); Diana defeated Carpaccio in competition for a commission from the *Scuola della Carità* (1508); Titian, Palma Vecchio and Pordenone all competed for a commission from the *Scuola di S. Pietro Martire*. Examples can be found outside Florence and Venice. At the court of Ferrara, there was a competition between Jacopo Bellini and Pisanello (1441), and at Milan, Leonardo, Bramante, Amadeo and others produced competing designs for the cathedral cupola (1490).[11]

Now the patron and the artist have been introduced to one another, it is possible to come to the main problem, that of their relationship, especially the influence of patrons and clients on the 'finished product'.

The testimony of contemporaries suggests that this influence was very great. Filarete described the patron as the father of the building he commissioned; the architect as the mother. The term *fecit* (he made) continued to be used of Renaissance patrons, rather than of artists, as it had been of medieval patrons. Titian, asking Alfonso duke of Ferrara for instructions, declared he was:

> convinced that the greatness of art amongst the ancients was due to the assistance they received from great princes content to leave to the painter the credit and renown derived from their own ingenuity in commissioning pictures . . . I shall, after all, have done no more than give shape to that which received its spirit – the most essential part – from Your Excellency.

He was, of course, flattering the duke; but the different forms flattery takes in different periods can provide valuable information for the historian.

More precise evidence about the role of patrons and clients for painting and sculpture is provided by the texts of contracts and commissions, scores of which survive for this period. It was quite common for artist and client to draw up a formal contract, attested by a notary, which provides valuable clues to the attitudes and expectations of both parties.[12]

In the first place, there was the question of materials to be settled. Sometimes the patron provided them at his expense, sometimes the artist. This question is extremely important because of the use of expensive items like gold, silver, and lapis lazuli, for paintings; marble and bronze for sculpture. The painter may well have been given an advance to buy his colours, or the sculptor his marble; and the sculptor may have had to do as Michelangelo used to, and contract with stone-cutters in Carrara to supply the marble, thus involving himself in administration as well as art. The same would happen to architects, on a larger scale. Contracts not infrequently specified that 'good' colours be used in a painting; the Michelangelo *Pietà* which he began in 1501 was to be 'of marble of Carrara, new, pure and white, with no veins in it'. Fra Angelico promised the linen guild in 1433 to use 'the best and finest colours that can be found'. More precisely, Andrea del Sarto promised to use at least five florins' worth of azure on his Virgin Mary. The great emphasis on materials is a clue to what the client thought he was buying.

In the second place, there was the question of price; 100 ducats, say, in which case the currency had to be specified – 'large' ones or papal ones. The price may have been paid on completion, or in instalments while the work was going on; it may not have been fixed in advance at all: sometimes the artist said he would take what the patron thought good to give him, and sometimes the work was valued afterwards by third parties, artists, one of whom may have been chosen by the patron and another by the artist. Payments in kind may have been included. Signorelli's contract for the frescoes at Orvieto cathedral gave him the right to a sum of money, to gold and azure, to lodgings and a bed – after negotiations he raised them to two beds.

In the third place, the question of delivery date, vague or precise, with or without sanctions if the artist did not keep his word. A Venetian state commission to Giovanni Bellini stated that the paintings should be finished 'as quickly as possible'. Beccafumi was given 'a year, or eighteen months at most' to finish a picture in 1529. Other clients were more precise, or more demanding. In 1460, Lippo Lippi promised a painting by the September of that year, and if he failed to produce it, the patron was given the right to ask someone else to finish it. Leonardo promised on 25th April, 1483, to deliver the *Virgin of the Rocks* by 8th December. Michelangelo's contract for 15 statues (1501) laid down that he was not to make any other contracts which would delay the execution of this one; it is surprising that more modern publishers do not imitate this stipulation. Raphael was given two years to paint an altarpiece, with a large fine (40 ducats, over half the price) if he was not on time (1505). The contract which Andrea del Sarto made in 1515 to paint an altarpiece within the year contained the clause:

that if he did not finish the said picture within the said time, the said nuns would have the right to give the said commission to someone else (*dictam tabulam alicui locare*).

An anonymous report to Lodovico Sforza in the 1480s on the qualities of different artists in Florence singles out Ghirlandaio as a 'fast worker' (*uomo expeditivo*).

In the fourth place, there is the question of size. This is surprisingly often left unspecified, perhaps an indication of sixteenth-century vagueness about quantities, though in a large number of cases the fact that a picture was a fresco on a particular wall, or a sculpture from the patron's block of marble or made for a niche, must have made details about measurements unnecessary. However, there are examples of precision. Michelangelo in 1514 promised to make his Christ Carrying the Cross 'life size'; and his bronze David, two *braccia* high (the marble David was made from a block provided by the *Operai del Duomo*, so the measurements are not specified). In 1540 Vasari promised to paint an altarpiece 6½ braccia high and 4 wide. Andrea del Sarto promised to make his altarpiece of 1515 at least 3 braccia wide and at least 3½ braccia high. Isabella d'Este, who wanted a set of matching pictures for her room at Mantua enclosed a thread in her letter commissioning painters so that they would know the measurements she required.

We come now, in the fifth place, to the question, crucial for us, of what actually went into the picture. Three kinds of thing happen in contracts which are relevant to this. The subject of the work may be spelled out in words; there may be reference to sketches and models; or the artist's or patron's initiative may be referred to. Some examples. The *Virgin of the Rocks* commission mentioned 'mountains and rocks' and also 'Our Lady in the middle. Her upper garment of ultramarine blue brocaded with gold.' Elaborate details are laid down by Giovanni Torna-buoni for the Ghirlandaios in the S. Maria Novella frescoes of 1485. For example, they were to paint the right hand wall of the chapel with seven scenes from the life of the Virgin: her birth at the bottom; above that her wedding; thirdly the Annunciation; fourthly the Nativity; fifthly the Purification; sixthly the infant Jesus disputing with the doctors in the temple; seventhly, the death of the Virgin. In this case a whole pictorial programme, whoever invented it, is legally laid down for the painters to follow. Even more interesting is the proviso which follows, in which the painters promise

> in all the aforesaid histories . . . to paint figures, buildings, castles, cities, mountains, hills, plains, rocks, clothes, animals, birds and beasts . . . just as the patron wants, if the price of materials does not prevent this (*secundum tamen taxa-tionem colorum*).

A more common formula in contracts is to find a relatively brief description of the iconographical essentials. Thus Andrea del Sarto agreed with the nuns of S. Francesco to paint:

> the image of the most blessed Mary ever a Virgin with her son in her arms and with two angels at the sides of the upper part who are crowning the said image of Mary the Virgin Mother . . . on one side there should be the image of the most blessed John the Evangelist and on the other St Bon-aventure dressed as a cardinal . . .

Sometimes the description in legal Latin of the details of a painting or sculpture seems to have been too much for the notary, and the document suddenly lapses into Italian. The Ghirlandaio paintings were to be, '*ut vulgariter dicitur, posti in frescho* (as they say in the vernacular, "frescoed").' For this reason, and perhaps also because patrons found the exact description of what they wanted too much of a struggle, it was often found simpler to refer to a painting or sketch or model. Sometimes the painting was by someone else, but had taken the patron's fancy. A contract between a certain painter

Barbagelata and the Confraternity of St Bridget at Genoa (1485) asks for a Crucifixion with the Virgin Mary, St John and the Magdalen, 'as they are customarily painted in such paintings (*ut depingi solent in similibus depincturis*)'. An interesting example of a direct demand on a painter to follow tradition, a 1429 contract for the church at Loreto, asks for the Virgin 'with her son in her lap, according to custom' (*seconda l'usanza*). The Barbagelata contract goes on to specify that the figures are to be painted in that manner, of the same nature, quality, goodness and perfection

> as those which are painted in the altarpiece of St Dominic for the late Battista Spinola in the church of the said St Dominic, made and painted by master Vincent of Milan (Foppa).

The will of the Venetian patrician B. Bragadin asked for a marble tomb in the church of SS. Giovanni e Paolo, 'like the one in the chapel of S. Elena', but with less gilding.

Again, a contract which Raphael entered into in 1505 to paint an altarpiece of the coronation of the Virgin laid down that it be:

> of that perfection, proportion, quality and condition of the painting existing at Narni in the Church of St Jerome . . . to resemble the said picture in colour, figures, number and ornaments.

There may have been a gradual rise of individualism in painting in this period (above p. 45) but there were certainly forces pushing it back.

More common are references to sketches or models provided by the painter or sculptor, and now lost. For example, Alvise Vivarini contracted with the *Scuola di S. Marco* to make a banner (1501), 'according to the order and form of the design which was made by him and seen by us'. Angelico contracted with the Linen Guild to paint a Madonna, 'with those figures that are in the design, as can be seen in the books of the said guild'.

Michelangelo's contract with the cardinal of Siena to make 15 apostles and saints laid down that:

before he begins to make these figures . . . he is obliged to
draw them on a sheet of paper, so that their clothes and
gestures can be seen . . . so that additions and subtractions
can be made if necessary.

The contracts Michelangelo made for the tomb of Julius II refer
to a 'designum' or 'modellum'; fortunately they go on to
describe the work as well, so that art historians have been able
to reconstruct the various stages of the project. The 'design'
may be in colour; when the duke of Milan was having his
chapel painted in 1474, his agent sent him two designs to
choose from, 'with cherubs or without' (cherubs cost extra),
and asked for the designs back, 'to see, when the work is
finished, whether the azure was as fine as was promised.'
Occasionally it may be the client who sends the sketch to the
artist. Isabella d'Este (see Pl. 11), who was extremely particular
about what she wanted, sent a sketch to Perugino in 1503 for
the 'battle of chastity against desire' which she wanted him to
paint.
    Besides these descriptions and drawings, there may be refer-
ences, more or less precise, to the initiative of the patron or
the artist. Tura contracted with the duke of Ferrara (1469) to
paint the chapel of Belriguardo 'with the histories which please
his said Excellency most'. When Perugino contracted for an
altarpiece with the monks of St Pietro in Perugia, the main
picture was described in some detail, but the predella was
simply to be 'painted and adorned with histories according to
the desire of the present abbot'. Isabella, in the Perugino
commission just mentioned, left the artist a restricted area of
freedom:

> If you perhaps think that these figures are too many for one
> picture, you may leave things out if you like, as long as you
> do not remove the foundation, which is these four main
> figures, Pallas, Diana, Venus and Love . . . you may leave
> things out if you like, but you are not to add anything of
> your own.

Foppa promised the priors of the confraternity of St John the
Baptist at Genoa to paint a chapel, 'well and with those figures
and images that the said priors want'. Raphael promised a

certain Andrea Baronci to paint a St Nicholas 'with figures just as the same Andrea says'. But the contract for Michelangelo's Christ carrying the Cross (1514) says simply that Christ should carry the cross 'in whatever attitude seems good to the said Michelangelo'. The commission from the Florentine Signoria for *Hercules and Cacus* (1538) gives him still more freedom: having mentioned that a certain piece of marble had been brought to Florence 'to make the image and figure of Cacus', it hands over the marble to Michelangelo, 'who is to make from it a figure together or conjoined with another, just as it pleases the said Michelangelo'. Such freedom seems an exceptional one in this period.

A last point which is made in contracts and commissions is about assistants. Some contracts are made with a group of artists, not an individual: the Venetian Signoria commissioned Giovanni Bellini and three others (Carpaccio being one) to paint pictures for the *Sala di Gran Consiglio*. Other commissions mention assistants, perhaps to pay them; in 1503, for example, the *Operai del Duomo* at Florence, commissioning Michelangelo to make 12 Apostles, paid the expenses of one assistant. In Flanders, at about this time (1519), a client once brought a suit against an artist (Albert Cornelis) on the grounds that he had employed assistants. He claimed that he was allowed to do this by custom, and that he was bound only to design the composition and paint the flesh parts himself. He won. I know of no similar lawsuit in Renaissance Italy, but the same conventions seem to have operated. Contracts do, sometimes, specify that the artist should produce all or part of the work 'with his own hand'. In the contracts with Perugino and Signorelli, for frescoes in Orvieto cathedral, it is laid down that all the figures 'from the waist up' should be by the master's own hand. Raphael promised to paint the figures of the altarpiece of the coronation of the Virgin (1505) with his own hand.

Finally, in one contract, that for the *Virgin of the Rocks*, there is a mention of a ten-year guarantee of good condition; if anything needs repainting before then, it is to be at the expense of the artist. One wonders whether Leonardo gave similar guarantees to the client for his *Last Supper*.

Contracts and commissions, however interesting, are incomplete evidence of the relationship between artist and client. They deal with intentions, but the historian, here as elsewhere,

wants to know what actually happened, whether the artist
was obedient, whether things went according to plan. In some
cases we know that they did not. In the case of Andrea del
Sarto's *Madonna of the Harpies*, both the contract and the
painting still exist, and there are serious discrepancies between
them. The contract refers to two angels; they do not appear
in the finished painting. The contract refers to St John the
Evangelist; he has become St Francis in the painting. Such
alterations may have been negotiated with the client – we do
not know. They are none the less a warning not to take one
kind of evidence too seriously. The best way to discover the
true balance of power between artist and patrons in this period
is surely to study the conflicts, which are likely to make
manifest tensions which exist in other situations too but are
latent there. The evidence for these conflicts is scrappy; sometimes extremely revealing letters from patron to artist have
survived, at other times one has to make do with anecdote.
Yet some sort of coherent picture seems to emerge.

There are two main reasons for conflicts between artist and
patron in this period. The first, which need not detain us, is
money. This was a special instance of the general problem of
getting someone of higher status to pay his debts. Mantegna is
said to have reminded Pope Innocent of his obligations
pictorially. Josquin des Près and Poliziano seem to have been
driven to similar expedients. Conflict about money might raise
the issue of the nature of artistic work as in the story of
Donatello and the merchant (above p. 95). The second reason
for conflict is the form of the painting or sculpture itself. What
happened when the artist did not like the patron's scheme, or
the patron did not like what the artist had produced? A few
examples will show. In 1436 the *Operai del Duomo* at Florence
commissioned Paolo Uccello to paint the equestrian portrait of
Sir John Hawkwood (referred to as 'Hauto') on the cathedral
wall. A month later they decided that the painting was to be
destroyed, 'because it is not painted as it should be' (*quia non
est pictus ut decet*). One wonders what experiments in perspective Uccello had been trying out. Again, when Cosimo Tura
was court painter at Ferrara, he had to repaint something
because the duke did not like it. Piero de' Medici objected to
certain small seraphs in the corner of a fresco by Benozzo

Gozzoli (*c.* 1456). A letter from Benozzo has survived in which he explains:

> I have only made one in a corner among certain clouds; one sees nothing but the tips of his wings, and he is so well hidden and so covered by clouds that he does not make for deformity at all but rather for beauty . . . I have made another on the other side of the altar but also hidden in a similar way . . . Nevertheless I'll do as you command; two little cloudlets will take them away . . .

In all these cases the artist simply gave way.[18]

In other cases, the conflict between patron and artist seems to have reached deadlock. There is a story about Piero di Cosimo, who once painted a picture for the Foundling Hospital in Florence. The director of the hospital, who commissioned the painting, wanted to see it before it was finished; Piero would not let him. The client threatened not to pay; the artist threatened to destroy the painting. Again, Julius II, the irresistible force, and Michelangelo, the immovable object, fought over the Sistine ceiling. One night, Michelangelo left Rome in secret and returned to Florence. One explanation given at the time was:

> that the Pope became angry with him because he would not allow any of his work to be seen; that Michelangelo distrusted his own men and suspected that the Pope . . . disguised himself to see what was being done.

Why did Piero and Michelangelo object to their work being seen before it was finished? Some artists today are touchy about laymen looking over their shoulder; but there may have been something more to these cases than that. Suppose an artist did not want to treat a subject in the way the client wanted. A possible tactic would be to hide the picture from him until it was finished, hoping that he would accept a *fait accompli* rather than wait for another version to be painted. For another Sistine ceiling the pope would have had to wait quite a while.

Giovanni Bellini was a painter who did not easily submit to the will of others. Bembo described him as one, 'whose pleasure is that sharply-defined limits should not be set to his style, being wont, as he says, to wander at his will in paintings (*vagare a sua voglia nelle pitture*)'. Isabella d'Este commissioned him to paint a pagan fantasy, just as she commissioned Mantegna and Perugino. It appears that he did not want to paint such a picture; nor did he want to lose the commission, or give offence to the princess. So he used delaying tactics, and at the same time hinted, through the agents Isabella used in her dealings with him, that another subject might not take so long. As one of them wrote: 'If you care to give him the liberty to do what he wants, I am absolutely sure that Your Highness will be served much better.' Isabella knew when to give way gracefully. She replied:

If Giovanni Bellini is as reluctant to paint his history as you say, we are content to leave the subject to him, provided that he paints some history or ancient fable.

In fact, Bellini was able to beat her down still further; she ended by accepting a Nativity. The fact that Bellini had an open shop, and that he was at Venice while she was at Mantua, probably helped him to win. Had he been attached to the court of Mantua, the outcome of the struggle might have been very different. Isabella seems to have learned this lesson, and soon afterwards took Lorenzo Costa into her permanent service.

These examples are simply some of the more dramatic or celebrated ones. They do not form a basis for generalizations by themselves. But there seems to be evidence that the balance of power between artist and patron was changing during the Renaissance, and that the patron was coming to play a more subordinate role. As the status of the artist rose, he was able to resist the patron (where necessary, more openly), and the patron made fewer demands. To Leonardo, Isabella made two great concessions: 'We shall leave the subject and the time to you.' A famous letter from the poet Annibale Caro to Vasari in 1548 acknowledges the artist's right to do as he pleases, like the poet (although he follows the acknowledgment with fairly precise instructions for an Adonis on a purple garment embraced by Venus):

For the subject matter (*invenzione*) I place myself in your

hands, remembering another similarity between poetry and
painting . . . which is that both the poet and the painter
carry out their own ideas and their own schemes with more
love and with more diligence than they do the schemes of
others.

This new freedom for artists may well be related to the
deliberate individualism of style in pictures of the sixteenth
century.[14]

One special problem has not been discussed so far: that of
the picture, whether mythological or historical, that requires
a literary knowledge of antiquity. Artists, as we have seen
above, usually lacked a classical education and so
could not have been responsible for these *invenzioni*. Nor is it
likely that the patron or client always had sufficient learning
to provide the idea. Consequently, since Warburg's essay
on Botticelli of 1893, art-historians have put forward the
hypothesis that there was an intellectual middleman between
artist and client, the humanist adviser. It has been argued, for
example, that Botticelli was advised by Poliziano; Bellini, by
Bembo; Correggio, by Giorgio Anselmi; Cossa, by Pietro Buono
Avogario or Pellegrino Prisciani; Perugino, by Francesco Matur-
anzio; Pinturicchio, by Nanni da Viterbo; Raphael, by Fabio
Calvo; and there are other examples. This hypothesis has also
been attacked, on the grounds that it is sheer assumption,
without any basis in fifteenth-century documents. The next
few paragraphs will consider some of the evidence for the
existence of the humanist adviser between 1420 and 1540.

Alberti advised painters to associate with poets and orators
who can help them with their *invenzioni*; but his treatise is
theory, not practice. The first concrete example of humanist
advice in the period concerns a Biblical subject, not a classical
one: the programme of the 'Gates of Paradise', the third door
of the Baptistery in Florence, executed by Ghiberti and
assistants. In 1424, months before Ghiberti was given the
commission, the patron, the Calimala guild, asked Leonardo
Bruni for a programme. His report, recommending twenty
'histories' and eight prophets, has survived. The report was
not followed, for the doors contain only ten 'histories'. Ghiberti
himself claimed in his memoirs that he was given a free hand:

The commission gave me permission to execute it in whatever way I believed would result in the greatest perfection, the most ornamentation and the greatest richness.

Yet it is curious that he makes mistakes when describing the doors. It is possible that the final design owes something to another humanist who opposed Bruni's programme, Ambrogio Traversari. At all events, we see a patron consulting a humanist about a programme before commissioning an artist.

A second case of humanist advice comes from Ferrara in the early fifteenth century, where Guarino of Verona was court schoolmaster. A letter of Guarino's to Leonello d'Este of 1447 survives, which suggests a possible programme for paintings of the Muses which Leonardo wanted.

There are several possible cases of humanist advice from the Medici commissions of the later fifteenth century. It is known that Botticelli's *Primavera* and *Birth of Venus* were painted for Lorenzo di Pierfrancesco de'Medici, a cousin of Lorenzo the Magnificent. His tutor was one of the most famous of all humanists, Ficino, and Gombrich has suggested that a letter from Ficino to his pupil in which he makes Venus a symbol of the humanist ideal, *humanitas*, is the key to the programme of the *Primavera*. Allusions to classical poetry in the two Botticelli paintings, make Warburg's suggestion that Poliziano helped with the 'invention' even more plausible than when he first put it forward. It is interesting to find Condivi declaring that the young Michelangelo made his *Battle of the Centaurs* at the suggestion of Poliziano, 'who explained the whole myth to him from beginning to end' (*dichiarandogli a parte per parte tutta la favola*).

Another milieu in which there is concrete evidence of humanist advisers is that of the court of Mantua, early in the sixteenth century. Isabella d'Este's correspondence shows that when she planned a series of 'pagan fantasies' or 'poetical inventions' for her study and grotto, it was the Mantuan humanist Paride da Ceresara to whom she turned for advice. It was he who provided the programme for the *Battle of Love and Chastity*, which a letter of Isabella's (above p. 116) shows her imposing on Perugino. Her Latin tutor Mario Equicola devised a programme of six 'fables or histories' to decorate a room at the court of Ferrara. Isabella also appealed to Bembo for *invenzioni*.

It would certainly be possible to add to these examples. In Florence in the early sixteenth century, according to Vasari, two groups of noblemen asked Andrea Dazzi and Jacopo Nardi to produce *invenzioni* for the floats for the Carnival. In mid-sixteenth century Rome, when Cardinal Farnese commissioned Vasari to paint the *Sala della Cancelleria* in the palace of S. Giorgio, the *invenzioni* were provided by Giovio. To sum up: there is some concrete evidence of humanists drawing up the programme or providing the 'invention' for works of art in this period, but not enough to say whether the practice was common or uncommon. Modern humanists like Warburg and Panofsky may have been tempted to exaggerate the importance of their Renaissance equivalents. Artists as well as intellectuals were called in to advise on works of art. Pisanello was an artistic adviser at the court of Naples, where he made sketches for the triumphal arch which was executed by a team of sculptors. Leonardo advised on the decoration of the ballroom at the Castello Sforzesco at Milan. In 1476, Gentile Bellini furnished Antonio Rizzo with designs for the bas-reliefs he was making for the *Scuola di S. Marco*, whether acting in his role of famous artist or in the role of patron (he was dean of the *Scuola*) is not known.

Humanists succeeded theologians as advisers when secular subjects began to replace religious ones, though some theologians advised painters in the period: Fra Sante Pagnini helped Michelangelo with the Sistine Chapel. After 1540, mythological dictionaries like the ones by Cartari, Giraldi and Ripa were published, and the artist no longer needed humanist advice so much. The humanist adviser, insofar as he existed, can be interpreted as a stop-gap, a means for coping with the sudden demand for classical mythology and ancient history which workshop traditions had not trained artists to provide.[15]

ARCHITECTURE, MUSIC AND LITERATURE

Architecture presents a special problem because the architect does not work with his hands: what does he provide, if not the 'programme'? This means that if the patron does take an active interest, the architect is likely to disappear between him and the master-masons. Some patrons certainly did take an interest in building; for example, they read treatises on architecture. When the triumphal arch project was being discussed, Alfonso of Aragon asked for Vitruvius to be brought to him. Ercole d'Este borrowed Alberti's treatise on architecture from Lorenzo de'Medici before deciding how to rebuild his palace. Federico of Urbino may have taken advice from Alberti personally – and Alberti may be classified at will as an architect or as a humanist adviser. Towards the end of the period, it would have been very much easier for small patrons to take an informed interest in the buildings they commissioned; Vitruvius was printed in 1486, and published in Italian in 1521. Alberti on architecture was printed just before Vitruvius (1485) but was not available in Italian until the end of the period (1546).

Filarete's treatise on architecture presents a picture, idealized no doubt, of the prince who cheerfully accepts the plans of his architect. There are also literary references to patrons giving instructions which architects simply carry out. For example, a panegyric on Cosimo de'Medici describes him as wanting to build a church and a house in his own manner (*more suo*) and telling the architect what to do:

> Such a skilled master notes it all down in his papers; he marks the house, here will be the porphyry gates, let there be a wide portico here, and here the first step of marble stairway . . .

A panegyric on Lorenzo went still further: 'How greatly he excels in architecture! In both private and public buildings we all make use of his inventions and his harmonies.' Lorenzo is a good example of the patron as amateur architect, for he submitted his own design in the competition for the façade of the cathedral in 1491. The judges were unable to choose his design or anyone else's, and so the façade was left unbuilt.

As with painting and sculpture, the clinching argument about the patron's importance would be his victory in a situation of conflict; but evidence of conflict is difficult to come by. In the Medici case there is simply the tradition that Cosimo preferred Michelozzo's design for the Medici palace to Brunelleschi's on the grounds that Brunelleschi's design was too ostentatious.[16]

As the classical style became popular among patrons, the retraining of architects must have presented quite a problem: here it was convenient to be attached to a court. Battista Covo, architect at the court of Mantua before Giulio Romano arrived, went to Rome to study in 1532.

In the case of music the situation is different again. Patronage of composers was rare, but patronage of performers was constantly necessary, and most Renaissance composers did sing or play as well. It may be useful to distinguish church, court and town musicians.

The Church was a great patron of singers, though not a particularly generous one. They were needed for sung masses and other parts of the liturgy, and they were needed all the time, as were organists. So the Church, a client for painters, was a patron for musicians. The composer and theorist Giovanni Spataro, for example, was choirmaster at St Petronio at Bologna for thirty years, 1512–41.

Cities also had a need for musicians, and took them into permanent service, though town musicians usually had another job as well. Cellini's father was one of the city musicians of Florence, playing the flute, but he was also an artist. Trumpeters were particularly in demand for processions at such civic events as the signing of treaties, state visits, or major religious feast-days. In Florence (until 1475) the trumpets sounded every Saturday at 11 p.m. in honour of the government. The best civic posts were at Venice. S. Marco was the doge's chapel, and so its choirmaster was a civic (which meant a political) appointment. The post was created in 1491 for a Frenchman, Pierre de Fossis. When he died in 1527 the procurators supported the claims of his former assistant, Lupato, to the appointment; but Doge Gritti forced through the appointment of an outsider, Adriaan Willaert, who stayed for 35 years, until his death in 1562. The musical importance of sixteenth-century Venice may owe something to the relative munificence of its civic patronage.

Court patronage was the least secure of the three main types, but had the possibility of the greatest rewards. Some princes took a great interest in their chapels: Galeazzo Maria Sforza, Ercole d'Este, Leo x. When Sforza decided to found a chapel, in 1472, he spared no effort to build it up. He wrote to his

ambassador in Naples with instructions to persuade some of
the singers there to come to Milan. He was to talk to them
and to make promises of 'good benefices and good salaries',
but in his own name, not the duke's:

> Above all take good care that neither his royal majesty nor
> others should imagine that we are the cause of these singers
> being taken away.

Presumably a diplomatic incident might have followed this
discovery. By 1474 the duke had at least acquired a certain
'Jusquino', perhaps Josquin des Près. The duke continued to
take a great interest in his chapel, which had to follow him
about to Pavia, Vigevano, and even outside the duchy. (Alfonso
of Aragon even took his chapel hunting with him!)

A still greater interest in music was taken by Pope Leo x.
He played and composed himself; a canon composed by him
still exists. His interests were known before he was elected
pope; and on the news of his election, many of the marquis
of Mantua's singers left for Rome. The most distinguished
composers in his service were probably Genet, who was in
charge of the papal chapel; Festa, most famous for his
madrigals; and the organist M. A. Cavazzoni. But there are
many stories of the pope's generosity to musicians, stories
which have been confirmed by an inspection of the papal
accounts. He took into his service a group of private musicians
(*musici secreti*) who numbered more than 15 in 1520. He paid
the famous lutenist Gian Maria 23 ducats a month, and made
him a count as well.

Isabella d'Este was interested in secular music as in secular
paintings; Marchetto Cara, who was a lutenist and a composer
of *frottole*, was at the court of Mantua from 1495 to 1525; and
Bartolomeo Tromboncino, another composer of *frottole*, was
in Mantuan service at the same time.

A fourth kind of patronage must not be forgotten: it was
possible for musicians to make their careers in the service of
private individuals. The organist Cavazzoni was at one time in
the service of a Venetian nobleman, Francesco Cornaro; at
another, in the service of the humanist and cardinal Pietro
Bembo. Willaert organized musical academies for a Venetian
lady, Polissena Pecorina, and a nobleman, Marco Trivisano.

In all these cases it is difficult to tell whether composers were hired because they could sing or play or because they could invent. There is a little evidence of interest in the activity of invention – but not much. Some pieces of music were dedicated to individuals or written in their honour. A certain Cristoforo da Feltre wrote a motet on the election of Doge Foscari (1423), for example. Heinrich Isaak, who was in Florence from 1484 to 1494, wrote an instrumental piece, 'Palle, palle', presumably for the Medici, since it refers to their cry and their emblem; he also set to music Poliziano's lament for the death of Lorenzo. Some pieces of music formed part of court festivities, the musical equivalent of the triumphal arches and fancy dress which artists like Leonardo had to design. Costanzo Festa, a distinguished composer of madrigals, wrote the music for the interludes for the wedding of Cosimo de'Medici duke of Tuscany. Alfonso della Viola, who was choirmaster to Ercole II d'Este, wrote music for the première of Giraldi's *Orbecche* and for other plays. There is also a fascinating letter about the hiring of a composer, written by a certain 'Gian' to Ercole I d'Este, about 1500. The choice lay between Heinrich Isaak and Josquin des Près.

> Isaak the singer . . . is extremely rapid in the art of composition, and besides this he is a man . . . who can be managed as one wants . . . and he seems to me extremely suitable to serve your lordship, more than Josquin, because he gets on better with his colleagues, and would make new things more often; it is true that Josquin composes better, but he does it when he feels like it, not when he is asked to; and he is asking for 200 ducats, and Isaak will be satisfied with 120.

In other words, the point that Josquin 'composes better' is recognized, but it is simply not the most important thing. The historian could hardly wish for a more revealing document on the relation of patron to artist.[17]

In the case of literature and humanism, patronage was less necessary than in the other arts, because so many writers were amateurs who had another means of livelihood and did not need rewards. But for some writers patronage was as much a necessity as it was for artists. Patronage was most necessary when it was least likely, when a writer was poor, young and unknown and wanted to study. In some significant cases it was forthcoming: Landino studied law at Volterra at the expense of a certain notary, Angelo di Jacopo Atti; Lorenzo de'Medici made it possible for Poliziano to study; Guarino was able to study at Verona thanks to a Venetian nobleman, Paolo Zane; Janos Lascaris's studies were financed by Cardinal Bessarion, who was a generous and discerning patron of scholars, Biondo, Poggio and Platina among them. One wonders how many promising careers came to nothing for lack of such patronage. Something was done for poor students at some universities: for example, Borso d'Este paid for their food and clothes at Ferrara. If Alfonso of Aragon found boys who were poor but able (says his official biographer Panormita) he paid for their education. Gifts to universities should be seen as indirect patronage of this kind for literature and learning; the most important was probably that of the Venetian government, which from the early fifteenth century onwards granted 4,000 ducats a year to the university of Padua.

Court patronage for writers who were established was certainly forthcoming because princes were interested in fame, and both princes and poets believed that poets could bestow it. It might, however, take a certain amount of intrigue as well as ability to acquire a post. As with painters, friendship and relationships made patronage easier to come by, and there were many intermediaries involved. Augustus could only be approached through Maecenas, and sometimes Maecenas could only be approached through various 'Mecenatuli', as the poet Panormita contemptuously called them. His own search for patronage led him up several blind alleys before eventual success. He tried Florence, dedicating a poem to Cosimo de'Medici as early as 1425, but failed to get anything; he tried Mantua, through a fellow-humanist, to find that they had Vittorino da Feltre and needed no one else; he tried Ferrara, through Guarino, who was established there, and was unsuccessful again; he tried Milan, through the archbishop, who wrote to the duke's secretaries for him; there at last he landed the post of court poet.

If one was a court poet or hoped to become one, a necessary activity – again following Virgilian precedent – was to write an epic about the prince, his family and deeds. Filelfo wrote a

Sforziad to celebrate the Sforza of Milan. Porcellio wrote a *Feltria* for Federico da Montefeltre of Urbino. Naldi wrote the *Volterrais* for Lorenzo de'Medici, an epic about the sack of Volterra after its rebellion in 1472. The same subject was attempted by another poet, Valentini, who hoped for a post at the university of Pisa; and Poliziano also intended to write on this theme. At Ferrara, T. V. Strozzi wrote the *Borsias* for Borso d'Este, the first of a series of epics for the family who were the patrons of Boiardo, Ariosto and Tasso. Ariosto made his hero and heroine Ruggiero and Bradamante ancestors of the house of Este. In his third canto, modelled on *Aeneid* vi, Merlin arranged a vision of the future in which Alfonso i, duke of Ferrara, and his ancestors Ercole, Leonello and Borso all appeared, and declared that the golden age would return under Este rule.

Court historians, like court epic poets, were in demand, again because they conferred fame (immortality, they claimed) on their patrons. Bartolomeo Fazio was appointed court historian to Alfonso of Aragon (see Pl. 10) at a salary of 300 ducats a year. Bernardino Corio, who wrote the history of Milan, was pensioned by 'il Moro', who also gave him access to the archives. Benedetto Varchi was commissioned to write his *History of Florence* by Duke Cosimo de'Medici. Machiavelli's *History of Florence* was commissioned by another Medici, Pope Clement vii, and dedicated to the pope by his 'humble slave'. Republics were aware of the value of official history too: Venice above all. Marcantonio Sabellico was official historian of Venice (at a salary of 200 *zecchini* a year); so was Bembo; so was Andrea Navagero.

Less politically useful works might be commissioned by patrons who had a taste for them or liked the company of the authors. Cosimo de'Medici gave Ficino a farm at Carreggi and a house in Florence, and encouraged him to translate Plato. Poliziano began a translation of the Iliad for Lorenzo de'Medici. His *Stanze per la Giostra* were written to celebrate a famous joust in which Lorenzo's brother Giuliano took part. Lorenzo also supported Luigi Pulci, whose company he enjoyed, and Pulci wrote his famous *Morgante* at the request of Lorenzo's mother Lucrezia. The lyric poets Bellincione and Visconti lived at the Sforza court producing verse letters and the like on demand. Poets like painters and musicians might have to help provide the entertainment at festivals: when he was in Mantuan service, Poliziano wrote his famous *Orfeo* 'to order' for a wedding. He also wrote begging poems to Lorenzo describing how his clothes had worn out, a poetic version of the hints which Mantegna and Josquin des Près apparently found it necessary to convey to their patrons. The verse request was a literary genre which reminds us of the importance of patronage in the cultural life of the time – and in the life of the individual writer.

Court patronage did not only mean something to live on; it meant status as a courtier, and – an important factor in Renaissance Italy – protection. Serafino of Aquila was in the service of cardinal Ascanio Sforza at Rome. He did not like the cardinal, so left his service and lived in Rome for a time without a patron. Then there was an attempt to kill him (he had a satirical vein); when he recovered, his contemporary biographer tells us, 'considering that to be without a protector was dangerous and shameful', he went back to Ascanio.

The problem for the writer who was not of independent means was that civic patronage was virtually non-existent; the choice was the Church, the court or a private individual. Court patronage and private patronage were insecure; if one had a benefice, at least it was permanent income. Hence we find Alberti, and Poliziano, and Ariosto, whom it is difficult to see as career clergymen, trying to get benefices. Poliziano was nearly a cardinal, and Bembo ended up as one. Castiglione, the complete courtier, died as papal nuncio and bishop of Avila. It should be added that it was possible for a layman who could write a good Latin letter to be paid by the Church, as Biondo and Poggio were, as papal secretaries.

The difficulties involved in depending on patronage for a living can be seen most vividly in the career of Aretino (see Pl. 7), who tried hard not to be dependent, but started as a shoemaker's son without money. He began his career under cardinal Giulio de'Medici, later Pope Clement VII. He then accepted an invitation from Federico Gonzaga to come to Mantua: wrote a poem in honour of the Gonzaga, and gave his play *The Marshal* a Mantuan setting. The pope did not care to see Aretino depending on someone else; but Aretino seems to have thought that two patrons gave him more freedom than one. In 1527 he nearly lost both; he broke with the pope, who then put pressure on Federico not to keep him at Mantua. He went to Venice, and became more independent than before. He was protected by Doge Gritti, and received gifts from a number of noblemen, without losing contact with Mantua. His position became firm enough for him to refuse an invitation to Florence from Alessandro de'Medici, and to break with Federico. Having many patrons (it is difficult to call them 'clients' because they did not pay Aretino for specific poems or letters) was something like having no master at all.[18]

Patronage of science can be passed over quickly. Most 'scientists' made their living through university teaching or the practice of medicine, and did not need anyone to take a personal interest in their research. But Pandolfo Petrucci, lord of Siena, was patron of Vannoccio Biringuccio, the metallurgist and engineer, who was to him what Leonardo was to Lodovico Sforza. Guidobaldo da Montefeltre, duke of Urbino, was patron of Luca Pacioli, who wrote on mathematics; and Lodovico Sforza invited Pacioli to Milan. Bartolomeo Eustachio was court mathematician to Guidobaldo della Rovere, a later duke of Urbino; it is a pity that we do not know what the duties of court mathematician were.

THE RISE OF THE MARKET

In the long run, the rise of printing involved the decline of the literary patron; the man of letters came to depend on the market (and his publisher) instead. But during the Renaissance, patronage and market systems coexisted. There is some evidence of the commercialization of patronage – the dedication of a book in the hope of instant cash reward. At the end of the period, one finds multiple dedications: Bandello dedicated each story in his collection to a different person. Sometimes they were friends of his (Castiglione, for example, and Molza) but more often they were great nobles – the Bentivoglio, the Colonna, the Farnese, the Gonzaga, and the Sforza – from whom he would have expected something in return. Printers sometimes needed patrons too: when Aldus Manutius published his famous edition of Virgil in 1501, he had several copies printed on vellum and distributed to patrons, among them (yet again) Isabella d'Este.

With the rise of the market in literature one finds some printers as extremely successful businessmen – the Giolito and Giunta firms, for example. One finds the printed book, originally thought of as just a manuscript 'written' by machine, being regarded as a commodity standardized in size (the terms 'folio', 'quarto', etc., go back to the Aldus catalogue of 1541) and price (the Aldus catalogue of 1498 is the first to give prices) and sold by means of advertisements, for example verses inserted by the printer at the end of one book to recommend the reader to go to his shop for others : 'Whoever wants to buy a "Furioso" (says one advertisement) or another work by the same author, let him go to the press of the Bindoni twins, the brothers Benedetto and Agostino.' One finds printers employing authors to write, translate, and edit for them : Gabriele Giolito did this. This is how the Venetian 'Grub Street' (just off the Grand Canal) came into existence in the middle of the sixteenth century; this was the time of the *poligrafi*, the first professional writers, men like Dolce, Domenichi and Ruscelli, who wrote (or plagiarised) anything that the printer thought might sell, and wrote for money. Aretino died just too soon : he would have been the greatest of them all.[16]

At much the same time, about 1550, we find the beginnings of Italian journalism – the commercialized newsletter, for example, which flourished at Rome – and of the professional theatre (which is what the term *commedia dell'arte* means literally).

In the visual arts, too, one can talk of the rise of the market, in the fifteenth and sixteenth centuries (coexisting with the personalized system of patrons and clients), provided one does this in sufficiently precise and qualified terms. By a market system I mean a system where clients do not commission works at all, but buy them 'ready-made', possibly through a middleman. Examples of the sale of uncommissioned works of art can be found already in different parts of thirteenth and fourteenth-century Europe. The demand for Virgins, Crucifixions or St John the Baptists was sufficiently great and sufficiently standardized for workshops to produce them before the customer turned up, but they might be left unfinished, in case the customer had some special demands. Some merchants dealt in works of art as in other commodities; the 'merchant of Prato' Francesco di Marco Datini, many of whose business letters survive, did this. Cheap painted stucco reproductions of famous sculptures were made in fourteenth-century Florence.

In the fifteenth century, one has the impression, difficult to document, that the ready-made work was more common. Merchants were appearing who specialized in the sale of works of art. In Florence, there was Bartolommeo Serragli, for example. He searched Rome for antique marble statues for one of the Medici; he ordered fabrics in Florence for Alfonso of Aragon; he dealt in illuminated manuscripts and terracotta Madonnas, chess-sets and mirrors. Donatello, Desiderio da Settignano and Fra Lippo Lippi worked for him. Vespasiano da Bisticci, the Florentine 'stationer' (seller of manuscripts) whose memoirs have made him famous, was also a middleman who arranged for illuminators, such as Attavante, to work for customers they did not know, such as Duke Federico of Urbino and King Mátyás of Hungary. One can also talk with confidence of a rise of a market in reproductions; woodcuts of devotional images, for example, began to be made in the early fifteenth century, before the invention of printing. Political woodcuts appeared in the later fifteenth century – for example the meeting of the pope and the Emperor in Rome in 1468. Then there was the glazed terracotta work of the Della Robbia workshop in Florence, especially after about 1470; cheap, standardized and so presumably uncommissioned. The Della Robbias produced miniature replicas of the Madonna of Impruneta (below, p. 258). There were the painted jars and plates from Bologna, Urbino, Faenza and elsewhere, often with classical motifs. This industry developed in the fifteenth century. When printing was established, in the 1480s and 90s, woodcuts became important as a means of illustrating books. Aldus produced a number of famous illustrated editions; of Dante, Petrarch, Boccaccio, of Herodotus, of the fantastic romance *Polifilo*, and so on. Other woodcuts and engravings were independent. Botticelli, Mantegna and Antonio Pollaiuolo were among the important artists who used the new media before 1500. What one would dearly love to know is how often fifteenth-century artists made something for which they had no commission, whether simply for their own pleasure or in the hope of selling it. Michelangelo wrote to his father from Rome in 1497 that he was working on a figure *per mio piacere*, 'for my own pleasure'. There are also examples of the sale of second-hand works of art. The auction of Medici property in 1495 included paintings.

In the sixteenth century the impression of the rise of the art market is still stronger. There is some evidence from the circle of Isabella d'Este at Mantua. For example, she bought the works of living artists from other people – she bought Michelangelo's sleeping cupid from Cesare Borgia in 1502. When Giorgione died (1510) she wrote to a Venetian merchant:

> we are informed that among the stuff and effects of the painter Zorzo of Castelfranco there exists a picture of a night (*una nocte*) very beautiful and singular; if so it might be, we desire to possess it and we therefore ask you, in company with Lorenzo da Pavia and any other who has judgement and understanding, to see whether it is a really fine thing and if you find it such, to go to work . . . to obtain this picture for me, settling the price and giving me notice of it.

However, the answer was that the two pictures of this kind in the studio had been painted as commissions, and the clients would not let them go – Isabella, here as elsewhere, was a little in advance of her time:

> . . . the said Zorzo painted one for Taddeo Contarini, which from my information is not very perfect as you would wish. Another picture, *de la nocte*, was made by the said Zorzo for one Victorio Beccaro, which I am told is better designed and better finished than Contarini's, but Beccaro is not at present in these parts, and, as I am informed, neither the one nor the other is for sale at any price, because they had them made for their own enjoyment.

The year after, it was an artist who took the initiative in a sale of uncommissioned work to the Gonzagas. Carpaccio wrote to Isabella's husband that he had a watercolour of Jerusalem; someone has made an offer for it (perhaps he was from the court of Mantua); the painter introduces himself anyway and describes the work. It is as if selling pictures in this way was coming in but was sufficiently unusual for an apologetic preamble to be necessary. Another Gonzaga, Federico, bought 120 Flemish paintings from a collection in 1535.

Isabella's agents (whom she employed in commissioning works as well as making offers for ready-made paintings) were not full-time specialist art-dealers: Lorenzo da Pavia, for example, was a maker of clavichords. In Florence, where there is some evidence of a market in paintings in the first half of the sixteenth century, there was such a dealer: Gian Battista della Palla. He is most celebrated for his activities as agent for François I, scouting round for works of art to send to France. For example, he bought a statue of Hercules by Michelangelo (not from the artist but from Filippo Strozzi's steward) and sent it to France in 1530. The same year he bought a statue of Mercury by Bandinelli and sent that to France too. He also bought a Fra Bartolomeo *St Sebastian* (from the client) and a Pontormo *Raising of Lazarus* for the French King. He wanted to buy some chests painted by Pontormo for a certain Borgherini and went to his house, but Borgherini's wife drove him out, shouting that he was 'a vile second-hand dealer, a fourpenny merchant' (*vilissimo rigattiere, mercatantuzzo di quattro danari*); it was worth risking a scolding, for there were great profits to be made selling to the King of France: Vasari says that 'the merchants' received four times what they paid Andrea del Sarto for a painting. There are other cases in early sixteenth-century Florence of the sale of uncommissioned works. When Pontormo died, a Madonna was found in his house; his heirs sold it to P. Salviati. Presumably, if the painting had been made on commission, the heirs would not have had to go to the trouble of disposing of it. Again, one finds one patron buying works of art originally commissioned by another; Ottaviano de'Medici, a keen collector, bought two paintings by Sarto which had been made for Ginori. From the same period, there are occasional references to exhibiting paintings in public, a form of advertising perhaps related to the rise of an art market. Bandinelli, Vasari tells us, painted St John the Baptist in the desert, and 'exhibited it (*lo messe a mostra*) in the shop of Michelangelo his father'. He painted a *Deposition of Christ*, and 'exhibited it in the New Market in the shop of the goldsmith Giovanni di Goro'.

In Venice as in Florence there is some evidence of the rise of the market. To return to the nativity scene which Bellini painted for Isabella when she wanted a pagan fantasy; at one point, when negotiations seemed to be breaking down, Bellini

told her that he had found someone who wanted to buy it –
o trovato uno che el vole comprare. Titian's portraits were
bought by people who were interested in the artist, not the
sitter; the first documented case of this comes from 1536,
when the duke of Urbino bought from Titian a portrait of a
'woman dressed in blue'. A certain 'Zuan Ram' seems to have
been active as an art-dealer in early sixteenth-century Venice.
Paintings were exhibited at the Ascension Week fair in Venice
– Lotto and the Bassanos were among the exhibitors – as they
were at St Anthony's fair at Padua.

In the sixteenth century, engravings became much more
frequent; the great centres were Venice and Rome – not, as one
might have expected, Venice and Florence. Giovanni da Brescia,
Jacopo de'Barbari, the Campagnolas, Agostino Veneziano and
Marcantonio Raimondi were among the famous engravers of
the time; engraving was becoming a specialist occupation.
Engraving was a way of making particular paintings better
known. Andrea del Sarto's painting of the *Dead Christ* was
engraved at Rome; Raimondi engraved, among other paintings,
Leonardo's *Last Supper.* Piracy developed. There exists a letter
of Giovanni da Brescia to the doge (1514) saying that he has
made some woodcuts of the Emperor Trajan and printed some
of them, but 'certain others' have taken the works to print
them themselves, which would be a grave loss to him; so he
asks for a ten-year monopoly of the woodcuts. At the same
time, the number of pieces surviving suggests that the maiolica-
industry was expanding. One should not forget the hand-made
copy: Vasari says that G. B. della Palla had copies made of
Florentine paintings and sculptures to send to France; he does
not say whether the copies were by someone else or by the
artists themselves.[19]

To sum up. It is easier to talk about the direction of
change than about its extent. There is no question of any
market system having displaced a more personalized system of
patronage in any of the arts by the middle of the sixteenth
century. That was to come considerably later in European
history – in the course of the seventeenth, eighteenth and nineteenth centuries, and in the Netherlands, France and England
rather than in Italy – though it was in Venice, in the early
seventeenth century, that the first commercial opera-house
opened. However, there were moves towards the commer-

cialization of the work of art, above all in Florence and Venice 1500–50, within the framework of the older system. For the artist it is likely to have meant greater freedom – and greater insecurity. For the work of art, it may well have meant a greater differentiation of subject-matter and a more deliberate individualism of style, the exploitation of the artist's unique qualities in order to catch the eye of a purchaser, at the same time that it meant the rise of reproduction and even 'mass-production' (though terracottas and maiolica had of course to be painted by hand) to appeal to a wider public at a cheaper price.

Conclusions

There remains the crucial yet unanswerable question of whether the arts flourished because of the patrons, or in spite of them. The question is unanswerable because one does not know what the same artists would have created in different circumstances. What one can discuss is the relation between patronage and the uneven distribution of artistic achievement between different parts of Italy.

Chapter Three suggested that art flourished in Florence and Venice because these cities produced many of their own artists, and that they were able to do this because talent was less frustrated among the sons of craftsmen than among other social groups. This is not the whole story: certain cities in Italy were more able to focus talent, to draw foreigners into orbit, than others. In the early fifteenth century Venice attracted Ghiberti, Uccello, Castagno and Alberti. Urbino, Mantua and Ferrara are famous examples of cities of moderate size without many important native artists, which became important centres of cultural happenings. In each case one can point to the court, to the prince or his wife, as the stimulus; the initiative lay with the patron. In Urbino in the time of Federico da Montefeltre, the arts were not important until he made them so. Laurana came to Urbino from Dalmatia, Piero della Francesca came from Borgo San Sepolcro, Francesco di Giorgio Martini came from Siena. It was only in the next generation, that of Bramante and Raphael, that important artists were born in or near little Urbino. Again, in Mantua

Isabella d'Este commissioned works from Bellini, Carpaccio, Correggio, Costa, Dosso, Francia, Giorgione, Leonardo, Mantegna, Perugino, Raphael, Titian. None of these artists was a Mantuan: the only Mantuan painter who worked for her was a much less important figure, Lorenzo Leombruno.

At these small courts, the patron seems to be calling art into existence where there was none before. But two points need to be borne in mind. The first is that such court patronage was in a sense parasitic on the art of the great centres like Florence. 'Parasitic' does not mean 'morally despicable' – the term is not being used as a value-judgement. But when discussing the relation of art to Italian society, we need to remember the cities in which artists were born or trained as well as the ones where they produced certain masterpieces.

The second point to make about the efficacy of court patronage is related to the first. Such patronage frequently did not last. A prince or princess might try to make their city or court a cultural centre but even if this actually happened, the achievement would not long outlive them. An interesting test-case is that of Alfonso of Aragon. He showed great interest in the arts and he ruled a great kingdom, but one which made a relatively small contribution to the Renaissance. How much could the king do for the arts, one might have asked at the beginning of his reign, and by what means? Alfonso was interested in the classics, in such authors as Seneca, Caesar, Livy, Horace, Lucretius, and Ovid. He took five well-known humanists into his permanent service: Panormita, Fazio, the two Decembrio brothers, and Valla. He founded a university at Catania. He was interested in music, built up a chapel of 22 singers and paid his organist the unusually large sum of 120 ducats a year. He was interested in the visual arts, invited Pisanello to court, and commissioned a grand triumphal arch on which such sculptors as Andrea dell'Aquila, Domenico Gaggini, Isaia da Pisa, and Francesco Laurana worked. Mino da Fiesole came and made the King's portrait in marble. He bought Flemish tapestries and Venetian glass and commissioned a great deal of table silver. When the king died, all this activity stopped. Two reasons can be given for this. In the first place, Alfonso had depended on men from outside his kingdom: Valla came from Rome, Fazio from Genoa, Pisanello and the sculptor Isaia from Pisa, and so on. In the second place, they had only the king's patronage; Alfonso's nobles do not seem to have followed his example and taken an interest in the arts.

In contrast to Alfonso, Lorenzo de'Medici had everything in his favour as a patron. Living in Florence, he had access to artists and did not have to attract them from faraway places. He was not a lone patron, but one of many, great and small. Patronage of the arts was traditional in such leading families as the Pazzi, Pitti, Rucellai, Strozzi, or Tornabuoni, perhaps a habit acquired in the days of civic patronage early in the fifteenth century. Lorenzo's patronage has been exaggerated in the past. The point to be made here, however, is not one about the extent of his patronage but about its facility. Patronage was structured; easy in some parts of Italy, difficult in others.[20]

5

The Functions of Works of Art

Chi volessi per diletto
Qualche gentil figuretta,
Per tenerla sopra letto
O in su qualche basetta?
Ogni camera s'assetta
Ben con le nostre figure.

Carnival Song of the sculptors of Florence.
('Who wants some elegant statuette for his
delight? You can put it above your bed or on a
stand. Our figures make any room look well.')

The idea of a 'work of art' is a modern abstraction, but
thanks to the existence of art galleries and museums we are
encouraged to project the idea back into the past. The title of
this chapter should have been 'the functions of painting and
sculpture, poems and plays' (there seems to be less to say about
music and buildings) for the people who looked at, listened to,
bought, used and enjoyed them.

For convenience in exposition, different functions will be
treated separately in this chapter. This does not mean that a
painting or poem had only one function, or that contemporaries
were always aware what that function was: there are 'latent'
functions as well as manifest ones.

PAINTING AND SCULPTURE

One thing is clear, and that is that Italians of the fifteenth and
sixteenth centuries did not look at paintings in the same way
as we do. For one thing, paintings might be regarded as
expendable. In the early sixteenth century, Filippo Strozzi,

making his will, asked for a monument to be erected in the family chapel in S. Maria Novella, in which there was a fresco by Lippi; he added, 'do not worry about the painting that is there now, which it is necessary to destroy, since of its nature it is not a very durable thing.'[1]

Functions may be divided for convenience into three: religious, political, and private. Religious paintings and sculptures may be sub-divided into those with a magical function, those with a devotional function, and those with a didactic function, though all these divisions obviously blur at the edges.

The term 'magical function' is used here to refer to images which are believed to have thaumaturgic or other miraculous powers, as in the case of certain famous Byzantine icons. There is a story in Vasari's life of Raphael which is the equivalent of the Byzantine icon legends. A painting of Raphael's was on the way to Palermo when a storm arose and the ship was wrecked. But the painting 'remained unharmed . . . because even the fury of the winds and the waves of the sea had respect for the beauty of such a work.' The nearest things to the thaumaturgic image are some gonfalons or processional banners, for example those painted by Bonfigli in Perugia in the later fifteenth century, gonfalons which seem to have been considered a defence against plague. The Madonna is shown protecting her people with her mantle against the arrows of plague. A verse on one gonfalon begs her 'to ask and help thy son to take the fury away'. The popularity of pictures of St Sebastian, who was associated with defence against plague (below, p. 183), suggests that the magical function of Renaissance art was not a negligible one. A kind of thaumaturgic image is the image to which an indulgence was attached. Sixtus IV attached an indulgence to images of *Maria in Sole*, Our Lady surrounded by rays.

Ex-votos appear in Italy during the fifteenth century. They may be described as having a quasi-magical function. The donor may believe that he was saved from disaster only because he made the vow to have the image painted, but he may just be saying 'thank you' to the relevant saint. Ex-votos include some well-known pictures of the period, for example Mantegna's *Madonna della Vittoria*, which was commissioned by Francesco Gonzaga after the battle of Fornovo, in which he had taken part, and which historians tend to regard as a draw rather than a victory. The Jews of Mantua actually paid for the painting, but not voluntarily. After the earthquake of 1504–5, Giovanni Bentivoglio of Bologna commissioned Francia to paint a picture of S. Cecilia. Raphael's *Madonna di Foligno* was commissioned by Sigismondo de'Conti in gratitude for his escape when a meteor fell on his house. Carpaccio's *Martyrdom of 10,000 Christians* and Titian's *St Mark Enthroned* were both commissioned to fulfil vows made in time of plague.[2]

There are cases of non-christian magic too. The Cossa frescoes in the Palazza Schifanoia at Ferrara, with their astrological themes, may well have been painted to ensure good fortune. It has been suggested that Botticelli's *Primavera* may have been a 'talisman', an image made in order to draw down favourable 'influences' from the planet Venus. When Leonardo painted the thousand-eyed Argus guarding the Sforza treasury, it is difficult to tell whether his intention was to work protective magic or merely to make an elegantly appropriate classical allusion.[3]

A second religious function is the devotional. Here the image is not itself the object of reverence, but inspires reverence for whoever is represented in it. The interest of the Christian clergy in the psychological effect of images goes back to Pope Gregory the Great at least, who wrote: 'When you see an image of Him, your soul is inflamed with love of Him whose picture you love to see.' In the fifteenth century, a particular interest was taken in images as a stimulus to devotion, perhaps provoked by the emergence of the woodcut. In France, Gerson, for example, approved the use of images, and in Germany Geiler von Kaiserberg explained how to use a religious woodcut:

> If you cannot read, then take a picture of paper where Mary and Elizabeth are depicted as they meet each other, you buy it for a penny. Look at it and think how happy they had been, and of good things . . . Then do them reverence, kiss the image on the paper, bow in front of the image, kneel before it.

S. Bernardino and Savonarola made a considerable use of the crucifix as a stimulus to devotion. In fifteenth-century Italy, a new kind of picture was the half-length picture of a religious subject, small enough not to be too expensive and with an intimate quality which made it suitable for private devotion. The term 'devotional pictures' (*quadri di devotione*) was current in Italy during the period. Perhaps the more naturalistic representation of Christ, Mary and the saints is associated with the increasing importance of this devotional function of art (see Pl. 19). With it goes the practice of commissioning religious works for a secular setting, a man's own house, rather than for a sacred setting, the church. Surviving inventories of the houses of rich laymen in the period suggest that there were images of Our Lady in almost every room. An inventory of the Uzzano castle in the early fifteenth century lists two paintings of the 'sudary' – Christ's face as imprinted on Veronica's towel – and immediately after one of them a predella is listed, as if people regularly knelt before the image. The increasing importance of the devotional image seems related to changing forms of religion, with the laity playing more of a part than before (below, p. 259).[4]

The third religious function is the didactic – teaching theology or ethics; pictures as the Bible of the illiterate. It was Pope Gregory the Great who gave the famous description of this function: 'Paintings are placed in churches so that those who are illiterate can read on the walls what they cannot read in books.' At the beginning of the fifteenth century, Cardinal Giovanni Dominici, writing on the education of children, suggested that parents should keep religious paintings and sculptures in the house because of their moral effect. The infant Jesus and St John would be good for boys; also the Massacre of the Innocents, 'in order to make them afraid of arms and armed men'. Girls should look at the eleven thousand virgins (whom the legend says accompanied St Ursula), and at Saints Agnes, Cecilia, Elizabeth and Catherine, 'who would give them a love of virginity, a desire for Christ, a hatred for sins, a contempt for vanities'.

A special case of the didactic is pictorial propaganda, the representation of controversial topics from one point of view. After the Council of Trent, as Emile Mâle has pointed out, paintings in Catholic churches tended to illustrate points of doctrine which had been challenged by the Protestants. Painting, like rhetoric, was a method of persuasion. This method was on occasion used during the Renaissance. In the fifteenth century, there was a conflict between popes and councils over the primacy; the popes won. Paintings commissioned by popes may reinforce their point of view. Botticelli painted the Punishment of Korah in the Sistine Chapel for Pope Innocent VIII (see p. 204 below). It has been pointed out that the bull of Pope Eugenius IV, condemning the Council of Basel, also makes reference to Korah. Similarly, Julius II used Michelangelo to support his primacy. The Sistine Ceiling contains a scene showing Alexander the Great kneeling before the priest of Jerusalem. Raphael's Heliodorus fresco carries a similar message. Many Renaissance pictures, in other words, were there not only to be looked at, or even meditated upon, but to be read.[5]

POLITICAL FUNCTIONS

One obvious political function of the portrait was to be used in marriage negotiations between princes. When Cosimo Tura was working at Ferrara, he painted three d'Este daughters, Lucrezia, Isabella and Beatrice, for their betrothals to Annibale Bentivoglio, Francesco Gonzaga and Lodovico Sforza respectively. Other portraits had what might be called a 'celebratory' function, the secular equivalent of devotion. The prowess of successful *condottieri* was celebrated by equestrian portraits: Donatello's Gattamelata at Padua, Verrocchio's Colleoni monument at Venice, Uccello's rather cheaper Hawkwood fresco at Florence. Letters were celebrated as well as arms; the portraits of Florentine chancellors were hung after their deaths in the *Palazzo del Proconsolo*. In Venice, the Republic was celebrated by means of the official portraits of doges and by the scenes of Venetian victories in battle in the *Sala di Gran Consiglio*. In sixteenth-century Florence, the portraits of the Medici bought by private individuals to hang in their houses – Francesco Rucellai, for example, bought several from Vasari – surely had a 'devotional' function, like the portraits of the Queen hung in Elizabethan country houses. Alfonso of Aragon's triumphal arch and his portrait-medal were intended to present a favourable image of his régime, as the inscriptions reveal. On the arch is written *Pius, Clemens, Invictus* (pious, merciful, unvanquished) and on the medal, *Triumphator et Pacificus* (victorious and a peace-maker). The king, who had only recently won the kingdom of Naples by force of arms, seems to be telling his new subjects that if they submit, they will come to no harm, but that in a conflict he is bound to win.

Court and civic festivals also tend to mix celebration of the régime with a little propaganda. Famous examples are all from the second half of the period; the 'feast of Paradise' at the court of Milan in 1490, Leo x's entry into Florence, or Charles v's entry into Bologna.

Political propaganda is not always easy to distinguish from the vaguer celebration, but some cases seem clear enough. In Filarete's ideal city 'Sforzinda', evil deeds and their punishments were to be painted in the cloisters of the *Palazzo del Podestà*, 'to frighten anyone who enters, to give an example to those who wish to take it, and to let those led here see quickly what their end will be'. Perhaps he was thinking of his own city, Florence, where in the fifteenth and sixteenth centuries the images of traitors and rebels were painted on the walls of public buildings. In 1440, Castagno painted the Albizzi and other rebels, hung up by the feet on the façade of the *Palazzo del Podestà*. He was given the nickname *Andrea degli impiccati* ('Andrea of the hanged men', or perhaps 'Andrew the Rope') as a result. In 1529–30, during the siege of Florence, Andrea del Sarto painted the images of the captains who had fled on the façade of the same building. One wonders why exactly this was done. Perhaps the aim was the magical destruction of rebels and fugitives who were beyond the reach of ordinary punishment, the same mechanism as the piercing of wax images of one's enemies. Perhaps the aim was to shame the wrongdoers and their families; perhaps the paintings were made primarily to give information, like a wall-newspaper or a 'Wanted' poster. Florentine art is particularly rich in (possible) political meanings. It has been argued that Masaccio's famous *Tribute Money* fresco, an unusual scene to paint, is related to the proposals made at that time, 1425, to introduce a new tax, the *catasto*. In their wars with greater powers, Milan and Naples, in the fifteenth century, Florentines saw themselves as Isaac saved from sacrifice, as David fighting Goliath, as Judith cutting off the head of Holofernes, as St George spearing the dragon. When the Republic was restored in 1494, political symbols of this kind reappeared. Michelangelo's *David* surely refers back to Donatello's *David*, and so to the dangers which the Republic had survived in the early fifteenth century. In 1503 the government commissioned the Leonardo and Michelangelo frescoes of the battles of Anghiari and Cascina for the new hall of the Great Council. The idea of a Great Council was borrowed from Venice, and the idea of decorating the hall with paintings of the victories of the Republic was clearly borrowed too. When the Medici returned, the hall and the paintings were destroyed. This destruction of art by the new régime suggests that its political function was taken very seriously.[6]

PRIVATE FUNCTIONS

Family portraits may be seen as 'pictorial eulogies' and certain works of art were certainly associated with important, ritualised moments of family history. The *cassone* was associated with weddings, for it contained the bride's trousseau. Pictures were often given as wedding presents : *quadri da spose*, 'wedding pictures' is a term used in the period. Other paintings were associated with births : the *desca di parto*, 'birth tray' on which refreshments were brought to the mother who had just given birth, was often painted with the *Triumph of Love*. To commemorate death, there were funeral monuments. Thus paintings and sculptures had their place in the ritual surrounding births, marriages and deaths, the three great *rites de passage*. Besides pictorial eulogies, there is one remarkable case of private pictorial defamation. Benaglio was once commissioned to go at night and paint obscene pictures on the walls of a nobleman's house at Verona, the enemy of his client, presumably to put him to public shame.

The distinctively private function of a painting or piece of sculpture was to give pleasure to its owner. This function was recognized by some contemporaries. Lodovico Dolce went so far as to suggest that the function of painting was 'chiefly to give pleasure' (*principalmente per dilettare*). In many cases, paintings appear to have given pleasure because they decorated a room. Even the Gonzagas seem to have thought of painting as a form of interior decoration. Isabella asked Bellini for a picture 'to decorate a study of ours' (*per ornamento d'uno nostro studio*), and Federico Gonzaga wrote to Titian in 1537 saying that the new rooms in the castle were finished, all that was lacking was the pictures 'made for these rooms' (*fatte per tali lochi*). But the Gonzagas, and others in the sixteenth century, sometimes express the desire for the work of a particular artist, and this implies that whatever secondary functions a painting may have, its primary function was simply that of being itself. The idea of the 'work of art' was just about thinkable in certain aristocratic milieux at the end of the period. It is possible that in these circles, paintings of subjects from classical mythology were thought of more as beautiful objects than as illustrations of a story with or without a moral – whatever the humanist adviser thought. It is significant that Isabella called her mythologies simply 'poetical inventions', and that Titian in the 1550s referred to some of his mythological paintings simply as 'poems', *poesie*.

An important question is whether the functions of paintings and sculpture changed in relative importance during the period. The increasing numbers of secular subjects (above p. 43) suggest that there was such a change, but alas the historian cannot measure it. The juxtaposition of two inventories may suggest the kind of change that took place. Both inventories are Florentine, both refer to the houses of patrician families. One is early fifteenth century, and refers to the town house and the castle of the Uzzano family; the other is early sixteenth century and refers to both the town house and the villa of the Capponi. The inventorist of the Uzzano goods takes little interest in pictures; on several occasions it is difficult to tell whether the *tavola* listed is a painting or a table. The only subjects mentioned are Christs and Virgins, in other words devotional images. There are fewer than a dozen works. In contrast, the Capponi had 54 works, counting furniture painted with scenes, and about 40 paintings and sculptures. There were three subjects from classical antiquity – Hercules, Midas and Scaevola. The inventorist sometimes noted the style as Flemish or German.[7]

LITERATURE

The main functions of literature were to teach, to persuade, and to delight. Castiglione's *Courtier* aimed at polishing its readers; Machiavelli's *Prince*, at the political education of its dedicatee. The beginning of Guicciardini's *History of Italy* declares that its readers will be able to draw many useful lessons from it, for themselves and the public good. Vasari declared that his *Lives* were written in order to educate young artists. Some plays were concerned with the religious or moral education of their audiences: the *rappresentazioni sacre* (the Italian equivalent of mystery and miracle plays) usually end with exhortations to the audience (delivered by angels) telling them to take to heart what they have just seen. At the end of *Abraham and Isaac* for example, the angel tells the audience about the value of 'holy obedience', *santa ubidienzia*.

The political function of literature may be divided into two – the panegyric and the satire, corresponding to celebration and defamation in the visual arts. The panegyric may be a formalized piece of flattery, or a rather more substantial piece of propaganda. Poetry written for festivals often contains panegyrics of princes, and perhaps princely festivals should be seen in general as a form of public relations, projecting an image of the ruler as powerful and generous, wise and virtuous. Poems were written to celebrate victories, like the Florentine victory at Anghiari in 1440. The historian could also be of value in establishing a good image for a republic or a principality – hence the number of official historiographers, especially in Florence and Venice.[8]

Satire (and here is a difference between literature and the visual arts) was as important a function as panegyric. In Florence, the herald had the task of writing what were called *cartelli d' infamia*, insulting verses on the enemies of the republic which would accompany paintings of them. The Castagno painting of Rinaldo degli Albizzi (above, p. 145) had the following verses attached:

> *Crudel ribaldo, cavalier superbo*
> *Privato di mia schiatta e d'ogni onore*
> *Ingrato alla mia patria e traditore*
> *Fra costor pendo il piú uniquo ed acerbo.*

(a cruel scoundrel, a proud knight, without family and without honour, an ungrateful traitor to my city, I hang here, the most wicked and bitter of all).

This is what might be called 'official' satire. There was also unofficial satire, anonymous criticism of rulers by their subjects, perhaps tolerated as a safety-valve. The classic Renaissance examples are the pasquinades (*pasquinate*), satires on papal policy which were attached to the pedestal of a fragment of a classical statue in Rome from the beginning of the sixteenth century.

Some Renaissance poems seem to have a political level of meaning, but perhaps not a political function. Was Pulci's epic the *Morgante* written to encourage a crusade against the Turks? Pulci had written to Lorenzo de'Medici in 1471 to persuade him to take part in such a crusade, and the poem does deal with deeds of heroism against the forces of Islam. Ariosto, in his *Orlando Furioso*, urges Frenchmen and Spaniards not to fight their fellow-christians when they could be fighting Muslims. The allusion to the invasions of Italy from 1494 onwards is obvious; what is not obvious is whether the poem has a political function or not.

A third function of literature is entertainment, or (to revert to the term when discussing paintings) pleasure. The author's pleasure, or the reader's. Machiavelli excused the frivolity of his *Mandragola* with a prologue saying that for him it was a means of passing the time. Writers of sixteenth-century prefaces often tell the reader that the author has aimed at his entertainment or pleasure (*comodo, diletto, piacere*, etc.). This seems a new stress, and one related to the commercialization of literature.

What is likely to strike the modern reader most in this account of the functions of the arts is how often they have purposes which he thinks of as 'additional' or 'subsidiary'; how much more a means than an end they are, and at the same time how much bound up with everyday life. Paintings have to be 'read', and books have to be read between the lines, if we are to see them as their creators intended.

ARCHITECTURE AND MUSIC

About the functions of architecture there is no need to say much, because the practical functions of buildings are obvious, and their prestige-function is the same as that of other works of art, if on a grander scale. The family palazzo had a celebratory function; it was designed more to impress outsiders than to provide the family with comfortable surroundings. There are only a few comments to be made. The first is that religious buildings might have secular functions. It was in Florence cathedral that Filelfo lectured on Dante in the 1430s; it was in the same place that a poetry-competition (on a secular theme, the praise of friendship) was held in 1441. This is not Renaissance innovation but a medieval tradition; not secularization but lack of specialization (below, p. 250). Different kinds of house or palace had different functions, and this may have affected architectural style. Palladio discusses this subject in the later sixteenth century, but his points seem relevant to an earlier period too. He suggests that the town house is for a life of work, 'the administration of the commonwealth and of one's own affairs' (this would apply to the ruling class of Venice and Florence, at least), whereas the country house was for relaxation, where a man 'tired of the bustle of cities, will restore and console himself', take exercise, or study. One would expect town houses to have a more utilitarian design than villas, and this does seem to be the case. Florentine town houses for leading families, the *palazzi*, have a heavy, severe, even grim look about them, especially from outside in the street. One has to remember that one of their functions was defence. They were really urban castles; this was the result of having a town-dwelling nobility. Villas tended to appear at a time when the danger of attack had receded, and could be built on a more open plan. Villas in different regions, however, might have different functions and this might affect their appearance. Venetian and Tuscan villas were for farming as well as for pleasure; Roman villas were not, and they were set among gardens rather than farmhouses.[9]

The functions of music are obviously related to the places where music was performed: the church, the palace, and the street. In church, music accompanied the liturgy: Mass, Matins, Vespers, and so on, more particularly on feast-days, such as the feast of the patron saint of the city – St Ambrose at Milan, St John the Baptist at Florence, and so on. In 1465 B. M. Sforza asked to borrow the *pifferi* ('pipers') of Borso d'Este, who refused because they were needed for 'the feast of Saint George, for which they are not just necessary but most necessary for our honour and that of the land'. In palaces, music accompanied great events for the family, such as weddings and important visits. Bembo describes a country-house wedding with music, singing and dancing in his *Asolani*. Music was important at some courts for the pleasure it gave – the court of Mantua in Isabella's time, or the court of Urbino in the time of Elisabetta Gonzaga and Castiglione. It accompanied plays, to distract the audience during intervals and to demand their attention, with sound of trumpet, when proceedings began again. The importance of the third milieu, the street, was that festivals took place in it and processions passed through it. Music played an important part in carnivals, state visits, victory celebrations, or such grand Venetian spectacles as the coronation of the doge or the annual 'Wedding of the Sea'.

Music was believed to have thaumaturgic powers; stories were current in the fifteenth century about cures effected by playing to the sick man. Some music may have been written with quasi-magical functions in mind. When he was working in Italy in the 1420s and 1430s, Dufay wrote two motets to St Sebastian as a defence against plague. Ficino played music to draw down astral 'influences'. For example, he played 'martial' music to attract Mars; a Renaissance 'Planets Suite'.

There was a lively debate about the functions of music in fifteenth-century Italy. The Carthusian Johannes Gallicus attacked Ockeghem and other modern composers for their 'new and vain song', on the grounds that the function of music was to please God. Tinctoris, who approved of the new music, suggested that music had a number of functions – he once listed twenty of them, such as curing the sick, exciting devotion, causing ecstasy – and emphasized that music existed for the sake of man. In music, as in painting, changes in form seem to have been related to changes in function.[10]

6

Taste

Every man has a certain natural taste as to
what is beautiful and ugly. (*In tutti è posto
naturalmente un certo gusto del bello e del
brutto.*)

Aretino in Dolce, *L'Aretino*

Neither the artist nor the patron was completely free to make
aesthetic choices. Their freedom was limited, whether they
realized this or not, by the need to take into account the
standards of taste of their time. Taste, wrote Sir Joshua
Reynolds, is 'the power of distinguishing right from wrong
. . . applied to works of art', a form of objective knowledge
'derived from the uniformity of sentiments among mankind'.
Insofar as they used the term, which was not nearly so fashionable in the fifteenth and sixteenth centuries as it became in
the eighteenth, Italian writers of the period would probably
have agreed with Sir Joshua. Their aesthetic judgements are
expressed in objective terms not subjective ones: 'this statue
is elegant', not 'this statue strikes me as elegant'. If Sir Joshua
is right, this chapter is unnecessary. But it is possible to argue
that what men consider beautiful varies according to the place
and time in which they live, and even that some societies do
not value what we call 'beauty'. If this second view is right,
then the historian has a job after all. He will want to discover
the standards of taste current in a particular society in a
particular period in order that we may see works of art, if only
momentarily, with the eyes of the artists' contemporaries. But
how can the historian see with the eyes of sixteenth-century
men? One operation that he can perform is the analysis of the
vocabulary of written acts of appraisal of paintings, buildings,
madrigals, poems, and other works. From Italy in this period
there survive a number of treatises on art or beauty, by

Alberti, Bembo, Dolce, Filarete, Firenzuola, Gauricus, Nifo, and others. These books are usefully explicit in that they discuss the criteria for aesthetic judgements, but they are often too abstract to answer the question of what men were looking for, and so seeing, in the works of the time. They can be supplemented by a more 'practical criticism', by judgements on individual works, which occur in a variety of places; in the lives of artists, in stories, in private letters, in contracts between artists and their clients.[1]

THE VISUAL ARTS

It would not be difficult to draw up a list of some fifty terms which came regularly to the lips and pens of Italians of the period when they were appraising paintings, sculptures, and buildings. Some are general, almost vacuous terms like 'beauty' (*bellezza*, *pulchritudine*) but most terms are more precise and so more revealing. It may be useful to distinguish five clusters of terms which refer to nature, order, richness, expressiveness, and skill.

Nature

The 'return to nature' is a favourite phrase of modern historians of Renaissance art. It does in fact correspond to a frequently-expressed formula of the time. Fazio praised Van Eyck for a portrait 'which you would judge to lack only a voice' and for 'a ray of the sun which you would take to be real sunlight'. Savonarola remarked of paintings that:

The closer they imitate nature, the more pleasure they give. And so people who praise any pictures say: look, these animals seem as if they were alive, and these flowers seem natural ones.

A contract for a painting of the visit of the three kings to the Christ-child demands that the figures should be painted naturalistically (*che le figure siano in forma comuna del naturale*). Vasari often praises painters for their naturalism; if someone mistakes art for nature this is related as a triumph. He tells a story, for example, of the painter Bramantino decorating stables with pictures of horses so well that a horse mistook the paintings for reality and kicked one.* Vasari praises the *Mona Lisa* because, 'The eyebrows were completely natural, growing thickly in one place and lightly in another and following the pores of the skin,' and because the mouth 'appeared to be living flesh rather than paint'. Vasari's comment on Leonardo's *Last Supper* was that, 'The texture of the very cloth on the table is imitated so skilfully that linen itself could not look more realistic' (*non mostra il vero meglio*). His praises of these particular pictures for their naturalism makes Vasari seem rather imperceptive to many of us, so it is interesting to find that Leonardo himself described the painter as 'imitator of all the visible works of nature' and declared that the closer a painting was to 'the thing imitated', the better. Again, Dolce's Aretino praises Bellini for his rendering of flesh and draperies which 'are not much different from the real thing' (*non si dicostano molto dal naturale*). Besides these references to paintings *al naturale*, or to *similitudine*, or to *il vero*, there are descriptions of the 'liveliness' of works of art, especially sculptures. Donatello is often praised in these terms. For Fazio, his achievement was 'to produce lively expressions' (*vivos vultus ducere*). Landino wrote that Donatello's statues had 'great vivacity' (*grande vivacità*) and that his figures all seemed in movement. Vasari and Gelli made similar comments about his *St George*. Another term which can be grouped in the 'naturalism' cluster is *rilievo*, meaning 'relief' or 'three-dimensionality'. Gelli, for example, criticized Byzantine art as being 'without any relief' (*senze rilievo alcuno*), with the result that figures looked like 'flayed skins' or clothes spread out on a wall rather than like men.

Not all Renaissance writers praise naturalism. Some who appear to do so in fact do not, thanks to the ambiguity of the term 'to imitate nature'. For 'Nature' in the Renaissance was a word with two basic meanings. There was the physical world, *natura naturata*; and there was the creative force, *natura naturans*. To imitate the first is 'naturalism' in the modern

* The story is obviously modelled on the ones about Greek artists in Pliny. But the kind of flattery surely reveals the standards of the flatterer – Pliny's and Vasari's.

sense; but what some Renaissance writers, such as Alberti, advocate is the imitation of the second. Alberti declared that nature rarely achieved perfection, and that the artists should aim at beauty (as nature does) rather than at realism (*simili-tudine*). In effect Alberti is saying that the artist should not imitate, but he uses the language of imitation to say so. Michelangelo came out still more strongly against naturalism. His objection to Flemish painting was that it was only 'to deceive the external eye'. When he designed the tomb for Lorenzo and Giuliano de'Medici, he did not represent them as 'nature had sculpted and created them' (*come la natura gli avea effigiati e composti*) but produced his own idealized versions. There is, therefore, both a naturalistic and an anti-naturalistic current in Renaissance taste.[2]

Order

A second cluster of evaluative terms refers to order or harmony. When Alberti tells the artist to imitate Nature the creator, he explains that Nature's aim is 'harmony' (*concinnitas*), 'a certain rational harmony of all the parts making up a whole so that nothing can be added or subtracted or changed for the better'. There were laws of harmony which consisted in quantity, quality and position. Similarly, Ghiberti wrote that 'only proportion makes beauty' (*la proportionalità solamente fa pulcritudine*). Again, for Pino, beauty is nothing but 'commensurability and correspondence of parts' (*una commensurazione e corrispondenzia di membri*). *Proporzione* is a favourite term of praise for works of art in this period, sometimes in a precise sense and sometimes in a vague one, as when Botticelli's paintings are described as having 'complete proportion' (*integra proporzione*) and Michelangelo's statues in the Medici Chapel as having 'a proportion' (*una proporzione*). Other terms in this cluster are *ordine* and *ordinato* – 'order' and 'well-ordered': Vasari described Michelozzo as the most *ordinato* of the architects of his day. Another popular term is *symetria*, 'symmetry'. Pacioli discusses the Medici Palace and other buildings in Florence in terms of symmetry. Landino declares that Cimabue revived symmetry. Francesco di Giolgio defines symmetry in terms of *proporzione* and of *misura*, 'measure', another *term in the cluster. *Misura* is a favourite word of Ghiberti's. Vasari wrote of Brunelleschi that he rediscovered the *misure* and *proporzioni* of the ancients. 'Rule' (*regola*) is another term in the cluster. The basic postulates implied by the use of all these terms may be summarized briefly. There are rules for beauty; these rules are mathematical or rational. Pacioli's geometrical aesthetics, his assertion that the only canon of beauty was the golden section, was simply an explicit statement of common Renaissance assumptions. Another important Renaissance idea was that correct proportions could be found in the (ideal) human body. Tables of proportions were produced by Alberti, Leonardo, Pacioli, Gauricus and others, usually following Vitruvius (4 palms make a foot; 6 palms make a cubit; 24 palms make a man, etc.). These proportions were applied not only to paintings and sculptures of the human figure, but to architecture too. Even gardens were ordered: Alberti suggests that, 'The trees ought to be planted in rows exactly even, and answering to one another exactly upon straight lines.' The little that is known about Italian gardens of the period suggests that he was expressing the conventional view. Topiary was revived in fifteenth-century Italy. The 'elegant ordination of vegetables', as Sir Thomas Browne calls it, is an important clue to the nature of Renaissance taste at a point where it diverges most from our own.

Not all artists and writers in the period believed in the virtues of harmony and proportion. In the 1480s, Sannazzaro's pastoral the *Arcadia* expressed a preference for nature in her wild state:

It is usual for high and spreading trees produced by nature in fearsome mountains to please those who look at them more than plants skilfully clipped and cultivated in elaborate gardens (*le coltivate piante, da dotte mani espurgate, negli adorni giardini*) . . . who doubts that a fountain that issues naturally out of the living rock surrounded by green plants is more pleasing to the human mind than all the other fountains, works of art made from the whitest marble and resplendent with much gold?

It is surely this attitude which underlies the popularity of landscape in the Venice region in the sixteenth century; at all events, the *Arcadia* is frequently reprinted in the same place and the same time as Giorgione, Titian, Dossi and others paint their landscapes.

From the 1520s on, there is a more general rejection of symmetry and of rules. Michelangelo's theory and practice are examples of this great change in values. Michelangelo condemned Dürer's book on proportion with the remark that 'one cannot make fixed rules, making figures as regular as posts' and declared that, 'All the reasonings of geometry and arithmetic, and all the proofs of perspective, are of no use to a man without the eye.' Vasari described Michelangelo's Medici Chapel in the following terms:

> He departed not a little from the work regulated by measure, order and rule (*misura, ordine, regola*), which other men did according to a common use and following Vitruvius and the ancients, to which he would not conform.

A favourite sixteenth-century term for the beauty which cannot be reduced to formulas or rules is 'grace' (*grazia*). Firenzuola suggested that it was not the women with the best figures who had the most grace; grace is not a matter of proportion. It is something more mysterious, 'born from a hidden proportion and from rules which are not in our books'. Thus the language of rules is used to argue that there are no rules. Varchi, later in the sixteenth century, contrasted grace and beauty; beauty was physical, objective, and based on proportions, while grace was spiritual, subjective and impossible to define. But how does one represent the spiritual in paint? Very often, in sixteenth-century writings on art (the term is much less popular in the fifteenth) 'grace' is used to mean something like sweetness or elegance or loveliness (*dolcezza, leggiadria, venustà*). It is associated with the paintings of Raphael and Parmigianino in particular. It would be uncharitable to conclude that the 'hidden proportion' merely consisted in making girls ten heads high, but there is no doubt that some sixteenth-century artists thought they had discovered the formulas that were not in their books.[3]

Richness

A third cluster of aesthetic terms centres on the notion of richness. There is the notion of variety, *varietà*; of abundance, *copiosità*; of splendour, *splendore*; of grandeur, *grandezza*; favourite adjectives, which it would be difficult and perhaps unhelpful to distinguish precisely, are *dovizioso*, *dignissimo*, *grande*, *illustre*, *magnifico*, *pomposo*, *sontuoso*, *superbo*. Bruni, called in to advise on the third baptistery door at Florence, suggested that they should be *illustri*, meaning that 'they can feed the eye well with variety of design'. Ghiberti, who designed the doors, tells us that he aimed at 'richness'. Alberti applied similar terms to painting:

> That which first gives pleasure in the narrative (*istoria*) comes from copiousness and variety of things . . . I say that narrative is most copious in which in their places are mixed old, young, maidens, women, youths, young boys, fowls, small dogs, birds, horses, sheep, buildings, landscapes and all similar things.

He objected to what he called 'solitude' in a narrative painting.

Judgements on works of architecture in particular employ terms taken from this 'richness' cluster. Poggio referred to a most 'magnificent villa' (*villa magnificentissima*) at Tusculum; Pius II, to 'magnificent palaces' in the harbour of Genoa, *magnifica in ipso portu palatia*. Filarete overworks the term *dignissimo* – 'most imposing', one might say – in his treatise on architecture. In the sixteenth century, judgements of this kind are still more frequent. Vasari will describe palaces with adjectives like *onoratissimo*, *sontuosissimo*, *superbissimo*, the superlatives adding to the effect of richness. Bandello describes buildings in similar terms in his stories. Vasari applies similar terms of praise to painting; for him, Michelangelo's *Last Judgement* is the great exemplar of the 'grand manner' or 'grand style' of painting, *maniera grande*, and he criticizes Raphael and Andrea del Sarto for lacking grandeur, *grandezza*.

Richness and magnificence are not universally admired qualities in the Renaissance, however. Works of art may also receive praise for their simplicity. Alberti usually comes down on this side. He described ornament as a secondary kind of beauty; quoted Plato and Cicero on the value of unadorned white temples, and added:

> For my own part, I am very ready to believe that purity and simplicity of colour, as of life, must be most pleasing to the divine being.

Elsewhere he attacks 'confusion' in architecture, which sounds like a defect related to the qualities of richness and variety. One of his terms of praise for works of art is 'modesty' (*verecundia*). He suggests that a sculptor will prefer pure white marble. It is as if whiteness was aesthetically pleasing to Alberti; the outward sign of reason, perhaps. Alberti's defence of simplicity suits the work of his friends Brunelleschi and Masaccio very well. Brunelleschi banished frescoes from his interiors, such as S. Lorenzo or the Pazzi Chapel. Pius II also placed a high value on light, whiteness and simplicity, as is clear from his comments on the cathedral he had built at Pienza. The walls, he wrote, gleam with a 'marvellous whiteness' (*candore mirabili*) and he issued a bull with the command, 'Let no one deface the whiteness of the walls and columns; let no one make any pictures,' presumably prohibiting frescoes, not just graffiti. Landino shared these values, and praised Masaccio's paintings because they were 'pure without ornament' (*puro senza ornato*).[4]

Expressiveness

For Fazio, this was one of the most important gifts of a painter. Pisanello, he wrote, excelled in 'expressing feeling' (*sensibus exprimendis*); for example, a Saint Jerome painted by him was remarkable for the saint's 'majesty of countenance'. Van der Weyden's *Crucifixion*, he wrote, was remarkable for the grief expressed in the tears of the bystander, and his *Passion* for its 'variety of feelings and emotions'. Alberti advised the painter to 'move the soul of the spectator', explaining that, 'These movements of the soul are made known by the movements of the body' – motion reveals emotion – and implying that to represent an emotion was to induce it, so that the beholder would 'weep with the weeping, laugh with the laughing, and grieve with the grieving' in the painting. Leonardo wrote that the good painter has 'two chief objects to paint, man and the intention of his soul', and that he must be able to represent the emotions, 'of anger, of pain, of sudden fright, of weeping, of flight, of desire, of command, of negligence, of solicitude'. His own comments on the subject of the *Last Supper* describe gestures and emotions, like the apostle who makes 'a mouth of astonishment', rather than the tablecloth which so struck Vasari. But Vasari noticed the expressive qualities of the *Last Supper* too, commenting that:

> Leonardo brilliantly succeeded in envisaging and reproducing the tormented anxiety of the apostles to know who betrayed their master; so in their faces one can read the emotions of love, dismay and anger, or rather sorrow, at their failure to grasp the meaning of Christ. And this excites no less admiration than the contrasted spectacle of the obstinacy, hatred and treachery in the face of Judas . . .

Again, Vasari gave Giotto the credit for being, 'The first to express the emotions, so that in his pictures one can discern expressions of fear, hate, anger or love.' He praised Michelangelo's *Last Judgement* because:

> In it may be seen marvellously portrayed all the emotions that mankind can experience . . . Michelangelo's figures reveal thoughts and emotions that only he has known how to express.

He praises Bramante for his *terribilità*, or awe-inspiring quality. This term is of course associated especially with Michangelo: and Aretino in Dolce's dialogue points out that sculptors remarked on the *terribilità* of Michelangelo's figures. Titian is praised in the same dialogue for giving his figures 'a heroic majesty' (*una heroica maestà*). Here the 'expressive' cluster and the 'richness' cluster overlap. A similar term is 'sublime': and Veronica Gambara, in a letter to Beatrice d'Este, praised Correggio's *Magdalen* for expressing *il sublime*.

Expressive qualities are clearly important for Renaissance

1   A portrait bust of
Filippo Brunelleschi
(from Florence Cathedral)

2 Pinturicchio (c. 1454–1513), a self-portrait from the
background to his *Annunciation*. A transitional stage in
the rise of the self-portrait suggesting a growing
self-consciousness among artists

3 Titian's portrait of Giulio Romano. The 'princely
   aspect' of the artist has attracted attention

4 *Above:* The training of the artist in the academy.
Agostino Veneziano's engraving of Baccio Bandinelli's
'academy' in Rome

5 *Below:* 'A building project is like a dance', wrote the
architect Filarete (c. 1400-69), shown leading his
apprentices (from the doors of St Peter's, Rome)

6 The training of the humanist at university. Woodcut of
   Landino lecturing

7 Titian's portrait of Pietro Aretino (1492-1556). A
spectacular example of a man who made literature pay

8 Two versions of the romantic artist (see Fig. 9) Palma
   Vecchio (c. 1480–1528), *Portrait of a Poet*. The idea of the
   poet as a melancholy genius goes back to fifteenth-
   century Italy, but no artist was portrayed in this way

9   A genuinely romantic portrait – Géricault's *Portrait of an Artist* (c. 1818) (see also Fig. 8). The painter can now aspire to the position of melancholy genius himself

connoisseurs: but so is harmony and proportion, and one set of criteria seems to conflict with the other. So Alberti can write that beauty is associated with calmness and self-control; an angry man lacks decorum. Vasari often plays down the expressive in the art he describes, even if Sir Anthony Blunt goes a bit too far in referring to Vasari's 'dislike of any kind of emotion in art'. Vasari certainly disliked some kinds of emotion in art, as his reactions to Pontormo's Certosa frescoes and Beccafumi's later paintings testify.[5]

Skill

The fifth and last cluster of terms concerns artistic skill. A work of art may be praised because of the effort which has gone into it; for Alberti, effort (*istudio, industria*) is a quality which makes it possible to achieve beauty by means of judicious selection from the visible world. Fazio praises Van Eyck for his 'skill' (*artificium*). A work of art may also be praised for its overcoming of difficulty, which is a sign of skill. The anonymous life of Brunelleschi praises him for the *difficoltà* which he had overcome in his *Abraham and Isaac*; Vasari praises Raphael's *Betrothal of the Virgin* for the temple which is shown in perspective, commenting that, 'It is marvellous to see the difficulties which he went out of his way to look for in this exercise.' The successful overcoming of difficulties is generally called 'facility'. Dolce's Aretino said that Raphael had sometimes been criticized as 'too facile' (*troppo facile*) but that these hostile critics did not know that facility is the chief excellence of art. There is an obvious paradox here. Artists who truly possessed facility might not be seen to have this quality because the spectator might not realize that there was a difficulty to be overcome. Some of them were not content with this, and wanted to draw attention to their skill. Pino tells young painters:

> In all your works, introduce at least one figure who is completely affected, mysterious and difficult (*sforciata, misteriosa e difficile*) which will show those who understand art how skilled you are.

T.I.R.I.   F

'Difficult' seems to be shifting from 'difficult to execute' to 'difficult to understand'. There is more than an element of artistic exhibitionism here. Perhaps the fight to raise the status of the artist had left its mark on aesthetics. Terms like Pino's suggest what it was the spectators were expected to look for in paintings by Pontormo or Parmigianino. It is interesting to find that in sixteenth-century Italian, the fashionable term *peregrino* (derived from the same root as the English 'pilgrim') could mean 'strange', 'foreign' or 'elegant'. The terms 'fantastic' and 'bizarre' appear in the art criticism of the 1530s (for an example, p. 199 below).

The frequent references to 'facility' and 'difficulty' in the sixteenth century suggest that artists and their public were becoming more conscious of technique and more interested in it. Pejorative terms tell the same story. Artists such as Vasari, laymen such as Gelli make considerable use of such terms as 'gross', 'rough' or 'clumsy' (*grosso*, *rozzo*, *goffo*) which they apply, for example, to medieval art. Vasari accuses Uccello of being 'dry' (*asciutto*); in other words, his painting does not flow, it lacks facility. Another popular term is 'draughtsmanship', or *disegno*, a term which has other meanings too; but when Michelangelo, for example, declares that Titian's *Danaè* lacks *disegno*, this is probably what he means. Vasari's *Lives* are full of technical points, like the texture of the tablecloth in Leonardo's *Last Supper* and the foreshortening in Michelangelo's *Last Judgement*, whether because he wrote the book in order to educate young artists or because he naturally saw pictures in this way. In other words, the study of the vocabulary of appraisal confirms the hypothesis (above p. 45) that there was an increasing interest taken in style during the period. The clinching example is the increasing use of the term 'style' itself: *maniera*.[6]

MUSIC

It was a commonplace that there are analogies between music and other arts, architecture in particular. Music, like architecture, is built on proportion; audible and visible proportions are analogous. A famous illustration of this attitude is Alberti's letter to his architectural assistant Matteo de'Pasti, about the church, S. Francesco, which they were building at Rimini. Matteo was apparently thinking of altering the proportions of the pilasters. Alberti wrote to warn him that if he did so, 'all that music would turn into discord' (*si discorda tutta quella musica*). In this period, musical terms like 'harmony', 'diapason' or 'diapente' were not infrequently used about buildings. The analogies were not simply metaphorical but were taken seriously. For example, the musical theorist Gafurius was on occasion called in as an architectural consultant. Analogies between music and the other visual arts were drawn, but were less precise. It was customary to remark that music was to the ear what painting was to the eye, without pursuing the analogy further. A sixteenth-century writer once compared Ockeghem to Donatello and Josquin to Michelangelo, though this was on account of their places in their respective arts, rather than on account of similarities in style. The important point is that the conventional wisdom of Renaissance aesthetics stressed analogies between the arts rather than the differences between them, the role of the medium.

The musical taste of this period is difficult to reconstruct, because treatises on music are much more concerned with technical matters, such as scales, modes, tones and so on, and much less concerned with aesthetic matters than treatises on art are; nor is there a musical equivalent of Vasari's *Lives*. There are fewer useful passages about music in private letters and other informal sources than in the case of the visual arts. Then as now it was more difficult for people to explain why they liked a particular piece of music than why they liked a particular painting. The following paragraphs consequently rely heavily on books by three authors writing between the late fifteenth century and the middle of the sixteenth: Tinctoris, Aron, and Vicentino.

The most heavily worked term of praise for music is 'sweet' or 'sweetness' (*soave, dolce, soavità, dolcezza*); but this tells us as little about the standards of judgement of the user as a term like *bellezza* does of the visual arts. More helpful for recovering Renaissance values is a group of terms centring on 'harmony', and having much in common with the visual cluster centring on 'order' and 'proportion'. The basic idea is that good music depends on rules, Tinctoris, for example, frequently criticizes the composers of his day for 'inexcusable errors', for breaking rules. He wrote a treatise on 'proportion' in music, the *Proportionale*, proportion being defined as the relation of two terms to another. Again, he defined counterpoint as a mixture of voices which is 'reasonable' (*rationabilis*). Again, Pietro Aron uses terms of praise like *ordinato, harmonica, stabile*.

An acute problem for the writers on music of the period was that of the discord. The problem springs from a fundamental difference between music and the visual arts, a difference disguised by their common use of the vocabulary of order and harmony. Discords, which occur in the music of this period, can be compared either to decoration or to asymmetry in the visual arts. In the first case they are good and in the second case they are bad. Tinctoris, for example, cannot make up his mind. At one point he compares musical discords to the figures of speech of the grammarians and rhetoricians; at another point he defines the discord as 'a mixture of two voices which naturally offends the ear'. His conclusion is that discords may be permitted, provided they are little ones – *discordantiae parvae*. In the early sixteenth century, Aron was prepared to go further in the direction of accepting discords than Tinctoris had been. For Tinctoris, a piece of music must begin and end with a perfect concord. For Aron, it is only necessary for it to end that way.

Another group of terms centres on the concept of expression. Here the analogy with the visual arts is an obvious one, but there seems to have been a time-lag : the expressive seems to have become important in theory and practice about 1500 or even later. Before this, people were interested in the psychological effects of music upon the listener, a subject on which Tinctoris wrote a short treatise, the *Complexus effectuum musices*. Castiglione has a comparison of the effects of two styles of singing on their hearers. One was practised by Bidon, a singer at the court of Leo x, and the other by Cara, in Mantua :

> Bidon's style of singing is so skilful, quick, vehement, rousing and varied in its melodies (*tanto artificiosa, pronta, veemente, concitata e di così varie melodie*) that everyone who hears is moved and set on fire . . . our Marchetto Cara is no less emotional in his singing, but with a softer harmony; he

makes the soul tender and penetrates it calmly and in manner full of mournful sweetness (*flebile dolcezza*).

The next stage is to move from the idea that music causes emotion to the idea that it also expresses emotion; that, for example, it reinforces the message of a text. Josquin's sad setting of Dido's lament from the *Aeneid* is a famous example. The madrigals of the 1530s and 1540s, by Festa, Willaert, Arcadelt and others, furnish many more. The fact that different stanzas of the same poem may express different emotions forces the composer of madrigals to break with strophic forms. For the theory behind these expressive songs, we have to wait till the 1550s, for Nicola Vicentino (a pupil of Willaert's) and Zarlino.

As Nicola Vicentino put it:

If the words speak of modesty, in the composition one will proceed modestly, and not wildly; if they speak of gaiety, one will not write sad music, and if of sadness, one will not write gay music; when they are bitter, one will not make them sweet . . .

The same points were made at much the same time by Gioseffe Zarlino:

Musicians are not supposed to combine harmony and text in an unsuitable manner. Therefore it would not be fitting to use a sad harmony and a slow rhythm with a gay text, or a gay harmony and quick and light-footed rhythms to a tragic matter full of tears . . . the composer should set each word to music in such a way that where it denotes harshness, hardness, cruelty, bitterness and other similar things the music be similar to it, that is somewhat hard and harsh, but without offending.

Harmony and expressiveness seem to have been the most important features of the musical taste of the time. There are others, which have their visual and literary analogies. Tinctoris suggested, with appropriate references to Horace and Cicero, that 'variety should be most diligently searched for in all counterpoint'; that *decorum* should be observed, for the music appropriate to a chanson was not appropriate to a Mass. Breaches of decorum of this kind were in fact rather common in the fifteenth century.

Most surprising of all, music, like painting, was expected to imitate nature. A composer setting the words of the Creed, 'he descended into hell . . . he ascended into heaven' would make the music go down and then up again at this point. Music sometimes imitated battles or hunting scenes: Isaak's *A la battaglia* is an example.[7]

LITERATURE

> There is a certain great affinity between poets and painters. A picture is nothing but a silent poem.

So Fazio wrote in the early fifteenth century. If the idea was not a cliché in his own time, it certainly became one not long after. The analogy between painting and poetry, usually supported by a quotation from Horace, 'as is painting, so is poetry' (*ut pictura poesis*), was one which people never tired of drawing. One might expect to find the canons of literary taste close to those current in the visual arts, and this is often the case. When Poliziano described Cino da Pistoia as the first who 'began to shun the old uncouthness completely' (*cominciò l'antico rozzore in tutto a schifare*), he sounds like Vasari describing Giotto, who 'evolved a delicate style from one which had been rough and harsh'. Five central concepts in the literary criticism of the period, the early sixteenth century in particular, all have parallels in the visual arts: decorum, grandeur, grace, variety and similitude.

Decorum (*decoro, convenevolezza*) played a greater part in literary criticism than in art criticism. In the visual arts, it meant avoiding such solecisms as putting an old head on an apparently youthful body, or, more controversially, making Christ on the cross look like a peasant. In literature, decorum involved the crucial problem of suiting the form (*forma*) to the content (*materia*). Bembo, formulating the conventional wisdom, distinguished three different styles (*maniere e stili*) and argued that the high, medium or low styles should be used according to the nature of the subject:

> If the subject is a grand one, the words should be grave, stately, sonorous, spectacular, brilliant (*gravi, alte, sonanti, apparenti, luminose*); if the subject is a low and vulgar one, they should be light, plain, humble, ordinary, calm (*lievi, piane, dimesse, popolare, chete*); if a middle one, the words should be in between.

The English term 'heroic couplets' is a survival of this kind of literary decorum. Bembo argued that Dante had broken decorum in his *Divine Comedy*, in picking an *alta materia*, a lofty subject, and then introducing 'the lowest and vilest things' (*le bassissime e le vilissime cose*). Bembo also criticized Boccaccio adversely, because in the *Decameron* he occasionally lacked judgement. Discussing this example, an ambiguity in Bembo's position becomes apparent. Is the low style right in its place or is it to be avoided altogether? He suggested on occasion that it was better to be silent than to choose a subject where the appropriate terms were 'vile', 'harsh' or 'spiteful' (*vili, dure, dispettose*). Vida formulated the principle of decorum much as Bembo did:

> *Verba etiam res exiguas angusta sequuntur.*
> When things are small the terms should still be so,
> For low words please us when the theme is low.

Another kind of decorum was emphasized by Daniello: the writer must put the appropriate kind of language into the mouth of each kind of person.

The discussion of decorum has already suggested that what pleased the critics most (and one assumes the reading public too) was a grand subject treated in the grand style. A second group of critical terms centres on this idea of grandeur, which has many synonyms: 'dignity', 'gravity', 'height', 'majesty', 'magnificence' (*dignità, gravità, altezza, maestà, magnificenza*). The contexts in which it is used suggest that the term 'sublime' (*sublime*) had a related meaning, without the association with terror which it acquired, or regained, in the eighteenth century.

One way of achieving the grand style was to sprinkle one's epic or tragedy (for these were the grand subjects) with these very adjectives, 'dignity' and the rest, in profusion. Another was to avoid scenes which did not express 'noble' emotions, such as those connected with love and war. The shepherds who consumed their food on stage while visiting the Christ-child (p. 41, above) certainly constituted a breach of decorum. Another recipe for the grand style, recommended by Daniello and Vida, was to use circumlocutions. A poet should not refer to 'the sea' but to 'Neptune'. He should not call the sun 'the sun', but rather 'the planet which marks the passage of time'. One reason for this was to lend humble things a borrowed splendour; for Vida, as for other poets of the time, the sun was humble and the sea had no poetic resonances. Another reason for circumlocution was linguistic; many names of things were considered too 'low' or 'common' (*basso, volgare*); examples which Daniello gives are the names 'owl' and 'bat' (*civetta, vipistrello*). It is difficult to be sure whether the names were considered common because the birds and animals were, or because many names of animals, as of flowers, had no standard Italian form, so that the poet was forced to use dialect. The important point is that circumlocutions, a great obstacle to the enjoyment of the modern reader, were positively welcomed by the sixteenth-century reader or listener. We think them 'artificial' in a pejorative sense; they thought them *artificioso*, a term of praise which it might be best to translate 'craftsman-like'.

A third cluster of critical terms centred on the concept of 'the pleasing' (*piacevolezza*). Approximate synonyms were 'elegance', 'grace', 'loveliness' and 'sweetness' (*leggiadría, grazia, vaghezza, dolcezza*). Perhaps the most important thing to say about these terms is that they referred to second-class beauties, the beauties of the low or middle style, lyric rather than epic, comic rather than tragic. Petrarch's *Canzoniere* and Boccaccio's *Decameron* were praised in these terms. Yet the same adjectives were used of paintings without any apparent second-class implications, another case where similarity of vocabulary masks important differences in the standards of taste applied to different arts.

Another important concept in literary criticism, corresponding roughly to the whole 'richness' cluster in the visual arts, is that of 'variety'. It refers both to subject-matter and to literary techniques. Vida, for example, told aspiring poets:

> *Quandoquidem, ut varium sit opus (namque inde voluptas*
> *Grata venit) rebus non usque haerebis in iisdem.*
> Tire not too long one subject when you write,
> For 'tis variety that gives delight.

Ariosto uses the idea of variety as a way of changing the subject, with the remark:

> *Ma perchè non convien che sempre io dica,*
> *né ch'io vi occupi sempre in una cosa . . .*
> But because it is not fitting that I should go on talking
> about and concerning myself with just one thing . . .

If a writer does have to go on saying the same thing, he is praised for saying it in different ways. Bembo gave Boccaccio a good mark for his skilful use of variation in the prologues to the hundred different tales in the *Decameron*. One of Daniello's arguments for circumlocutions was 'to avoid monotony' (*per fuggire la satietà*). Savonarola recommended the Bible for its 'marvellous variety' – 'diversity of stories, multiplicity of meanings, variety of figures'.

Another critical term is 'similitude' or 'imitation'. 'Imitation' is an ambiguous term in the period. It may refer to the imitation of other poets, which is a means of achieving a beautiful effect rather than an end in itself. It may also refer to the imitation of nature. In this second sense, unlike contemporary art criticism and subsequent literary criticism, it is quite rare. For examples one is forced to have recourse to relatively minor critics. Gauricus argued that the subject-matter of literature 'should not be far removed from ordinary life' (*non longius a cotidiana consuetudine remota*) and, more positively, that fiction should resemble fact (*haec quae confingentur veri simillima videri debebunt*). Giovanni Britannico da Brescia argued that fiction should, in the phrase beloved of the art critics of the time, 'imitate nature' (*debet enim fictio artificiosa naturam imitari*). The rarity of this idea in literary criticism is something that needs explaining. One reason may be that realism was left to history. Obvious contrasts between history and poetry were, according to Pontano and other writers on the subject, that history followed the order of events themselves, while the epic poet did not – he usually began in the middle; and that the historian presented people as inconstant and unstable because this is what they were really like, while the poet or dramatist maintained constancy of character.

The last few paragraphs have summarized the main doctrines of literary taste as it can be learned from sixteenth-century treatises. A great deal of literary practice appears to correspond to this theory, but not all. These rules exclude some mystery plays, and it is quite difficult for them to accommodate Dante, Boccaccio, and even Ariosto, whom Bembo tried to persuade to write not a 'romance' but a true epic in the Virgilian manner. But Dante, Boccaccio and Ariosto were in fact extremely popular in Italy in this period, as a count of the editions published shows. There must have been another set of standards of taste in which 'grandeur' counted for less; one can only regret that it did not find a formal spokesman.[8]

VARIETIES OF TASTE

So far, this chapter has been concerned with common Renaissance assumptions, with a common language of taste. It might be summed up, crudely, in a formula : beauty=nature= reason=antiquity. These different values were not consistent with one another in the way that the formula implies; but they were very often treated as consistent by contemporaries. This is not to say that there were no aesthetic disagreements during the Renaissance, but only that the disagreements took place, like disagreements in every age and on every subject, within a common framework of assumptions which was all the more powerful for being unconscious. Thought was free – within limits. There existed what might be called 'invisible barriers' to thinking beyond those limits. Thought that passed the barriers appeared self-evidently absurd to contemporaries.

Yet within the common framework there *were* differences. Differences between one individual and another; differences between Florence and Venice; differences between the fifteenth century and the sixteenth; differences between the qualities looked for in a painting and those looked for in a piece of music. Vasari and Michelangelo belonged to the same milieu, but Michelangelo had little time for the successful imitation of the outward world in which Vasari took so much pleasure. Florentine and Venetian taste differed in that the Venetians cared more about colour, and the Florentine about draughts-manship, *disegno*. There are important differences between the arts concerning what was appreciated and what condemned. Whatever might be said about the resemblance between columns and trees, it was clear that architecture was not an imitation of the visible world in the same sense that painting could be. In the case of music, it was difficult to decide whether a dissonance was analogous to ornamentation or to a breach of decorum, a problem which suggests that analogies between the arts could be far from obvious. As for differences between the taste of 1420 and the taste of 1540, they are somewhat obscured by the fact that changes in the vocabulary of taste took place less quickly than changes in taste itself. The term 'variety' was used by Alberti in the 1430s to praise paintings, and the same term was used to praise paintings in the 1530s. Although the term is the same, the paintings are not; 'variety' now demands a higher degree of complexity. Here language masks change instead of revealing it. Again, it has been suggested that the traditional vocabulary of art criticism was inadequate for describing what was most appreciated in Giorgione. But one shift in taste within the period has left verbal clues to its existence, and that is the reaction in the 1520s against 'measure, order and rule', a revolt against reason which is associated with a greater stress on the eye, rather than the brain, and on internal, subjective criteria rather than on exterior ones.

The most striking instances of disputations about taste come from an examination of attacks on the arts during the period, attacks which were far from infrequent. To revive a useful Oxford term of the early sixteenth century, there were 'Trojans' as well as Greeks in Renaissance Italy. The Trojans put forward three main arguments which tended to cut across the arts. In the first place, the arts are 'vanities' in the sense of things unimportant in themselves which become evil because they distract people from what is truly important, God. In the second place, they are idolatrous, whenever they illustrate the actions of pagan gods. In the third place, they are provocations to immorality whenever they glorify sexual activity. In the context of arguments about taste, the first attack is too radical to be important, for it does not allow the arts to exist at all. The second and third arguments are more relevant because they involve preferring some works of art to others.

The most famous Trojans of the period were S. Bernardino and Savonarola. It was the argument about the glorification of sexual activity in the arts to which they returned most. Bernardino condemned the 'bestial errors' of Boccaccio, and the 'poison' mixed with the 'honey' of Ovid. Savonarola denounced 'a certain kind of religious art'.

> You painters do ill . . . you fill the churches with every vanity. Do you believe that the Virgin Mary went about dressed as you paint her? I tell you that she went dressed like a poor girl, simply, and veiled so that her face could scarcely be seen . . . You show the Virgin Mary dressed like a whore.

In 1497, Savonarola inspired a famous 'burning of vanities' at Florence. It was customary to have bonfires at carnival time, and S. Bernardino had encouraged bonfires of vanities, but this time, as Nardi records, the bonfires were fed with

> lascivious and indecent books (*libri lascivie e disonesti*), and all sorts of figures and paintings which could arouse people to wicked and indecent thoughts.

Books which included Boccaccio's *Decameron* and Pulci's *Morgante*. According to Vasari, the painter Baccio della Porta, later and better known as Fra Bartolommeo, was a devotee of Savonarola's, and hearing him

> shouting every day in the pulpit that lascivious pictures and music and books about love are often a temptation to evil, was persuaded that it was not good to keep paintings of male and female nudes in the house, where there were children.

So that when the burning of vanities took place, which included 'paintings and sculptures of nudes, many by the hand of excellent masters . . . which was a great pity', Baccio brought to the pyre 'all the drawings of nudes which he had made, and Lorenzo di Credi did the same'. Cronaca was another devotee of the friar's, but fortunately he was an architect. Benivieni destroyed many poems after his conversion by Savonarola. G. F. Pico gave up reading poems:

> I felt my soul to be softened by them. But what is more detestable is that most poets mixed into their verses the greatest wickedness and impurities.

Savonarola also suppressed the traditional carnival songs. Music was as always freer from this sort of pressure than the other arts; some lutes were added to the bonfire of vanities, but Savonarola and his supporters seem to have thought, like St Francis, that it was a pity the devil should have the best tunes, and turned some popular songs into hymns. Lorenzo de'Medici's famous 'quant'è bella giovinezza' (how beautiful is youth) with its hedonistic sentiments was given words beginning:

> *Viva viva in nostro core*
> *Cristo re, duce e signore.*
> (May Christ the King, Leader and Lord live in our hearts.)

Again, the art-loving Leo x was followed as pope in 1521 by Adrian vi, a Dutchman of rather more severe tastes. A contemporary described how the pope:

> while reading a certain elegant work in Latin the other day happened to remark, 'this is the work of a poet', as though he were ridiculing eloquence. And again, when he was shown the Laocöon in the Belvedere as a wonderful and excellent thing, he said, 'Those are the idols of the ancients.'

During the reign of his successor, Clement vii, Marcantonio Raimondi made engravings of Giulio Romano's illustrations to Aretino's *Postures*, poems on the different positions for copulation. Matteo Giberti, a leading Catholic reformer and secretary to the pope, had Raimondi imprisoned for this. Pope Paul iv was another enemy of indecency in the arts, and had draperies painted on some of the nudes in Michelangelo's *Last Judgement*. However, the frequency of naked bodies in religious paintings before 1540 suggests that the Trojans were in a minority before that time.[9]

TOWARDS A SOCIOLOGY OF TASTE

One way in which taste is related to society is through language. In this period as in others the language of taste was related to the language of social behaviour. The aesthetic vocabulary of the educated Italian of the fifteenth and sixteenth century widened, and the new terms often came from books on conduct. *Decorum*, a word frequently in the mouths of the critics of the period, was for Cicero, from whom they borrowed it, a moral ideal. 'Grace' was a term applied to deportment before it was taken over by the art critics, and even *maniera* was originally more associated with 'manners' than with 'style'. The use of such terms underlines the fact that the taste of 'the time' was the creation of particular social groups and expressed their social prejudices. It was considered a breach of *decorum* to use technical terms when writing in the high style, because artisans were low-status people, so the cultivated writer should not show too exact a knowledge of their 'mechanical' occupations. It was also a breach of *decorum* to use new words, because 'new men' were not acceptable socially. Vida makes this analogy explicit:

> But yet admit no words into the song
> Unless they prove the stock from whence they sprung.

Bembo's discussions of vocabulary suggest that he was preoccupied with what was U and what was non-U. His preoccupation was brilliantly parodied by Aretino, a writer who did not come from the upper classes, in his story of the courtesan who felt strongly that one should call a window *balcone*, never *finestra*; a door, *porta*, never *uscio*; and a face, *viso*, never *faccia*. Again, when Alberti discusses the importance of 'dignity' in painting, the social overtones of his aesthetic term are obvious. I do not want to suggest that social standards

entirely determined aesthetic ones. A man who liked complexity in painting could defend his liking by using the
vocabulary of 'richness', a term of praise obviously associated
with riches. The man who preferred simplicity would keep
away from the pejorative term 'poverty', but he could defend
his preference by using a term like 'modesty' instead.[10]

This last point may prompt the question, whether varieties
of taste are correlated with differences in social status. In the
case of twentieth-century taste, it has proved possible to
investigate this problem empirically. In Evansville, Indiana, for
example, 1,200 people listened to records of eight different
kinds of music, and their reactions were measured on a five-
point scale. They were also classified according to age, sex,
income, and other criteria, and it turned out that some kinds
of music appealed more to some social groups than to others,
while other kinds of music cut across social groupings.[11]

It will be no surprise for the reader to learn that the evidence
does not exist for such a study to be made of the arts in Italy
during the period. All that can be done is to assemble a few
fragments and hope for a few more. It is obvious, for example,
that houses built for people of different incomes will look
different for that reason, and Filarete declared that he could
design a house for 'every class of persons' (*ciascheduno facultà
di persone*). He went on to describe a gentleman's house with
Doric proportions, a merchant's house with Corinthian proportions, and an artisan's house with Ionic proportions. Whether
Filarete or anyone else ever made such distinctions in practice
is another matter.

In the case of music, theorists did suggest that different
musical styles were suitable for different audiences. As Nicola
Vicentino, explained, in antiquity :

The chromatic and enharmonic genera was rightly reserved
for other uses than the diatonic. The latter was sung at
public feasts, in public places, for ordinary ears (*vulgari
orecchie*): but the two former were used in private enter-
tainments of lords and princes for cultivated ears (*purgate
orecchie*).

He seems to be suggesting that the more expressive style, the *musica reservata* of his own day, should in fact be 'reserved' for an élite. Again, one must not read a recommendation of the 1550s as if it were the description of actual practice between the 1420s and 1540s. We know that there were close links between popular songs and songs composed in a court milieu. But we also know that striking innovations in secular vocal music occurred in the early sixteenth century, especially at the court of Ferrara; it is plausible to suggest that these innovations widened the gap between music for the élite and popular music. And here we have a composer suggesting that such a gap is in fact a good thing and a characteristic of antiquity.

In literature, we have seen that there was a hierarchy of styles: high, middle, and low. This hierarchy was a moral one in antiquity, but a social one in the Renaissance. Aristotle had said in his *Poetics* that tragedy dealt with good men, comedy with the ordinary; he was interpreted as saying that tragedy dealt with men of noble birth, and comedy with men of humble birth. The language of comedy was low: ordinary colloquial language. Thus it was acceptable for Ruzzante to compose his comedies in Paduan dialect. The language of tragedy, and epic, was more controversial: some scholars thought that the elevated style must be literary Latin – that the vernacular was 'vulgar' (the term *volgare* did in fact carry both meanings). Others, like Bembo, argued the case for a purified or ennobled vernacular. The implication of these arguments was that literature in the high style was literature for the élite, and that this élite was at once intellectual and social.

This was the theory: what happened in practice? Modern sociologists can study theatre audiences to see if a particular age-group or social class is dominant; historians have to be content with what scraps of information have survived. It is plausible to argue that tragedies, when they were performed, were attended by high-status audiences; the evidence is from the places in which they were performed – at court or in noblemen's houses. However, on the same grounds it can be argued that the Roman-type comedies of Ariosto, Bibbiena, Machiavelli and others were also for a predominantly noble audience, at least until towards the end of the period. For the 'multitude' there were the miracle and mystery plays. In the mid-sixteenth century, however, the existence of a playwright like Anton Francesco Grazzini, an apothecary by trade, suggests that the taste for the classical comedy had become more widely diffused.

The sociology of the reading public is a little easier to reconstitute than the sociology of theatre audiences, thanks to the survival of library inventories. Two popular books in Italy in the period (as before and since) were Boccaccio's *Decameron* and Petrarch's *Canzoniere*. But Boccaccio seems to have been popular above all among Tuscans, merchants and women. Petrarch seems to have been popular with young noblemen all over Italy. It is interesting to find the most vigorous attack on 'Petrarchism' coming from one of the few writers who was not from the upper classes, Pietro Aretino.

In the case of painting, Frederick Antal (above, p. 29) argued that in Florence in the early fifteenth century, there were two kinds of taste in the visual arts, each characteristic of a particular social group. The old nobility, he argued, were conservative in art as in politics, and they liked plenty of decoration, so Gentile da Fabriano appealed to them. The wealthy merchants were more prepared to accept innovation, and they liked rationality and simplicity in painting, so they preferred Masaccio. A study of the contemporary vocabulary of appraisal suggests one argument in favour of this thesis: that Alberti defended the simplicity of paintings (above, p. 159) by using the term 'modesty' (*verecundia*), as if buying a Gentile da Fabriano was a sign of conspicuous consumption, while buying a Masaccio was a sign of sobriety, even thrift. But there are more serious arguments against this thesis. The first is that contemporaries did not suggest that different styles of painting suited different social groups, whereas they did make such suggestions about music and literature. The second argument attacks the permanent association of simplicity with any social group. Within the Italian art of the period, there were two movements from complexity to simplicity, one in the early fifteenth century and one in the early sixteenth (from Ghirlandaio to Leonardo). In the second case (below, p. 333) there are reasons for thinking the change associated with an aristocratic ethos. It must not be assumed that simplicity is always 'bourgeois'. The third argument against the Antal thesis has been discussed already (above, p. 29); it is that the Florentine patricians whose patronage he studies are one social group rather than two. It is a pity to have to abandon a hypothesis which promised a fruitful comparative approach to the sociology of taste, but it is a poor sociologist or historian who does not let the evidence have the last word.[12]

7

Iconography

Invenzione means devising poems and histories
by oneself, a virtue practised by few modern
painters, and it is something I regard as
extremely ingenious and praiseworthy.

Pino

Iconography is the study of the meaning of images, an approach
to art-history which goes back to the mid-nineteenth century
but became important in the early twentieth, a reaction led by
Emile Mâle and Aby Warburg against the purely formal
approach to works of art. There was a parallel movement in
literature, a study of 'imagery' in the metaphorical sense, more
particularly of the traditional image, *topos*, or cliché, associated
in particular with Ernst Curtius. Fifteenth- and sixteenth-
century Italians may not have known that they were studying
'iconography', but some of them were extremely interested in
what they called 'inventions' or 'stories' (*invenzioni, historie*),
the message which the work of art was intended to convey.
Appropriately enough, Mâle and Warburg did not preside over
the birth of a discipline but over its rebirth.[1]

MANIFEST CONTENT

It seems useful to distinguish two levels of meaning in art and
literature, the manifest and the latent, and to begin with the
manifest. The obvious question, in a book concerned with the
social history of art, is that of the relative popularity of
different images. This question is not as easy to answer as it
looks. It is necessary to avoid placing too much emphasis on
the isolated image; a saint or Madonna which we look at in a
museum may once have been part of a polyptych with a

complex programme, and much of its significance will be missed by treating it out of context. Then there is the practical problem that even if one limits oneself to the relatively manageable field of paintings, it is to find that there is no catalogue of all Italian paintings produced between 1420 and 1540, not even of those which survive. What does exist is a catalogue of dated European paintings which includes 2,229 dated Italian paintings for the 120 years 1420–1539; the subject of 2,033 of these paintings is described. Of these 2,033, 1,796, or about 87 per cent, are religious in subject, and 237, about 13 per cent, are secular. The religious paintings can be broken down into a few broad categories: about 50 per cent are mainly concerned with the Virgin, nearly 25 per cent with Christ and nearly 23 per cent with the saints, and there are only a few paintings mainly concerned with God the Father or the Trinity or with Old Testament scenes. Of the 237 secular works, about 67 per cent are portraits.[2]

Before going any further, it is necessary to discuss the reliability of this sample. Surviving pictures and dated pictures may not be representative of the rest in other respects. Surviving pictures may be a biased sample leading one to underestimate the number of secular paintings produced, because works commissioned for churches had a better chance of survival than works commissioned for private collections in that the Church never died. It might also be that surviving pictures lead one to underestimate the numbers of portraits, in particular; many would have been lost because for a long time they were of family interest only. Hence the figures given above for secular paintings in general and portraits in particular should be taken as minimum figures and no more.

Does the fact that a painting is dated (and only a minority of Renaissance paintings are dated) make it unrepresentative in other ways too? Some artists date more than others. Bicci di Lorenzo always dated, Domenico Veneziano never dated. Some artists paint a higher proportion of secular pictures than others, so bias may be introduced; but with paintings by more than 400 artists in the sample, the personal biases should cancel out. Might portraits be dated more often than other works? This seems plausible because of family interest in such matters, and might compensate for the likely loss of portraits just mentioned. More serious is the fact that the number of dated paintings tends to increase every decade between 1420 and 1519, from 31 (1420–9) to 441 (1510–19). There is a very real danger of making generalisations about the whole period on the basis of evidence taken more from one part of it than from another, a danger which in fact threatens all students of Italian culture during this period. Another point to be borne in mind is that all the figures are less precise than they look. Occasional pictures may have been counted twice, for example.

Another way of building up conclusions about the relative popularity of certain motifs or genres would be to take the work of particular artists and to classify it. To take seven painters who were at work in different generations and different parts of Italy, one might look at Uccello, Antonello da Messina, Mantegna, Botticelli, Carpaccio, Luini, and Dosso Dossi. The main conclusion which emerges is the obvious one of the variety of individual patterns, contrasting with the main trends. Dossi painted 41 religious paintings and 40 secular, whereas all the others painted far more religious paintings. Uccello painted no known Madonnas and Antonello da Messina painted very few (six known, compared with ten Christs), while Botticelli and Luini painted a great many (45 Marys compared to 18 Christs in Botticelli's case; 94 Marys compared to 55 Christs in Luini's).[3]

Let us return to the 1,796 religious dated pictures, and look at them in a little more detail.[4] The main categories were images of Mary, nearly 50 per cent of the total; images of Christ, nearly 25 per cent: and images of the saints, nearly 23 per cent. The reader may be surprised to see that Christ was of no more pictorial importance than the saints, but in thirteenth-century France he had been much less important. During the period 1420–1540, pictures of Christ became rather more popular and pictures of the saints somewhat less popular, while Mary's rating did not change. Here is a comparison between the first half of the period and the second half:

	Mary	Christ	Saints
1420–79	52 per cent	18 per cent	30 per cent
1480–1539	53 per cent	26 per cent	20 per cent

The most popular ways of painting Mary are the simplest; either a Virgin and Child, or simply a Virgin. The child may be asleep; the Virgin may be enthroned, or holding a book; adoring the child (a fourteenth-century innovation) or feeding him. Other popular subjects are the Annunciation; the Coronation of the Virgin in Heaven; her Dormition and Assumption. Another popular type is the Mother of Mercy, with people sheltering under her cloak. Other scenes from the life of the Virgin are more rare: her birth and marriage, and the Visitation. There are also pictures of her associated with particular cults: the Virgin of the Rosary, the Virgin of Loreto, the Virgin of Siena, the Virgin of Victory, the Virgin of the Earthquake. There are pictures of her saving a child or saving boats. In most of these, as in the case of the Mother of Mercy type, the emphasis is on Mary as 'mediatrix of all graces', the mediator between God and men. A number of these pictures look like ex-votos (above, p. 141).

Pictures of Christ frequently represent his birth, passion and death, but rarely anything in between. There are some Baptism of Christ scenes, and, much more rarely, a picture like Mazzolino's *Christ driving the buyers and sellers from the temple*, 1524. The most popular category of all is that of the Nativity, which should be treated as three scenes rather than one: the actual birth, the adoration of the shepherds, and the adoration of the kings or wise men. The death-scenes can be divided into the Crucifixion itself, the deposition, the *pietà*, the burial. The Resurrection and Last Supper are also popular. Then there are scenes from the Passion, like the Agony in the Garden and the Scourging at the Pillar, or the Man of Sorrows, a picture of Christ with the instruments of the Passion and the Five Wounds. More rarely one finds the Circumcision, the Marriage Feast at Cana, the Transfiguration, the Ascension. Another type is the *Salvator Mundi*, with globe, cross, and crown of thorns; and there are also such symbols of Christ as the Pelican, the Lamb of God, and the Host.

This thematic pattern is not essentially an Italian one, though a comparative study might reveal variations in different parts of fifteenth-century Europe. The pattern is linked to the liturgy and the institutions of the Church. The birth, passion and resurrection of Christ are preferred to his public life because Christmas and Easter are the great events of the Church year. The Adoration of the Kings is a separate scene because it has a separate feast, the Epiphany. The Baptism of Christ is an important theme because of the sacrament of baptism, and the Last Supper because of the sacrament of the eucharist. The stress on the sufferings of Christ the man, rather than on the majesty of Christ the king, is something found all over Europe in the fourteenth and fifteenth centuries. There is perhaps a little less emphasis on the sufferings in Italy than in some other European countries.

There was a luxuriant variety of saints painted in Italy in the period, a variety which can be quite bewildering. What modern art-historian, or what sixteenth-century bishop, for that matter, would be confident in his ability to identify the attributes of (say) SS. Eusuperio, Euplo, Quirico or Secondiano? Yet each of these saints had a church dedicated to him in sixteenth-century Pavia. Some saints had great importance in one area but were little known elsewhere, like S. Ansanus, a patron of Siena, and S. Petronius, patron of Bologna. In a limited space, it is best to concentrate on the most popular saints, and again statistics from Errera provide some guidance. There are exactly 100 identified saints in the 1,796 dated religious pictures of the period, of whom 22 occur seven or more times. The 'top ten' are as follows : St John the Baptist (51 times); St Sebastian (34); St Francis (30); St Catherine of Alexandria (22); St Jerome (22); St Anthony of Padua (21); St Rocco (19); St Peter (18); St Bernardino (17); St Bernard (15) ties with St Michael (15). The exact numbers should not be taken seriously, but the odds are that these were the most popular saints in Italy during the period. It remains to explain why this was so.[5]

St John the Baptist occurs in four main forms. He may be wearing a hair-shirt, as in his desert days, and carrying a cruciform staff. He may be playing with the Christ-Child, still carrying a small cross. He may be baptizing the adult Christ, or being beheaded by request of Salome. St John, the last prophet and the bridge between the Old Testament and the New, the precursor of Christ, was one of the greatest saints in the Middle Ages. His name was invoked in the litany immediately after the archangels. His popularity in this period is neither new nor surprising. It should only be added that he was one of the patron saints of Florence, and of the great *Calimala* guild in particular.

St Sebastian, a Roman centurion in the time of Diocletian, was said to have been martyred by being shot with arrows.

This made him, by an interesting association of ideas, the patron of archers. He was also one of the patron saints of Rome. None of these facts seems sufficient to account for his popularity, but he was also invoked as a patron against plague, a custom which goes back to the seventh century at the latest. The reason for his efficacy against plague seems to be that the attacks of the plague were often visualized as arrows launched by God, in the Middle Ages as in Homeric times. Sebastian as a defence against plague stepped into the shoes, or rather the sandals, of Apollo. So Gozzoli painted a fresco in a church at S. Gimignano to commemorate the plague of 1464, with God shooting arrows and broken arrows surrounding St Sebastian. Another reason for Sebastian's popularity at this time may have been the excuse he afforded for introducing a naked young man into a religious painting. A story told by Vasari in his life of Fra Bartolommeo suggests that such a painting might have been more of a distraction from devotion than a stimulus to it.

The popularity of St Francis poses no problems; he was an Italian saint and the order he founded was flourishing in Italy during the period. The cult of St Francis was strongest in his native region, Umbria, and it was also very strong in Tuscany; but many important towns elsewhere had Franciscan churches dedicated to him – Cremona, Ferrara, Mantua, Padua, Pavia.

St Catherine of Alexandria's popularity apparently dates from the thirteenth century. Even in Italy, St Catherine of Siena was not a serious rival. The main reason for her popularity seems to have been her patronage of young girls. In the fifteenth century, the story grew up of her 'mystic marriage' to Christ, and this was a favourite way of representing her, for example by Lotto and Parmigianino. This made her an appropriate subject for paintings given as wedding presents. Outside the mystic marriage context, she was recognizable by the wheel on which, legend said, she was to have been martyred – the first Catherine wheel.

St Jerome was represented in two different ways, which suggests that he had two different 'images' and appealed to two kinds of people. He was most often represented as a penitent in the desert, knocking at his breast with a stone; Jerome the ascetic. He was also represented sitting in his study writing; Jerome the scholar, the translator of the Bible into Latin. In both cases, his cardinal's hat and his lion are not far away.

The story about how St Jerome came to have a lion as a pet is retailed in the *Golden Legend*, a thirteenth-century Italian book of stories about the saints which was extremely popular in the period and tells most of the stories which painters liked to illustrate. St Jerome was much more popular in the Veneto than elsewhere; but then he was born near Aquileia. Humanists liked him as a fellow-scholar, with an enthusiasm for Cicero, even though he repented of this; but he had a wider appeal too, of which the most obvious evidence is the spread, in late fifteenth-century Italy, of printed vernacular lives of him which placed special emphasis on his death and miracles: there are 13 editions before 1500 preserved in the British Museum alone. St Jerome in the desert was also a good excuse for painting a rocky landscape, but the penitence was often taken seriously; he was the patron of groups of hermits in Lombardy and elsewhere (below, p. 254). Whether hermits were allowed to commission paintings I have not been able to discover.

St Anthony of Padua was another Franciscan, not an Italian but a Portuguese, who preached at Padua and died there in 1231. Quite why he should have been so popular it is difficult to say. There seems to be no evidence of belief in his gift for finding lost objects in this period. He was revered as a miracle-worker, and among his most famous miracles, sculpted by Donatello and Tullio Lombardo, were the miracles of the mule and the leg. In the first, he converted a heretic when a mule knelt before the blessed sacrament; in the second, he was confessing a man who said he had kicked his mother. St Anthony said that he deserved to have his foot cut off. The man went away and cut it off, but the saint stuck it on again. One might regard St Anthony as an equivalent of St Francis but for the Veneto. His cult owes something to the preaching of another Franciscan, St Bernardino, and there is a Francis-like story of his preaching to the fish.

St Rocco was, like St Sebastian, a patron against plague. He was a fourteenth-century Frenchman, from Montpellier, who went to Italy and ministered to plague victims at Acquapendente. He too was particularly popular in the Veneto, especially after the translation of some of his relics to Venice in 1485. (The Scuola di S. Rocco existed at Venice in this period, though Tintoretto's paintings for it come later.) It is interesting to find that he was not canonized until the seventeenth century;

evidence of the popular rather than official nature of his cult in the fifteenth and sixteenth centuries.

The surprise with St Peter is not that he is in the top ten, but that he shares the seventh place with St. Rocco. One reason could be the relative unimportance of Rome, and weakness of the papacy, until the later fifteenth century.

St Bernardino, a third Franciscan, and a Sienese, lived in the early part of this period (he died 1444) and was a great preacher. If the Errera pictures are a fair sample, he was popular in his own century, but this popularity declined sharply about 1500.

The tenth place is shared by St Bernard and St Michael. St Bernard does not seem an obvious choice for a popular Renaissance saint; the scene that attracts painters and patrons is his vision of Our Lady, which suggests that he owes his popularity to her. St Michael, as the liturgy reminds Catholics to this day, is a protector against 'the wickedness and snares of the devil' and often appears destroying the devil in the form of a dragon.

The next ten saints in popularity are saints who are on the way down, or the way up, or of some specialist importance. On the way down are Christopher, James, Martin and Nicholas, all great saints of medieval Christendom; St Nicholas having been the centre of a specially Italian cult since the eleventh century, when his relics were transferred to Bari. St Christopher, in other places and times a celebrated patron against earthly dangers, has perhaps been squeezed out by SS. Sebastian and Rocco. Saints who are rising are St Paul and St Mary Magdalen, both popular in the sixteenth century but not the fifteenth. St Paul's popularity is a reminder of the importance of the Catholic Reformation, and the debates over justification by faith which continued up to the Council of Trent. The Magdalen's popularity may well be due to her association with the sacrament of penance; it grew still further after the end of the period, during the Counter-Reformation. Other saints in the top twenty are St Augustine, St Stephen, St George (the patron of Genoa and armourers, and a patron of Venice) and Venice's chief patron St Mark.

A conspicuous omission is that of any Dominican saint. St Dominic himself occurs only twice in the list; and the most popular Dominican saint, St Peter Martyr, occurs only five times. He was a thirteenth-century inquisitor from Verona, and it was after him that the humanist Pietro Martire d'Anghiera, and, more ironically, the heretic Pietro Martire Vermigli, were named.

There is no doubt that the majority of paintings commissioned in Italy throughout the period were religious in subject, and this fact is enough to correct a simple view of fifteenth-century Italy as essentially a secular culture. All the same, there is evidence of a rising interest in the secular. Federico Gonzaga, commissioning something from Sebastiano del Piombo in 1524, wrote:

> I don't want saints' stuff (*cose di sancti*) but some pictures which are attractive and beautiful to look at.

He was part of a trend; between 1480 and 1539, the proportion of dated Italian paintings which were secular in subject rose every decade from 5 per cent, 1480–9, to 22 per cent, 1530–9. Perhaps this change is to be related to a secularization of a world-view (below, p. 245) but more likely the explanation is that the functions of paintings were changing.

Two hundred and thirty-seven secular paintings are listed in Errera for the period. The number is too small for a breakdown by subject-matter to be a reliable guide to the subjects of paintings which were not dated. But 159 pictures, about 67 per cent, were portraits, and this point confirms a general impression that the portrait, a secular version of 'saints' stuff', was in fact the most popular secular genre. Before the mid-fifteenth century, secular portraits were rare; this is what gives its point to the opening lines of a poem by Leonardo Giustinian: he tells his beloved that he has made a painting of her on a little sheet (of vellum, or paper) as if she were one of God's saints:

> *i't'ho dipinta in su una carticella*
> *come se fussi una santa di Dio.*

Then came the series of portraits of 'famous men', heroes of antiquity or of the modern world: Castagno painted a famous series in Florence. Dante was much painted; there were famous *condottieri*, and famous lawyers. The next stage (logically if not chronologically, one cannot be certain of the dates) was the painting of princes (and their wives) in their own lifetime, as Bonifazio Bembo painted Francesco Sforza, Piero della Francesca painted Federico da Montefeltre. The last stage was the democratization of the portrait, to represent merchants and their wives, sons, daughters. Unfortunately so many surviving portraits are unidentified that we cannot say how far down the social scale the custom spread. Looking back, we can see the beginnings of this trend in the rising importance of the donor's portrait in religious pictures, from Scrovegni to Portinari to Vendramin. At the end of the period, Aretino made an interesting and characteristic outburst against the democratization of the portrait, though on the grounds of merit not birth. Leone Leoni had struck a medal of Molza the poet; Aretino wrote to him, in 1545 :

Portray men like this, not people who are scarcely known to themselves, let alone to anyone else. Fame should portray a man before the sculptor does; I do not believe that the decrees of the ancients allowed unworthy people to have their images made in metal. It is the disgrace of our age that it tolerates the painted portraits even of tailors and butchers.[6]

The portrait may have been the most popular secular genre; but the one with the highest status was the *istoria*, the 'history', by which was meant the narrative picture. It is useful to distinguish at least three sorts of narrative picture : i, the mythological scene; ii, the allegorical scene; iii, the historical painting proper.

The scenes from classical mythology include some of the best-known paintings of all, like Botticelli's *Birth of Venus*. Favourite sources for the stories were Ovid's *Metamorphoses* and Lucretius's *On the nature of things*, whether it was the painter, the client or the humanist-adviser who read them. Titian's *Bacchus and Ariadne* illustrates Ovid, Book VIII; Dossi's *Circe* illustrates Ovid, Book XIV; a number of paintings by Piero di Cosimo illustrate Lucretius. These scenes shade into another class of paintings, the allegories, which may be defined as paintings built around personifications, which do not tell stories so much as illustrate ideas. Petrarch's *Triumphs* are popular subjects for allegorical paintings; the triumphs of love, chastity, death, fame, time, and eternity. These are relatively easy to identify; for example, Cossa's frescoes in the Palazzo Schifanoia at Ferrara. Other allegorical paintings are more difficult to interpret, and some of the best art-historical detective work of our time has gone into their decipherment. Does Botticelli's *Pallas and the Centaur* represent wisdom taming the passions? Does Giorgione's *Tempest* represent Fortitude and Charity? The historian turns with relief to a third class of secular paintings, history-paintings in the narrow sense, where at least the manifest content is not controversial; Uccello's *Battle of San Romano*, Piero della Francesca's scenes from the life of Constantine, or Raphael's pictures of incidents in the history of the popes.

It is difficult to decide how seriously all these subjects were taken. At the beginning of this century it was argued that in Italy in the fifteenth and sixteenth centuries, there was a rising interest in the form of paintings at the expense of their content, and that in many cases the content was just a 'pretext'. How can we know this? It is difficult to show that a St Sebastian, say, or a sleeping Venus, is just a pretext for painting a nude figure, because the picture would not look any different whether this was the case or not. In some sixteenth-century cases, paintings of St George and St Jerome show the main figures as very small, and that may be evidence that the subject was not taken very seriously. It is also possible to appeal to literary sources. There is the evidence, quoted above (p. 45), of increasing interest in pictorial technique. In a small number of cases we do know how some contemporaries saw particular works of art, or genres, or artists. It turns out that in the sixteenth century, unlike the fifteenth, some mythological paintings were no longer seen as 'histories' but as 'poems', a term which suggests that they were not so much illustrations to a text as free fantasies on the part of the painter. Titian called some of his mythological scenes poems (*poesie*). It has also been argued, on the basis of one interesting text, that it was possible in the 1520s to think of painting in genre terms. Paolo Giovio described some of Dossi's paintings as 'oddments' (*parerga*) consisting of:

sharp crags, thick groves, dark shores or rivers, flourishing rural affairs, the busy and happy activities of farmers, the broadest expanses of the land and sea as well, fleets, markets, hunts and all that sort of spectacle.

It was just such details that Giovanni Tornabuoni demanded from the Ghirlandaios in 1485, in frescoes which were to illustrate the life of the Virgin (above, p. 114). It does seem that within the 'history' the importance of the story was diminishing.[7]

Connected with this diminution, surely, is the rise in this period of two secular genres which are not narrative at all, but (if the inescapable literary metaphor may be continued) descriptive – the landscape and the still-life. In each case the genres achieved independence about 1500; they were, in a very few instances, emancipated from the backgrounds of narrative pictures. In each case one cannot be sure exactly when this emancipation occurred; one of the problems is that of knowing whether paintings which have survived were formerly part of a decorative ensemble or not. Uccello's *Hunt at night* at Oxford has one significance if it is just a painting on a panel, another if it was part of a painted *cassone*. Jacopo de'Barbari's painting of partridges is more important in the history of art as it is than if it were part of a scheme for illusionistic interior decoration – but it may have been just that. At this point it is necessary to turn to texts for help; to try to find out when the concepts of landscape and still-life first appeared.

In the case of landscape, one should perhaps include pictures of towns as well as country; in an urban civilization like Italy, it is not surprising to find townscapes appearing first. The duke of Mantua, Isabella's husband, collected them. In 1493, Gentile Bellini arranged to send him pictures of Cairo and Venice; in 1497 he was trying to obtain a picture of Genoa; and in 1511 Carpaccio offered him a picture of Jerusalem. The term used for these pictures was usually 'views' (*vedute*). It is intriguing to know that at Giorgione's death there was a picture in his studio which Isabella's agent called 'a night' (*una nocte*); was this a landscape? It may equally well have been a 'holy night', that is, a Nativity. Correggio's *Nativity* of 1530 has often been called 'Night'. But then the use of this term to describe religious pictures in the sixteenth century is itself an argument in favour of the 'pretext' thesis. The first known use of the term 'landscape' in Italian comes from about this time;

in 1521 Michiel recorded the existence of 'many little landscapes' (*molte tavolette de paesi*) in the collection of Cardinal Grimani. It is curious that the first reference to 'landscape' in German comes from the same year. It is also Michiel who described Giorgione's *Tempest* as

> The landscape on canvas with the tempest, with the gypsy-girl and soldier. (*El paesetto in tela cum le tempesta, cum la cingana et soldato.*)

This does not prove that *The Tempest* is not an allegorical picture; it was possible for sixteenth-century observers, like modern ones, to miss the point of the picture. But it is significant that Michiel can describe the picture as if it were a landscape without surprise. In the early sixteenth century, in the Veneto, there were painted a number of pastoral scenes which probably did not illustrate any story in particular, but simply evoked the Arcadian mood.

In the case of the still-life, the clues lead back once more to the circle of Isabella of Mantua. In 1506 a certain Girolamo Casio wrote to her that he was sending her 'a picture full of fruit' (*uno quadro pieno de fructi*) by Antonio da Crevalcone. The date fits nicely with a painting of partridges by Jacopo de'Barbari, of 1504, and with the beginning of the career of Giovanni da Udine, described by Vasari as learning from a Fleming how to paint 'fruit, leaves, and flowers'.[8]

In sculpture, as in painting, the fundamental unit was the programme; not 'Moses' but 'the tomb of Julius II', though the dispersal of the elements and loss of some of them often makes this seeing-as-a-whole almost impossible. As with painting, the predominant themes in sculpture were religious : the Virgin and Child, but in marble or terracotta this time; the *pietà*; the images of the saints, either alone in a niche or whole sculptured scenes from their lives, as in the case of the Donatello miracles of St Anthony at Padua. There is a similar rise of new genres in sculpture as in painting; the portrait-bust and the portrait medal appear at much the same time, the mid-fifteenth century, as the rise of the painted portrait. There is a similar trend towards the autonomy of the statue as of the painting. This is most obvious in the making of statuettes for collectors, by such sculptors as Riccio and 'Antico', but these statuettes are part of a wider movement, that of the emancipation of the statue from the niche.

In the case of architecture, one might have thought there was nothing to say about iconography at all; in what sense do buildings have 'subject-matter'? In the literal sense, they do not; but architectural forms in more than one culture have been influenced by the desire to create symbols. This is true of the Indian *stupa*, the medieval cathedral, and the Renaissance church. The cross-plan of the medieval church was commonly interpreted as a symbol of the crucifixion. The medieval cathedral was (at least sometimes) seen as the image of the cosmos, or of heaven. Abelard, for example, compared the heavenly Jerusalem with the earthly, more specifically with Solomon's Temple, which in its perfect proportions was an appropriate image of heaven. The sculptures on the façade of St-Denis suggest that it was intended to represent the gate of Heaven, the threshold of eternity. These ideas were still very much alive at the Renaissance. Writing a memorandum in 1534 about the construction of a new church in Venice, Francesco Giorgi, a Franciscan, referred to Solomon's Temple and the image of the cosmos:

> When God wished to instruct Moses concerning the form and proportion of the tabernacle which he was to build, He gave him as model the fabric of the world . . . Pondering on this mystery, Solomon the Wise gave the same proportions as those of the Mosaic tabernacle to the famous Temple which he erected.

As for the gateway, when Alberti designed S. Francesco at Rimini he borrowed the façade design from a Roman triumphal arch; the obvious implication is that Christians triumph over death. Thus he managed to allude to Roman architecture, Petrarch's triumphs, and medieval building tradition in one motif.

Another symbol in Renaissance architecture was the circular plan. For example, an anonymous drawing of *c.* 1500 of an ideal city makes it circular, with streets radiating like the spokes of a wheel. This made the city the image of the cosmos, or of the sun (a theme taken up *c.* 1600 by Campanella, who called his utopia the *City of the Sun*). Some Renaissance architects broke with the Latin cross-plan, symbol of the crucifixion, and built churches with a circular or at least a centralized, Greek-cross plan, such as Brunelleschi's S. Maria degli Angeli; Michelozzo's SS. Annunziata; Sangallo's S. Maria delle Carceri, and others. The circle was a symbol of perfection, of the cosmos, and of God, and the circular plan was as much a christian symbol as the cruciform plan. But not everyone during the Renaissance, not even all educated men, shared this view. Filarete seems to have seen circular plans as pagan; he points out that in antiquity they did not use the cross-plan because they were idolaters and had no respect for it (*perché erano idolatre non avevano rispecto*). Pius II saw Alberti's S. Francesco as pagan. It is not only Ruskin and the moderns who see Renaissance churches as worldly.⁹

It would be stretching the meaning of the term 'iconography' in an unhelpful way to apply it to literature; but some of the more obvious similarities and differences between the subject-matter of literature and the visual arts are worth noting. One genre – the religious drama – does deal with the same themes that are popular in religious paintings : Abraham and Isaac, Tobias and the archangel Raphael, the Annunciation, the Nativity, the Last Supper, the Resurrection, the Last Judgement, St John the Baptist, St Barbara, St Ursula; one has the feeling reading them that one is looking at a Renaissance painting, and scholars have argued for most of the century as to which form influenced which. One might compare portraits and self-portraits with biographies and autobiographies. Apart from this, the differences are more remarkable than the similarities. A favourite pictorial genre like the mythology does not have many literary equivalents, though some poems by Lorenzo de'Medici on Pan, Mars and Venus do correspond neatly with paintings made for him and his circle; and there are passages in Poliziano which correspond in detail as well as mood to Botticelli's *Birth of Venus* and *Primavera*. The lack of more precise literary equivalents can be explained by the fact that books like Ovid's *Metamorphoses* were in circulation, so there was no need to write more. Then the pictures of battles and other state occasions from Uccello to Vasari have their parallels in the rhetorical descriptions of battles in the humanist history, from Bruni to Guicciardini; the equivalent of the landscape background is the descriptive passage in the narrative poem, such as those of Ariosto. There are also cases where painters illustrate modern poets, particularly Dante, Petrarch and Boccaccio; and Dossi, at the court of Ferrara, illustrated his fellow-citizen and contemporary Ariosto. But there is an obvious discrepancy between the visual arts and literature. In this period most paintings were religious in subject, whereas most works of imaginative literature were secular. We return to one of the main themes of this book, the fact that there were 'two cultures' in Italy. Most religious paintings were produced by ordinary people, craftsmen, for ordinary people, in the sense that many were displayed in churches where everyone could see them. Imaginative literature was produced by an élite for an élite. The one case of close correspondence between art and literature is the case of the religious drama, a traditional and popular form, and one which by 1540 did not have long to live.

LATENT CONTENT

Contemporaries were used to looking for hidden meanings in literature, if only because they were often told from the pulpit (e.g. below p. 210) that the Bible had not only a literal meaning but three others: allegorical, moral, and anagogical. They certainly looked for hidden meanings in works of secular literature, even if they did not always distinguish the kinds of hidden meaning as carefully as Biblical commentators. Landino, for example, in his commentary on Horace's *Art of Poetry*, wrote of poetry that:

> When it most appears to be narrating something most humble and ignoble or to be singing a little fable to delight idle ears, at that very time it is writing in a rather secret way the most excellent things of all, which are drawn forth from the fountain of the gods.

Again, Vellutello argued that the chief aim of comedy is:

> under the veil of joyous and pleasant discourse, to hide always some useful and appropriate morality.

A number of commentaries were written which bring out in detail the kind of hidden meaning they were referring to. Landino's Commentaries on Virgil and Dante; Beroaldo's commentary on Apuleius, *The Golden Ass*; Pico's commentary on the poems of Benivieni; Vellutello's on Petrarch are all examples from this period. The hidden meaning is often a religious one, or a neoplatonic philosophical one (which is not very different from the religious) underlying the apparently secular or frivolous.

Why so much secrecy? If one had asked a humanist, he might well have replied that one ought to hide mysteries from the vulgar; or that (as Macrobius put it) 'a frank, open exposition of herself is distasteful to nature'. One might add that when the moral message is a banal one, it needs to be hidden to make it interesting; that the allegorical habit of mind was a central characteristic of late medieval culture, and could not be abandoned in a hurry; and that it had an important function, that of reconciling the apparently irreconcilable, paganism and christianity – that was how the system had grown up in the days of the early Church. In the early fifteenth-century, Dominici attacked humanists for paganism; Salutati, who defended humanists against him, wrote a book on the allegorical meaning of the Hercules myth, to show that pagan forms carried christian meanings.

Two examples of the allegorical approach to literature at the Renaissance are the commentaries on Ovid and Ariosto. Ovid is a useful example to take here because his *Metamorphoses* furnished the subject-matter, as we have seen, for a number of Renaissance paintings. He had been studied a great deal from the twelfth century on, and provided with allegorical interpretations; the thirteenth-century French *Ovide Moralisée* is famous. In Italy the favourite interpretation seems to have been that of Giovanni de Bonsignore in the fourteenth century; the Italian editions of the *Metamorphoses* printed at Venice in 1497 and 1533 print his allegorizations. In Book I, for example, there is the transformation of Daphne, fleeing from Apollo, into a laurel. We learn that Daphne stands for prudence; the laurel (because it is evergreen) for virginity. This of course allegorizes the parts at the expense of the whole – for Daphne is not transformed into a virgin, she is transformed in order to remain a virgin. In Book x, there is the story of Orpheus and Eurydice. Eurydice stands for 'good judgement'. So the devil tempted Orpheus, he strayed from the right path; that is, he lost his judgement, his Eurydice. He repented and prayed to God; his judgement was restored on condition that he did not yield to temptation ('look back') again.

In the case of the *Metamorphoses*, we have an ancient author, a medieval commentator, and both popular in the Renaissance. But did contemporary writers intend their own works to be understood allegorically? Were they so understood? The Venice, 1542 edition of Ariosto's *Orlando Furioso* has, as it says on the title page, 'some allegories added for each canto', presumably by Dolce, since he is responsible for the glossary of difficult words and passages. Canto 1, the flight of Angelica, he interprets as showing 'the ingratitude of women'. Canto 34, in which Orlando recovers his lost wits, which have to be brought back from the moon, is supposed to show that 'once a man has lost his wits (*l'intelletto*) he cannot regain them by human aid without the special grace of God'. Canto 45, Ruggiero's combat with Bradamante, shows in Ruggiero 'the qualities of a perfect knight'. This is a rather different kind of hidden meaning, whether Ariosto intended it or not, from the ones attributed to Ovid; the characters are not made to personify abstract qualities, but their actions and predicaments are simply turned into generalizations.

It seems that in the period, an accepted way to read a poem was allegorically, using the term loosely to cover the whole complex of non-literal meanings. It is always possible that a work of the period which the twentieth-century reader naturally interprets literally had, for its author and his first readers, one or more hidden meanings. Poliziano's *Orfeo* may simply be a celebration of a great artist from antiquity, but it is more likely to have several meanings. It may be a story about the loss of a man's judgement, which was Bonsignore's interpretation of the Orpheus story. Given the fact that the play was written for wedding celebrations and that Poliziano moved in the circle of Ficino and Lorenzo de'Medici, it is more likely that the play is saying something about the nature of love, and something of which Plato would have approved. Turning to the speech of Phaedrus in the *Symposium*, we find that the story of Orpheus is given another interpretation; whereas

Alcestis had the courage to die for love, Orpheus, 'as is only natural in a musician', had not, but entered Hades alive; hence he was not given Eurydice but only shown a ghost of her. Pico della Mirandola discussed this passage in his commentary on a love poem by Benivieni, comparing the act of love to dying and human love to love of God.[10]

If the common reader of the period was likely to look for hidden meanings, so was the man who looked at paintings; as is poetry, so is painting. The most obvious occasions to look for such meanings were in cases where the painting lacked a more literal meaning; cases such as Perugino's *Combat of Love and Chastity*, or Dossi's *Three Ages of Man*. But in the majority of cases, paintings had a literal meaning and it was up to the spectator to read between the brush-strokes. For example, a number of paintings and sculptures of the period represented subjects taken from the Old Testament. But the Bible was commonly interpreted in three non-literal ways, and in particular characters from the Old Testament were taken to be 'types' or 'figures' of characters in the New Testament. Eve and Judith, for example, were considered to be types of the Virgin Mary, to 'prefigure' her. The story of Judith comes from the *Apocrypha*; when Holofernes, the chief captain of Nabuchodonosor, King of the Assyrians, attacked Israel, Judith, a Jewish widow, went to him in his tent, made him drunk and beheaded him with his own sword. Thus it was possible to compare Judith and Mary; Judith liberated Israel by her victory over Holofernes, Mary liberated mankind by her victory over Satan. But according to the Biblical commentators, the relationship between Judith and Mary was closer than mere similarity or analogy. It was believed that God had so arranged things that Judith killed Holofernes because Mary would be victorious over Satan; a kind of dumb prophecy, not *in verbis* but *in rebus*. Similarly with the types of Christ, of whom many were discovered in the Old Testament. Adam : Christ was the second Adam because man's state before the Fall prefigured his state after the Resurrection. David : his victory over Goliath prefigured Christ's victory over Satan. Jonah : his three days in the whale prefigured Christ's descent into hell. Isaac : his sacrifice prefigured the Crucifixion. Moses : his leading of Israel to the Promised Land prefigured the Redemption, and so did

Noah's saving of his family in the ark. These typological meanings go far towards explaining why some Old Testament themes were so much more popular in art than others.

Sometimes it is a relatively minor incident from the Old Testament that is endowed with figural significance. To take a subject which was extremely popular in fifteenth-century Italian paintings: Tobias and the angel. The story comes, once more, from the *Apocrypha*, from the *Book of Tobit*. It says that the boy Tobias 'found Raphael, who was an angel' and went on a journey with him, and on his advice took a fish which leaped out of the river, and with its gall cured his father's blindness. St Augustine's interpretation of the story was that 'Christ is that fish which came to Tobias'.

Sometimes it is extremely difficult to decide whether a painting should be interpreted typologically or not. Fra Pietro da Novellara, writing to Isabella of Mantua in 1501, described a sketch by Leonardo as follows – the 'may be' is significant:

A cartoon of a child Christ, about a year old, almost jumping out of his mother's arms to seize hold of a lamb. The mother is in the act of rising from St Anne's lap, and holds back the child from the lamb, an innocent creature which is a symbol of the Passion (*significa la passione*), while St Anne, partly rising from her seat, seems anxious to restrain her daughter, which may be a type of the Church (*forsi vole figurare la Chiesa*) who would not hinder the Passion of Christ.

Secular paintings, like secular poems, may carry a moral, allegorical or 'spiritual' meaning. The pagan gods and the planets associated with them were often taken to stand for moral qualities. Mars stood for courage, Venus for love; or, as Ficino once suggested, 'Mars stands for speed, Saturn for tardiness, Sol for God, Jupiter for the law, Mercury for reason, and Venus for humanity (*humanitas*).' This suggestion occurs in a letter to the man who commissioned Botticelli's *Primavera*, so it has been conjectured that the Venus in that painting stands for 'humanity'. The *Birth of Venus* may also carry a moral message. Boccaccio's *Genealogy of the Gods* describes the birth of Venus from the sea, described her as carrying (rather than standing upon) a seashell, and comments that this Venus symbolizes 'the life of lust' (*la vita lasciva*). The pejorative overtones may be inappropriate in interpreting the Botticelli, but the fundamental equation may be the same.

By the mid-sixteenth century, if not before, a whole symbolic language had been elaborated for secular paintings, as Vasari's notebooks show. He employed about a hundred animals, birds and reptiles; the lion standing for courage, the serpent for envy (or health or deceit) and so on. He employed about 40 vegetables, some of them with meanings which have survived to the twentieth century, such as the olive, symbol of peace; others with more esoteric meanings. He also expressed himself in the language of minerals (the emerald stands for virginity, the diamond for courage) and in that of astrology, as well as that of moralized classical mythology. A convenient example of Vasari's method in composing a painting with a hidden meaning comes from a letter he wrote in 1533 to Alessandro de'Medici, explaining the significance of his portrait of Lorenzo. For example, he says that he has painted a vase full of roses and violets.

This vase will have a spout for pouring water, which will pierce a beautiful mask crowned with laurel, and in front, or on the spout, there will be these words, *Praemium virtutis* (the reward of virtue). On the other side there will be a lamp in the classical style, also looking like porphyry, with a fantastic foot and a bizarre mask on the top . . . showing that the magnificent Lorenzo, by his remarkable method of government . . . enlightened his descendants, and this magnificent city.

Such a painting may be regarded, to use a term of the 1530s, as an 'emblem', a design which could be translated into a sentence. Emblems became fashionable in the sixteenth century, as the popularity of the first emblem-book, Alciati's, showed. But the idea existed before the word. Some fifteenth-century humanists designed emblems, modelled on what they thought hieroglyphs meant; for they interpreted the writing of the Egyptians as a metaphorical language, not a literal one; as a set of devices, or rebuses, or *imprese*. Alberti, for example, adopted the device of the winged eye, and put it on the reverse of his portrait-medal. It would be tempting to interpret this device as saying something about devices; they convey a message to the eye, in a flash, whereas to listen to the same message in words would take much longer. But the motto, *quid tum*, suggests that the emblem represents the speed of divine retribution.[11]

Pictures which taken as a whole have only one level of meaning may contain objects which have more than one. The classic account of this 'concealed or disguised symbolism' has been given by Panofsky in his book on *Early Netherlands painting*; he suggests that the problem in the fifteenth century was to reconcile the new naturalistic art with christian symbolism, and the solution was to introduce 'apparently naturalistic artifacts' which were not just themselves but also, in a phrase he quotes from Aquinas, corporeal metaphors of things spiritual (*spiritualia sub metaphoris corporalium*). Thus if a Madonna is represented in a church, the church may represent The Church: a pot of lilies in an Annunciation scene is not only interior decoration but a symbol of chastity; and so on. The problem (for contemporaries as well as for modern art historians) must have been not just spotting the symbol, but deciding whether the artist really meant it, whether one was being over-subtle. But in some cases the arguments really do carry conviction. For example, a picture in the Brera, by Piero della Francesca or from his studio, representing the Madonna, in which an egg hangs from the ceiling of the church in which she sits. Now (as some fifteenth-century antiquarians knew) in ancient Laconia, Leda's egg hung from a temple ceiling. By implication, Leda is a type of Mary; for Leda conceived by a swan, Mary by a dove. Again, when a Crivelli Christ-child holds an apple, one is probably meant to think of it as Adam and Eve's apple, the fruit of the tree of knowledge, and of Adam as a type of Christ. When Leonardo paints an Adoration of the Magi with an aqueduct in the background, the more learned contemporary spectators might remember that St Bernard compared the Virgin to an aqueduct, because she is the mediatrix of all graces. When Dossi paints a Christ-Child playing with a cock, rather more contemporaries might see the cock, associated with the new day, as a symbol of the Resurrection.[12]

ICONOGRAPHY AND IDEOLOGY

So far, the hidden meanings discussed have been religious and moral ones. Hidden political meanings also existed. A scene from ancient history might be intended to suggest to the spectator a parallel with modern events, even if the relationship between the two sets of events was not conceptualized in the same way as that between the Old Testament and the New, in terms of prefiguration. Iconography may conceal ideology in the sense of ideas manipulated for political purposes.

To be sure not to project on to works of art meaning which their creators never intended, it is best to start with literature, with explicit discussions of implicit and hidden meanings. To return to Ariosto. The publisher of the 1542 edition, Gabriel Giolito, wrote a preface to the *Orlando Furioso* in which he pointed out the political message of the poem:

Here the prudence and the justice of an excellent prince, here the rashness and the negligence of an unwise king accompanied by despotism.

Ariosto, in his seventeenth Canto, introduces an explicit parallel between the barbarian invasion of Italy in Charlemagne's day and those of his own day, but Giolito goes further than this. His point is not one about topical allusions but about political education. But did contemporaries read the *Furioso* as if it were comparable to Machiavelli's *Prince*? Machiavelli had pretensions as a poet; did Ariosto have pretensions as a political theorist? If he did, there would have been nothing surprising to his contemporaries in this. Machiavelli quoted Virgil as if he were an authority on politics, bringing in Dido's apology to Aeneas as evidence that a new prince has to be harsher than one who is well established. With any literature of this period, it is always worth the reader's while asking himself whether the events of the poem or story, true or imaginary, set in the recent or the remote past, might not refer to the events of the writer's own day. If the writer is a man of affairs, the likelihood is all the greater that this is one of the right ways to read his book. To take Lorenzo de'Medici's play about Saints John and

Paul, for example. The play is much concerned with the political problems of the Emperor Constantine. Does Lorenzo identify with him? The rebellion of Dacia and its suppression by Gallicanus is reminiscent of the rebellion of Volterra against Lorenzo and its suppression by Federico da Montefeltre. Constantine emphasizes that he did everything for the common good. Was Lorenzo writing propaganda for himself?

Painting and sculpture may also carry political meanings, which are that much harder for the historian to decode; there are no lines for him to read between. Such decoding is bound to be speculative and interpretations are often controversial; hence it may be wise to start with one of the most explicit examples, Raphael's frescoes in the Vatican, executed for Julius II, and, after his death, for Leo X. There is a fresco, painted about 1511, of the Expulsion of Heliodorus from the Temple. This subject is yet again taken from the *Apocrypha*, but it is difficult not to connect it with Julius II's expulsion of the Bentivoglio family from Bologna, an event which took place at about the same time as the fresco was painted: 'the Temple' becomes a symbol of the States of the Church. The Bentivoglio are seen as profaning the Temple; this is the papal version of the conflict. Art is here fulfilling the function of propaganda, just like the modern poster (above, p. 145). Again, Leo I and Attila the Hun are represented: to make the hidden meaning not too difficult to discover, Leo I has been given the features of Julius II. Julius and others often spoke of the French and other invaders of Italy as the 'barbarians'; the historical parallel is the same as Ariosto's. In this painting, of about 1512, the Huns are probably the French. Again, there is a fresco of the coronation of Charlemagne by Leo III. This time the pope, all the more appropriately called Leo, has the features of Leo X: Charlemagne has the features of François I. In other words, with a change of pope came a change of policy; friendship with France, the signing of the Concordat of Bologna in 1515, at about the time this picture was painted.

The Raphael frescoes are an unusually elaborate and transparent example of political meaning in the arts. There are many cases where the meaning is less clear. It has been argued (more particularly by Frederick Hartt) that a number of early fifteenth-century Florentine sculptures refer to the wars between Florence and her much more powerful enemies.

Abraham and Isaac on the Baptistery doors: the Florentines hoped for deliverance from the Milanese threat by divine intervention at the last moment, just as Isaac had been delivered. Donatello's *David* of *c.* 1408 probably represents Florence; Goliath being Ladislas of Naples. The inscription on the statue reinforces this interpretation; it reads:

> to those who bravely fight for the fatherland the gods will lend aid even against the most terrible foes.

Donatello's *St George* is another possible symbol of Florence; the dragon representing her enemies. In a similar way, in Sweden, when the regent Sten Sture had defeated the Danes in 1471, he commissioned a figure of St George from Bernt Notke for the church of St Nicholas in Stockholm. Donatello's *Judith and Holofernes* seems to have carried a political rather than a religious message. At any rate Piero de'Medici had a political moral inscribed under it in the mid-fifteenth century:

> *Regna cadunt luxu, surgunt virtutibus urbes*
> *Caesa vides humili collis superba manu.*
> (Kingdoms fall through luxury;
> cities rise through the virtues;
> you see a proud neck struck by a humble hand.)

It has been suggested recently that this was an attempt by the Medici to show the Florentines that they were still citizens, that they were not thinking of turning themselves into princes. By 1476 this point no longer seemed plausible. At any rate, when in that year the Florentine government acquired Verrocchio's *David* and put it in the courtyard of the Palazzo Vecchio, it was inscribed with a harmless moral referring to foreign policy, not to domestic affairs:

> Whoever defends his own country will be victorious. The power of God will destroy the anger of the enemy. Behold, a boy has conquered the awful tyrant. Conquer, oh citizens!

One could go on almost indefinitely with possible political interpretations of works of art of this period. Botticelli's *Pallas and the Centaur* may refer to Lorenzo de'Medici's victory over the Pazzi, who had conspired against him. It has been argued that the Sistine Chapel frescoes are a manifesto for the pope in his conflict with the church councils of the fifteenth century. For example, Botticelli painted for the pope the scene of the punishment of Korah, taken from the Book of Numbers; Korah and his men, the Bible says:

> Gathered themselves together against Moses and against Aaron, and said unto them, Ye take too much upon you, seeing that all the congregation are holy, every one of them, and the Lord is among them; wherefore then lift ye up yourself above the congregation of the Lord?

In response to the prayers of Moses, the earth opened, and swallowed the rebels up. Michelangelo created two marble symbols of the Florentine Republic. His famous marble *David* was commissioned in 1501, during the revived republic. Vasari considered it to be a symbol of 'just government' and it was in fact set up outside the seat of government, the Palazzo Vecchio. Michelangelo's *Brutus*, which he made about 1539, was commissioned by Cardinal Niccolò Ridolfi, a member of a prominent Florentine family, and at the instance of Giannotti, a Florentine republican, exile, and writer on politics, so it is plausible to interpret it as an affirmation of republican ideals against the restored Medici rule.[18]

ICONOGRAPHY AND SOCIETY

For the social historian of art, two questions about iconography are paramount. The first question is, who understood the meaning of works of art in the period? The evidence does not allow of a straight answer, but a few comments can still be made. It is likely that the urban population, which had access to regular sermons, had little difficulty in reading religious paintings. The essential clues to the attributes of saints, to St Sebastian's arrows and St Catherine's wheel, are usually to be found in their legends, and such books as the *Golden Legend* were well known in fifteenth-century Italy. For those who could not read there were religious plays, which so often dealt with the very themes most popular in paintings.

The iconography of secular paintings was probably intelligible to a minority only. Scenes from ancient history and classical mythology would be easy to recognize if one had read one's Livy or one's Ovid; this virtually meant having gone to a grammar school, and only a minority of Renaissance Italians can have done that. This educational fact gives some basis to the favourite Renaissance division of the public into two parts, 'the multitude' and 'those who understand'. 'Those who understand' would not have included many artists; hence the need for the humanist adviser. We know that some painters did not understand the iconography of works by some other painters: Vasari's puzzlement at some paintings by Giorgione is just as great as that of modern critics:

> As far as I am concerned, I have never understood them; nor have I, by asking around as I have done, ever found anyone who does.

It is also likely that the proportion of people who understood secular iconography increased during the period, as humanist education spread. But the great breakthrough came just after the end of the period, with the publication of three Italian mythological reference books between 1548 and 1556 – Giraldi, Conti and Cartari.[14]

The second question about iconography and society is that of explaining the dominance of certain images, or kinds of image, in the period. Why were most paintings religious? Why were no pure landscapes or still-lifes painted in the fifteenth century? For painters take an obvious interest in landscape or still-life backgrounds to narrative scenes.

The obvious explanation is the functional one, outlined earlier (p. 140). Most paintings were religious in subject-matter because they were intended to fill religious functions, whether they were hung or painted on the walls of churches or private houses. More will be said about the religious life of Renaissance Italians and the place of art in it in Chapter 9 (p. 250). Landscapes and still-lifes did not appear till the end of the period because it was not till then that patrons began to think of paintings as objects worth having for their own sake – a crucial change of function.

Another relevant point is that different types of subject, pictorial and literary, had different social statuses. In literature, for example, the epic and the tragedy were high-status genres; the romance, the lyric, the novella and the comedy came lower down. This is why a printer found it necessary to apologize to his patron for an edition of Ariosto's *Orlando Furioso*. Gabriel Giolito, dedicating the 1542 edition to the dauphin, remarked that Ariosto:

> had raised the baseness of romances (*la bassezza de romanzi*) to such a height on the wings of his rare and happy wit.

This hierarchy of genres should alert us to the fact that one function of the theory of hidden meanings was a social one; to show that (as Landino and Vellutello argue, above p. 194) 'low' themes were really high ones in disguise, just as profane ones were really religious, and pagan themes really christian.

In the course of the sixteenth and seventeenth centuries a similar hierarchy was established for paintings, with the 'history' or narrative picture at the top; then the portrait; then the landscape and still-life. It seems plausible to argue that in the fifteenth century such a view was held implicitly, though not stated, and that this was another reason for the absence of landscapes and still-lifes as genres.

Of course this explanation does not go far enough. The obvious next question is, 'Why was there this particular hierarchy of subject-matter?

The 'history' was presumably high-status because it was the visual equivalent of the highest form of literature, the epic; the epic was high-status because the ancients had said so, and because the greatest poets, Homer and Virgil, had written epics as their masterpieces. But this is not the whole story. Writing on beauty, Nifo suggested that only the human body was really beautiful. Here the hierarchy of genre seems to reflect a hierarchy of values. Paintings which represent the actions of men have a higher status than paintings of trees or fruit, because men are nobler than, have a higher status than, trees and fruit. Thus the art and literature of the age reflects the central values, the world-view of the age, and cannot be fully understood until that value-system or world-view is examined and described. This will be done in the next chapter.

World-Views: Some Dominant Traits

The subject of this chapter has many names. Marx called it 'ideology', Wölfflin *Lebensgefühl*, Mannheim *Weltanschauung*, and Febvre called it *outillage mental*. The idea common to all these historians and sociologists is that a social group, large or small, tends to have certain attitudes in common; attitudes to God and to the cosmos, nature and human nature, life and death, space and time, the good and the beautiful. These attitudes may be conscious or unconscious; few people seem to be aware that they have 'a' conception of space or time, but rather more are conscious of their attitude to the state.[1]

It has often been suggested that the relation of art and literature to society is not direct, but that it is mediated through a world-view. To quote only historians of the Renaissance, von Martin and Antal both wrote as if this were the case. There are three implicit hypotheses here, which all need to be tested against the evidence. First, that there *are* world-views; that attitudes are structured, so that one can usefully talk of 'Renaissance attitudes', 'Italian attitudes' or 'clerical attitudes'. Second, that art and literature in a given period express some dominant world-view; that they are not 'out of step'. Third, that a social explanation can be given for the predominance of a given world-view : for example, that different social groups or classes have different ways of seeing the world, and that the dominant view of the period is the view of the dominant class. There are obvious problems for anyone trying to verify these hypotheses. The most explicit evidence of attitudes is literary, whether formal treatise or private diary – but these sources are richer for Tuscany than elsewhere, richer for the end of the period than the beginning, and richer for some social groups, like nobles and wealthy merchants, than for others, like craftsmen and peasants. There is also the problem of studying attitudes of which people were not conscious; one has to practise reading between the lines, or, as sociologists call it, 'content analysis', using the frequency of recurrence of certain fashionable terms as a clue to shifts in values. In the early fifteenth century, fashionable terms of praise were terms like 'delicate' or 'elegant', whereas in the early sixteenth century, 'grand' and 'heroic' were fashionable.[2]

Renaissance Italians lived in a mental universe which was animate rather than mechanical, moralized rather than objective, and organized in terms of correspondences rather than causes.[3]

A common phrase was that the world was 'an animal'; as we would say, 'organic'. Leonardo developed this idea in a traditional way when he wrote:

> We can say that the earth has a vegetative soul, and that its flesh is the land, its bones are the structure of the rocks . . . its blood is the pools of water . . . its breathing and its pulse are the ebb and flow of the sea.

Similarly, Alberti wrote that a building is 'like an animal', and Filarete that, 'A building . . . wants to be nourished and looked after, and through lack of this it sickens and dies like a man.' Hence Michelangelo's insistence that an architect know anatomy. Even Frank Lloyd Wright could not match this organic theory of architecture. The operations of the universe were described in terms of love; magnetism, for example:

> We see the magnet is loved so greatly by the iron, that notwithstanding the size and weight of the iron, it moves and goes to find it.

Dante's famous phrase about 'the love that moves the sun and the other stars' was still taken seriously. Besides love, or 'sympathy', there was also natural hatred or 'antipathy': cold hated hot, moist hated dry.[4]

On occasion a mechanical model of the universe might be employed. Fontana, who wrote on water-clocks, once referred to the universe as this 'noble clock'. Leonardo wrote that 'the bird is an instrument operating by mathematical law', an assumption necessary to his attempts to construct flying-machines. He described the tendons of the human body as 'mechanical instruments', and the heart as a 'marvellous instrument invented by the supreme master'. Machiavelli and Guicciardini, applying mechanics to politics, thought in terms of the 'balance of power'. But this kind of analogy was rare, and the 'mechanization of the world-picture' was the work of the seventeenth century.[5]

The universe was 'moralized' in the sense that it was divided into different strata with higher or lower status. It was thought better or higher to be warm than cold: 'the warm is much more noble and perfect than the cold, because it is active and productive'. Again, it was considered better not to change, like the heavens, than to change, like the earth; better to be at rest than to move; better to move in a circle than in other ways; better to be a tree than a stone, an animal than a tree, a human being than an animal, a man than a woman, a nobleman than a peasant.

The parts of the universe were related to one another symbolically rather than causally, in terms of 'correspondences'. The most famous of the correspondences was that between man, the 'microcosm' and the universe in general, the 'macrocosm'. Thus Fontana wrote that a man's right eye corresponded to the sun, his left eye to the moon, his ears to Jupiter and Mars, his nostrils to Mercury and Venus, his mouth to Saturn. Leone Ebreo suggested that a man from waist to feet corresponded to the sublunary world; from neck to waist, to the heavenly world; his head corresponded to the 'intelligible world'. Numerology played a great part in these analogies; if two sets contained the same number of units, this was not put down to accident but was taken to prove correspondences. The fact that (as men believed in this period) there were seven planets, seven metals, and seven days of the week suggested that there were connexions between them. There were twelve apostles and twelve signs of the zodiac, hence an apostle was allocated to each sign. Other correspondences were derived from letters of the alphabet. Benivieni made a great deal of his discovery that the five letters in the name 'Maria' corresponded to the five stages of the spiritual life. M. corresponded to *Memoria mortis*, awareness of death; A. to *Abrenuntiatio omnium terrenorum*, the renunciation of all worldly goods; R. with *Rectitudo cordis*, righteousness of heart; I. with

Illuminatio divina, divine enlightenment; and A. with *Amor*, love. Again, St Bernardino preached a sermon on the name 'Jesus'; he had the letters YHS painted in gold on a blue background, with twelve rays coming from them, and he interpreted this device, like the scriptures, in four ways. In the first place it meant 'Jesus'; in the second place the three letters signified the Trinity, and the twelve rays the twelve apostles; in the third place YHS signified the Church, and its fourth sense, the moral sense, was written on our hearts. This elaborate system of correspondences had a great advantage for artists and writers; it meant that their images were not 'mere' images, their symbols not 'mere' symbols; symbolism was the language of the universe and God its creator.[6]

Belief in correspondence helps explain the interest which was taken in 'prodigies', out of the ordinary events which were interpreted as 'portents', signs of future events. A typical example is Infessura's record that in 1472 'the comet was seen in heaven with a great tail, and it was said that it means the death of great lords'. Thus Landucci recorded the birth of deformed children in his diary, with comments like 'such signs signify great trouble in the city where they take place.' The deaths of famous men, Lorenzo de'Medici for example, were 'seen' to be accompanied by portents. The French invasion of Italy in 1494 was preceded by fearsome prodigies, recorded by Guicciardini :

> In Apulia, at night, there were three suns in the middle of the sky but cloudy all about them and with horrible thunder and lightning; in the territory of Arezzo, for many days infinite numbers of armed men on great horses passed through the air, with a terrible noise of trumpets and drums; in many places in Italy holy images and statues sweated openly; many monstrous men and other animals were born everywhere.

Prodigies were usually taken to signify disasters, not good fortune, which suggests that considerable insecurity underlay the consciously-expressed world-view in Renaissance Italy.[7]

Views of the cosmos

The conventional picture of the cosmos was the Aristotelian-Ptolemaic one. The fundamental distinction was that between Heaven and Earth.

'Heaven' should really be in the plural: the earth was surrounded by seven 'spheres' or 'heavens', and in each of them moved a planet: Moon, Mercury, Venus, Sun, Mars, Jupiter, and Saturn. The planets were animate; each was moved by an 'intelligence', a being often equated with the appropriate classical god or goddess; this fusion of planets and deities had permitted the 'survival of the pagan gods' into the Middle Ages and Renaissance. Men's lives were subject to planetary 'influences'. As the planets sang in a carnival song written by Lorenzo de'Medici, 'from us come all good and all evil things,' and rich and poor were alike subject to them. So were the days of the week: Monday was influenced by the moon, Tuesday by Mars, Wednesday by Mercury, Thursday by Jupiter, Friday by Venus, Saturday by Saturn. To discover what the future might have in store one could consult specialists, astrologers, who calculated the configuration of the heavens at a particular time; calculations were made easier by the division of the paths of the planets into twelve sections, each represented by a sign, the signs of the zodiac, and a subdivision into thirty-six decans. An example of this kind of calculation is Fracastoro's explanation of the outbreak of syphilis in Europe in terms of a conjunction of Saturn, Jupiter and Mars in Cancer.

These beliefs had considerable 'influence' on the arts. Borso d'Este, duke of Ferrara, had a room in his Palazzo Schifanoia decorated with the signs of the zodiac and the images of the decans. Alberti and Filarete advised the choice of a 'good constellation' for laying the foundation of a building. Filippo Strozzi had the foundations of his palace laid (on 6th August, 1489) only after consulting 'a man learned in astrology'. When a Florentine committee was discussing where to put Michelangelo's *David*, one speaker suggested that it should replace Donatello's *Judith*, which was 'erected under an evil star'. Ficino studied how to capture the 'spirit' of the planets by means of images and music. For each planet one could make an appropriate 'talisman', an image engraved on a precious stone under a good constellation. Mars, for example, was susceptible to an image of a young man with a girl. Music too had to be appropriate to the planet. For Mars, the music should be 'martial'; for Venus, Ficino recommended that it be 'voluptuous with wantonness and softness'. Against this background of ideas it is possible to interpret Botticelli's *Primavera* as a kind of talisman, and to take literally Vasari's remarks about creativity:

> The greatest gifts may be seen raining on human bodies from celestial influences, often by natural means and occasionally by supernatural ones.[8]

Astrology was allowed by the Church; it was not considered incompatible with Christianity. Pope Paul III, for example, took a great interest in astrology; he summoned to Rome Luca Gaurico, the astrologer who had predicted his election, knighted him and made him a bishop. The power of the stars did not detract from God's power:

> *Giove é pianeta, che 'l suo ciel sol muove,*
> *Ma più alta potenzia muove Giove.*
> (Jupiter is a planet, who moves only his own sphere,
> but there is a higher power which moves Jupiter.)[9]

At the same time, it might be argued that theology and astrology formed two systems which did in practice compete with one another, which occupied the same heavenly space. The saints presided over certain days; so did the planets. Should one sing planetary music or sing Mass? consult an astrologer or consult a priest? Into this space was also inserted the angelic hierarchy in its nine ranks – angels, archangels, principalities, powers, virtues, dominations, thrones, cherubim and seraphim. One attempt at reconciling the different parts of the traditional world-picture was made by Fontana, who declared that angels dwell in the signs of the zodiac and in the decans and move the planets.

Reconcilable or irreconcilable with Christianity, astrology was not taken equally seriously by everyone. Cavalcanti thought that, 'It is not reasonable that divine providence should move the heavenly intelligences for such a small matter as the weakness of a mere man, who is nothing but a breath of wind.' Pius II scoffed at the duke of Ferrara for taking astrology seriously. Giovanni Pico della Mirandola declared that 'astrology offers no help in discovering what a man should do and what avoid.' Guicciardini thought it foolish to take astrology seriously: 'Astrologers do not know what they are talking about; they are never right except by accident.' Long before Jonathan Swift, Aretino produced a parody-prognostication for the year 1527.[10]

Above the seven heavens, beyond the sphere of the 'fixed stars', there was God. In the writing of the time, God is indeed almost everywhere. Even bills of exchange began with the monogram YHS. In private letters, God constantly recurs, as in those of Alessandra Strozzi:

> Please God free everything from this plague . . . it is necessary to accept with patience whatever God wants . . . God give them a safe journey.

And so on. Of all the ways in which Christians have imagined God, two seem particularly characteristic of Renaissance Italy. The first, which corresponds to much of the painting of the time, is the image of the second person of the Trinity, God the Son, the 'affective leader' as we might say. Christ can be seen as a king, as a redeemer, as a man of sorrows, and so on; all these aspects appear in the art and literature of the time; what is particularly striking is the tone of much of the poetry (Savonarola's, for example), full of endearments, such as 'my dear Lord', *signor mio caro*, or 'sweet spouse', *dolce sposo*. In other words, the emphasis on the 'sweetness of God' (*dulcedo Dei*) and on the 'pathetic tenderness' of writing about Christ, which Huizinga noted for France and the Netherlands in the later Middle Ages, can be found in Italy as well.

The second image of God characteristic of the period is the image of the first person of the Trinity, God the Father, the 'instrumental leader', who occurs in paintings, when he occurs at all, usually in the form of a benevolent old king. The favourite images from this period are not those of the father or ruler so much as those of the merchant or architect. Renaissance Italians projected their own concerns on to the heavenly world. *Messer Dominedio* is seen as the head of a business, with whom one may keep an account, which is rendered at death. 'You, oh God, sell us every good thing for the price of labour,' wrote Leonardo. Sometimes it is man who works in the shop, while God (p. 236 below) owns the business. At the other times, it is God who is the steward, who administers the world for man, and 'turns the annual yield over to us with large interest'. Or God is seen as the architect of the universe. Lorenzo de'Medici writes:

> *Magno Iddio per la cui constante legge*
> *E sotto il cui perpetuo governo*
> *Questo universo si conserva e regge . . .*
> *Bellissimo Architetto il mondo bello*
> *Fingendo prima nell'eterna mente,*
> *Fatto hai questo all'immagine di quello.*

(Great God, by whose unchanging law and under whose eternal rule this universe is governed and preserved, most beautiful architect who imagined the world in his eternal mind and created it in that image.)

Men differed about the degree to which God intervened directly in His universe. The traditional view was that He intervened a great deal. For Landucci, this is clear. When plague struck Florence, he wrote in his diary, 'It pleased God to chastise us.' When the French invasion of 1494 left Florence virtually unharmed, he wrote, 'God never removed His hand from off our head.' Again, Savonarola declared that Charles VIII was able to march through Italy with such ease in 1494 because of the sins of the Italians; God was punishing them. But some educated laymen rejected this view of God. For Machiavelli, the 'sin' of the Italians in 1494 was reliance on mercenary armies. For Guicciardini, God's ways were beyond comprehension.[11]

Earth

Earth, or Nature, was the lower world, composed of the four elements, earth, water, air and fire, as painted, for example, in Vasari's Room of the Elements in Florence. Earth, the heaviest, lay at the centre; above it came water, then air, and finally fire, just below the Moon. The elements were themselves composed of the four contraries (hot, cold, moist, dry); thus cold and dry together made earth, hot and moist made air, and so on. There were also four levels of earthly existence: human, animal, vegetable, and mineral. This was the famous 'great chain of being' as Pope and Lovejoy have called it; 'scale' or 'ladder' of being might be a better term, since it makes the social hierarchy of being more apparent. A plant was 'higher' than a stone because stones had no souls, while plants had 'vegetative souls', animals had 'sensitive souls' and man an 'intellectual soul'. Animals, vegetables and minerals, like men, had their own hierarchies; the precious stones were higher than the semi-precious, the lion was the king of beasts, and so on. Many animals, vegetables and minerals had generally-accepted symbolic meanings, and many paintings and poems cannot be understood unless one knows that the emerald stood for virginity, the elephant for piety, and so on. There were other beings whose place on the ladder was less certain. 'Demons', for example, who lived midway between the earth and the moon. They are fairly rare in Italian art, and some writers, like Pomponazzi, doubted whether they existed at all. There were fairies, whom some thought a kind of demon, others thought spirits of the dead. There were the wood-demons who lived in lonely places and would eat boys, as Poliziano's grandmother used to tell him when he was small. There were the nymphs, who wander, or flee, through the poems of Poliziano and Lorenzo de'Medici. It is necessary to remember that all these creatures were not poetic fictions, but were believed to exist.[12]

An important earthly power was fortune, a way of describing whatever on earth was outside human control, but seen as possessing positive characteristics. Two popular images of fortune associated it (or rather, her) with winds and with a wheel. The phrase 'fortune of the sea' meant a tempest, a paradigm case of sudden and uncontrollable changes in affairs. The Rucellai family used the device of a sail, where the wind represented fortune, and the sail, the power of the individual. Guicciardini, reflecting on the 'frequent variations of fortune', saw human affairs as a sea roused into movement by the winds. The other common way of seeing fortune was as a goddess, often with a wheel, and with a forelock which must be seized quickly, because she was bald behind. So Machiavelli defends impetuosity on the grounds that fortune is a woman, 'and to keep her under it is necessary to beat her and strike her', and Guicciardini suggests that it is dangerous to try to make con-spiracies foolproof because 'Fortune, who plays such a large part in all matters, becomes angry with those who try to limit her dominion.' Is the goddess necessary to the argument here, or is she simply employed to decorate conclusions arrived at by other means?[18]

To understand and manipulate the world of earth, a number of techniques were available, including alchemy, magic and witchcraft. Given the world-view as described so far, belief in alchemy is not surprising. It depends, for example, on the ideas that there is a hierarchy of metals, with gold as the noblest, and that a 'social' mobility' or transformation of metals is possible. It also depends on treating inorganic matter as if it were organic. It was believed that metals grew (slowly) in the mines, and that they were 'engendered'. Gold, for example, was engendered by mercury and sulphur. All the alchemist had to do was speed up the natural process, and his catalyst, if he could find it, was also the cure for all illnesses. Alchemy was connected with astrology, because the seven planets and the seven metals were associated: gold with the sun, silver with the moon, mercury with Mercury, iron with Mars, lead with Saturn, tin with Jupiter, and copper with Venus.

Burckhardt thought that alchemy 'played only a very sub-ordinate part' in Italy in the fifteenth and sixteenth centuries. It is dangerous to make general assertions about the popularity of such a deliberately esoteric subject as alchemy, but the odds are that he was wrong. The Venetian Council of Ten clearly thought that alchemy did not play a subordinate enough part, and passed a decree against it in 1488. A number of Italian treatises on alchemy from the later part of the period have survived. The most famous is a Latin poem, published in 1515 and dedicated to Leo x, Augurello's *Chrysopoeia* – there is a story that the pope rewarded the poet with an empty purse. A certain 'J. A. Pantheus', priest of Venice, also dedicated an alchemical work to Leo, before inventing a new subject, 'cabala of metals' or 'Voarchiadumia' which he carefully distinguished from alchemy – perhaps the Council of Ten were still hostile. The hermetic philosopher Lazarelli also wrote on alchemy, but he did not publish his ideas. Some people were sceptical about the claims of the alchemists. St Antonino held that the transmutation of metals was beyond human power. The metallurgist Biringuccio thought that alchemy was (probably) 'a vain wish and fanciful dream' and its adepts, 'more inflamed than the very coals in their furnaces' with the desire to create gold, were misguided; it was better to go mining as he did.

There are some tantalizing indications of the impact of alchemy on the arts, a subject which does not seem to have been studied very much in modern times. Alchemy had its own symbolic system, in which, for example, a fountain stood for the purification of metals; Christ for the philosopher's stone; marriage for the union of sulphur and mercury; a rose for the colour red; Venus for copper; a dragon for fire. It may well be that the famous 'archaeological romance' the *Polifilo*, which makes use of some of these symbols, has an alchemical layer of meaning as well as others. We know from Vasari that Parmigianino studied alchemy:

> He left off painting altogether and began to study alchemy, thinking he would soon become rich by congealing mercury.

One wonders whether Parmigianino made use of alchemical symbolism in his art, whether there is a link between the esoteric arts of alchemy and Mannerism, which were also associated at the court of Rudolf II in the later sixteenth century.[14]

Magic was discussed more openly than alchemy, at least in its white form; for

> Magic has two forms, one of which depends entirely on the work and authority of demons, a thing to be abhorred, so help me the God of truth, and a monstrous thing. The other, when it is rightly pursued, is nothing else than the utter perfection of natural philosophy . . . as the former makes man the bound slave of wicked powers, so does the latter make him their ruler and lord.[15]

One might define magic, cross-culturally, as the attempt to produce changes in the world as the result of performing certain ceremonies and of writing or uttering certain 'spells', 'charms' or 'incantations', verbal formulas which request or demand that these changes happen, or making certain images in order to produce these changes. So defined, a belief in the efficacy of magic seems a natural part of a view of the world as animate, whether it is believed that the rain itself hears the magician's demand that it fall, or that a spirit does this. In terms of this definition, the most influential group of magicians in Renaissance Italy were, no doubt, the clergy, who were experts in ceremonies and in spells (prayers, at least when directed towards specific material ends); who were trained to cast out evil spirits (exorcism); who were the custodians of objects of great magical powers (relics), which often cured people from illness. St Bernardino's famous 'YHS' surrounded by rays was a kind of talisman, and Bernardino suggested that, 'In the name of Jesus you will heal the sick and the poisoned, and avert storms or pestilence.' Another magical image, much in use at the time, was the Agnus Dei, an image, usually in wax, of the Lamb of God, which was widely believed to protect its owner from shipwrecks, storms, and the dangers of child-birth. Certain paintings and sculptures of Christ and the saints, and more especially of Our Lady, were believed to have similar powers. Landucci records that in 1483 the image of Our Lady of Impruneta was brought to Florence, 'for the sake of obtaining fine weather, as it had rained for more than a month. And it immediately became fine.' Of course, one finds the clergy – Bernardino, for example – opposing magic. Books of spells figured in his bonfires of 'vanities' as they did in Savonarola's. Perhaps the clergy resented unofficial competition.

There were two other reasons why the Church might regard magic with suspicion. The first concerns ends; magic might be 'destructive' as well as 'productive' or 'protective', to use the convenient distinctions of modern anthropologists. The second reason concerns means: how did magic work? If crops and winds and sickness simply responded to commands or requests, there was no problem; but it might be that the magic worked because the magician had induced spiritual beings to intervene; that he acted by means of 'demons'. In other words, magic might be 'natural' or 'demonic'. A common view, though not a universal one, was that magic was demonic, and that demons were evil spirits. Thus Fontana, who made a number of mechanical devices to produce spectacular effects, gained the reputation of a necromancer who had assistance from 'spirits from hell', much as John Dee gained a sinister reputation in sixteenth-century Cambridge as a result of the too successful 'effects' he contrived for a performance of Aristophanes. No doubt many of their contemporaries thought the same of Brunelleschi and Leonardo. At a more learned level, the philosopher Nifo argued that the marvels of magic showed that, contrary to Aristotle's belief, demons really existed.

Ariosto's *Orlando Furioso* is full of magic. The sorceress Alcina and the sorcerer Merlino are important characters; Angelica has a magic ring; Astolfo is turned into a tree; Atlante's castle is the home of enchantment, and so on. One needs to imagine the book's first readers, knights and ladies, as people who did not take magic too seriously, but did not take it too lightly either.

However, there were sceptics about magic as there were about astrology. Pomponazzi, defending the Aristotelian position, suggested that demons did not exist, and that the common people simply attributed to demons actions which they could not understand. He recognized that certain phenomena presented serious problems for his theory: the apparent extraction of arrows by means of incantations, and the cure of the 'king's evil' by the kings of France. But Pomponazzi thought that these phenomena could be accounted for in naturalistic terms. He thought the same about some of the miracles recorded in the Bible, and about cures by means of relics, arguing that the cures may have been caused by the faith of the patient, and that dogs' bones would have done just as well. It is not surprising that the book was not published in Pomponazzi's lifetime.[16]

Witchcraft might be regarded as the poor man's magic, or rather, the poor woman's. The witch (*strega, maliarda, fattucchiera, incantatrice*) was most often associated with destructive magic, but practised the other kinds as well. If a child was ill, the mother might go to a witch for a charm on a parchment scroll for the child to wear. It was commonly believed that a witch made a pact with the devil, and was given in return the power to turn into an animal, the power to ride through the air, the power to cause and cure illnesses. There are examples of women confessing to such practices early in the period.

In Rome in 1427, two witches confessed that they turned into cats, murdered children and sucked their blood, all common accusations. But in Italy, as elsewhere in Europe, the 'witch craze' in the sense of belief in the numbers, power and malice of witches seems to have spread in the later fifteenth century and after. In the early sixteenth century G. F. Pico della Mirandola wrote a dialogue on witches between an unbeliever, who finds it a laughing-matter that old women are believed to ride through the air faster than the wind and to have intercourse with demons, and a man who takes it all very seriously. The sceptic is eventually convinced. One kind of argument which figures largely in Pico's book makes it easier to understand why the Renaissance was a period in which belief in witchcraft seems to have revived: the argument from antiquity. As the believer points out, Homer and Pindar, Horace and Virgil and other classical writers all mention witches.

For popular beliefs in witchcraft, Pico's book is not a good source. For these it is necessary to look at the actual confessions of witches, however distorted by the prejudices of the interrogator. To take one example; Chiara Signorini, a peasant woman from the Modena area, was accused of witchcraft in 1520. She and her husband had been expelled from their holding, whereupon the lady who owned the land had fallen ill. Chiara offered to cure her on condition that they were allowed to return. Who knows how to cure illness knows how to cause it, went a proverb current at the time. A witness deposed that she had seen Chiara place at the door of the owner's house:

> fragments of an olive-tree in the form of a cross . . . a fragment of the bone of a dead man . . . and an alb of silk, believed to have been dipped in chrism.

When Chiara was interrogated, she described visions of the Blessed Virgin, which the interrogator tried to interpret as a diabolical figure. Chiara was tortured until she in fact agreed that the devil had appeared to her and that she had adored him, but she would not admit having gone to a 'sabbath'. This case shows how witchcraft might have a social function, that of the peasant's last defence against the landlord; and also that one man's religion is another man's witchcraft, a conflict of interpretations in which the torturer had the last word.[17]

VIEWS OF SOCIETY

The first thing to say about the view of society in Renaissance Italy is that in the most literal sense there was no unified system. It was not until the later seventeenth century that the term 'society' came to be used regularly in its modern sense (as opposed to meaning 'sociability' or 'association') in Italian as in English, French and German. But there was a strong political consciousness and men saw what we call the 'social' largely in terms of the political. Common terms in the mouths of Italians were *republica* (republic) and *principato* (principality). The existence in Italy of both republics and principalities made people aware of the fact that societies could be organized in more than one way. The form of organization was called the *governo*, or the *ordini*, or the *reggimento*, which might be translated as 'the form of government', 'institutions' or 'the constitution'. In Florence in 1494, for example, there were discussions, reported by Guicciardini, on the relative merits of *governo ristretto*, *governo universale* and *governo popolare*; that is, of oligarchy, democracy, or a compromise between the two. So Italians were aware that institutions could be changed, and this awareness is central to the existence of the literature on the ideal city-state. Alberti's and Filarete's treatises on architecture are social as well as architectural utopias. Leonardo's designs for an imaginary city express the same awareness that things can be different, that men can plan their social life. It was this awareness that Burckhardt referred to when he called his chapter on politics 'Der Staat als Kunstwerk' – 'the state as work of art'. Given this awareness of the possibility of change, there was need for terms to express the difference between political organization and its specific forms, republican or monarchical. There was the term *commune*, 'the common', but this remained tied to the meaning of the city in its political aspect. There was the term *corpo politico*, 'body politic', expressing the idea that the constitution was an organism, which corresponded to the microcosm and macrocosm; the political sector of the animate universe. Thus monarchy could be defended on the grounds that:

It is a more natural form of government . . . more like God's, who rules the universe alone . . . in our body, all the members obey the rule of the heart . . . deer, cranes and many other birds, when they migrate, always choose one leader.

And Giannotti wrote that, 'every republic is like a natural body', and the same image, which was not just an image, underlies many other political statements, like Machiavelli's remark that political disorders begin by being difficult to diagnose but easy to cure, and end by being easy to diagnose but difficult to cure; a variation on the *topos* of the ruler as physician of the state, which depends on the idea of the 'body politic'. It would be interesting to know whether Machiavelli thought he was drawing an analogy or describing a correspondence. That this correspondence was taken less seriously in Italy than elsewhere is suggested by the early development of a rival concept; that of the *stato*, which was changing in the fifteenth century from its original meaning of 'state of affairs' to its modern political sense. Thus Lorenzo de'Medici represents the Emperor Constantine wondering whether to let a mere subject marry his daughter; if I do not, he says to himself,

> . . . *in gran pericolo metto*
> *Lo stato* . . .
> (I will put the state into great danger.)

Machiavelli uses the term *stato* 115 times in the *Prince*; in only five cases does he use it in the traditional sense.[18]

Men were aware, often acutely, of differences in what we call 'social stratification' and they called 'the grades and distinctions of men'. They tended to work with two-class and three-class models, and the three-class model, traditional elsewhere in Europe, seems to have been the most popular. Thus Filarete refers to three types of man, the *gentili uomini* (nobles), the *populari* (citizens) and the *contadini* (peasants), pointing out that they correspond to three types of stone – the precious, the semi-precious and the ordinary – and explaining that in his ideal city they would be dressed in different colours as well as living in different kinds of house. Giannotti described the inhabitants of Venice as divided into three 'orders' (*ordini*):

gentiluomini, *cittadini* and *populari*. Machiavelli described Florence as divided into three groups. At the top came the *grandi*, or *nobili*. Then came the *popolari*, or *popolo grasso* ('fat people'), or *mediocri* ('middle class'). At the bottom came the *plebe*, the plebs, or *popolo minuto* ('little people') or *popolo basso* ('lower class'). That the three-class model was a stereotype is clear from the fact that people agree more often that there are three groups than on what the three groups are. Sometimes peasants are included, sometimes omitted; the same with the lower class; sometimes the merchants are separated from the nobles, sometimes not. One specially Italian feature of this stereotype deserves emphasis. Elsewhere in Europe the popular tripartite model was that of the 'three estates', those who pray, those who fight, those who work the land. In Italy in the fifteenth century, it had taken the form of the upper, middle and lower classes, which is still with us. In this system the superiority of the nobleman was justified by argument from correspondence.

> Nature has implanted in everything that hidden seed which gives a certain force and quality of its own essence to all that springs from it, making it like itself : as we can see not only in breeds of horses and other animals, but in trees as well, the shoots of which nearly always resemble the trunk.

But if this was the case, social mobility was not justified. At this point the common belief in nobility of birth clashed with the other common belief (to be discussed below) of the importance of individual achievement; birth versus worth.[19]

Another aspect of the Renaissance view of society is its image of the past. With the idea of the malleability of institutions is associated an awareness of change over time, a sense of anachronism. Lorenzo Valla, for example, was conscious that language had a history, that 'modes of expression' (*stilus loquendi*) were subject to change. Flavio Biondo argued that the modern Romance languages had developed out of Latin; he was also interested in changes in cities, and wrote a book, *Rome Restored*, in which he tried to reconstruct classical Rome on the basis of both surviving remains and literary evidence. In another book he discussed the costume of the Romans and the way in which they brought up their children; in other words, he began to write what we call 'social history'. In the later fifteenth century, antiquarian sensibility became fashionable and began to affect the arts. The *Polifilo*, in which a lover searches for his beloved in a landscape of temples, tombs and obelisks, might be called an 'antiquarian romance', and is written in a consciously archaic Latinate Italian. Artists whose work illustrates the interest in antiquarianism include Mantegna, Riccio, Raphael, and Giulio Romano. Dolce's *Aretino* praises Raphael for a cartoon in which Jewish women are represented in historically correct costume. Vasari comments on Giulio Romano's picture of Constantine in battle, that the artist had done historical research by looking at Trajan's column, from which:

> he profited greatly for the costumes of the soldiers, the armour, ensigns, bastions, stockades, battering rams and all the other instruments of war.

It is clear that Vasari too was interested in getting the details right. This might have been expected, for his *Lives* are organized around the idea of development in time, from the 'Greek Manner' to Michelangelo. It has been shown that Vasari drew a medieval-type frame around a drawing by Cimabue in his possession, which suggests his sense of historical appropriateness. Although he believed in progress in the arts, he also thought that artists should be judged by the standards of their own time, not his, writing that

> my intention has always been to praise not absolutely but, as the saying is, relatively (*non semplicemente ma, como s'usa dire, secondo ché*), having regard to place, time, and other similar circumstances.

The sense of historical perspective is surely connected with the stylistic self-consciousness of this period. Men found their artistic identity by rejecting their immediate predecessors and imitating the ancients. There was an even more literal kind of imitation; the fake antique seems to be a Renaissance invention, and the making of classical sculptures and Roman coins flourished in Venice and Padua in the early sixteenth century. Presumably it was a response to the craze for antiquity and the rise of the market in works of art; but faking also depends, like the discovery of fakes, on a sense of period style.

The growing sense of historical perspective also worked to undermine the imitation of the past. Filarete recommended artists not to dress their contemporaries in Roman costume, and Guicciardini gave students of politics similar advice:

> How mistaken are those who quote the Romans at every step. One would have to have a city with exactly the same conditions as theirs and then act according to their example. That model is as unsuitable for those lacking the right qualities as it would be useless to expect an ass to run like a horse.[20]

The modern reader may well be surprised by the fact that Italians who were aware of changes in government, costume, language and art were not conscious of still greater social and economic changes. Where we give explanations of events in social terms, they tended to give explanations in terms of the will of God or the qualities of outstanding individuals. Like the concept of 'society', the concept of 'the economy' was lacking in Renaissance Italy; the term *economia* refers to household management.[21]

Another surprise for the modern reader is that where we tend to be prejudiced in favour of change, of the new, Renaissance Italians tended to be prejudiced against. The term *anticato* meant old; it did not yet mean 'antiquated' in the sense of 'out of date'. In debates in Florentine committees, it is taken for granted that *modi nuovi*, 'new ways', are undesirable, and that 'every change takes reputation from the city'. In Guicciardini, the term *mutazione* (change) seems to be used in a pejorative sense, and when he describes a man (like Julius II) as *desideroso di cose nuove* (desirous of new things) it is with an overtone of disapproval. The great paradox is that at a time when Italian culture was strongly marked by what might be called 'the propensity to innovate', innovation was, in theory, considered a bad thing. So when Filarete praises Renaissance architecture and condemns Gothic, it is the Gothic which he calls *moderno*. It is only at the end of the period that one can find someone (Vasari for example) cheerfully admitting to being *moderno* himself.

One kind of change *was* widely considered as acceptable, but that was 'renovation' not innovation; and also change of a final kind; the millennium. Millenarianism has been usefully defined as a movement inspired by the belief in a salvation which is collective, terrestrial, imminent, total, and supernaturally accomplished. In Italy in this period, the form that it took, which owes a great deal to the Apocalypse and the writings of Joachim of Fiore, was that there would be a 'scourge', the loosing of Satan, followed by the renewal. The renewal would be presided over by an ideal pope (the Angelic Pope) and an ideal Emperor (the Second Charlemagne) and it would include the conversion of the Turks, the political unification of the world, the binding of Satan, and the return of the Golden Age. Florentines tended to include the expansion of the Florentine empire in the programme, and to refer to their city as the 'New Jerusalem' or 'City of God'. The most famous millenarian prophet of the time was, of course, Savonarola, but his ideas were part of a Florentine tradition. He interpreted the invasion of 1494 as the arrival of a new Cyrus, Charles VIII, to scourge the Church. He declared Christ 'King of Florence'. He announced that:

> Florence will be more glorious, richer, more powerful than she has ever been. First, glorious in the sight of God . . . Second, oh Florence, you will have innumerable riches, and God will multiply all things for you. Third, you will spread your empire, and thus you will have power temporal and spiritual.

Cardinal Egidio of Viterbo identified the Angelic Pope successively as Julius II, Leo X, and Clement VII. In 1516, a certain Fra Bonaventura declared that he was the Angelic Pope, and excommunicated Leo X. The sack of Rome in 1527 was widely interpreted as the scourge which was to precede the great renewal.

These ideas too made an impact on the arts. In a copy of St Augustine's *City of God* illuminated in Florence in the 1470s, the City of God was given the appearance of Florence. Botticelli's *Mystical Nativity* belongs to this millenarian movement, as its inscription reveals:

I Sandro painted this picture at the end of the year 1500 in the troubles of Italy in the half time after the time according to the eleventh chapter of St John in the second woe of the Apocalypse in the loosing of the devil for three and a half years. Then he will be chained in the twelfth chapter and we will see him trodden down as in this picture.

In the *Orlando Furioso,* Ariosto wrote about a world-emperor 'of the blood of Austria and Aragon' (that is, the young Charles v) suggesting that God wishes

> ... *che sotto a questo imperatore*
> *Solo un ovile sia, solo uno pastore.*

(that under this emperor there should be one flock and one shepherd.)[22]

It is difficult to know how seriously this prediction was intended to be taken. It could be no more than a courtly gesture; but at much the same time, Egidio of Viterbo was writing very seriously indeed about Charles v as the 'second Charlemagne'. Again, it is possible that the poets round Cosimo and Lorenzo de'Medici who wrote of the return of the golden age under Medici rule were doing something more than turn a decoratively flattering or flatteringly decorative phrase. The Renaissance idea of the Renaissance may also owe something to the millenarian idea of the 'renewal of the world' (*renovatio mundi*).

VIEWS OF MAN

A useful summary of ideas about the physical constitution of man can be found in the *Triumph of the four complexions,* written for a Florentine Carnival. The four complexions or temperaments are the traditional classifications which go back to the Greek medical writer Hippocrates: choleric, sanguine, phlegmatic and melancholy. The choleric complexion was explained by the preponderance of bile ('choler') in the body; it made men brave, proud and angry. In the system of correspondences, it was associated with fire, Mars, and summer. The sanguine complexion, explained by the preponderance of blood, made men quiet, happy, and easily disposed to love, and was associated with air, Venus, and spring. The phlegmatic complexion was explained by a preponderance of phlegm; made men fat, placid and somnolent; was associated with water, the moon, and with winter. Finally, the melancholic complexion was explained by the preponderance of the 'black bile' from which the term 'melancholy' is derived, made men thin, timid, serious and 'ingenious', and was associated with earth, Saturn, and autumn. Aristotle suggested that all great men were melancholics. Ficino joined this idea to Plato's concept of inspiration as 'divine frenzy', suggested that creative people (*ingeniosi*) were *malinconici* or *furiosi*, and thus helped create the modern myth of the artist as genius and bohemian. Ficino was probably thinking of humanists, but Vasari applied his doctrine to artists.[23]

Another way of relating appearance to character practised in this period was the art of face-reading, which depended on the assumption that a man looked like whatever animal he resembled in character. In the great correspondence-system, animals tended to be associated with moral qualities. Thus a brave man was supposed to look like a lion, because lions were brave and symbolized courage. A celebrated face-reader of the early sixteenth century was Bartolommeo della Rocca, called 'Cocles'. An example of his diagnoses, unfortunately recorded after the event, is that of Savonarola. Cocles quoted Savonarola as an example of the rule that eyes placed lengthwise show a man to be hot in complexion and deceptive in character. Physiognomical theory naturally influenced portraits. The *condottieri* Gattamelata and Colleoni, and Cosimo de'Medici duke of Tuscany, were all given distinctly 'leonine' features by Donatello, Verrocchio and Cellini respectively.[24]

The self-consciousness of Renaissance man is one of the great Burckhardtian themes, and for evidence one can point, like Burckhardt, to the number of self-portraits, autobiographies and diaries dating from this period. Self-portraits are usually not pictures in their own right, as they were to become, but occur in pictures of something else. Among the more secure identifications are the self-portraits of Ghiberti, Gozzoli, Michel-angelo, and Pinturicchio (see Pl. 2); among the less certain, those of Botticelli, Leonardo, Masaccio and Raphael. Parmigia-nino painted a picture of nothing but himself, and so, after

1540, did Titian and Vasari. Autobiographies from this period include one by Alberti (if his authorship is accepted), Pius II's *Commentaries*, and Guicciardini's *Ricordanze*. They all three have a rather detached manner. Alberti and Pius even write about themselves in the third person – why? The example of Caesar seems relevant, but is not a satisfying explanation. For more intimate autobiographies one has to wait until just after 1540, for Cardano and Cellini. Diary-keeping was much more widespread, particularly in Florence; famous examples are the ones kept by Goro Dati, Luca Landucci, Bernardo Machiavelli and Giovanni Rucellai. They were kept for more practical reasons than autobiographies, to record expenses for example, so that it may be argued that they are not evidence of self-consciousness at all. This may well be the case with some Venetian diaries, almost exclusively concerned with outward and public events, like those of Priuli and Sanudo. In the Florentine diaries, however, a personal note does creep in, and the fact that memoranda are organized in this way around the life of the writer may be significant.

Evidence of self-awareness is also provided by the existence of such 'how to do it' books as Machiavelli's *Prince*, Castiglione's *Courtier* and Aretino's *Ragionamenti* (della Casa's *Galateo* is too late for inclusion). Implicit in these books is the idea which Pico's God makes explicit when He tells man that 'as though the maker and moulder of thyself, thou mayest fashion thyself in whatever shape thou shalt prefer'. The sculptural metaphor makes one wonder about connexions between Renaissance self-awareness and Renaissance art. Books of advice to princes existed long before Machiavelli, but Machiavelli's emphasis on techniques is new, and so is his presentation of alternatives which implies that a prince can choose his personal political 'style'. The idea of personal style is absolutely central to Castiglione, where it is taken as far as it can go – logically and psychologically. It is the graceful style that the courtier is urged to cultivate, and to do this it is necessary

to avoid affectation as much as possible; and to coin a term, to use in everything a certain carelessness (*sprezzatura*) which conceals skill, and shows that whatever is said or done has been done without pains and virtually without thought.

He goes on to compare the courtier to a painter, who must know when to stop. It is possible that Castiglione borrowed the term 'grace' (*grazia*) from Alberti, applying it to life instead of art. Lifemanship imitates artmanship. At any rate, he was much interested in 'the presentation of self in everyday life', and thought of the self as a consciously-planned work of art. With Aretino's dialogue we move from the *cortegiano* to the *cortegiana*, from the courtier to the whore. The main difference is that the courtier is instructed to mould his whole self; the whore only her outward self. Nanna instructs Pippa in 'pretences and flatteries', in deceiving men, in giving kisses to all but her heart to none. The two roles may have been more alike than Castiglione would have admitted; the art of flattery was far from useless at court. And both roles demanded a high degree of self-consciousness.[25]

It is always dangerous to argue from a small number of texts to the style of thought of an age. How typical were Machiavelli, Castiglione and Aretino? There is linguistic evidence that some of their concerns were shared fairly widely. The term 'style' (*maniera*) is applied to behaviour in the early fifteenth century, and is used more commonly in the later fifteenth century. Thus Leonardo Giustinian refers to the *zentile maynere* of his beloved (perhaps 'fine manners' would be an appropriate rendering) and Lorenzo de'Medici told his lady,

> *Se tu vai, stai o siede*
> *Fa d'aver sempre maniera.*
> (Whether you are walking, standing or sitting,
> try always to do it with style.)

In the early sixteenth century, when Machiavelli, Castiglione and Aretino were writing, the term was used most of all.[26]

A concern with identity appears even in practical jokes. There is a story that Brunelleschi persuaded a fat carpenter that he was not himself but a certain Matteo, and that Matteo was he. A whole circle of friends, Donatello included, joined in, putting the carpenter in the position of the man in the psychology experiment, surrounded by stooges, who all say that the straight line is crooked until he disbelieves his own eyes and says the same. The carpenter was persuaded that he was not himself and began to think, 'what shall I do if I have become Matteo?'[27]

It is tempting to discuss the importance of the mirror in promoting self-consciousness, although such a discussion can be little more than 'speculation'. Flat, non-distorting mirrors were first produced in quantity in fifteenth-century Venice, so the dating makes the argument plausible. The idea that mirrors do stimulate self-consciousness is suggested by Gelli, in a carnival song he wrote for the mirror-makers of sixteenth-century Florence.

> Scorgono i suoi difetti in lo specchiarsi,
> Non facili a veder come gli altrui;
> Onde può l'uom da sè ben misurarsi,
> E dir, 'Miglior sarò da quel ch'io fui'.

(A man's own defects can be perceived in the glass, defects which are not easy to see like those of others. So a man can take his own measure and say, 'I will be a better man than I have been.')

The mirror can be dangerous, for mirror-image may not correspond to self-image. It has been argued that the portrait developed in the fifteenth century as the answer to the mirror, a reaffirmation of the self-image.[28]

A common view of man at this period was that he was essentially self-assertive, competitive, and thirsty for fame; as the social psychologist might say, that he had a strong 'achievement drive'. Burckhardt argued that 'the modern sense of fame' was new in fifteenth-century Italy; Huizinga asserted that, on the contrary, it was 'essentially the same as the chivalrous ambition of earlier times'.[29] The romances of chivalry do indeed suggest that the desire for fame was one of the leading motives of medieval knights; perhaps one should say no more than that new forms of self-assertion appeared in Italy, that glory was demilitarized. However, it may also have been the case that men were becoming more self-assertive, or that more men were becoming self-assertive. In the Italian literature of this period, it is certainly remarkable how often self-assertion words occur; words like 'competition' (*concertazione, concorrenza*); 'emulation' (*emulazione*); 'glory' (*gloria*); 'envy' (*invidia*); 'honour' (*onore*); 'spur' (*sprone*); 'sweat' (*sudare*); 'shame' (*vergogna*); and, above all, 'valour' or 'worth' (*valore, virtù*). It seems likely

that if these words occur with great frequency in a particular
text, as they do in Alberti's *On the family*, its author has an
above-average achievement drive. It is for comparative content
analysis to test the hypothesis that the fifteenth century was
more self-assertive than the fourteenth, Florence more than
Milan, or Italy more than France. A high achievement drive
in Florence might help explain the remarkable creative record
of that city, the sharp tongues, the envy, and the institutionalization of competitions between artists.

At any rate, self assertion was an important part of the
Renaissance image of man. For example, life was often seen
as a race. Bruni suggested that some, 'do not run in the race (*in
stadio*), or, when they start, become tired and give up half-
way'. Alberti saw life as a regatta in which there were only a
few prizes :

> Thus in the race and competition for honour and glory in the
> life of man it seems to me very useful to provide oneself
> with a good ship and to give an opportunity to one's powers
> and ability (*alle forze e ingegno tuo*), and with this to sweat
> to be the first.

Leonardo recommended artists to draw in company :

> First, if you are inadequate, you will be ashamed to be seen
> among the number of men drawing, and this mortification
> is a motive for studying well. Secondly, a sound envy will
> stimulate you to become one of the number who are praised
> more than you, and the praise of others will spur you on.

Vasari declared that :

> Rivalry and competition, by which a man seeks by great
> works to conquer and overcome those more distinguished
> than himself in order to acquire honour and glory, is a
> praiseworthy thing.

Vasari admitted that this stress on rivalry leads to envy, and
his lives of Castagno and Bandinelli read like caricatures of the
competitive, envious Tuscan. His story about Castagno's murder
of Domenico Veneziano has turned out to be a myth not

history, but it is a myth which reveals central Tuscan values. Envy is the natural complement of the drive towards achievement. So, when Cosimo de'Medici ruled Florence, he is said to have taken care to make his desires appear to have come from others, 'to avoid envy as much as he could'. His grandson Lorenzo, projecting his own feelings outside himself, wrote of Fortune as 'envious' of his success.[30]

It was not only in Tuscany that fame was the spur. In Castiglione's *Courtier*, somone remarks that:

> It is wrong to defraud oneself of due honour and to refrain from seeking the praise which is the only true reward for great deeds.

In the South, the poet Tansillo wrote of Icarus (instead of blaming him for presumption):

> *Questo aspirò alle stelle, e s'ei non giunse,*
> *La vita venne men, ma non l'ardire.*

(This man aspired to the stars, and if he did not reach them, it was life and not ardour which gave out.)

Quotations of this kind could be multiplied. So far, they have been taken from contexts of approval, but men who did not accept the 'fame ethic', as it might be called, still recorded the fact that it existed. Pius II, himself not backward in the struggle for high place, gave an unsympathetic account of it in his book on *The miseries of Courtiers*, in which life appears more like a rat-race than a boat-race.

> In the courts of princes the greatest effort is devoted to pushing others down and to climbing up oneself . . . there is no trust among courtiers; a brother is not safe from a brother, a son is not true to his father, a father to his son.

Landucci, whose place in society was a modest one, moralized in his diary about the ambitions of the great, 'ambitious men who are not contented with the state of life to which God has called them' (*lo stato che da Iddio*), but risk dangers all 'to obtain a short-lived fame on this earth'.[31]

Associated with the ideas of the self-conscious and self-assertive man is the idea of the unique man. At the court of Urbino, Accolti had the nickname of *L'Unico*, 'the unique one'. An anonymous Milanese poem declares that there is only one God in Heaven, and only one 'Moro' (Lodovico Sforza) on earth. In his biographies, Vespasiano da Bisticci often refers to men as 'singular' (*singolare*). Vittoria Colonna referred to Michelangelo as *unico*. Thus there was a place for eccentricity in Renaissance Italy, although more conformist ideals, like those of citizen and courtier, seem to have been relatively more important.

Another associated emphasis was that on a man alone, rather than as a part of a family. Family pride was still strong, but it had a competitor. Vasari has a story (inaccurate, but revealing of the values of the time) about how the Sangallos got their name, saying that Lorenzo de'Medici conferred it on Giuliano, who protested at the loss of his family name but was told that Lorenzo

> would rather that on account of his abilities (*virtù*) he started a new family than depend on another.

A favourite Renaissance debate concerned the relative importance of achievement and descent, worth versus birth. The result was usually inconclusive, but this, in a Europe dominated by the values of 'blood', was an achievement in itself. It is interesting to find that several leading figures of the period were illegitimate – Alberti, Ghiberti and Leonardo among them – men who would be likely to emphasize achievement over birth and also to succeed in a society which did the same. But the emphasis on the isolated individual should not be exaggerated. Portraits seem to express it; but they were often hung in family groups. Signatures on paintings seem to express it, but may have had the function of a workshop stamp. Diaries seem to express it, but some of them were more like family chronicles, and Landucci's diary was in fact continued after his death. The illegitimate Alberti was the author of a treatise on the family.[32]

Another essential part of the image of man at this time was the idea that he was essentially a rational, calculating, prudent animal. 'Reason' (*ragione*) and 'reasonable' (*ragionevole*) are terms one finds over and over again, usually with overtones of approval. It is necessary to distinguish other meanings of *ragione*, but these meanings are connected with the idea of rationality. *Ragione* may mean 'accounts'; merchants call their account-books *libri della ragione*. *Ragione* may mean 'justice'; the 'Palace of Reason' in Padua was a court. Justice too involves calculation, as the classical and Renaissance scales-image reminds us. *Ragione* also meant 'proportion' or 'ratio'. A famous early definition of perspective in the anonymous life of Brunelleschi calls it the science which sets down the differences of size in near and far objects *con ragione*, which can be and has been translated either as 'rationally' or 'in proportion'. Reason was also associated with speech; in Italian, *ragionare* still means 'to talk'. But then speech was a sign of rationality which showed man's superiority to animals.

The habit of precise calculation was ingrained in Italian life. Burckhardt's examples are good ones; he pointed out that in fifteenth-century Florence and Venice, an interest was taken in statistics of imports and exports, population and prices. In Rome, budgets of the Church have survived for the years 1480 and 1525. Double-entry book-keeping was already widespread in Italy before 1400.

With the emphasis on reason and calculation, went the regular use of such words as 'prudent' (*prudente*), 'carefully' (*pensatamente*), and 'to foresee' (*antivedere*). The implication behind their use is made explicit by Giovanni Rucellai when he writes :

It does not please me to act hastily in any matter, but rather to do everything prudently and after taking thought.

The habit of calculation was applied to personal relationships. Men appear to have been more concerned than before to control themselves and to manipulate others. The attitude to time changed. The old way was to divide the day by what was happening in it; 'task-oriented time', this has been called. Short amounts of time were counted in *Aves*, the amount of time it took to say a 'Hail Mary'. However, in the later fourteenth century, mechanical clocks came into use, and the division of hours into minutes and seconds became common. In our period, the importance of clocks increased. About 1450 a clock was made for the town hall at Bologna; in 1478 one was made for the Sforza castle in Milan; in 1499 a clock was placed on Piazza S. Marco in Venice; and so on. In the late fifteenth century, portable clocks came in (*horologi portativi*). In Filarete's utopia, the schools for boys and girls had an alarm-clock (*svegliatoio*) in each dormitory; this idea at least was not utopian, for at Milan in 1463 the astrologer Giacomo da Piacenza had an alarm-clock by his bed.

The link between the new conception of time and the general rationalization of life is made apparent in Book III of Alberti's treatise on the family. In this book Giannozzo, the merchant, advocates a careful use of body, soul, and time. In the morning, he says, he organizes himself for the whole day. Although he never quite says (like Benjamin Franklin) that 'time is money', he does use a whole set of related expressions. Time is 'precious', it must be 'spent' carefully and not wasted, and this involves 'thrift' (*massarizia*). Giovanni Rucellai, echoing Giannozzo, advises his family to 'be thrifty with time, for it is the most precious thing we have'. The same point was made in more religious language by Giannozzo Manetti, who is quoted as being in the habit of saying that,

> 'Of the time which is given us in this life we must give an account of every moment,' basing his argument on a text in the Gospel which declares that Almighty God is like the master of a business who gives money to his treasurer and requires him to render an account as to how it may have been spent. So God wills that when a man quits this life he shall account for how he has spent his time, even to the glance of an eye.

The examples so far have been Tuscan ones, However, F. M. Visconti was described in 1443 as 'a most attentive and thrifty user of his time who does not waste a moment', and Vittorino da Feltre, hating to waste time, drew up a time-table for the studies in his school.

It seems plausible to suggest a link between conceptions of time and conceptions of space. Renaissance Italians seem to have had a more precise, quantitative notion of both than their predecessors and contemporaries. The discovery of perspective, which involves the idea that space is measurable or calculable, and the idea that time is like money are related aspects of

Italian culture. Brunelleschi made clocks as well as discovering perspective. Just as many people still measured time in *Aves*, so Italian measures were still rather vague by modern standards. Men measured in 'arms' and 'palms', and the *braccio*, or arm's length, tended to vary between 22 and 26 inches. Such a tradition makes Brunelleschi's achievement even more astounding than we usually think it.[33]

It is not surprising to find the praises of self-control in some writings of the time. In Alberti's book on the family, the humanist Lionardo suggests that it is good 'to rule and control the passions of the soul' and Guicciardini declares that there is greater pleasure in controlling one's desires (*tenersi le voglie oneste*) than in satisfying them. This did not mean a habit of mild behaviour, for

> It is perfectly all right to avenge yourself even though you feel no deep rancour against the person who is the object of your revenge.

The account-book model of psychology is in evidence in Guicciardini:

> Be careful not to do anyone the sort of favour that cannot be done without at the same time displeasing others. For injured men do not forget offences; in fact, they exaggerate them. Whereas the favoured party will either forget or will deem the favour smaller than it was. Therefore, other things being equal, you lose a great deal more than you gain.[34]

The reasonable is often identified with the useful, and a utilitarian approach is characteristic of a number of writers at this time. In Valla's dialogue *On pleasure*, one of the speakers, the humanist Panormita, defends an ethic of utility. He argues that the virtues are not, as commonly thought, ends in themselves; their purpose is utility (*utilitas*). All action – here he sounds like Bentham – is based on calculations of pain and pleasure. Panormita need not represent Valla's own point of view; what is interesting here is what was thinkable in the fifteenth century, not who thought it. An emphasis on the useful·can be found over and over again. It echoes through Alberti's book on the family. Filarete created in 'Sforzinda' a utilitarian utopia in which the death penalty is abolished because criminals are more useful to the community if they are condemned to hard labour for life, and they are treated just harshly enough for this punishment to be an adequate deterrent. The idea that the moral virtues are not ends in themselves is usually implicit in Machiavelli's *Prince*, and occasionally explicit. Machiavelli writes of cruelty 'well used' or 'badly used', and warns the compassionate prince 'not to make a bad use of this compassion'. His criterion for good and bad use is the 'utility of the subjects' (*utilità de'sudditi*).

There was an anti-rational side to Renaissance thought, even if it was only in a minor key. It can be seen, for example, in Florence in the late fifteenth century. Ficino emphasized the irrational element in poetry, the poet's inspiration (*furor*) akin to melancholy and madness. He advocated the approach to God through the negation of the intellect. There was a Dionysian as well as an Apollonian side to the Renaissance, to use terms which Ficino would have understood as well as Nietzsche. Again, Giovanni Pico wrote in praise of blind love and against reason, 'Love was described by Orpheus as without eyes because love is above the intellect.' Pico was interested in the Platonic science of numbers, but – like a true nobleman – he was eager to distinguish it from 'the arithmetic of traders'. Where Bruni had argued that the essential human characteristic was the use of reason, Savonarola declared that it was the contemplation of God, emphasizing that, 'the christian life is not founded on the natural light of reason alone.'[35]

In the ladder of being, man was a central rung. Yet in a sense he was not part of the ladder at all, for he had free will and could move down or up; he could be an ape or an angel if he wished. His free will, together with his reason, made the dignity of man. A favourite subject for Italian writers of the period was the 'human condition' (the phrase is theirs, *humana conditio*), and they frequently emphasized the dignity of man. Valla, with characteristic boldness, called the soul the 'man-God' (*homo-deus*) and wrote of the soul's ascent to heaven in the language of a Roman triumph. Palmieri revived Origen's idea that all the damned would be saved eventually. Pomponazzi suggested that those (few) men who had managed to become almost completely rational deserved to be numbered among the gods. How could a man move up the ladder?

According to the humanists, study as well as virtue was relevant, and especially the study of grammar, rhetoric, history, poetry, and ethics. These were called the 'humanities' (*studia humanitatis*) because they made a man complete – there was no distinction made between the complete human and the complete humanist. The underlying assumptions here are that man is a rational animal, and that rationality is developed by the study of language – hence the importance of grammar. Self-knowledge was also considered necessary to the completion of man. Ficino, for example, quoted the Delphic oracle's 'Know thyself' with approval. The self-consciousness which was such an important part of the Renaissance view of the world here received its justification.

It is easy to exaggerate the importance and the novelty of these striking statements. It is tempting to take Pico's treatise on the dignity of man to symbolize the Renaissance, and to contrast it with Pope Innocent III's treatise of the misery of man, taking the latter to symbolize the Middle Ages. To imagine that the contrast was as simple as this is to misunderstand both Renaissance and Middle Ages. In both periods man's misery and his dignity were recognized. Many Renaissance arguments for the dignity of man, such as the beauty of his body, his upright posture, and the fact that God became man, are commonplaces from patristic and medieval as well as classical tradition. The themes of dignity and misery were considered complementary, not contradictory; Pope Innocent had intended to write a book on the dignity of human nature. Conversely, Innocent's book on man's misery was reprinted several times in Venice in the early sixteenth century, which suggests that his views were not generally abandoned. But Michelet and Burckhardt were not completely wrong to talk about the Renaissance 'discovery of man'. The sudden popularity of the dignity-of-man genre in fifteenth-century Italy suggests that an important shift of emphasis was taking place from one of the two complementary themes to the other. Burckhardt needs to be qualified rather than rejected.[36]

Important evidence for the spread of this confidence in man comes from the growing use of such adjectives as 'divine' or 'heroic' to describe princes, painters and other mortals. Alberti had called the ancients 'divine', and Poliziano had coupled Lorenzo de'Medici with Giovanni Pico as 'heroes rather than men', but it is only in the sixteenth century that this language becomes commonplace. Vasari described Raphael as a 'mortal god', and wrote of the 'heroes' of the house of Medici. Aretino, typically, called himself 'divine'. Bandello wrote of the 'heroic house of Gonzaga' and of the 'glorious heroine' Isabella d'Este. The famous description of Michelangelo as 'divine' was really rather a commonplace kind of praise.

The arts were affected by the ideas of the dignity of man, and the divinity of particular men. Where Innocent III had held man's nudity against him, Manetti argued that man was born 'for the sake of the fitting and the beautiful'. Nifo went still further, and defended the proposition that 'nothing ought to be called beautiful except man'. (By 'man', he meant woman, and Jeanne of Aragon in particular.) Paintings of the idealized naked human body might be expected in a society where such views were expressed. The whole application of the language of behaviour to the arts rests on the assumption that what is human can be beautiful; and a painter could hardly show *grazia*, the most popular of late Renaissance qualities, without representing the human body. The derivation of architectural proportions from an idealized human body also depends on the assumption of the dignity of man. It is interesting to find both Alberti and Filarete quoting the Greek sophist Protagoras with approval: 'Of all things the measure is man.' The 'grand manner' was dominant in Italian art in the early sixteenth century, at the same time that the term 'heroic' was overworked in literature, and Vasari contributed to the diffusion of the heroic ideal in both media. It looks as if changes in taste can be related to larger changes in world-views.[37]

A philosophy of life is tested by its attitude to death. In this period two attitudes to death coexisted, which may be linked to the themes of the misery and dignity of man respectively. The first view, the traditional one, was that death showed the vanity of the things of this world, and that life was simply a preparation for death. At a Florentine carnival one of the floats consisted of corpses, who told the spectators,

> *Fummo già come vo'sete,*
> *Vo'sarete come noi.*

(Such as ye, such were we;
such as we be, such shall ye be.)

Savonarola developed the theme of death in his sermons, urging his hearers to visit cemeteries; to think of every day as if it was their last; 'to take a skull in one's hand and contemplate it often'; in brief, to look at life through 'death-coloured spectacles' (*occhiali della morte*). The visual equivalents of this attitude are the woodcuts of the Dance of Death, of which 32 known examples have survived for the period 1488–1543.

The second attitude to death, the new one, secular and self-assertive, assumes that it is possible to triumph over death. Fame triumphs over Death in Petrarch's *Triumphs*, which were often illustrated by fifteenth-century painters. Life was seen by some men not so much as a journey towards death as a brief space in which something could be achieved. It is difficult to tell how far the new attitude to death, surely linked to the achievement drive, had spread before 1540; but it may be significant that in fifteenth-century Italian tomb sculpture (unlike similar sculpture elsewhere) the macabre is almost entirely absent. The coexistence of the two attitudes to death can be documented from the same family, in two reactions to the death of Matteo Strozzi in 1459. His mother Alessandra drew comfort from the fact that Matteo had made a 'good death' and could expect a 'good place' in Heaven. For Marco Strozzi, the lesson was that 'men of worth (*valenti uomini*) do not let themselves be overcome by fortune.'[38]

A favourite subject for debates was the relative merit of the active life and the contemplative. The traditional view was that the contemplative life, that of the monk, was better than the active life of the layman. In this period, there was a strong tendency to reverse this judgement. Leonardo Bruni formulated the contrast as one between the 'life of business' (*vita negotiosa*) and the 'life of idleness' (*vita otiosa*). Monks are attacked for their idleness in Poggio's dialogues, much as 'abbey-lubbers' were attacked in Reformation England. This stress on the active life is associated with the achievement drive and with the new sense of 'clock-time'. The hatred of idleness is obvious in Alberti's book on the family, in the diaries of Goro Dati, and Giovanni Rucellai, in the treatises on education by Vegio and

Vergerio. The sculptor Gauricus declared, emphasizing conscious planning at the same time as the virtue of hard work, that:

> Since I was a boy, I planned my life so that as far as it was in my power I never wasted any of it in idleness.

For Alberti, even the villa was associated with the active life, not the contemplative; with agriculture, not with escapism. 'Buy the villa to feed your family.' But in the later fifteenth century, the villa was often prized because one can study there in solitude, or attain tranquillity of mind, or simply enjoy oneself. The praises of the villa became the praises – in secular terms – of the *vita contemplativa*. As one mid-sixteenth century writer put it, in the country you could 'cultivate your garden' (*coltivare il vostro giardino*).[39]

Associated with the praises of the active life one often finds the praise of wealth, in place of the traditional defence of poverty. Bruni, Poggio, Alberti and Palmeri all make this point. In Alberti's book on the family, the merchant Giannozzo refers again and again to 'holy thrift' (*santa masserizia*). Poggio's dialogue *On avarice* contains a defence of avarice by one speaker, half-playful, but half in earnest. If men do not produce more than they needed, he says,

> All the splendour of cities will be removed, divine worship and its embellishments lost, no churches or arcades built, all the arts will come to an end . . . What are cities, commonwealths, provinces, kingdoms, but public workshops of avarice?

Again, it is with an air of deliberate paradox, but with a serious intention, that Machiavelli undertakes the defence of meanness in his *Prince*. The prince should be mean because that is to exercise liberality towards all those from whom he does not take, who are many, rather than to those to whom he would have given, who are few. Such a 'thrift ethic', had it been general among princes and noblemen, would obviously have discouraged art patronage. Landucci, recording the fact that 70,000 florins were spent on Leo x's entry into Florence in 1515, commented with disapproval, 'all for things of no duration'. However, there was a rival economic ethic, the ethic of liberality or conspicuous consumption. It can be found even in Alberti, in whose book on the family the virtue of 'magnificence' (*splendore*) competes with that of thrift. It can be found in Cosimo de'Medici, who said that

> His greatest mistake ever was not to have begun to spend his money ten years before he did,

and in Giovanni Rucellai, who declared that it was more pleasant to spend money than to make it. This propensity to consume conspicuously is even more obvious at the courts of princes. It underlies the outlay on rich clothes, on entertainment, on banquets, and – last and perhaps least – on the arts.[40]

An important cluster of concepts referring to an ideal style of life are 'valour', 'loyalty', 'courtesy' and 'honour' (*valore, fede, cortesia, onore*), and their less precise opposites 'villainy' and 'shame' (*viltà, vergogna*). One might have expected a full exposition of such qualities in Castiglione's *Courtier*, but in that book they are referred to only in passing, as if any cultivated reader was bound to know about the fundamental qualities already. It is easier to illustrate this complex of values from fiction, from Ariosto's *Orlando Furioso*. For example, the recurrence of particular adjectives to describe the heroes and their actions adds up to a value-system, from the first Canto onwards, with its references to 'bold enterprises', 'famous deeds', 'valiant paladin' and so on (*audaci imprese, chiari gesti, paladin gagliardo*). More important still, the story is deliberately contrived to make the heroes and heroines face conflicts of values, so that a world-view is implicit in the structure of the poem. The last two cantos are organized around conflicts of loyalty and courtesy. Ruggiero has been captured and owes his life to his rescue by Leon; this is a great courtesy which demands repayment. Charlemagne has declared that whoever wants Bradamante to be his wife must fight all day with her without being defeated. Leon asks Ruggiero to fight Bradamante for him, not knowing that Bradamante is Ruggiero's beloved. Ruggiero is torn between loyalty to Leon and loyalty to Bradamante. He decides that his duty is to agree to Leon's plan; to do otherwise would be faithless, *mancar di fede*. He disguises himself, fights Bradamante and wins. Now it is

Bradamante who has a moral dilemma. She did not expect to be defeated by anyone but Ruggiero. Now she has to choose between private loyalty to her lover, and public loyalty to her 'word of honour'. She is about to choose the former (*servar fede al mio amante*) when Heaven helps her out of the dilemma. For when Leon learns of the true situation, he will not have Ruggiero outdo him in courtesy and so yields the lady, thus resolving two sets of moral conflicts with one gesture, and allowing the poem to end happily.

Machiavelli's discussion of 'keeping faith' in the *Prince* makes a dramatic contrast to the values of Ariosto:

> Everyone knows how praiseworthy it is for a prince to keep faith and act with integrity rather than with cunning; nevertheless experience shows that in our time the princes that have cared little about keeping faith have done great things . . . and have overcome those who based themselves on loyalty.

Again, when he heard that Charles v had captured Francis i at Pavia, Machiavelli wrote to Guicciardini that 'it will be a good plan for the King to promise everything in order to be free,' as Francis in fact did, breaking his word soon after. Guicciardini seems to have taken breaches of faith rather more seriously. When Oliverotto was murdered by Cesare Borgia at Sinigaglia, Guicciardini's comment was that 'it was very just that he should die by treachery,' seeing that he had come to power in Fermo the same way.[41]

WORLD-VIEWS AND SOCIAL CLASSES

The attitudes described so far have touched the arts at many points, but with the accumulation of detail has come the danger of losing sight of the main aim of this chapter, to determine whether the major changes of style which make this period different from the thirteenth and fourteenth centuries can be explained by major changes in world-view, and whether these changes in world-view are associated with particular social groups or classes. At this point it may be a good idea to stand back from the Renaissance world-view and to try to 'place' it historically.

But is there a 'Renaissance world-view' at all? As this chapter has shown, some men thought that God was near, others that he was remote; some that astrology was reliable, others that it could not be trusted; some that the active life was better than the contemplative, others the reverse; some that the study of Greece and Rome was desirable, others that it was useless or dangerous. Confronted with this variety, it is tempting to give up the attempt to explain altogether; but this should not be without asking whether the variety is not structured in some way. In fact, it seems to be structured in more than one way.

Ideas about the stars, about God, about politics, about art, and about man formed a 'belief system' in the sense that many of them supported one another. If a man believed in the analogy of microcosm and macrocosm, it was not likely to be difficult to convince him that a building or a state was also like a body. It was natural to imagine the invisible as like the visible; God as the head of a large firm, the New Jerusalem in the form of Florence. Do witches really fly through the air? Reflecting on this problem, a Dominican friar concluded that this flight was 'by no means impossible, as demons can move a man from place to place'. As evidence he quoted legends of St Ambrose, St Martin and St Peter. When Pomponazzi wanted to argue that many happenings which are attributed to magic are in fact natural, he too appealed to other parts of a common belief-system. The laurel tree has the power of repelling lightning by natural means: perhaps some men have similar powers. The friar and Pomponazzi both argued from analogy, and towards opposed conclusions, so the Renaissance belief system cannot have been monolithic. Had it been, it would have been very difficult for it ever to have changed; for intellectual change, like social change, seems to be engendered by contradictions within the system.

In a longer perspective, that of European thought from the thirteenth century (say) until the seventeenth, it is possible to distinguish traditional from modern views within this period. The idea of God's direct intervention in the universe; of correspondences; of the animate universe; of the moralized universe – all these are 'traditional'. The idea of the universe as subject to natural law; of causes; of the mechanical universe; of the objective universe – all these are 'modern'. The views of Alberti, Fontana, Guicciardini, Leonardo, Machiavelli, Pomponazzi and Valla, some of which were shocking to their contemporaries, were to become commonplace later.

Another hypothesis about the structuring of world-views is that different views are characteristic of different social groups or classes; it has often been said that the values of the Renaissance were associated with one class in particular, the 'bourgeoisie'.[42] The great problem is that of verification. To relate world-views to social groups involves sorting both into tidy heaps. A simple model of the social structure (but a little more complex than the models used at the time, as we have seen) sees it as divided into five groups: the clergy; the nobles; the merchants and professional men; the artisans and shopkeepers; the peasants. To classify world-views is more difficult, but the concept of 'syndrome' may be a useful one here. A syndrome may be defined as a pattern of biases. Biases may be defined as tendencies towards one pole or the other along an axis of bias. Axes of bias which seem relevant to Renaissance thought are natural versus supernatural; achievement versus birth; arms versus letters; thrift versus splendour; active versus contemplative; fortune versus *virtù*; faith versus reason; the dignity of man versus his misery. Renaissance values might be described as the pattern resulting from the bias towards the natural, towards achievement, towards letters, towards thrift, towards the active, towards *virtù*, towards reason, and towards the dignity of man. The point is not that most men in the period would be biased in these directions, but that what made the fifteenth and sixteenth centuries different from the centuries before was the tendency towards these poles.[43]

Each social group has its own syndrome, as well as the society as a whole. One may attempt to discover these group syndromes in two ways. The first way, which is a short cut, is to argue that there is an affinity between a particular social group and a certain set of attitudes. Thus one might expect from the clergy an emphasis on the supernatural; on the contemplative life; on faith; and on man's misery without God. The clergy might be said to have a professional interest in these views, in the sense that their social position depended on them. Again, one might expect from the nobility a stress on birth, on arms, and on splendour; for without these stresses there would have been no nobility. From merchants and professional men one might expect a stress on achievement, thrift and reason, since their way of life was based on competition and calculation. From the lower classes one might expect a stress on man's misery and the power of fortune; hardly because it was their 'interest' to hold such views, for it would have been in their interest to achieve a higher position, but because it is likely that people at the bottom of the social ladder will see the ladder as being more difficult to climb than the people on the middle or top rungs think. This doctrine of affinities between ideas and social groups would make it possible to explain changes in the dominant world-view at different periods in terms of the changing importance of different groups. One might compare twelfth-century France and fifteenth-century Italy, for example, and suggest that in France the dominant view was a fusion of the views of the priest and the knight, while in Italy the dominant view was that of the merchant, or a fusion of the merchant and the noble into the urban patrician. Of course, in fifteenth-century Italy the merchants were not a majority of the population, or of educated men; the 'dominance' of their view would have to be explained by its rubbing off on members of other social groups, in particular the marginal members of such groups, such as nobles whose noble descent did not go back very far, or clergy without a vocation.

The long way round, which is the surer, of relating world-view and social groups, or rather, of deciding whether or not they are related, is the empirical, the quantitative. It consists in examining the attitudes of one individual after another to see whether members of a particular social group tended in practice to accept a certain syndrome. This is a task to keep a team of researchers happily occupied for a long time; in fact the work has not been done. The nearest approach to it comes in C. Bec's book *Les marchands écrivains*, a study of the culture of Florentine merchants in the late fourteenth and early fifteenth centuries. He shows that in this group, a stress on prudence and reason and a confidence in the powers of the individual were in fact fairly widespread. One can only regret the absence of similar studies for other regions, periods and groups.

Until such studies are made, one can illustrate the 'affinities' just discussed, and not establish that they really existed. The clerical view, for example, could be illustrated from the writings of Bernardino of Siena and Savonarola, who both stress the supernatural over the natural, the contemplative life over the active, faith over reason, and man's misery over his dignity. The view of the nobility can be illustrated from the writings of Ariosto and Castiglione – not in an extreme form, for no literary man is going to be a perfect representative of the values of arms as opposed to letters. But Ariosto's heroes are well-born and valorous, and in *The Courtier* the sense of the meeting seems to be in favour of birth and arms. Both writers appreciate splendour. Castiglione's stress on spontaneity implies no very exalted view of calculation, perhaps because he associates it with merchants. Ariosto virtually omits religion from the *Orlando Furioso* altogether, and although he introduces enchantments, his tone is not always too serious. The views of merchants might be illustrated by Giovanni Rucellai, but as he often follows Alberti, it might be better to choose him. The views of Alberti and Guicciardini, both members of an urban patriciate, are similar; they both stress achievement, calculation, and to a lesser extent thrift; they both stress the natural as opposed to the supernatural. All these examples suggest that the short cut did not take a fundamentally wrong turning.

One might illustrate the views of the artisan-shopkeeper class from the diary of Landucci; apart from his emphasis on thrift, his world-view is much like that of the clergy. In his world God intervenes directly and often; man is presumptuous and weak and needs to know his place. Landucci was in fact an admirer of Savonarola, before the excommunication of the friar. Landucci was an apothecary; but so was Palmieri, whose view of the world is much more like Alberti's. How can one decide which view is the typical one? In fact, Palmieri's political activities show that he should be allocated to the urban patriciate, but the fact remains that it is very difficult to discover how far Landucci's attitudes were typical of the group to which he belonged. And we are still more in the dark about the attitudes of the peasants, although they were a majority of the population of Italy; and about the attitudes of women.

One last consideration about the relation of world-view to social groups; the explanation of innovations. The seven men whose views stand out as unconventional are Alberti, Fontana, Guicciardini, Leonardo, Machiavelli, Pomponazzi and Valla. By their social origin and their own occupation, these men do belong to the merchant-professional class, with the stress on the 'professional'. Alberti practised as a humanist and an architect, and was from a patrician family with a tradition of commerce. Fontana was a physician. Guicciardini practised as a lawyer and administrator and was from a patrician family with a tradition of commerce like the Albertis. Leonardo was the son of a notary, and practised as an engineer, besides painting. Machiavelli was the son of a lawyer and was himself a diplomat and administrator. He once described himself as 'unable to talk about gains and losses, about the silk-guild or the wool-guild'. Pomponazzi was a professional academic and the son of another professional academic. Valla was the son of a lawyer and, although a cleric, had a professional career as secretary to princes and professors in universities. Thus, provided that one thinks of professional men first and merchants second, there is something in von Martin's explanation of humanism as 'bourgeois' after all.

9

The Social Framework

If a modern Christian could visit Renaissance Italy, he would probably be very much surprised by what he found going on in church, and even an Italian Catholic might raise an eyebrow. For example, 'in churches people walk about as they do on the piazza.' Gasparo Contarini describes them as they walked, 'talking among themselves about trade, about wars, and very often even about love'. One might expect to find beggars in church, or small boys being taught by a schoolmaster without a school, or even horses, and it might be used for a storehouse for grain or wood. A visitation of the diocese of Mantua in 1535 reported on the church of S. Lorenzo in that city:

> In the upper part of the church the chaplain has a kitchen, beds and other things which are not very appropriate for a holy place; but . . . he may be excused because his dwelling is very small.

In early sixteenth-century Rome, each May, a pig was let loose in the church of SS. Philip and James, and whoever could catch it could keep it. Valuables might be kept in the sacristy of a church. The bags with the names of citizens who were eligible for the Florentine Signoria were kept in the sacristy of S. Croce. In 1527, Piero Gondi asked Michangelo's permission to hide his valuables in the sacristy of S. Lorenzo (which Michelangelo was rebuilding), 'by reason of the dangers which now threaten us'. There were few other safe places and modern architectural specialization, like modern institutional specialization, had not developed. If religious art seems informed by a secular spirit, that should not surprise us. The distinction between the sacred and the profane, like the distinction between the public and the private, was not drawn in the same place, and was not drawn as sharply as it was to be drawn later. But the distinction was drawn: rights of sanctuary, for example, still existed in Italy in this period. St Antonino's manual of confession makes a great deal of sacrilege, that is offences against holy people, places and things. In 1463, the bishop of Modena forbade people to walk through the cathedral during Mass, and in 1530 the duke of Milan forbade walking through churches altogether, especially during services.[2] Bloch's remark about the Middle Ages, that men were inclined 'to treat the sacred with a familiarity which did not exclude respect', remains true for this period, though one should add that the familiarity did not always include respect either.

Similarly, the clergy were not always sharply distinguished from the laity. They did not have a distinctive education; seminaries were rare. There were many marginal cases men in minor orders, like Poliziano and Ariosto. There were also priests who wore laymen's clothes, who carried weapons, who hunted, who begot and raised children. But it seems impossible to discover how many such clergy there were, and so answer the rhetorical questions of a speaker at the Lateran Council of 1514:

How many do not wear the clothes laid down by the sacred canons, keep concubines, are simoniacal and ambitious? How many carry weapons like soldiers and lay rascals (*secularazzi*) and threaten people with them? How many go to the altar with their own children around them? . . . How many hunt and shoot with crossbows and guns?

But Pope Eugenius IV complained that at Venice, in 1433, the greater part of the notaries and scribes were clerics. The Roman census of c. 1526 records a friar working as a mason (*il frate muratore*). The pope was a prince. It does not even seem possible to calculate the approximate numbers of the Italian clergy at this period, though the priest/people ratio is obviously a key factor in the spread of religious knowledge. In the city of Bologna in 1570, 5 per cent of the population were clerical; out of 60,000 people, there were 1,000 priests, friars and monks and 2,000 nuns. In one quarter of Rome in 1526 (Monti) some 8 per cent of the people were clergy, but Rome is a special case. In Venice in 1563, 2 per cent of the population were friars and nuns; the number of secular priests are not known. The reason there were so many nuns was that it was much cheaper to put a daughter into a convent than to marry her off, complete with dowry; convents too required dowries but they might be only 20 per cent of what husbands expected.

Again, it is not possible to make very precise statements about the social origins and the education of the clergy in the period. But the clergy may be divided into four groups. In the first group, the bishops. A study has been made of the Italian bishops who went to the first sessions of the Council of Trent between 1545 and 1547; 71 bishops, of whom 56 were not members of religious orders. Of these 56, about 70 per cent were of noble family, especially so in the Veneto (where bishops had names like Contarini, Foscari, Soranzo) and least so in the States of the Church. What frequently happened was that a nobleman would be appointed when he was a child when his elders were still in a position to help him. Alvise Pisani was made bishop of Padua at the age of six. An elder relative, an uncle for example, would resign his bishopric in his nephew's favour, retaining the income and the authority during his own lifetime. The result of this resignation system was to make some bishoprics virtually hereditary in certain families. Similarly Pius II, Calixtus III and Sixtus IV all appointed their nephews cardinals, and these cardinals became popes: Pius III, Alexander VI and Julius II. Leo X and Clement VII were cousins. The other common means of rising in the Church hierarchy was via the clientèle rather than the family. A man would take a doctorate in law, enter the household of a prominent cardinal, serve him as secretary or vicar-general, and obtain a bishopric through his influence. The sale of ecclesiastical offices (like lay ones) was not unknown. In Naples in Alfonso's time the archbishop of Benevento paid the court 500 ducats for his see; the bishop of Catania paid 4,000 for his. As far as education was concerned, bishops were likely to be well trained in law but not in theology. Some of them never set foot in the diocese, like the Estes, uncle and nephew, archbishops of Milan from 1499 to 1550.

The second group of clergy is that of the 'rectors', the holders of benefices. A monastery or a family might have the right to appoint. To obtain a benefice patronage was often important. Bernardino da Feltre's guide to confession asks penitents 'if being a patron you have presented an unqualified person', and 'if you have received a reward for presenting someone' as if these situations were recurrent. So were pluralism and non-residence. What does not seem to be known is the extent of either, whether enough to cause a shortage of parish clergy in a country which was full of clergy.[3]

Non-resident bishops confided their diocese to a vicar-general; non-resident rectors appointed a 'chaplain' to do their duty in the parish, often for a small proportion of the income. This is the third group of clergy. Some chaplains in the diocese of Milan in the early sixteenth century had an income of 40 lire per year, which was less than unskilled labourers earned. The chaplains were often ignorant; again, we do not know how often. The visitation records of the diocese of Mantua between 1535 and 1553 make 57 explicit judgements about the parish clergy, of which 22 are unfavourable, such as 'he knows nothing' or 'he is illiterate'. At the Visitation of the diocese of Pisa in the mid-fifteenth century, the Vicar-General was shocked to find some priests had no breviaries. It would not be surprising if these priests were typical, in a period before printing had been invented. Stories of the ignorance of the parish clergy were common; in his sermons, S. Bernardino tells of one who said the Hail Mary at the Elevation, and another who used to say 'hoc est corpusso meusso'. Some of them engaged in other employment, like horse- and cattle-dealing; it was a way of making ends meet.[4]

The fourth group of clergy were the members of the religious orders. There were many complaints about them too; about friars who were more like soldiers than friars, and nuns who were more like prostitutes than nuns. But the educational level of some of them, especially the Dominicans and Franciscans, was higher than that of the parish clergy, and their social origins were probably higher too, even if Albert of Sarteano (a Franciscan who studied under Guarino of Verona) and S. Bernardino of Siena (the son of a nobleman) cannot be taken as typical. The number and variety of the religious orders needs emphasis. There were five mendicant orders: the Dominicans; the Franciscans; the Austin friars, including Luigi Marsigli, the friend of Salutati and Niccoli; the Carmelites, devoted to Our Lady of Mount Carmel, who included the poet 'Mantuan' and Fra Lippo Lippi; and the Servites, also devoted to the Blessed

Virgin, and founded at Florence in the thirteenth century. Then there were monks, notably the Benedictines, who in Italy included the Vallombrosans and the particularly strict Camaldolese, one of whom was Ambrogio Traversari, a great student of Greek and translator of the Greek fathers. There were the Hieronymites, a federation of groups of hermits (and another illustration of the devotion to St Jerome in Italy in this period; they were particularly strong in Italy and Spain). The Hieronymites included the hermits of St Jerome of Lombardy and the hermits of St Jerome of Fiesole, whose first house was built at the expense of Cosimo de'Medici.

It was the Dominicans and the Franciscans, however, who made the greatest impact on the laity. The Dominicans included S. Antonino, Fra Angelico, and Savonarola, three very different types of men. In the late fourteenth century, the order had been particularly associated with an emphasis on penitence, on the fear of God rather than the love of God. Angelico's frescoes in S. Marco are in marked contrast to this emphasis, but at the end of the century Savonarola returned to the stern tradition. The fifteenth century was more the century of the Franciscans; the study of new foundations confirms what the study of iconography has suggested (above, p. 184). In 1420 there were about 30 communities of 'Observants', Franciscans who wanted to reform their order. By 1517, when the order was officially split into two, there were about 1,260 Observant communities, some taken over from the other wing, the 'Conventuals', the others new foundations. The most famous of the Italian Observants were S. Bernardino of Siena, Bernardino of Feltre, and John of Capistrano, great preachers all of them.

It was the friars who ensured the importance of sermons in Italian religious life, at a time when many of the parish clergy seem to have been too ignorant to preach, 'dumb dogs that will not bark', as a sixteenth-century Puritan described their English equivalents. S. Bernardino even told his congregation that if they had a choice between Mass and a sermon, they should choose the sermon. When he (or another famous performer) came to town to preach, legal proceedings were sometimes postponed so that everyone could hear him. Sermons were sometimes taken down in shorthand. Some preachers had little to learn from actors; one read a letter from Christ to his congregation, and one Franciscan preaching for a Crusade entered the pulpit dressed in armour. The travelling preacher, like the strolling players, bridged the gap between the small supply (for not all the friars preached, let alone well) and the large demand. But the parish clergy resented competition from the friars, who conducted funerals without their permission, and took away fees and alms which were their living.[5]

> It seems to me that men set up shop nowadays and sell the blood of Christ . . . How many priests sell burials, and take money for ringing the bells, for carrying the cross before the dead, for saying the office of the dead, for the sacraments of the Church?

This denunciation of commercialized religion gives a good impression of what the laity wanted from the clergy, of what they were prepared to pay for. Similarly a parish priest told the visitor of his diocese, Pisa, that his duties were 'to give the people candles and holy oil'. Religion meant ritual. In the first place, the ceremonies associated with the rites of passage; baptism with birth, confirmation with growing up, matrimony with marriage; for death there were all the ceremonies just quoted, together with the masses for the dead, often provided for in wills. Then there were the ceremonies associated with the different times of the year: Advent, Christmas, Lent, Easter, Pentecost; and with the feasts of the saints. S. Bernardino told his hearers that good works were worth more on feast days, and 'the greater the feast the greater the merit'. Guides to confession asked whether the penitent had worked or made someone else work *in festa*. Guild statutes laid down that members must not work on 'the feasts laid down by Holy Mother Church', but turn up for the procession instead. The number of feasts observed varied from place to place; but there would be some 40 odd altogether.[6]

Feasts may be roughly divided into those concerned with Christ, Mary and the saints. Feasts concerned with Christ included Christmas, the Epiphany, Palm Sunday, Easter, the Ascension, Pentecost, the Circumcision, Holy Cross, and Corpus Christi. The feast of Corpus Christi was growing in importance in the fifteenth century. It was celebrated with special magnificence by Pius II and his cardinals at Viterbo in 1462; the decorations included a fountain which ran with water and wine, and, 'a youth impersonating the Saviour, who sweated blood and filled a cup with the healing stream from a wound in his side'.[7] A new devotion was the adoration of the host displayed on the altar for the 'forty hours', which began at Milan in 1527 as a reaction to the sack of Rome, and spread through the Church.

Processions were an important part of all these feasts. In Rome on Easter Sunday, the pope was carried in procession to St Peter's before celebrating High Mass and blessing the people from his balcony. In Venice, the great festival was the Ascension, the day of the wedding of the sea. In Florence, Palm Sunday was a great day, with a procession led by a painted Christ on an ass, with an umbrella carried over it. On the feast of Corpus Christi, the host was carried in procession, as in the famous painting by Gentile Bellini of the procession in Piazza S. Marco. It might also be carried in procession in times of danger. In 1527, when the Florentine government feared that the imperial army would invade Tuscany, 'Every Friday they had a procession with the body of Christ and the whole city followed, often with great devotion.' An important part of the devotion to Christ centred on relics of the Passion. At Turin, the Holy Shroud was displayed; at Rome, a piece of the Cross, the Holy Lance, with which Christ was pierced, and the 'Veronica', that is, 'The miraculous likeness of Jesus Christ imprinted on the towel which the celebrated woman Veronica is said to have offered him.' Fragments of the Cross were venerated all over Italy; in fact, as S. Bernardino commented, 'If all the pieces of wood that are shown belonging to Christ's cross were put together, six yoke of oxen could not draw them.' Another famous relic, at St John Lateran in Rome, was the whole staircase up which Christ was led to Pilate. A German pilgrim described the custom there: 'We crawled up these steps on our knees, saying a Pater Noster on each step.' Plays about Christ were performed for some of these festivals. At Florence there were performances of plays about the three kings at Epiphany; at Rome, there was a Passion Play every year at the Colosseum.

This was acted by living people, even the scourging, the crucifixion, and how Judas hanged himself. They were all

10 In the manner of Piero della Francesca, *Alfonso of Aragon*, king of Naples and important patron of the arts

11   Leonardo da Vinci, *Isabella d'Este*. Marchioness of
Mantua whose art patronage was, as Edgar Wind put it,
'dictatorial, fanciful and pedantic'

12 Bronzino (1502–72), *Ugolino Martelli*. A private patron
from Florence whose interests in architecture, sculpture
and literature are all referred to in this portrait

13 Raphael, *Leo X* (1518) (detail). His importance as a patron has often been exaggerated, but his interest in music is, at least, undeniable

14 Woodcut of Adriaan Willaert (c. 1490-1562) from his *Musica Nova*, 1559. A Fleming and choirmaster of St Mark's, he was an important link between Josquin des Près and the Venetian School

15 *Above:* Lorenzo Vecchietta (c. 1412–80), *The Sermon to the Confraternity* (*see also Fig. 17*)

16 *Below:* Raphael's workshop. Stucco relief showing members of Raphael's studio plastering, painting and decorating the Loggie in the Vatican

17 Battista Dossi, *Madonna with saints and confraternity*.
Together with Plate 15 shows the importance of
collective patronage at this time – especially the
religious confraternity, a group of laymen meeting
regularly for religious and social reasons

18 Castagno (c. 1421–57), a leather shield depicting the
   youthful David (1450). An example of the practical
   functions of the 'work of art'

19 Carpaccio, right-hand panel from *The Reception of the English Ambassadors and St Ursula talking to her Father*. The devotional picture in a domestic setting

the children of wealthy people, and it was therefore done orderly and richly.[8]

There were fewer important feasts associated with Mary; the main ones were her Nativity, Annunciation, Purification ('Our Lady of the Candles') and Assumption. In Rome, on 25th March, the feast of the Annunciation, the pope would pay state visits to two churches dedicated to Our Lady, S. Maria sopra Minerva and S. Maria del Popolo. In Florence, the image of the Virgin at Impruneta, six miles south of Florence, was often brought into the city (above, p. 218). Every 15th August, the feast of the Assumption, there was (and in fact still is) a great festival at Siena, a city which had become the vassal of the Virgin in the thirteenth century. On that day attendance at Mass in the cathedral was compulsory for Sienese, and there was a horse-race in honour of the occasion. At Mantua, on the same day, there was a pilgrimage to S. Maria delle Grazie, a church outside the city wall with a picture of the Virgin supposedly painted by St Luke. The most famous relic of the Virgin was probably her girdle, preserved at Prato. The story went that after her assumption, Thomas doubted whether she was really in Heaven, so she threw down the girdle to convince him; the scene is painted by Ghirlandaio in the cathedral at Prato. Another famous relic was her house at Nazareth, displayed at Loreto; it was supposed to have been transported there miraculously in the thirteenth century. Pope Paul II was cured of plague at Loreto, and in the fifteenth century the cult of the 'holy house', as it was called, increased in importance. In Leo x's time, Andrea Sansovino and Baccio Bandinelli worked on the shrine at Loreto.

Mary was worshipped under many forms: Our Lady of Good Counsel, Our Lady of Mercy, Our Lady of the Snows, and so on. The popular devotion to the rosary was associated with her rather than with Christ; the Life of Christ was seen through her eyes. Many stories of her miracles were in circulation, sometimes collected into book form. These stories have some interesting common characteristics; for example, the miracles are often associated with an image of the Virgin; and they are often concerned with worldly help, so that the man who has recourse to Mary's intercession wins a lawsuit or makes a fortune. Mary seems to have been particularly 'miracologenic', and particular miracles often started local cults: Our Lady of the Fire at Forlì, Our Lady of the Oak at Viterbo, Our Lady of the Pillar at Mondovi, and so on. At Genazano, near Palestrina, where there was a church of Our Lady, in 1467 (according to a writer fourteen years later), 'an image of the blessed virgin miraculously appeared on the wall of the said church' and became the object of a cult. In Rome in 1470, near the Capitol, an image of Our Lady 'began to work miracles', so a church was built on the spot and the image painted by Antoniazzo Romano. One of the most famous images of all was that of S. Maria Impruneta, which was brought to Florence regularly to stop the rain or to solve political problems between 1354 and 1549. Terracotta reproductions of it, made by the della Robbias, were popular. Ex votos were often vowed to Our Lady; the Church of La Madonna del Monte at Cesena still has 246 of them from the fifteenth and sixteenth centuries. All these examples illustrate the variety of the functions of what we call 'works of art'. The popular nature of these cults of the Virgin deserves emphasis. In a number of cases, shrines were built after the Virgin had appeared to someone of low status; at Genoa in 1490 to a shepherd, for example, at Savona in 1536 to a labourer.[9]

The popularity of the saints was also very great. The Golden Legend went through at least seven editions in Italy between 1483 and 1533. Saints dominated the major feast-days; of the 42 days when the cloth-workers of Vicenza were not allowed to work, 25 were saints' days, including the feasts of Saints Catherine, George, John the Baptist, Mark, Martin, Nicholas, and, jointly, Peter and Paul. This list overlaps considerably with the saints who are painted most frequently, in spite of the absence of Saints Jerome, Rocco and Sebastian. One might compare the evidence of children's names. In the creative élite the most popular were the following: John, Anthony, Francis, Andrew, Bartholomew, Bernard and Jerome. A number of popular places of pilgrimage were associated with saints. People went to Bari to see the tomb of St Nicholas, with a stream of oil flowing from it; to Assisi to see the tomb of St Francis; to Padua to see the tomb of St Anthony. One of the attractions of Rome was the gridiron on which St Laurence was roasted, preserved in the church of SS. Lorenzo e Stefano; another was the head of St John the Baptist.

The great function of saints was their patronage. 'You can't get to heaven without saints,' as a Maltese proverb has it, picturing the next world in the image of this one, where petitions need the backing of the powerful. Mary was the universal patroness, but the saints were specific ones, associated with particular towns and crafts, so that devotion to a saint was a way of expressing civic sentiment or professional consciousness. Painters, for example, had a special devotion to St Luke. St Ambrose was the patron of Milan, St Mark of Venice, St John the Baptist of Florence. St Ambrose was not only associated with the city but with the republican form of government. The short-lived 'Ambrosian Republic' invoked his name and arranged great processions on his feast-day. The Sforza, like the Visconti, did not favour the cult much, but before the assassination of G. M. Sforza in 1476, the conspirators swore an oath together before a picture of St Ambrose. In Venice, the troops of the republic marched under the banner of St Mark, which was ceremonially handed to the commander in the church of St Mark. There were images of St Mark in the towns within the Venetian Empire as a sign of Venetian domination, and for the same reason the images were defaced when the French took Cremona, Crema and Bergamo in 1509. The stewards of the guild of ships' caulkers at Venice had to lay on trumpeters and pipers for a special Mass on St Mark's day. In Florence, 24th June, the feast of St John the Baptist was celebrated with races, jousts and bull-fights. The subject towns of the Florentine Empire sent deputations to the capital, and there were the usual floats, men walking on stilts made to look like giants, tight-rope walkers, jugglers, tooth-drawers, and so on. Such feasts were events on which civic prestige depended and during which communal values were reaffirmed. The decline of devotion to St Ambrose and St John which has been observed in fifteenth-century Milan and Florence thus looks like an indicator of declining civic sentiment.[10]

The forms of devotion to saints suggest that the laity, or some of them, had considerable influence in the Italian Church. Much of this influence was exercised through religious confraternities, societies which developed in Italy in the thirteenth century and became still more popular in the fourteenth and fifteenth. At least 80 were founded in North and Central Italy in the thirteenth century; 202 in the fourteenth century; 218 in the fifteenth century. The importance of these confraternities as patrons of art has been discussed already, but here is the place to emphasize the forms of their devotion. A popular one in the fifteenth and sixteenth centuries was devotion to Corpus Christi, the body of Christ. Confraternities with this dedication were founded at Parma in 1486, Perugia in 1487, Orvieto in 1488, Genoa in 1490, Bologna in 1491, Ravenna in 1492, Brescia in 1494, Verona *c.* 1517, and Rome in 1539. The impulse to a number of these foundations came from Bernardino da Feltre, who was, like Bernardino da Siena, a great apostle of Christocentric devotion. Perhaps the rising popularity of pictures of Christ owes something to the Observants. Some fifteenth-century Florentine pictures of the Adoration of the Magi were almost certainly made for members of the Confraternity of the Magi, which included Landino and Lorenzo de'Medici.

It was not only as patrons of paintings that the confraternities made their impact on the arts. They performed plays. It was the Confraternity of the Gonfalon which performed the Good Friday Passion Play at the Colosseum – Antoniazzo Romano was a member and painted the scenery. It was the Confraternity of St John which performed Lorenzo de'Medici's play about Saints John and Paul at Florence. Confraternities often sang *laude*, hymns in praise of the Virgin, in their processions and in special meetings in church, and these hymns were sometimes important examples of religious poetry, and might be set to music by famous composers such as Dufay. They also listened to lay sermons. On one occasion at least the preacher was Machiavelli, whose 'exhortation to penitence' delivered to the Confraternity of Piety in Florence has been preserved. It has been argued that the Platonic Academy in Florence was modelled as much on these confraternities as on Plato's original Academy.[11]

These confraternities were social clubs as well as devotional ones. The statutes laid down the duty of visiting sick members, and aiding them if they were in need. They also aided non-members, and in this period, these works of charity seem to have been increasing in importance; the 'seven works of temporal mercy', that is:

To visit the sick. Feed the hungry. Give drink to the thirsty. To clothe the naked. To succour prisoners. To bury the dead. To give lodging to pilgrims.

The names of some of the new foundations illustrate these aims. The Confraternity of St Martin was founded in Florence in 1441 to help paupers – for St Martin divided his cloak with a beggar. Names like 'the confraternity of mercy', 'the confraternity of charity' were common. In Milan, a confraternity organized weekly visits to prisoners. At Cremona, another concentrated on men condemned to death. One at Rome was founded to provide dowries for poor girls. These foundations are part of the evidence for the transformation of religious ideals in fifteenth-century Italy, an increasing social consciousness which has been called 'civic christianity'. Ludwig Pastor compiled a table of charitable foundations – hospitals, almshouses, orphanages and so on – in Italy between 1400 and 1524; he listed 334 of them, 103 in South Italy; 90 in Lombardy; 50 in the States of the Church; 37 in the Veneto; 23 in Liguria; 22 in Piedmont; 11 in Tuscany. One wonders why Tuscany does so badly, whether there is an inverse correlation between art patronage and works of charity. It is also possible that new foundations is a misleading index of charity, which should take new gifts to old foundations into account as well. If the distribution of church property in Pistoia in the fifteenth century is compared with its distribution in the thirteenth century, a rise in the relative wealth of hospitals and other charitable organizations can be seen. Charity at Pistoia was advertised by means of art; on the façade of the Ospedale del Ceppo, from 1525 on, there was a coloured terracotta frieze of *The works of mercy*, made by G. della Robbia and S. Buglioni.[12]

It is not yet possible to generalize about the wealth of the Italian church at this period. A study of the property owned by the churches of Florence in certain parts of Tuscany has revealed that its holdings increased from 13 per cent of the land in 1427 to 23 per cent in 1498. But in Lombardy the trend was the opposite way. There the laity were successfully taking property away from the Church, and the lay administrators of church property paid a rent of which the real value was less every year. In the mid-sixteenth century, the Spanish government found that the Church possessed only from 10 per cent to 15 per cent of the land of Lombardy.[13]

THE STATE

Burckhardt devoted a celebrated chapter, his first, to what he called 'Der Staat als Kunstwerk' (the state as a work of art), meaning by this phrase that Renaissance Italians offer many examples of political awareness, reflection, and calculation. Has this picture stood up to the test of more than a century of research?

It is convenient to look at republics and principalities separately before coming back to the question of the existence of a 'Renaissance state'.* In the twelfth and thirteenth centuries, North and Central Italy were full of republics; some seventy odd. By the fifteenth century, most of them had lost their independence and were under the control of a prince or part of a larger empire. But of the 'Big Five', two states were republics, Florence and Venice, the Renaissance cities par excellence.[14]

The Venetian constitution was celebrated for its stability and balance. These qualities are related; it is difficult for a system in equilibrium to change. The Venetian pyramid of power – to consider its formal structure – had the doge at the top. He was elected, but held office for life. He took decisions in consultation with two bodies: the Council of Ten, and the College of Sages (six 'great sages', who took it in turn to prepare business for the college, and ten others). Below the College came the Senate, with 120 ordinary senators (60 chosen by the outgoing Senate, 60 by the Great Council) and about the same number of members *ex officio*. The main function of the Senate was legislative. Below the Senate came the Great Council (*Maggior Consiglio*), with about 1,300 members. Its function was to choose the magistrates, the 800-odd important offices like senator, ambassador, judge, naval officer. Most offices were held for six months at a time, but membership of the Great Council was for life. There were also permanent

* With regret, I have had to omit consideration of the small states; republics like Lucca and principalities like Ferrara.

professional civil servants, such as the staff of the three chanceries.[15]

The Florentine pyramid of power – again, the formal structure – was topped by the Signoria of nine men, the Gonfalonier of Justice and eight priors. Next came two colleges, the Gonfalonieri (16 men) and the Buonomini (12 men). All these were the legislature. There were also two councils with legislative functions, the Council of the People and the Council of the Commune, but they had lost much of their importance in this period. There were special-purpose executive and judicial committees such as the Six, who dealt with trade; the Eight, who judged criminal cases; the Ten, who dealt with peace and war, and so on. When they were needed, *pratiche* (councils without fixed membership) and *parlamenti* (general assemblies of citizens) might be called. There was also a chancery staffed by professional civil servants. Offices rotated even more rapidly than in Venice; the Signoria were in office for only two months at a time. This created 54 vacancies every year, and these were filled not by election as at Venice but by lot: the names were taken out of bags kept for this purpose.

The Florentine political system was not stable, but altered so much that change can be considered part of its structure. As a Venetian observer put it:

> They have never been content with their constitution, they are never quiet, and it seems that this city always desires change of constitution, so that any particular form of government has never lasted more than fifteen years.

He commented, rather smugly, that this was God's punishment for the sins of the Florentines. Dante's diagnosis of the Florentine system was not so different; he had compared Florence to a sick woman twisting and turning in bed, comfortable in no position. And so, in this period, in 1458 a Council of Two Hundred was set up; in 1480 it was replaced by a Council of Seventy; in 1494 the Medici were driven out, and a Great Council on the Venetian model was created; in 1502 the gonfalonier of justice was made a life appointment, turning him into a kind of doge; in 1512 the Medici returned, in the baggage of a foreign army, and the Council of Seventy returned with them; in 1527 the Medici were again driven out, and in 1530 returned again; in 1532 a Great Council and a Senate were set up, though it was the duke who now exercised power.[16]

The other three members of the Big Five, Milan, Rome and Naples, may be regarded as monarchies, ruled by a duke, a pope and a king respectively; two hereditary rulers, and one, the pope, an elective one. In contrast to the republics, the key institution in all three cases was the court, which served both private and public functions, the household of the prince and the administration of the state. Courts numbered hundreds of people; in 1527 the papal court was about 700 strong. A court was an extremely heterogeneous collection of people, a point which emerges vividly from such documents as the account-books of Alfonso of Aragon king of Naples, the lists of people paid by the duke of Milan in 1476 and 1498, and of people given mourning-cloth on the death of the pope in 1447 and 1503. The lists begin with men of high status; at Milan the marquesses of Mantua and Monferrato; at Naples, the seven great officers – constable, admiral, protonotary, chamberlain, justiciar, seneschal, chancellor; at Rome, three great officers, the vice-chancellor, the grand penitentiary, and the chamberlain. The lists continue through ambassadors, castellans, doctors, secretaries, gentlemen of the bedchamber, university professors, chaplains, pages, tutors and governesses, heralds, trumpeters, men-at-arms, cooks, bakers, barbers, falconers, fools, midgets, shoemakers, singers, stableboys, tailors, and the servants of the higher officials. It may be useful to divide this great crowd of men into three groups: the noblemen, or 'courtiers', high-status amateurs; the officials, high-status professionals; and the servants (or the servants of the servants), low-status professionals. Most of these people lived in one place, though it might be possible to live out and draw an allowance in lieu of free accommodation. When Lodovico Sforza was living in the Castello Sforzesco, it also housed his relatives (legitimate and illegitimate), his favourites, his personal servants and his civil servants – the chancery, for example, occupied the ground floor. The court ate together, though high officials might have their meals sent to their rooms, and hangers-on might appear at mealtimes. Lodovico once had to forbid the distribution of wine to people who did not have the right to it.

When the prince moved, most of the court moved with him. When the court of Milan went to the country in Lodovico's time, it took 500 horses and mules to support it; and the court often went to Pavia, to Lodovico's favourite Vigevano, and to smaller castles, summer residences and hunting lodges like Abbiategrasso, Binasco, and Cusago. Similarly, Alfonso of Aragon was often on the move, not only within his kingdom of Naples but outside it, in Tuscany or Catalonia, and officials were kept on the move too; in December 1451, for example, Alfonso summoned his council to Capua, where he was hunting, in order to decide a dispute between the Crown and the city of Barcelona. As for popes, Pius II's memoirs give a vivid picture of a court almost permanently on the move.

It will be clear from this brief account that Lorenzo de'Medici did not have a court in the same sense as the popes or the Sforzas; he had a small household and that was all, a point which may help explain the lack of large-scale art patronage on his part.

In principalities, the legislature was the prince, for his will was the law. But he often asked for advice, and sometimes took it, so an important political function was that of counselling, institutionalized, as language reminds us, in 'councils'. In Milan under Lodovico there was a Privy Council (*Consilio Segreto*), which had twelve members in 1490. In Naples under Alfonso the council was larger; as described by a visitor in 1444, it included the seven great officers of state *ex officio*, as well as a number of other nobles and some doctors of law. In Rome, the council was called the College of Cardinals, which met, together with the pope, in Consistory. There might be some 20 or 30 cardinals at any one time. In 1483, for example, there were 23 cardinals resident in the diocese of Rome, and 9 more who were not.

Justice and finance tended to be administered by separate bodies of specialists. At Milan there was a Council of Justice; at Rome, the Rota; at Naples, the Holy Council (*Sacro Consiglio*) was set up in Alfonso's time. All these were supreme courts of appeal. There were also travelling judges in the provinces, in areas where the local aristocracy did not control justice themselves. Financial institutions were not unified but diverse. In Milan, there was a main treasury, but the salt-tax had its own officials, and the duke his own treasurers, who attended him wherever he went to make payments on the spot where necessary. In Naples, the Chamberlain was the great officer traditionally in charge of finance, but there were other treasuries; the sheep-tax had its own officials; and Alfonso set up the Council of Finance (*Consilium Pecuniae*) as a supreme financial body without, however, abolishing the office of Chamberlain. In Rome, the Chamberlain was in charge of finance, but besides his 'Chamber' (*Camera*) there was a 'privy treasury' with its own treasurer.[17]

Thus in formal terms there were considerable differences between republics and principalities and the ways in which they organized legislative, judicial and administrative bodies. In theory, the 'people' had power in one type of state, and the prince in the other. In practice, there was less difference between them. The apparent rule of prince or people may mask the reality of control by a ruling élite or oligarchy. It has been argued that such an 'iron law of oligarchy' exists in all institutions, and it is worth testing this generalization against evidence from Renaissance Italy. In any case, the social historian is bound to be interested in the types of men who exercise power in different regimes. This attempt to pierce beneath the surface of political reality, fascinating as it is, is very difficult. It has been argued that in the interests of clear thinking we should not speak of a 'ruling élite' in any society unless there is a well-defined minority group in that society whose preferences regularly prevail in cases of conflict on key political issues. Too much evidence has disappeared for the historian of Renaissance Italy to meet these criteria completely, and this point needs to be borne in mind throughout the following pages.[18]

Venice was a society much like England in its love of hiding change behind the fiction of continuity and of hiding conflict behind the fiction of consensus. The fifteenth-century tourist might understandably have mistaken the doge for a monarch. One of them described the doge going in state to S. Marco:

> There preceded him . . . 14 minstrels, 8 with silver bassoons, from which hung golden cloths with the arms of St Mark, and six pipers with trumpets, also with rich hangings.[19]

To pick up a book printed in Venice might reinforce the illusion of monarchy, for the colophon sometimes contains a phrase like 'in the reign of the illustrious prince Andrea Gritti'. What this really shows is that the Venetians had developed the distinction (in Bagehot's famous formulation) between the 'dignified' and the 'efficient' parts of the political system. For the power of the doge was severely limited, above all by the Council of Ten. To take one example of conflict over key political issues (peace versus war in this case) when Doge Francesco Foscari went ahead with his own policy against the wishes of the Council of Ten, they forced him to resign, in 1457. Venice was not a monarchy. On the other hand it was not a democracy either. The membership of the Great Council was laid down at the end of the thirteenth century; it included all males over 25 years old whose families were inscribed in the Golden Book, about 200 families in all. These families filled all the magistracies, making Venice quite definitely into an oligarchy. Within this oligarchy there was an inner circle of families who intermarried and held most of the highest offices. For example, one comes to expect Venetian ambassadors to be called Badoer or Contarini, or Morosini, or Soranzo, or Tiepolo. Offices might rotate rapidly, but they rotated among the same families, about 4 per cent of the population at most.

Where Venice excluded craftsmen and shopkeepers from political life, Florence allowed them a role – but a small one. The still more rapid rotation of office and the habit of choosing officials by lot made the system more open than the Venetian one. But not everyone was eligible for office. Only citizens were eligible; that is, those adult males who belonged to one of the 21 guilds. Being politically adult meant being 14, not, as at Venice, 25; a difference which helps explain both Venetian stability and Florentine experiment. It was the names of these guildsmen that went into the bags; about 4,000 people, again a minority of the population. There were some 3,000 offices to be filled annually, but they varied greatly in importance, and seven out of the nine *signori* had to come from the greater guilds, and a similar proportion of the two colleges. In other words, a minority of the citizens, the *popolo grasso*, filled the majority of the high offices, leaving about 25 per cent of these offices for the others. In practice, not all eligible names went into the bags; Guicciardini says that Lorenzo de'Medici 'made sure the bags were filled with men dependent on him'. By the mid-fifteenth century, high office was restricted to some 350-odd families. Real power was restricted still further, to a small inner circle.

The Commune was governed at dinners and at desks (*alle cene e negli scrittoi*) rather than in the Palace; many were called to office, but few were chosen to govern (*molti erano eletti agli uffici e pochi al governo*).[20]

As Niccolò Soderini put it in a speech in 1465, it was the rich who controlled the offices. One might describe the government of Florence as Marx described the modern state, as 'a committee for managing the common affairs of the whole bourgeoisie'. Giovanni Rucellai had a similar idea, remarking that 'to desire to administer the state as if it were one's own shop' is a dishonest thing (cf. p. 271).

Within the inner circle, men competed for office; as much for status – to make a figure in the city – as for power. Among the patricians, as Guicciardini put it in a famous phrase, a man was hardly regarded as human unless he had held high office at least once.

Republics in practice were not ruled by everyone, and similarly, principalities were not ruled by one man alone. The nobles believed that the prince should rule in consultation with them, and that this was what the council was for. In Milan, there were powerful families like Maino, Stampa, Trivulzio to reckon with; in Rome, the Orsini and the Colonna; in Naples, the Caracciolo, the Caraffa, or the Gaetani. To evade noble control, rulers tended to rely on a small inner ring of advisers, men they could trust, professional officials, perhaps men they had 'raised from the dust' to the disgust of the noble amateurs. Thus at Milan, the Privy Council developed out of a larger council, but even the Privy Council was too large for Lodovico Sforza, who tended to rely on one adviser, Calco. In Naples in Alfonso's time there was a large council with little more than ceremonial functions and an inner ring whose advice the king took. In Rome, the College of Cardinals was tending both to increase in size and decrease in power, and again an informal inner ring developed, composed of some cardinals who were particularly close to the pope, and some officials who were not cardinals at all.

Republics and principalities can have seemed little different from the point of view of the subject areas, and Florence, Venice, Milan, Rome and Naples were all empires in the sense of territorial states; all had towns and countryside subject to them. Florence ruled Arezzo, Livorno, Pisa, Pistoia, Volterra. Venice ruled Bergamo, Brescia, Cremona, Padua, Verona, Vicenza. Milan ruled Alessandria, Como, Novara, Pavia. Rome ruled Bologna, Orvieto, Perugia, Urbino. The Kingdom of Naples included Bari, Brindisi, Lecce, Otranto, Salerno. The existence of these subject territories involved the appointment of a whole host of administrators; castellans, judges, tax-collectors, 'sages of the terraferma' and governors with such different titles (and powers) as capitano, justiciar, legate, podestà, vicar.

All governments may be oligarchies, but some oligarchies are smaller than others. The impression persists, if only because of the literature on politics written at the time, that there was wider political involvement in Florence and Venice than there was elsewhere.

So far, the Italian states have been considered in relation to Aristotle's types: monarchy, aristocracy, democracy. Another important typology is that of Max Weber, concerned not with how many people have power but with the way in which they exercise it. Weber distinguishes three types of 'domination' (*Herrschaft*): the charismatic, the patriarchal, and the bureaucratic.[21]

Charismatic domination is domination by an outstanding individual, a Christ or a Napoleon, on the basis of personal 'magnetism' or 'glamour'. The charismatic leader 'seizes the task for which he is destined and demands that others obey and follow him by virtue of his mission'. This mode of domination depends on personal loyalty. It is unsystematic and unspecialized; the followers do what the leader demands, but his demands are not predictable. It is also unstable, since it depends on the wishes and ultimately on the life of an individual. Weber did discuss the possibility of transmitting charisma; when this happens, there is a move towards the second type, the patriarchal.

Patriarchal domination is also based on personal loyalty and on personal favour, and again lacks clearly defined spheres of authority, systems of appointment, regular rewards. But it is more stable than the charismatic type, because obedience is based on tradition as well as on the personal relationship. The officials, members of the household of the ruler, hold permanent positions even if they are given tasks from day to day. They are recruited from men bound to the ruler by personal ties;

relatives or clients.

The third type of domination is the bureaucratic; the rule of the office. The bureaucratic system, in contrast to both the others, depends on the separation of private from public, the man from the role or office. There is a formally-defined hierarchy, and a man obeys a higher official because he holds that post and not because of his personal or family qualities. There is departmental specialization, together with formally defined spheres of competence. There is much use of written records, whereas under charismatic and patriarchal domination most business was oral. Officials are professionals, with formal training, an ethos of their own, appointment and promotion by merit rather than 'favour', and a fixed salary, usually in money. In a word, the system is impersonal or 'rationalized'. These three types of domination are types, not to be found in a pure form in historical societies. It is not surprising to find that Renaissance Italy was, in varying proportions, a mixture of all three.

The most obvious example of a charismatic leader is surely Savonarola, who may be regarded as virtual king of Florence (though Christ officially held the title) from 1494 to 1498. He ruled by virtue of his personal prophetic gifts, and was deserted by his followers when that virtue left him. A secular example might be that of Cesare Borgia, who had the power to fascinate his contemporaries, notably Machiavelli, though his success did not depend on his personal qualities to the same degree as Savonarola's. Then there are the possessors of institutionalized, or as Weber says, 'routinized' charisma; above all, the popes. A pope like Julius II has personal magnetism too, but his office has charisma – at any rate, the assumption that it has makes better sense of the ceremonial and the adulation surrounding popes than the contrary assumption does. Similar is the charisma of royalty; that of the kings of Naples, for example. Princes like the dukes of Milan had something similar – but perhaps weaker. Royal charisma seems less important in Italy than elsewhere in Europe, no doubt because Italy was not a kingdom and most of its princes were relatively new. This fact may have made it easier for Italians to make relatively cool, detached analyses of political structures and techniques. Machiavelli's *Prince*, Guicciardini's treatment of the career of Savonarola, and Pomponazzi's discussion of touching for the king's evil are all examples, even if Machiavelli was somewhat carried away by Cesare Borgia. It would seem that the charismatic type was not the dominant mode of domination in Renaissance Italy, although it was present.

It may be more useful, with respect to Weber, to work with two models rather than three, and to regard charisma as an 'extraordinary' mode of domination which can coexist with bureaucratic systems (under Napoleon, Lenin, Hitler) as well as with patriarchal ones (Muhammad, Genghis Khan). An advantage of working with two models only is that it enables a sharper formulation of contrasts, thus :

patriarchal	bureaucratic
personal	impersonal
amateur	professional
informal	formal
oral	written
general	specialized
traditional	rational

Language seems to lend itself to dichotomies rather than trichotomies.

A strong case can be made for the dominance of the bureaucratic system, above all in Florence and Venice in the fifteenth and sixteenth centuries. The distinction between public and private was drawn by some contemporaries, like the distinction between sacred and profane. References to the common good, the honour of the commune or its hurt are frequent, using such terms as *la cosa pubblica, il bene pubblico, honore pubblico,* or *danno di commune*. In the confession-manual of Bernardino da Feltre, lords are asked 'whether you have appropriated what belongs to the public' (*le cose commune*), perhaps common lands. There was a steadily-increasing use of the term *stato* in its modern meaning of 'the state' (as opposed to 'state affairs') or ('status'). One character in Alberti's dialogue on the family declares :

I do not want to consider the state as if it were my own property, to think of it as my shop, to treat it as if it were part of the dowry of my daughters, or in any way turn the public into the private.[22]

Professional officials were numerous and increasing in number, and a doctorate in law was something like a professional training for them, in the sense that it was relevant to their work and considered as a qualification. In Milan under the Sforza some 20 per cent of the Privy Council were lawyers. In Naples under Alfonso, lawyers were prominent in government. When the appeal court was set up in Naples, six permanent members were appointed, all lawyers. They were forbidden to engage in private legal practice, but were paid 500 ducats a year each. Fixed money salaries were quite common in the government of the Big Five. In Venice, *c.* 1500, secretaries in the chancery averaged 125 ducats a year, about the salary of branch managers of the Medici bank. There was an attempt to ensure appointment by merit. In Naples in the early sixteenth century, a succession of decrees ordered provincial governors and other high officials not to solicit judicial offices for their clients, forbade officials to accept presents (food and drink excepted), and made them swear that they had not given or promised anything for their offices. In Milan, the governor declared in 1543 that it was his firm intention

> That every office of whatever kind should not only be exercised personally and not by proxy, but that it should not be possible to obtain it in any way by money or other promises.[23]

In Florence, Milan and Naples, the professional standards of officials were enforced by the institution of *sindacato*, better known under its Spanish name of *residencia*. When an official's term of office expired, he had to remain behind for a week or a month while his activities were investigated by special commissioners, or 'syndics'.

In the greater Italian states, there was considerable demarcation of function between officials. In Milan under Lodovico Sforza, there was a secretary for ecclesiastical affairs, a secretary for justice, and a secretary for foreign affairs, who had clerks under him specializing in the affairs of different states, such as France or Venice. In Florence and in Venice specialist committees existed, for trade, for naval affairs, and so on. Overlapping jurisdictions and immunities were being eliminated, centralization and rationalization were taking place.

In the fourteenth and fifteenth centuries, the Florentine commune and its courts and officials extended their powers at the expense of such rival institutions as the Church, magnates, guilds, and religious confraternities. In fifteenth-century Milan, the dukes attacked the immunities of the Church, and laid down that there were to be no private jurisdictions within the duchy and that no subject should accept foreign titles without the consent of the duke, who would not have his dogs wearing other men's collars. To the delight of the modern historian, the importance of written records was increasing; records such as the minutes of debates (the Florentine *Consulte e Pratiche*), and social surveys undertaken to assess taxes (the Florentine *Catasto* of 1427, the Roman census of *c.* 1526, the Sienese 'alliramenti' of 1509 and 1531). A last example of stress on impersonal and rational criteria for the selection of office-holders, and of what the sociologist calls 'universalism' as opposed to 'particularism', comes from a dialogue by Guicciardini in which one character declares that, ideally, all offices in Florence

> should not be chosen by quarter but by the whole city, because in such matters the distribution by quarters makes no sense; the point is not to make the quarters equal but to choose the most worthy.

The social background to this idea is the shift within Florence from a federation of quarters and other associations which had to be balanced against one another, to a more centralized system.[24]

Yet the patriarchal type of domination was still deeply rooted in Italy, especially at courts, where administration was household-based, loyalty was focused on a man, not on the state, and the ruler might bypass the normal course of government whenever he wanted to grant favours to personal suitors. The princes' favour was the prime necessity in appointments and promotions. As Pius II remarked, 'at the courts of princes, what matters are personalities not services' (*non enim servitia in curiis principum sed personae ponderantur*).[25] When professional lawyers were appointed members of the appeal court at Naples, the nobles protested, and the king appointed some of them too. Nor was it only courts which were run in this way. Although many officials did in fact have law degrees, there was no examination system as there was in China at this time, nor even the kind of training which was compulsory for officials in the Ottoman Empire. The personal ties of father and son, patron and client still counted in politics. Key offices might be given to the 'familiars' or clients of high officials. The popes often relied on their nephews, not to mention closer relatives, in the government of the Papal States. Castellanships and other positions of trust were often transmitted from father to son, with the consent of the prince. In spite of numerous decrees, offices were in practice treated as property and bought, sold and inherited. In Venice in 1528, the high office of procurator of St Mark changed hands for 20,000 ducats. This was exceptional only because the office was a high one; offices which were not 'magistracies', secretaryships and stewardships, were regularly bought, sold and given as dowries in Venice.[26] In Milan, Naples and Rome, offices were also sold; in Rome, the department of the datary grew up to deal with this business.

When a man bought an office, he might exercise it in person, but he might equally well 'farm' it; that is pay a substitute to perform the duties for a fraction of the proceeds. On a larger scale, governments often farmed the taxes, that is sold the right of collecting them to businessmen. In other words, the rector-vicar system existed in the lay world as well as in the Church. An office, like a piece of land, was an investment. Like land, it might confer status, but was also expected to bring in an income. Official salaries were often inadequate. In Milan *c.* 1450 the chancellor of the duke's council was paid 68 lire a year, slightly more than the average wage of an unskilled labourer. Hence the stress by officials on presents and fees; again, the analogy with the clergy holds good. To get a letter from the chancery of Milan, for example, the client had to pay a fee called euphemistically 'the emolument of the seal'. Officials might have the right to a proportion of confiscated goods. Common perquisites were presents of wine and food from clients, before or after the favours they requested. A final example of the lack of a sharp distinction between public and private concerns government documents. These were still often considered the private property of officials. Late in the sixteenth century the Venetian ambassador to Rome, Paruta, observed that on the death of a pope, many documents were taken away by his relatives.

Thus the Italian states were a mixture of bureaucratic and patriarchal modes of domination, with a dash of charismatic. Looked at from a twentieth-century industrial society, it is the patriarchal aspects which stand out most clearly. Looked at from the tenth century, say, or from the point of view of an anthropologist studying tribal societies, what is most striking about Renaissance Italy is the emergence of the bureaucratic system. Although systematically comparative research on this problem has not been undertaken, it is likely that bureaucratic elements developed in Italy earlier than in other parts of Europe. The concept of the 'state' was more likely to develop in a city-republic, where there was no individual person to focus loyalties. In Italy, there were more educated laymen than elsewhere who might develop the peculiar ethos of the professional bureaucrat, and Bologna was already a famous law school in the twelfth century. It seems as reasonable to speak of a 'revolution in government' in Renaissance Italy as in Tudor England. Burckhardt's language has an old-fashioned ring today, but in his chapter on 'the state as a work of art' he put his finger on the same salient features of political organizations as Max Weber did, and noted their early development in Italy. To the (limited) extent that the bureaucratic mode of domination had developed, it is useful to speak of a 'Renaissance state'.

But is the Renaissance state related to the culture of the Renaissance? Were republics or principalities better for the arts? What were the cultural consequences of the rise of bureaucracy?

The question about forms of government and the arts was discussed by contemporaries, naturally enough, since their eyes were on Greece and Rome. Pius II suggested that:

> The study of letters flourished most of all at Athens, while it was a free city, and at Rome, while the consuls ruled the commonwealth.

Leonardo Bruni expressed similar opinions (above, p. 15). The opposite point of view was maintained by Giovanni Conversino da Ravenna, c. 1400:

> Where the multitude rules, there is no respect for any accomplishment that does not yield a profit; accomplish-

ments that make money are accepted, those of leisure are rejected. For when everyone is either engaged in piling up money, or is indifferent to a name beyond the city walls, everybody has as much contempt for the poets as he is ignorant of them, and will rather keep dogs than maintain scholars or teachers.[27]

The fact that the two great republics, Florence and Venice, were the cities where most artists and writers originated is the obvious point in favour of the first thesis. But it is not enough for a historian to record a correlation; he must attempt to explain it. Two points suggest themselves. One might expect the achievement drive to be greater in republics than in principalities, because republics work on the principle of political competition, so fathers are more likely to bring up their sons to try to excel others. One might expect the achievement drive to be stronger in Florence, where the system was more open, than in Venice, where one social group monopolized the magistracies. The myth of democracy would be more important than the reality, for it is the myth which would affect upbringing. A second point is that in communities where the level of political participation is relatively high, a political education is easier to come by, and so one might expect to find more and better historians, given that historians wrote mainly about politics in the period. In fact the Florentines predominate even more in the writing of history than in other arts. There was Bruni (a Tuscan working in Florence), Machiavelli, Guicciardini, Nardi, Nerli, Segni, Varchi, and others.

The conclusion seems to be that it is better for a writer or artist to be born in a republic than in a principality; he is more likely to develop his talents. When they are developed, however, he needs patronage; and in the field of patronage it is less easy to say which political system benefits the artist most. In Republics, there was civic patronage. The most spectacular cases come from Florence in the early fifteenth century, where artisans still participated in the government, and where Brunelleschi was one of the priors in 1425. As the political importance of the *popolo minuto* declined during the fifteenth century, so did civic patronage. In Venice there was the state, but (see p. 101 above) it was not a very munificent patron. It is not surprising that a number of artists who were born and trained in republics were attracted to courts: Leonardo to Milan, Michelangelo to Rome, Agostino di Duccio to Rimini, Jacopo Bellini to Ferrara, Sebastiano del Piombo to Rome, and so on. An enterprising prince who was willing to spend the money could make his court an artistic centre fairly quickly, by buying up artists who were already trained and practising. In the visual arts, 23 per cent of the creative élite surveyed in this book are known to have worked at courts at some point in their career.

A vivid impression of the court milieu can be obtained from some literary sources, of which the most famous by far is Castiglione's *Courtier*, published in 1528. His picture is an idyllic one, and coloured by nostalgia. A good corrective is Pius II's little book *The miseries of Courtiers*, written in 1444. Castiglione was deliberately writing a 'complete courtier', the equivalent of Plato on the ideal republic. But he does communicate a sense of what it might have felt like to be one of a group of young men and women living for months on end in a huge palace, with the leisure and the gifts necessary to spend their time in singing and dancing, argument, parlour games, and flirtation. The atmosphere is something like what one imagines a seventeenth-century salon to have been. Castiglione stresses the fact that at courts 'many things were done to please the ladies', so that music and poetry flourished. Perhaps Urbino was an exceptional case in this respect, because Duke Guidobaldo was sickly and went to bed early, leaving his wife to preside over the evening discussions. One wonders what the evenings were like in the time of Guidobaldo's father, the famous *condottiere* Federigo. One of the speakers in the dialogue describes other courts, reminiscent of the modern prep school or barrack-room life, where the courtiers throw food at one another or make bets on who can eat the most revolting things.

To turn to Pius II is to come down to earth with a bump. His book is a mixture of literary and moral *topoi* and wry personal observation. If a man seeks pleasure at court, he writes, that man is in for a disappointment. There is music at court, but it is when the prince wants it, not when you want it, and perhaps just when you want to sleep. The servants never bring the food on time, and they whisk the plates away before you have finished. You cannot sleep comfortably because the bedclothes are dirty, there are several others in the same bed, your neighbour coughs all night or pulls the bedclothes off you, or because you are sleeping in the stables. You never know when the court is going to move. You make ready to leave, only to find that the prince has changed his mind. Solitude and quiet are impossible. Whether the prince stands or sits, the courtier always has to stand up. These do not sound like the conditions most likely to stimulate creativity, but they are the conditions in which writers like Ariosto or Bellincione must have worked. Artists could at least escape to the environment of their own workshops, but they too were not allowed to forget that it was their job, together with the fools and midgets, to divert the prince.

It is likely that the arts were affected by two features of Italian political systems which cut across the division into republics and principalities: imperialism and bureaucracy. The growth of the Florentine, Venetian and other empires, the shift from city-state to territorial state, favoured the concentration of wealth and population in the capital, because the country-side was often taxed at higher rates. At the same time, political and economic lines of communication made it likely that an artist would be drawn to the capital of the empire in which he was born. Leonardo Bruni and Vasari came to Florence from Arezzo, Fra Angelico and Castagno both came to Florence from the Mugello. Giorgione came to Venice from Castelfranco; Titian from Cadore; Paris Bordone from Treviso; Bonifazio Veronese from Verona; Giorgio da Sebenico from Dalmatia, then part of the Venetian terraferma; Palma Vecchio from near Bergamo; Coducci again from near Bergamo; and so on. Artists thus came to be concentrated in relatively few centres partly as a result of political forces. Arezzo's or Bergamo's loss was Florence's or Venice's gain, and perhaps that of the world, in that the concentration of gifted men is likely to produce a favourable milieu for artists to learn and work.

The rise of the territorial state encouraged the rise of the bureaucratic mode of domination, since an increase in the numbers of professional civil servants made greater specialization possible. It increased the number of jobs available to the educated layman and thus both reflected and contributed to the secularization of Italian culture. Leonardo Bruni and Bartolommeo Scala were chancellors of Florence; Antonio

Loschi was employed in the chancery of Milan; Machiavelli and Guicciardini were professional civil servants for an important part of their lives; Alberti, Biondo and Valla held posts in the papal bureaucracy; Panormita, Pontano and Valla were civil servants at Naples. The rise of bureaucracy encouraged the rise of humanism, which was a set of ideas well suited to become the ethos of civil servants.[28] For humanists tended to stress the power of the word, the importance of education, merit as against birth, reason as against tradition, letters as against arms, and this world as against the next. The bureaucrat, like the merchant, lived by a rational calculating approach to human problems. This association of humanism with a social group of increasing importance may have contributed to the success of both, and to the changes in world-view which historians think of as characteristically 'Renaissance'.

THE SOCIAL STRUCTURE

One important reason that the trend towards bureaucratic government did not go further was that impersonal administration in the modern sense would have been impossible in what was basically still a face-to-face society. At the end of the period, only two towns, Naples and Venice, had populations over 100,000, the size of Cambridge, England, in 1968. Florence was about 70,000, the size of Bedford; Perugia was about 20,000, the size of Newbury, Berkshire.* In a town of 70,000 people, it was obviously not the case that everyone knew everyone; but at this time the division of towns into quarters still meant a great deal. Florence was divided into four quarters – S. Maria Novella, S. Croce, S. Giovanni, and S. Spirito. Venice was divided into six 'sestieri' – Castello, S. Marco, Cannaregio, S. Polo, S. Croce, and Dorsoduro. Rome was divided into thirteen 'rioni', and so on. These quarters were a focus for religious and political loyalties. Within them, the parish was a meaningful unit, and so often was the street, which might be

---

* These figures, like those on p. 302 below, are extremely rough estimates. Professor David Herlihy, who is now working on the *catasto* records, informs me that 'the true figure of the Florentine population in the fifteenth century probably lies between 40,000 and 70,000 persons.'

dominated by a particular trade. The Florentine woodworkers clustered in two streets, one of which, the present Via Torna-buoni, was then called 'via larga dei legnaiuoli'. In Rome, the goldsmiths clustered in via del Pellegrino. Cities were small enough for the sound of a particular bell to be enough to tell everyone to start work or to stop work or rush to the piazza. In Florence, when a man wanted to transfer funds, he would not write a cheque (though cheques did exist) but would be likely to go to the banker's table and tell him in person what to do. Fifteenth-century commercial law was biased in favour of oral contracts and against written ones. Teaching and learning in universities were essentially oral, 'lectures' really were 'readings' from basic texts, and examination was by 'disputation', the oral defence of a particular proposition or 'thesis'. Official impersonality was made impossible because citizens knew officials in their private roles. A Florentine might know the man who had assessed his taxes, and complain as Cavalcanti did :

> He knows very well that it is impossible for me to pay such an outrageous amount; if he wanted my place, why did he not offer to buy it from me?[29]

The intimate, village quality (as it seems now) of Renaissance society is brought home when one remembers that Guicciardini was held at the font by Ficino, and corresponded with Machiavelli; or reads the discussion about the placing of Michelangelo's *David*, in 1503; thirty men present, including Leonardo, Botticelli, Perugino, Piero di Cosimo, the Sangallos, Andrea Sansovino, Cosimo Rosselli, all recorded in the minutes of the meeting as taking up one another's suggestions.

Yet Italian society was certainly complex enough to split into many groups, to need some kind of classification. Classifications are arbitrary, but they have important consequences; according to the scheme used, some aspects of social reality is made to stand out sharply, but at the price of blurring others which may be no less important.

The working model of the social structure which has been used throughout this book distinguishes five main social groups: the clergy; the nobles; merchants and professional men; artisans and shopkeepers; and finally, peasants. Three of these groups, clergy, nobles and peasants, are the traditional three Estates, and can be defined in legal terms; the other two groups are more like classes, simpler to define in economic terms. But the chief criterion for distinguishing these five groups is not legal or economic, but social: the Weberian concept of a typical 'style of life'. I am not suggesting that there were exactly five sharply defined styles of life in Italy, merely that it is useful to distinguish five. There were social hierarchies and other differences within each group, and a blurring of the frontiers between them. It was possible for a given individual to be a nobleman (because his parents were noble), a cleric (because he had received the tonsure) and a merchant (his actual occupation) and his personal style of life might be a combination of elements from all three groups, though such a combination is unlikely to have been a common one. In the description which follows, I shall try to bring out what is *characteristic* of each group, what makes it different from the rest, even at the expense of presenting the behaviour of the group's average member, insofar as this is known. It is to be regretted that the proportion of the Italian population belonging to each of these five groups cannot be calculated. It may be possible to do this in the near future for much of fifteenth-century Tuscany, but hardly for Italy as a whole.[30]

The clergy have been described in detail already (above, p. 252ff). Here it is only necessary to make three or four points. The legal definition of a cleric was a man who had taken the tonsure, was therefore immune from lay jurisdiction, and who should have been over seven, legitimate and unmarried. A definition in terms of style of life would count as clerics men who performed certain social roles: friar, monk, parish priest, bishop and so on, adding that such men were normally recognizable by their dress. The legal and social definitions of the clergy overlapped but did not coincide; it has been seen that there were many Italians who were legally clerics who lived in the manner of laymen. There was a complex social hierarchy within the clergy: pope, cardinals (not to distinguish different kinds of cardinal), archbishops, bishops, abbots, priests, and so on. In social as opposed to legal terms it is more useful to distinguish the higher clergy as a whole from the lower clergy, and perhaps to make room for a clerical 'middle class' of canons and rectors whose benefices were worth more than a certain amount. But the social history of the Italian clergy remains to be written.[31]

The second major social group was that of the nobility. Legally, a noble was the son of a noble, or a man who had been ennobled by a prince. In Venice, a noble was a man whose family was in the 'golden book', a social register which was closed at the end of the thirteenth century. But in Italy as in England in the period, men accepted the style of life definition and accepted as nobles men who 'lived nobly'. The most important feature of living nobly was not to work; the nobles were a leisure class. 'The unemployed' (*scioperati*) is a term sometimes used to describe the nobles in this period. Machiavelli expanded on the definition, describing gentlemen (*gentiluomini*) as

> Those who live in idleness from the abundant revenues of their possessions, without worrying about agriculture or any other work necessary to gaining a living.[32]

A leisure class has the opportunity to develop more than one style of life, and the Italian nobles took advantages of this opportunity. The different styles are grouped together here because they were practised by men who treated one another as social equals, sometimes by different members of the same family.

The traditional pursuit of the nobleman was war. War had become a business in fifteenth-century Italy, but this did not stop a proportion of the nobility from engaging in war on either an amateur or a professional basis. A famous military leader of the early sixteenth century was Fabrizio Colonna, who came from one of the leading families of the papal states. In Genoa, as in Venice, the nobility had a tradition of naval service, and the great naval *condottiere* Andrea Doria came from one of the chief Genoese families. Castle-guard was an important part of the military way of life, and in Lombardy, for example, castellans tended to be drawn from the old noble families of the duchy. The military way of life seems to have been strongest among the nobles of the South and of the papal states. In both areas nobles still had feudal vassals, *fideles*, men who held their lands in return for military service. It is not surprising to find private warfare still flourishing in both areas;

between the Orsini and the Colonna, for example, or between the counts of Capaccio and Lauria in Calabria in Alfonso's time.

The more peaceable noble had some five or six respectable careers to choose from. He might live on his estate and take a personal interest in its management. Alvise Cornaro the Venetian is the most famous of those who did so; a Calabrian example is that of Luca Sanseverino, duke of S. Marco. The patricians of fifteenth-century Florence did this part-time, spending several months in the country each year. Other nobles relied on their stewards to run the estate and simply came for the hunting – dogs and birds were an important part of the noble style of life. In principalities, an attractive way of life for many nobles was that of courtier. In republics, a leisure class is likely to be the group which occupies unpaid, time-consuming, honourable offices. Some became officials, and many posts in the Milanese bureaucracy were held by members of old noble families, exercising in the name of the prince powers which had once been their own. Ambassadors were very often noblemen. A nobleman might enter the Church, particularly if he had a relative who was a bishop. He might become a lawyer, a career which seems to have become more attractive to the nobles of Milan and Naples and the patriciate of Florence about the year 1500: Gaspare del Maino of Milan is a famous example of the nobleman turned lawyer. Finally, in some parts of Italy it was possible for a nobleman to go into trade, provided that it was wholesale and not retail. This was true not only of Florence and Venice but of Milan; in the late fifteenth century Gian Stefano Brivio, for example, joined with two citizens of Milan to make silks, brocades and cloth of gold and silver, and Bartolomeo Grassi formed an association to trade in ironware. But the nobleman in business seems to have become rarer towards the end of the period.

What held the nobles together as a social group, despite this variety of possible occupations, was their common system of values which was expressed in their way of life. They regarded themselves as the only people capable of 'honour' (*onore*). Honour meant esteem; the qualities which made a man worthy of esteem, such as courage, loyalty and generosity; and the outward signs of esteem, such as titles and offices. This ambiguity in the term played into the hands of the nobles and thus helped maintain the social structure, for it implied that all men with honours were men of honour. Honour could be lost by cowardice, treachery, insult or the adultery of one's wife, but in the last two cases it could be restored by a duel, a formalized mode of aggression which was replacing more disorderly and spontaneous noble combats during the sixteenth century. From the cultural historian's point of view, the most significant element in this constellation of noble qualities is generosity, for this was proved by means of conspicuous consumption, whether on alms, clothes, horses, hospitality or patronage of the arts, especially commissions for palaces and funeral monuments which would bear witness to the wealth and status of the family and make its fame long-lasting, if not eternal.

Stratification within the nobility was important to its members, who included dukes, marquesses, counts, knights, and simple gentlemen. Or, to adopt an economic rather than a legal criterion of stratification (and both criteria were relevant to a man's status) they were divided into large, medium and small landowners.[33]

It remains to discuss those who were neither clergy nor nobles, the men who elsewhere in Europe were usually lumped together into the miscellaneous category, the 'third Estate'.

In the first place, merchants and professional men. 'Merchant' tended to be a rather unspecialized occupation at this period. Such a man might sell goods of very different kinds, both wholesale and retail, and he might act as a banker and an insurance man into the bargain. A man describing himself as a merchant and owning a shop might manage the business himself (as some nobles managed their estates) or he might employ a factor to do this for him. In one sense of the term Lorenzo de'Medici was a merchant, for his fortune came from the Medici business, which included cloth manufacture, the exploitation of the papal alum monopoly, and, above all, banking; but he does not seem to have taken much interest in the running of the business, leaving this to his managers. A man who was brought up to be a merchant would, after learning to read and write, go to an 'abacus school', learning how to calculate discounts and interest, and how to keep accounts, and would then be apprenticed to a merchant, perhaps starting by sweeping the shop, and graduate to working as the firm's representative in Antwerp, Bruges, Lyons or London.

'Professional men' is a useful general term (which was not used in the period) to cover doctors, lawyers, judges, notaries, university teachers (often, but not always, doctors or lawyers), full-time officials such as the staff of chanceries (often with a legal training). A university education, usually in law, was a distinguishing mark of this group. Some notaries went to university in this period, others did not, which makes them somewhat marginal members of this group. It was the lay equivalent of the clergy (at least the educated clergy), with the obvious difference that professional men could bring up their sons to follow them.

It may well be asked whether merchants and professional men are part of the same group. One answer to this question is that social groups do not exist; it is the historian or sociologist who groups people and it would certainly have been possible to divide Italian society into six groups rather than five. Whether this is done or not, some important similarities between merchants and professional men are worth bringing out. They did not work with their hands. They tended to be the best-educated men; they needed literacy. Only a minority of the clergy and the nobles had a similar education, and their status did not depend on it to the same extent. They wore similar clothes, long black gowns, though the clergy wore these too. It is plausible to argue that they had common values, such as an attachment to hard work and a rational, calculating approach to life, but this hypothesis needs to be tested by more empirical research, such as the study of library inventories. They did not have an ethos which was compulsory and protected by sanctions like the ethos of the nobility, but they may have happened to think in similar ways which set them apart from other groups. I have left till last the two most important criteria of group membership: a common consciousness, and intermarriage. When the Florentines spoke of the *popolo grasso*, the fat ones, they tended to mean the members of the seven greater guilds. Five of these were different kinds of merchant, but two, the guilds of the 'judges and notaries' and 'doctors and apothecaries', contained professional men. (Confusingly, the 'doctors and apothecaries' included painters too.) Intermarriage is the best test of whether one social group regards another as its equal, and intermarriage has not been studied systematically to answer this question in the case of Renaissance Italy. My impression, without figures, is that the sons of professional men tended to marry the daughters of merchants, suggesting that professional men were considered somewhat superior. Similarly, it is easy to find examples of merchants who had their sons brought up to be lawyers, as Alciati's father did, but difficult to find lawyers who meant to make merchants of their sons. The lawyer had a better chance of ennoblement. However, stratification within this group was more complex. Merchants, one imagines, were stratified by wealth; again, the study of marriages would test this hypothesis. Among professional men, judges and lawyers took precedence, and notaries came at the bottom. Lawyers were called 'Messer', but notaries merely 'Ser' (hence Brunelleschi was known by contemporaries as 'Filippo di Ser Brunellesco'). Lawyers were often younger sons of nobles, or of ruling families in the cities; notaries were often recent immigrants from the countryside.[34]

It is worth moving from types to reality for a moment to point out the difficulty of classifying the ruling élites of Florence and Venice. Machiavelli put his finger on the problem when he wrote that Venice was ruled by gentlemen, but that they were gentlemen 'more in name than in fact' because their wealth came from trade rather than from land. The same point could be made about Florence. On the one hand it is difficult to call these groups 'noble' because of their interest in trade and industry, their ethos of hard work and thrift, their calculating mentality. On the other hand, it is difficult to call them members of the merchant-professional group, since they ruled empires, engaged in conspicuous consumption, put their names in a golden book (as in Venice) or engaged in the occasional tournament (as in Florence). It is possible to create a new category and call them a 'patriciate', but to do this is not all that useful, because we have to do here not with a new style of life but with a fusion of elements in two others, a little closer to the nobles in Venice, a little closer to the merchants in Florence.

The fourth group distinguished here is that of the artisans and shopkeepers. In many cases there was no distinction between the two; a man might make swords, say, and sell them in the workshop. In other cases the artisan (like many weavers at Lucca, for example) sold all he produced to an entrepreneur who retailed the goods to the public. The great variety of crafts and trades is apparent from the list of the lesser Florentine guilds : the sword-makers, the armourers, the shoemakers, the key-makers, tanners, smiths, masons, carpenters, bakers, butchers, tavern-keepers, oil-sellers. A much longer list could be compiled from the Roman census of *c.* 1526. In one quarter alone, Regio de Ponte, about 8,000 people were employed in about 80 trades and crafts, from the obvious 56 tailors, 36 innkeepers and 34 shoemakers to the water-sellers, mattress-makers, perfumiers, ropemakers, saddlers, spurriers, and two rosary-sellers. It would be interesting to know to what extent all these men had a common 'artisan culture', common attitudes, a common style of life. They all worked with their hands. They all left school early, to be apprenticed. But there were important differences within this group. Some were literate, others were not. There was a crucial economic difference between the masters, small employers who worked in the businesses they owned, and the apprentices and journeymen who worked for them. Some masters were small entrepreneurs, with an extra workshop and equipment which they hired out to poorer workers. Some owned land; 'a piece of land' is often mentioned in the tax returns of Florentine craftsmen, for example Verrocchio. Beccafumi, Moretto da Brescia, Paris Bordone and other painters bought land. There were big differences of wealth and status within the artisan-shopkeeper group. The tax-assessments of Siena in 1509 and 1531 show that the normal assessment for an artisan was from 100 lire to 200 lire. Artists were a little above average; of 17 painters, 16 are assessed at 250 lire (like Beccafumi) or below, and one, Pinturicchio, at 425 lire. But one goldsmith is assessed at 1,400 lire. Among shopkeepers, some *merciai* (clothes-sellers) and *pizzicaioli* (food-sellers) were assessed at 1,000 lire or more, but others below 250 lire. At the bottom of the artisan hierarchy came unskilled workers such as the washers of wool, who had no guild, the men who had participated in the famous rising of the Ciompi in Florence in 1378.

There are a number of people who do not fit easily into this group, nor into the final group, that of the peasants. For example, actors, clowns, undertakers, and teachers of the abc, to quote groups who have in common the fact that they were expressly excluded from the guild of judges and notaries in Florence. There are part-time rural craftsmen. There are domestic servants, a large group (8 per cent of the population of Venice in the later sixteenth century) and probably highly stratified according to their place in the household and the place of the household in society. A still more numerous group is that of the poor, whose misery was recorded when it was exceptional, in time of famine. Da Porto wrote of Vicenza in 1528:

> You cannot walk down the street or stop in a square or a church without multitudes surrounding you to beg for charity; you see hunger written on their faces, their eyes like gemless rings, the wretchedness of their bodies, with skins shaped only by bones.

From the point of view of style of life, it is perhaps sufficient to ask whether all these people were urban or rural, and classify them in the fourth or fifth group according to the answer. Even so there are problems. Some men did rural work in an urban setting, like the numerous gardeners employed in sixteenth-century Rome. Others did urban work in a rural setting, that is, they were full-time craftsmen, blacksmiths for example. Did they identify themselves as peasants or as craftsmen? We do not know. Some groups, notably beggars, soldiers and students, often wandered about between country and town, lacking a fixed place in the community both geographically and socially. The existence of marginal occupations is another reminder that to divide the population into five groups is inevitably to simplify and involves writing about ideal types, not individuals, or even individual occupations.[35]

The last group, the peasants, were the majority of the population but the group the historian knows least about, as well as the group on which the Renaissance made least impact – if, indeed, it made any impact at all. The peasants were very far from being a homogeneous group. Legally, they were divided into the free and the serfs. Serfdom had declined relatively early in Italy, but it had not disappeared altogether. In Friuli, Liguria and Sardinia, serfs still existed in 1420, though serfdom in Friuli disappeared in the later fifteenth century. In practice, even 'free' peasants might find it difficult to leave the land they were working, at least in a period of labour shortage. The commune of Florence ordered in 1415 that

> No peasant (*laborator*) can leave the land he has worked or reject the terms on which he has worked for a year or more without the consent of the landowner (*dominus poderis*); he is bound to work the land on the terms agreed.

Thus it would have been difficult for many peasants to leave for the city and become artists, as Castagno and Beccafumi did. Yet there is no doubt that many did leave, or the *condottieri* would have had no troops; the typical mercenary was a mountain peasant.*

From the economic point of view, peasant society was highly stratified. At the top was a group of kulaks, known as *contadini grassi*, or, in the South, as *borgesi*, who owned more land than they needed to support themselves and their families. They might act as *fictaiuoli*, rural middlemen who leased land from the Church or nobility and subleased it to labourers. One would expect millers and stewards to belong to this group. Below it came the peasants with enough land to support themselves and families; those with some land, but not enough to support themselves; and the *lavoratori*, landless agricultural labourers. Regional research has not gone far enough to tell us what proportion of the peasantry belonged to each group, only that the variation between some villages and others was very great; there were villages where most peasants owned land, and others where almost all the land was in the hands of the rich landlords. There was great variation in the system of land tenure. Land might be leased to the man working it for an indefinite period, for thirty years, or for less. The rent might be paid in money, in kind, or in labour services.

In spite of these differences, there was a common peasant style of life, following the rhythm of the seasons. The labours of the months, as painted on terracotta plaques in the ceiling of Piero de'Medici's study, were as follows: January, felling trees; February, grafting fruit trees; March, pruning vines;

* Professor Herlihy informs me that the Florentine *catasto* 'gives the impression of considerable labour mobility in the countryside'.

April, training vines; May, scything grass; June, reaping corn; July, threshing corn; August, ploughing; September, gathering grapes; October, sowing corn; November, gathering olives; December, digging. What this representation leaves out is craft activity; above all the spinning and weaving, by peasants or their wives, on which the Florentine cloth industry, for example, depended. One imagines, reasoning by analogy, that there was a common peasant culture, folktales, songs and proverbs, a local and magical version of Christianity, with memories of occasional visits to towns on the occasion of great festivals. But even less is known about the thought-world of the Italian peasants of this period than about their economic and social life.[36]

It may be useful to try to sum up economic differences in two tables. In the first place, the pyramid of wealth in Florence, in 1457, as taken from the tax records. The tax consisted of 0·5 per cent of the wealth of each household, after the deduction of allowances.

2 per cent households paid 10 florins or more		source:
16 per cent	2 to 10 florins	de Roover,
54 per cent	5 soldi to 1 florin	*Medici Bank*,
28 per cent households were too poor to pay tax.		p. 45ff

The second table is an attempt to calculate the range of variation in income between different social groups in Florence, Milan and Venice. The standard Florentine coin was the florin (first minted in Florence); the standard Venetian coin was the ducat (first minted in Venice); the standard Milanese coin was the Milanese ducat. To make comparison easier I have converted all these currencies into lire (the 'money of account' used at this time) at rates varying between 4L to 7L to the florin or ducat according to the currency and period. This table may be misleading for several reasons. It does not take account of short-term fluctuations, which were considerable. The averages sometimes cover wide variations. The table does not take account of perquisites, which are incalculable. But it would have been still more misleading not to provide a table at all. The annual figures are sometimes conversions of daily rates: I have multiplied by 250, not 365. I have not made any allowances for changes in prices: the Price Revolution struck Italy at the end of the period, about 1550.[37]

77,000L, great merchant, Venice *c.* 1500
73,500L, great ecclesiastic, Venice *c.* 1500
21,000L, Doge of Venice, *c.* 1500
12,500L, ambassador, Venice, *c.* 1500
 3,750L, captain of infantry, Milan *c.* 1520
 2,500L, well-known professor, Venice *c.* 1500
  900L, secretary in chancery, Venice *c.* 1500
  900L, master shipwright, Venice *c.* 1550
  700L, engineer, Venice *c.* 1500
  600L, branch manager, Medici Bank, Florence, *c.* 1450
  400L, silkweaver, Florence *c.* 1450
  300L, experienced bank clerk, Florence, *c.* 1450
  250L, soldier, Milan *c.* 1520
  250L, court trumpeter, Milan *c.* 1470
  200L, young bank clerk, Florence *c.* 1450
  150L, soldier, Venice *c.* 1500
  125L, silk-weaver, Milan *c.* 1450
  120L, mason or carpenter, Milan *c.* 1450
   75L, labourer, Venice *c.* 1500
   70L, shop-boy, Florence *c.* 1450
   60L, labourer, Milan *c.* 1450
   50L, servant, Venice *c.* 1500 (board included)
   50L, apprentice shipwright, Venice *c.* 1550
   50L, labourer, Florence *c.* 1500
   40L, servant, Florence *c.* 1400 (board included)
   40L, chaplain, Milan *c.* 1500

The difference between the income of the chaplain at the bottom of the table and the richest Venetian cardinal (at 140,000L p.a.) is a difference of 35,000 to one. No doubt there were still richer men in Italy. In the USA *c.* 1900, the difference between the incomes of the richest and the poorest was about 100,000 to one.

Differences in income form one criterion, though only one, for arranging different occupations in a social pyramid. This arrangement is necessary because men in Renaissance Italy, as in other traditional societies, were acutely aware of differences in status, and because the different statuses which different societies attach to such roles as soldier, clerk, merchant, teacher, artist have a great effect on what men of ability in those societies choose to do. But a social hierarchy is not easy to reconstruct. Unlike the modern sociologist, the historian cannot ask the men he studies how they classify themselves or anyone else; he has to make do with the scraps of information that happen to have been recorded. The best evidence comes not from words but from behaviour. Men made reverence to their 'betters' in the street. It was noted as a mark of revolutionary situation in Lucca in 1532 that when the common people passed a noble citizen in the street:

> Not only did they not deign to make him reverence, as is the custom in Lucca to honour the ruling élite (*i grandi del governo*), but they stared at him with anger and contempt.

In Florentine processions, knights walked first, followed by lawyers, then merchants and notaries;; and the processions of the time, given the stress on precedence, may be regarded as materializations of the social hierarchy. Intermarriage makes a good test of whether one family regards another as equal or not. The fact that Lorenzo de'Medici married Clarice Orsini, from one of the great Roman noble families, can be taken as a sign that the Medici had 'arrived'. But intermarriages have not been studied systematically from the point of view of the reconstitution of the Italian social hierarchy. A more careful examination of the typical income of particular occupations would also furnish valuable clues.

Until more systematic studies have been made, any account of the Italian social hierarchy must remain impressionistic; here is one such impression. At the top, the higher clergy and the titled nobility. Then the gentlemen and patricians, irrespective of their occupation. In the next place, lawyers who were not nobles, followed by other professional men – officials, doctors, professors, notaries. Cathedral canons and prosperous merchants would have a place about here. Then lesser merchants and the most prosperous of the master craftsmen, such as goldsmiths. Then, perhaps, the rich peasants; but the rural and urban worlds did not meet often enough for this to be certain. Then the majority of master-craftsmen, the schoolmaster, the chaplain; the journeymen, apprentices and middle peasants; at the bottom the unskilled, urban and rural, and the poor.

To understand a given society it is important to know how open it is; the amount of social mobility. On the answer to this question depends some explanations of the Renaissance. One would expect to find a relatively mobile society associated with respect for achievement and for innovation and with high creativity. But was Italy in general and Florence in particular a more mobile society than most others? Individual cases are striking. There is Giovanni Campana, a shepherd boy who became a university lecturer in Perugia, and was made a bishop by Pius II. There is Scala, the miller's son who became chancellor of Florence. Scala's coat of arms figured a ladder; his motto was 'gradatim' (by degrees). These were obvious heraldic puns on his name, but also an appropriate symbol for the socially mobile intellectual. Scala's *Apologia* discusses great men of humble birth. Less spectacular to contemporaries, but of still more interest to moderns, are the peasants turned artists, such as Beccafumi and Castagno. However, there is no precise information about the rate of social mobility in Italy; this is particularly unfortunate in a field where the historian who does not make a quantitative statement says virtually nothing at all, for no society has zero social mobility, and no society has perfect social mobility, which would mean that there was no chance of predicting a man's status from that of his father. All societies are somewhere in between these two poles, so that the point is, precisely where. The sources give the impression, which systematic research will one day confirm or deny, that for Europe in this period, North and Central Italy, especially Florence, were extremely open societies. This is related to the importance of the towns, where the birth rate was lower; the towns maintained their population by recruitment from the countryside, and this necessarily resulted in social mobility. Hence the competitiveness, the envy, and the emphasis on achievement which was characteristic of the Florentine social character (above, p. 232). A second impression, equally strong, is that Florentine and indeed Italian society was becoming less open. In Florence, in the later fifteenth century, the merchant patriciate was crystallizing into a nobility. No new families were let into the group led by the Medici and including (to mention only families which married into the Medici in the fifteenth century) the Albizzi, the Bardi, the Pazzi, the Ridolfi, the Salviati, the Strozzi and the Tornabuoni. These were the 'best people', the *ottimati*. Historians have noticed a similar closing of the ranks in other cities, such as Lucca, Pistoia, Padua and Brescia. With this apparent decrease in social mobility went a change in the life-style of the Florentine and Venetian patriciates; a gradual withdrawal from trade which made them more like the European nobilities than they had been.[38]

Society can be seen as a pyramid of strata; it can also be seen as divided into 'classes' in the sense of 'conflict groups'; haves and have-nots, rulers and ruled, exploiters and exploited. This too was a contemporary view of society, not often explicit but revealed in moments of conflict between town and country, landlord and tenant, employer and employee, noble and commoner. The Venetian patrician Priuli took conflict between town and country as axiomatic, writing that the peasants of the *terraferma* were pro-Venetian precisely because the citizens of the subject towns were anti-Venetian, 'since citizens and peasants are always contrary to one another' (*essendo li cittadini e villani contrarii sempre l'uno a l' altro*). A number of anonymous printed poems of the early sixteenth century remark on the ignorance, filthy habits, malice and general unreliability of the peasants; 'don't trust the peasant' (*de villan non te fidare*) is the refrain of one of them. The villein was a villain. Ruzzante's comedies about rural life in the country round Padua appealed to the same prejudices. In fact, the countryman had better reason to hate the townsman than the other way round, for he tended to pay higher taxes, imposed by the town government, which was also likely to force down grain prices to benefit citizens at the expense of peasants.

Town versus country easily passes into landlord versus peasant, since many citizens of Florence and Venice, to mention only these two, owned land in the *contado*. The evidence of peasant hostility to landlords is in actions rather than words. In 1438, for example, the local peasants attacked Ravenna. In 1455, it was the turn of Pistoia; in 1462 of Piacenza. Particularly violent was the peasant war in Friuli in 1511. At Udine there was a massacre of noblemen, and in the countryside a number of castles were burned down. In most cases one has to guess at the grievances of the peasants, helped out by texts like a surviving song which attacks the share-cropping system in Tuscany:

Noi ci stiàm tutto l'anno a lavorare
E lor si stanno al fresco a meriggiare;
Perchè s'ha dar lor mezza ricolta,
Se n'abbiam la fatica tutta noi?

(We work all year, while they lie in the shade; if all the work is ours, why should half the harvest be theirs?)

In the towns, while there was no movement in this period as spectacular as that of the Ciompi in Florence in 1378, there were risings of workmen against employers. There were such disturbances in Florence in 1435 and 1464. In Venice in 1460 there was a clash between the caulkers and the ship-owners. In Lucca in 1532 there was a revolt of the silk-weavers, the *straccioni*, which developed into a general conflict between rich and poor, rulers and ruled, because the great silk-merchants in fact governed the city. Cities were the scene of what Machiavelli called 'the deep but natural conflict between the commoners and the nobles', because the nobles wanted to command, and the commoners did not want to obey. Cavalcanti is another Florentine witness of the 'hatred between the patricians and the lower classes', in which he was certainly not on the side of what he called the 'beastly multitude'. The contemptuous references to 'vile' and 'mechanical' occupations, so common in sixteenth-century Italy, are as much rationalizations of class conflict as anything, and a sign that the nobles were becoming more conscious of their nobility.

It is thus not difficult to find instances of social conflict which did not follow the lines of the three Estates, as well as some which did. There were conflicts between rich clergy and poor clergy, which sometimes led the poor clergy to take part in popular risings. But Italy in this period was not a class society, because conflict groups based on economic interests were not dominant. At least equally important was the old conflict between clergy and laity and the rivalry between one family and another, one guild and another, one town and another. The 'vertical' tie between patron and client mattered as much as the 'horizontal' tie between two artisans or two peasants. Patronage in this wide sense of the term sometimes affected the arts; it explains how Beccafumi, Castagno, Vasari and others from humble backgrounds got their start in life. Patronage was an important force working against the bureaucratic mode of government; an official was likely to bestow the subordinate offices which were often in his gift to his junior relatives, to his 'familiars' (members of his household) or to other clients of his. The importance of this system of patronage here on earth, in Church and State, helps explain the importance of the system of patron saints among the mental structures of Renaissance Italians. Indeed, some of the civil disturbances just mentioned can be explained – in part – in terms of patronage and its characteristic political organization the 'faction' (*setta, parte*). The civil war in Friuli in 1511 began as a conflict between two factions, the *Zamberlani* and the *Strumieri*. The first supported Venice, the second the Emperor; but the conflict between the factions also expressed the rivalry of two leading local families, the Savorgnan and the Torriani. The peasants were on the side of the *Zamberlani*, so their attack on the palace of the Torriani, leaders of the *Strumieri*, can be interpreted in factional terms; but they also sacked the castles of some nobles who were members of the same faction as they were. Faction was well known in fifteenth-century Italian politics. In Perugia the Oddi fought the Baglioni; in Pistoia the Panciatichi fought the Cancellieri; in Florence there were the Medici and Uzzano factions early in the fifteenth century and the supporters and opponents of Savonarola late in the century. It was local rivalries which still gave substance to the venerable party terms 'Guelf' and 'Ghibelline' in the sixteenth century. Bergamo, for example, was still divided in this way. In Genoa, the distinction between Blacks and Whites (originally Guelph and Ghibelline) still mattered; offices were divided equally between the two groups. Historians have tended to lament faction as a cause of civil war. It might equally well be argued that faction was part of a system of cross-cutting allegiances which sometimes broke down but often played an important part in preserving the social equilibrium.[39]

Yet another focus of allegiance was the family. For Guicciardini, the eternal glory of 'our family' (*casa nostra*) was one of the two things he declared he wanted most in the whole world. Michelangelo's letters are full of references to his efforts to help his family. The object of such allegiance was not just the nuclear or conjugal family of husband, wife and children, which a late twentieth-century Englishman is likely to associate with the term 'family'. It was an extended family which included brothers and sisters, uncles and aunts, nephews and nieces, grandparents and cousins; the 'house' (*casa, domus*), or the 'relations' (*parentado*). It was a particular type of extended family; the agnatic. That is, relationships were traced legally through the male line, excluding in-laws or mother's brothers. Socially the importance of women was that they linked 'houses' by the bonds of affinity. Guicciardini tells us that he married a Salviati because an alliance with such a powerful house would advance his career. The 'house' was a group of people with the same surname, descended from a common ancestor. The distinction between such a house and a family in the modern sense emerges clearly from a document from sixteenth-century Lucca about a tomb constructed 'for certain families of the house of Pagnini' (*per quasdam familias domus Pagnine*). The happiness of individual members was often sacrificed to the good of the house. Whom a girl married, and whether she married (since convents were cheaper than husbands) were collective, not individual, decisions. Wills sometime instruct executors whom a daughter is to marry. In this period marriages without the consent of the parents were not valid according to canon law. Property was primarily family property; there is a story of a dying man telling the friars around his bed that his property was not his to give them, because his father gave it him in trust to pass on to his children.

The importance of such extended families in this period varied with the region and the social group. It has been customary for historians to emphasize the large household idealized by Alberti, and certainly documentary evidence of households of 17 or even 40 persons can be found. But recent research on fifteenth-century Tuscany has shown that the average size of household was quite small. In Florence in 1427 mean household size was 3·75, in Arezzo it was 3·5, in Pistoia it was 3·6. In rural districts it was somewhat larger: 5·1 in the area round Florence. Household size is only one kind of evidence for the importance of the extended family; links between separate but neighbouring households may be strong. But these figures are enough to make one wonder whether the Italian system was not like the traditional Chinese family system in which everyone idealized the extended family but only the upper classes generally achieved it. The house was the group of people with the same surname; surnames were not common among peasants or even artisans, which suggests that their family sense was not 'extensive'.

It is from the nobility and merchants that most of the evidence comes for the importance of the *casa* during the Renaissance. A dramatic example is that of the nobility of Genoa. In fifteenth-century Genoa there were some forty-odd noble houses, called *alberghi*. The Spinola di San Luccà numbered 81 households in 1465, the Doria numbered 59, the Lomellini 46, the Grimaldi 41. The members of an *albergo* bore the same surname and the same coat of arms; so they were essentially a lineage, a group of agnates. They were not in fact all blood relations, because adoption was permissible and because clients, servants, and even slaves were considered part of the *albergo*, and might use its surname, though they did not have voting rights at family councils. The group lived in separate households but in the same quarter. They lived near because one of the functions of the *albergo* was to defend its members; it was an alliance in the military sense. It was also an economic unit. Taxes were levied on the *albergo* as a whole, not on the household which made it up, and funds were held in common to dower girls and send young men to study. The *albergo* was also a political unit which was ruled by governors who settled internal disputes and represented the group in dealing with the outside world. Such a highly-organized lineage is reminiscent of South China or West Africa in this century.

The Genoese *albergo* was not typical of Italian family organization, even among the nobility, but at once compensated for and contributed to the weakness of the Genoese commune. Its equivalent in Florence, the *consortería*, was less important in the fifteenth century than it had been a hundred years before. Individual magnates often left their *consortería*, changing their name and coat of arms and going to live in another quarter, so as not to be held responsible by the commune for the violent actions of their kinsmen. In Florence brothers often lived apart, owned property separately and were taxed separately. Commercial companies might be organized on a family basis but they did not need to be. It was still possible to list the great 'houses' (*casate*) in Florence in 1494. The Altoviti had 66 men (presumably corresponding to the Genoese 'households'); the Albizzi had 65; the Rucellai had 60; the Strozzi 53. The structure still existed, even if the functions had been attenuated. In Lucca the decline of the great house was also apparent. By 1520 there was only one such grouping left, that of the Poggi, feared by the other members of the governing élite on account of its numbers and cohesion, and forced to change its surname after an unsuccessful rising in 1522. In Siena the lineage seems to have retained more importance. In the early sixteenth century, such old noble families as the Piccolomini (Pius II's family) and the Tolomei tended to form *consorterie*, to cluster in a particular quarter in nearby palaces and to be assessed together for tax purposes. In between the Genoese and Florentine patterns came the Venetian *fraterna*. In the fifteenth century in Venice, among the patricians, brothers tended to live together and the basic unit of business life was the family partnership. But the *fraterna* lacked the formal organization and the political and military functions of the *albergo*, just as the Venetian state was more powerful than the Genoese.

Certain major regional variations are clear. There is still room for argument about the precise importance of the lineage and especially about its political function. Its importance is implied by the fact that in Florence there were laws in force throughout the period which kept the chief offices from being filled by more than one man from the same *casata*. The political activities of a single household might lead to reprisals against the whole lineage; all the Pazzi suffered as a result of the conspiracy of a few of them. On the other hand, it is possible to find brothers on opposite sides in Florentine politics; when Filippo Strozzi opposed the Medici, Alfonso Strozzi supported them. This kind of division might be no more than a family insurance policy; in 1510, during the war between Venice and the Emperor, one Veronese nobleman confessed as much:

We are four brothers; two with the Emperor and two with the Venetians. If the Emperor wins, we will save our possessions, and if the Venetians win, the other two will.

In other cases, conflict between branches of one family was obviously serious. In Perugia in 1460, for example, Braccio Baglioni murdered his cousins Galeotto and Pandolfo. The 24 Baglioni households of 1511 cannot be regarded as a political unit, whereas the 59 Doria households of 1465 can. The absence of primogeniture was likely to lead to quarrels over the division of property. Giovanni de'Medici's property passed to his two sons jointly. Two generations later there was still a certain coolness between the two Lorenzos, cousins, about the way the property had been divided.

One reason for the importance of family groupings as compared to the individual (in the age of Burckhardt's 'individualism') was that individuals were expendable. Renaissance Italy, like most traditional societies, had a high birth-rate and a high death-rate. It was normal, though tragic, for children not to survive infancy. Pius II's family offers a dramatic example; his mother Vittoria produced 18 children, of whom only three survived to adulthood. As for general trends, in Pistoia in 1427, there were 3,364 children aged four years or less for 2,877 women of child-bearing age, so fertility was, by modern standards, remarkably high. It would be interesting to know whether this was a short-term trend, the reaction to the plague of 1423, or the normal pattern for Tuscany at that time.[40]

The Italian social structure as described in this section touches the arts at many points. The importance of the aristocratic lineage and the value set on its cohesion helps explain the importance of the family chapel and its tombs, the focus of 'ancestor worship'. No ancestors, no lineage. The fact that the family was, in all probability, rather less cohesive in Florence than elsewhere helps explain Renaissance 'individualism' both in the sense of self-consciousness and in that of competitiveness. The ambiguous status of the painter, the musician, and even sometimes of the humanist, turns out to be part of a general social problem, that of accommodating in the social structure, as the division of labour progressed, all roles other than those of priest, knight and peasant – those who prayed, fought and worked – the only roles which the traditional picture of society admitted. If the status of the artist was uncertain, so, if to a lesser degree, was that of the merchant. But Florence and Venice were cities of merchants and shopkeepers, and it is probably not coincidence that it was in these cities that the artist was accepted most easily. It was probably easier for achievement-oriented merchant cultures to recognize the worth of artists than for birth-oriented military cultures like France, Spain, or Naples. To put it another way; in Italy, where the nobles were no longer great fighters, and the clergy no longer very holy, there were more opportunities for civilian laymen such as the lawyer, the humanist and the artist than there were elsewhere.

ECONOMIC AND GEOGRAPHICAL BACKGROUND

The population of Italy in 1540 was something like nine million or a little more. As for the situation in 1420, there is really no basis for a reasonable guess, beyond saying that it was probably smaller. A likely pattern is that of a fairly steady growth of population between the 1440s and the 1520s, then a drastic fall during the plague of 1527–31, and finally a recovery. The regional distribution of the population was approximately as follows:

The South	3,600,000
Papal States	1,600,000
Veneto	1,600,000
Lombardy	750,000
Tuscany	600,000
Piedmont	600,000
Liguria	400,000

(total adds to 9,150,000, a speciously precise figure)

An important social fact about this population was the extent to which it was urban. From our point of view overwhelmingly rural, from the point of view of contemporaries Italy was an incredibly urban society. In Italy about 1550, 40 towns or so had a population of 10,000 or more. About half of these had a population of 25,000 or more; in the rest of Europe, from Lisbon to Moscow, there were probably no more than another 20 towns of this size. Seven towns had a population of 60,000 or more – Naples, Venice, Milan, Palermo, Florence, Genoa, Bologna. About 26 per cent of the Veneto was urban, and about the same proportion of the population of Tuscany. Only Flanders is likely to have had a higher proportion of townsmen. However, the historian should be cautious in talking about a movement of 'urbanization' in the fifteenth and sixteenth centuries. Of the bigger towns, Florence, Naples, Venice and Rome all grew very considerably during the period; Naples numbered about 40,000 people in 1450, but about 210,000 a century later. Florence had 40,000 people in 1427, and perhaps 70,000 a century later. But it is unlikely that the urban population generally grew at the expense of the rural. In the fifteenth century, in Lombardy at least, the population was rising in the countryside rather than in the towns. The greater cities were growing at the expense of the smaller. Venice, for example, grew at the expense of other towns in the Veneto, and Florence at the expense of other towns in Tuscany. Even so, Florence in this period never topped 70,000, so far as we know, compared to its population of about 100,000 in the early fourteenth century. Two more qualifications to the picture of urbanization in Renaissance Italy are necessary. The first is that the peak period of urban growth was as far back as the years 1150–1200. The second is that, as the figures in the table show, the whole movement is a miniature one compared to the growth of towns in nineteenth-century Europe. In 1550, in a population of about nine million, only three-quarters of a million lived in towns of 50,000 people or more.

Naples	210,000	Lucca	25,000
Venice	160,000	Messina	25,000 (1505)
Milan	70,000	Piacenza	25,000
Palermo	70,000	Siena	25,000
Florence	60,000 (70,000 in 1520)	Bergamo	20,000
Genoa	60,000 (1530)	Parma	20,000
Bologna	60,000 (1570)	Perugia	20,000
Verona	50,000	Trapani	20,000
Rome	45,000 (55,000 in 1526)	Taranto	20,000
Ferrara	40,000	Pavia	15,000
Mantua	40,000 (1559)	Modena	15,000
Brescia	40,000	Turin	15,000
Cremona	35,000	Catania	15,000
Lecce	35,000 (1561)	Nicosia	15,000
Padua	30,000	Udine	15,000
Vicenza	30,000	Castro-giovanni	15,000

Italy in 1550: towns of 15,000 and over
Source: Beloch vol. 3, especially p. 327 ff. Figures to nearest 5,000

The relatively great size and number of Italian towns is obviously linked with the relatively great importance of merchants, professional men, craftsmen and tradesmen in the Italian social structure. But why were towns so important? In the short-term, towns maintained their importance by their economic policies. Cities often had political control of the countryside around them, and enforced at the expense of that countryside a policy of cheap food, mitigated only by smuggling. At the same time, the countryside was forced to pay more than its share of taxation, which must have been an incentive for the more prosperous peasants to emigrate to the city. Citizens might also have legal privileges which countrymen lacked. In the sixteenth century, pregnant women used to travel to Lucca from the *contado* so that their children would be born in the city. But, of course, these policies do not explain how the cities came to grow up where they did in the first place. The siting of important Italian towns naturally owed much to the sea, rivers, and the heritage of Roman roads. Genoa, Venice, Naples and Palermo are all seaside towns. Pavia and Cremona are on the Po, Pisa and Florence on the Arno. The Roman Via Emilia, still followed by the railway, links Piacenza, Parma, Modena, Bologna, Imola, Faenza, Forlì and Rimini. These geographical factors do not provide the whole explanation either. Towns develop in response to demands from other places, either their immediate surroundings or more distant areas, because they perform services for those places. In pre-industrial Europe, it is useful to distinguish three types of service and three types of city. In the first place, the commercial city, usually a port; Venice and Genoa are obvious examples. The hinterland they served was not just the Veneto and Liguria respectively; in a sense it was the whole of Europe, because Venetian and Genoese merchants were middlemen in the trade between Europe and the East, and had, until the Portuguese began to use the Cape route, no serious competitors. In the second place, there was the craft-industrial city, such as Florence or Milan. In the third place, there was the capital. Naples and Rome are examples, the centres of lay and clerical bureaucracies respectively. In the case of Naples, the hinterland for the 'services' provided was the Kingdom of Naples or in the reign of Alfonso of Aragon, his whole empire. In the case of Rome, the hinterland was sometimes the papal

States, sometimes the Roman Catholic world. Rome was, as its contemporary critics remarked, 'a shop for Christ's things (*una bottega delle cose di Cristo*); its invisible exports were indulgences and dispensations. Whether citizens, subjects and Christians saw the masses of officials in Rome and Naples as providing services or as parasites is, of course, not the issue here; the point is simply to explain the growth of cities. Florence and Venice also had officials, and Rome also had all the kinds of artisan mentioned in the 1526 census, but these are not the reasons why they grew. The largest craft in sixteenth-century Rome was that of the tailors, who worked not for export but for the city population itself.[41]

Industry, trade, and agriculture. The description which follows concentrates on the larger towns at the expense of the smaller ones and of the countryside, because of the cultural importance of those larger towns.

In Lombardy the chief industries were arms, cloth, silk and building. 'Arms' meant swords, suits of armour, and cannon. Brescia and Milan were the chief centres of manufacture; a Venetian ambassador commented that the Milanese 'always wanted war in order to dispose of their products' (*per dar spazamento a le robe sue*). The iron ore came from the hills behind Brescia and Bergamo. Some of the finished products were exported outside Italy, to South Germany for example. The industry reached its height during the fifteenth century, to decline as a result of competition from Nuremberg and later as a result of changing methods of warfare; but locksmiths remained important in Milan and artistic ironwork increased in importance. The second important Lombard industry was cloth-making. The leading towns were Milan, Como and Cremona, the last town specializing in fustian, a fabric made from cotton woven on a linen warp. Some of the raw materials came from the backs of sheep pastured in the mountains of North Lombardy, some from England, some from South Italy. Like the armaments industry, the Lombard cloth industry began to decline about 1500. Its place was taken by silk, an industry which had been encouraged by the dukes of Milan in the fifteenth century, who had ordered the planting of mulberry trees and given tax privileges to immigrant manufacturers, but which became really important to the economy of Lombardy only in the sixteenth century. The building industry was also a local speciality, and Lombard masons could be found at work in many parts of Italy. A famous example is Pietro Lombardo, from Carona on Lake Lugano, master mason of the doge's palace at Venice and founder of a dynasty of architects and sculptors. There are many others. Masons from the Lugano valley were at work in Siena in the early sixteenth century, and in Lucca most of the building was done by Lombards.[42]

Venice was much less of an industrial city than Milan, but the manufacture of glass, ships and books was important there all the same. Glass was an old Venetian industry, which had moved outside the city to Murano about 1300 to minimize the risk of fire. In the earlier fifteenth century, products tended to be utilitarian; for example, phials, mirrors and spectacles. In the later fifteenth century, luxury products such as drinking glasses and chandeliers came to dominate the industry. Shipbuilding was another traditional Venetian industry, giving employment to some 6,000 craftsmen in 1420. The wood usually came from the Dolomites. Within the industry there was considerable division of labour; woodcutters, sawyers, shipcarpenters, house-carpenters (who built the cabins), caulkers who fastened the timbers, caulkers who filled the seams, oarmakers, mast-makers and pulley-makers, not forgetting the stevedores who moved things about in the shipyards, or the ironsmiths, or the sail-makers, usually women, headed by a 'mistress of the sail-makers'. In the field of printing, from the 1490s to about 1520 Venice was the chief city in Europe, both for quantity and quality. The Aldine press has gone down into history, but quite a number of other presses, such as that of the Gioliti, were famous in their day. At the end of the period, the Venetian cloth-industry shot into importance. Whereas in 1516 only some 1,300 odd 'pieces' of cloth were produced, by 1540 the amount had risen to 7,000. Other towns in the Veneto such as Padua and Verona had a longer tradition of cloth-making.

In the fifteenth century, Venice was the greatest merchant city in the world. In the early fifteenth century, she exported 10 million ducats' worth of goods a year. Much of this trade was with the Levant, and especially with Alexandria and Beirut. The Venetians imported spices (such as pepper), cotton, potash and silk, and in return exported cloth (English and Italian), making up the balance with silver coins specially minted for the purpose. About 1500, 2½ million pounds of spices came to Venice from Alexandria every year, and 300,000 ducats, besides merchandise, went back in return. Most of the spices were bought to re-export westwards. Trade with the Empire, by a land route through Friuli and over the Alps, was important in the Venetian economy; hence the building of the 'Germans' Warehouse' (*Fondaco dei Tedeschi*) which Giorgione and Titian decorated early in the sixteenth century. The merchants of Augsburg, Nuremberg and Bruges all bought spices from Venice, again mainly for resale. In the later fifteenth century, Venetian trade had to face two major threats. The first was the western advance of the Turks, which damaged the Levant trade as well as involving the Venetians in expensive wars. The second threat, to Mediterranean trade in general and to Venice in particular, was the Portuguese discovery of the Cape route to the Indies. By 1505 the Venetian government was concerned enough to set up a committee to study this problem. One Venetian response to shrinking trade was to expand the cloth-industry; another was to invest more heavily in land, a trend which underlies the rise of the villa in the Veneto in the age of Palladio.[48]

Like Venice, Genoa was predominantly a trading city, but here again there were local industries, of which the most important were silk, cloth, arms, ships, and paper. Genoese silks had an international reputation, and Genoese silkmakers were also in demand. Louis XI, for example, tried to attract them to France. Silk-making was one of the most specialized industries in Europe at this time. At Genoa, when the raw silk arrived (usually from Grenada) it went through six main processes, each of which was a specialized occupation. The silk was wound on to reels by a *faccitrice*; it was spun by a *filatore*; it was boiled, to remove the gum, by a *cocitore*; then it went to the warper, the *orditore*; then to the weaver, the *testore*; finally to the dyer, the *tintore*. Genoese silk came in a variety of colours and textures. Different craftsmen specialized in the weaving of brocade, damask, samite, taffeta and velvet. The silk might be painted by specialist silk-painters, but the black silk was the most famous Genoese export, produced for a market of widows, clerics and officials. The arms, ship-building and paper-making industries were all rural. Iron from Elba was taken to forges at Voltri, Varazze and still smaller places, to be made into cannon and suits of armour. The ship-building industry was dispersed along the Ligurian coast, at Sampier-darena, Savona and elsewhere; and the paper-mills clustered round Voltri.

Tax records show that the great days of Genoese trade were in the thirteenth century, not the fifteenth, but Genoa was still an important commercial power. There was the grain trade, for example. Genoese merchants imported grain from a wide variety of places: from Andalusia, from the Black Sea region, from Flanders, from North Africa and from Provence. Some of this grain was consumed in Genoa itself, but most of it was re-exported to other parts of Italy, and some was even sent back to Spain. Salt was exported to Milan, Nice and elsewhere; Lombardy and France were also important customers for Genoese-made silks and suits of armour. In the course of the fifteenth century, Genoese trading interests began to shift west-wards. It was not so much the fall of Constantinople that was responsible as the fall of Caffa, the famous Genoese trading post on the Black Sea. As the Turks advanced, so Genoa's trade with France and Spain began to replace her trade with the East. The Genoese imported wool and raw silk from Spain; they shipped marble from Carrara, in Tuscany, to Spain; the Genoese Columbus discovered the New World for Spain; and at the end of the period, Genoese bankers were becoming essential to Spanish government finance, a role they retained till the seventeenth century.[44]

Florence was the Italian industrial town par excellence, and cloth-making her chief industry, well ahead of such rivals as silk, wood-working, goldsmith's work and stone-dressing. A description of Florence in the later fifteenth century lists the numbers of workshops as follows: 270 for woollen cloth, 84 for wood-carving and inlay, 83 for silk, 74 for workers in gold (goldsmiths and gold-beaters) and 54 for stone-dressers. From the art historian's point of view, the economic importance of what we call the 'applied arts' is significant. From the point of view of the economic historian, it is cloth which deserves most attention. Cloth-making was the industry in which the division of labour was most highly developed. Contemporary treatises distinguished some twenty-odd steps in the process of turning a fleece into a piece of cloth, and most of these stages involved a specialized occupation. First the fleeces were beaten with willows by the *battitore*; then the wool was sorted by the *sceglitore*; then washed by the *lavatore*; beaten again by the *battilano*; oiled and combed by the *petinatore*, or carded by the *scardassatore*; spun by the *filatrice*, usually a woman; woven into cloth by the *tessitore*; its knots removed by the *dizzeccolare*; the cloth washed by the *purgatore*; fulled by the *calcatore*; stretched by the *tiratore*; napped by the *garzatore*; sheared by the *cimatore*; dyed by the *tintore*; mended by the *emendatore*.

Cloth-production naturally involved the Florentines in trade. The marketing of cloth as well as its manufacture was controlled by the wool-guild, the *Lana*. The *Seta*, or silk-guild, did the same for silk. But there was a third guild, the *Calimala*, which imported cloth from France and Flanders, arranged for it to be 'finished' (that is, napped, sheared, dyed and mended) and re-exported it. Florence became more of a trading power in the course of the fifteenth century. The Florentines bought the port of Livorno from Genoa, took over the port of Pisa, set up the 'Consuls of the Sea' and moved into the Levant trade. By 1472 there were 51 Florentine agents in three Turkish towns alone, in Adrianople (Edirne), Bursa and Istanbul. There were sizeable colonies of Florentines in Naples, where they had a resident consul; in Lyons, the chief market for Florentine silk; in Antwerp and in Seville. But Florentine trade still did not equal that of Venice and Genoa.[45]

In Rome and Naples, and generally in the States of the Church and in the South, industry was much less important than in the North, and the import-export trade was mainly in the hands of foreigners; Catalans, Florentines, Genoese, and others. When, in the mid-fifteenth century, alum mines were discovered at Tolfa, in the Papal States, it was to the Medici that the running of the alum business was confided. Even the pope's bankers came from outside the Papal States; the Medici at one time, the Sienese Agostino Chigi at another. The one export industry in the pope's dominions apart from alum was the paper-making industry at Bologna, which helps explain why Bologna was more populous than Rome.

The Italians produced the typical Mediterranean combination of grain, olives and wine. Fruit-growing was important in some areas, and rice and maize could also be found. Within the period two opposite trends are visible. In the Po valley, agriculture prospered. In Central and South Italy, it was gradually declining.

Although both Lombardy and the Veneto were mountainous towards the North (Bergamo and Belluno, for example), most of these two regions coincided with the Po valley, one of the great plains of Europe, fertile and with a well-distributed rainfall. In the course of the fifteenth century, canals were dug in Lombardy for the purpose of irrigating the land and waste land was brought into cultivation. By the year 1500, in the area between Pavia and Cremona, some 85 per cent of the land was under cultivation, an extremely high proportion for the time, when marshes and woods were much more widespread than they are today. Dairy farming was becoming important, and in the fifteenth century, Lombard butter was exported to Rome. The Venetian tradition had been 'to cultivate the sea and leave the land alone', but in the later fifteenth century, Venetians were investing in property on the *terraferma*, and improving the estates they had bought. Alvise Cornaro is the man best known for his interest in what he called 'the enterprise so important for this state : to bring waste places into cultivation', but he was far from being the only patrician to think in this way.

South of the Po valley the picture was less rosy. In Tuscany, though the hilly terrain restricted agriculture, the interior valleys were fertile. The Valdarno was best known for grain, the Valdichiana for wine, the Mugello for fruit, and the Lucca region for olives. But in the fifteenth century, land in southern Tuscany was going out of cultivation, perhaps a result of the decline in the population of Florence. Between 1300 and 1500, and mainly in the fifteenth century, 10 per cent of the villages of Tuscany disappeared. Further south, the rocky terrain and the low rainfall in the growing season have always been obstacles to a prosperous agriculture. These permanent obstacles should not be exaggerated; the area round Naples was well known for its fruit, Apulia was called 'the granary of Italy', Sicily was known for its grain and sweet wines, and the Kingdom of Naples as a whole exported grain, olive oil and wine to Spain, Venice and elsewhere. But Southern agriculture was slowly declining thanks to competition from German grain, Portuguese wine (from the Madeiras, colonized in the early fifteenth century) and Lombard butter (an alternative to olive oil). There was a gradual shift from arable to pasture, encouraged by Alfonso of Aragon, and accompanied by a decline in population. As in sixteenth-century England, the sheep were eating up the men. A similar trend from grain to wool can be seen in the Roman Campagna. Noble landowners like the Colonna encouraged the conversion of arable to pasture, to keep food prices up by keeping production down. The popes, from Sixtus IV to Clement VII, opposed this policy in the interests of the consumer, and tried – by decree – to encourage the cultivation of grain. Although 25 per cent of the villages in the province of Rome had disappeared between 1300 and 1500, the Roman Campagna was able to supply the city with food until the end of the sixteenth century.

Changes in the countryside were obviously connected with changes in the towns. To maintain Italy's high urban population, it was necessary for many farmers to produce for the market. The concentration in Venice of some 160,000 people who did not grow their own food entailed the commercialization of agriculture not only in the Veneto but in Mantua, in the Marches, even, perhaps, in Apulia. The commercialization of agriculture went furthest in Lombardy, where the Visconti and Sforza rulers encouraged change, and land passed from rentiers to entrepreneurs, from traditionalists to innovators. Share-cropping spread during the period, in Tuscany for example, which suggests that more and more landlords were willing to think like businessmen. Italian cloth exports involved the growing of woad for the market in Lombardy, as well as the keeping of sheep in Tuscany, in the Roman Campagna, and in the South.[46]

It would be fascinating – if it were only possible – to study the Italian economy in fully quantitative terms; to calculate the Gross National Product and the different regional products, to calculate the average income per head and its variations, to discuss the balance of payments between Italy and the rest of the world, or between one region and another. From this we could discover who ultimately footed the bill for the Florentine Renaissance: the Frenchmen or Neapolitans who bought Florentine cloths and silks, the woolcombers and weavers who helped produce them, or the sharecroppers of Tuscany. In practice, it is impossible to go beyond fairly vague statements about the Italian economy as a whole (to use this convenient modern abstraction). It looks as if Italy had a favourable balance of trade with Western Europe, but an unfavourable balance with the East. It also seems that the South of Italy was exchanging food and raw materials, especially wool and raw silk, for the manufacturers of the North, and that this trade was accentuating the already considerable social differences between the two halves of the peninsula.

Another intriguing and essentially quantitative question is that of Italian prosperity, or productivity, in the fifteenth century, as compared with the period before the Black Death. One influential modern view is that the fifteenth century was a period of slow recovery from disaster, that by 1500 the economy had not yet climbed back to the level attained in the early fourteenth century. To take some Florentine examples; in fifteenth-century Florence, the output of cloth never rose above 30,000 pieces a year, whereas in 1338 it had been 80,000 pieces. In 1458 the biggest enterprise in Florence, the Medici Bank, had a capital of about 30,000 florins, whereas the Peruzzi Bank, early in the fourteenth century, had had a capital of 100,000 florins. There was land reclamation in Southern Tuscany before the Black Death, but this land went out of cultivation and remained waste during the fifteenth century. In Genoa, maritime trade seems to have been at its height at the end of the thirteenth century, to have been at a low ebb for more of the fifteenth century, improving suddenly between 1475 and 1510. In Sicily, wheat exports declined during the fifteenth century.

This interpretation of economic history, the 'stagnationist' view as it has been called, has been challenged. It has been argued that silk production increased in the course of the fifteenth century in Florence, Genoa, Milan, Venice, and elsewhere; that agriculture prospered in Lombardy during the same period; that Venice was developing new industries; and that Sicilian wheat exports may have declined only because population, and so internal demand, increased. It is difficult to choose between these rival interpretations because there are only fragments of evidence about specific industries, specific cities, and specific moments. It is impossible to calculate whether the expansion of the silk industry was greater than the contraction in the woollen cloth industry, for example, or to assess the relative importance of Tuscan losses and Lombard gains.

Another controversial and important question is whether the economy of Renaissance Italy was essentially capitalist. Capitalism has been defined in many different ways; it might be useful to operate with a model which emphasizes two main features, the concentration of capital in the hands of a few entrepreneurs, and the institutionalization of a rational, calculating, impersonal approach to economic problems. Given these common characteristics, it might also be useful to distinguish commercial, financial and industrial capitalism from one another.

It is not difficult to find examples of rich entrepreneurs in this period. In 1428 Averardo di Bicci de'Medici left a fortune of 180,000 florins. It was possible for entrepreneurs to accumulate capital in this way because in some leading industries, many of the workers were in practice dependent on them. In Florence, the Medici took over the Wool Guild, much as they took over the state, without altering traditional forms but making sure that they controlled the key offices. In the cloth industry, a number of processes, such as beating, sorting and combing, were carried out in large workshops (which it is tempting to call 'factories') by men who were paid daily wages. Much of the spinning was done by the wives of peasants in the villages around Florence, but they were dependent on the entrepreneur who supplied them with the raw material, paid them, and disposed of the finished product. In fifteenth-century Genoa, the washers and weavers of cloth were dependent on the drapers, who were themselves dependent on great merchants. The silk-merchants provided not only the raw material but also spinning-machines and workshops which they hired out to spinners who worked for them. Similar conditions prevailed in the silk-industry of sixteenth-century Lucca. In the textile industries, where division of labour had gone so far, it is difficult to see how co-ordination would have been possible without the entrepreneur.

The rational, calculating approach has already been illustrated from contemporary writings (above, p. 234); more important here is the institutionalization of such attitudes, the existence of a complex credit structure which depended on abstraction and calculation and included banks, bills of exchange, companies, insurance, and a public debt. Banking was an Italian speciality in this period. There were banks in Bologna, Genoa, Milan, Naples, Palermo, Pisa, Rome and Venice. Some like the Medici Bank had branches in different cities. Banking was closely associated with foreign exchange; to avoid the Church's ban on usury, lending money was disguised as an exchange transaction. There were also *Montes Pietatis*, communal pawnshops which were encouraged by the Church. They began at Orvieto in 1463 and by 1491 had spread to Perugia, Viterbo, Savona, Assisi, Mantua, Cesena, Parma, Lucca, Verona, Padua, Piacenza and Ravenna. These *Montes* borrowed money as well as lending it, and paid regular interest. They were modelled on the public debt, the *Monte Commune*, which had existed in Florence from the middle of the fourteenth century onwards and had made its citizens into investors in the state. Florentine identification with their commune had an economic basis. It was also possible to invest in companies, without taking part in their management, and with only a limited liability in case of the company's failure; the name for such a company, in which capital and management were separated, was the *commenda*. It was possible to insure against loss of ships and loss of life. Venice was the great centre of marine insurance in the period, while in Genoa it was possible for a husband to insure his wife's life against the risk of death from pregnancy. Bills of exchange were widely used, and it was also possible to draw cheques on one's bank.

It would give a false impression not to mention the more traditional aspects of Italian economic organization. Most industries were organized more simply than the cloth and silk industries; in many, the craftsman and the entrepreneur were the same person. In industries where capital was required, because the raw materials were expensive or because the finished product might take years to make, the usual method was for the customer to finance the operation, and hire master masons or ship-carpenters as he needed them. Even in the cloth industry, the direct control of the entrepreneur extended only to a few processes and a few people; in Florence, dyeing and fulling were subcontracted. The cloth-industry was not polarized into rich merchants and poor workmen; both groups existed, but in this industry too there existed the small masters who both worked themselves and employed others. Thus to speak of 'industrial capitalism' in Renaissance Italy is likely to be misleading. The great fortunes of the time were made in trade and in banking, not in industry. Rich entrepreneurs like the Medici were unspecialized; they imported goods, sold them wholesale and retail, engaged in banking, and helped organize production – functions which were divided among specialist firms after the Industrial Revolution. Again, the existence in Italy of business techniques which had a great future should not lead us to overestimate their importance then. The *commenda* existed, but it lasted for only two or three years at a time. The more permanent unit was the family business, which blurs the distinction between the firm and the household, the public and the private. Goro Dati's *Libro segreto*, part diary, part account-book, illustrates this blurring. So does the habit of forming partnerships in the name of children, as the Medici sometimes did; the equivalent in economic life of making a child a bishop or a cardinal. Families rather than individuals were members of guilds, and widows carried on with their husband's business. At a time when credit instruments like bills of exchange and cheques were in use in cities, many peasants paid their rent in kind, under the share-cropping system. In the early sixteenth century, some officials in Milan were paid in salt, and small fees were often paid in kind. Guicciardini received a ducat and a goose a year as his retainer from the canons of Florence cathedral. Instances can be found of rural clergy who received the income from their benefices entirely in sacks of grain. It is hardly surprising that criticisms of the way of life of the clergy, buying and selling like merchants, went unheeded.

As with bureaucracy, so with capitalism. The term describes an ideal type or model, to which reality never more than approximates. Italy in this period approximated more closely to both than did other European societies, but in Italy too large-scale and small-scale enterprises coexisted, as did specialized and unspecialized institutions.[47]

It is not difficult to find links between the state of the economy and the state of the arts, but the historian is faced with the usual choice between a narrow precision or grandiose vagueness. Art often followed the trade routes. Venice exported art and artists to the Empire as well as other commodities; Jacopo de'Barbari went to Nuremberg, Paris Bordone and Titian went to Augsburg. Tuscan artists also followed the trade routes,

Rosso and Leonardo to France, Torrigiani to England. In Torrigiani's case, it is known that Florentine merchants with English contacts arranged for him to go. Again, it is known that a famous picture by Hugo van der Goes, now in Florence, was taken there by Tommaso Portinari, manager of the Bruges branch of the Medici Bank. Sebastiano del Piombo left Venice for Rome at the invitation of the banker Agostino Chigi; thanks to his business connexions with Venice, Chigi had come to know the artistic scene there.

At the other extreme of generality, there is the Marxist view (above, p. 26) that in this period, as in all others, the cultural 'superstructure' was in fact determined by the economic 'base', and that the Renaissance was a sort of 'bourgeois revolution' in the arts which expresses the rationalizing tendencies of capitalism. It is true that some works of art, such as palaces, which cost a great deal of money, are more directly related to the state of the economy than, say, lyric poems. It seems plausible to explain the decline of building projects in Florence in the 1430s by the expense of the war with Milan. But, in general, the economy seems to affect the arts much more by indirect than by direct means; to be mediated through the social. In Florence in the fourteenth and fifteenth centuries one can find new forms of economic organization, thought, and art. Are they connected? It was in Florence that perspective was rediscovered, and it was also in Florence that fifteenth-century children were most likely to study geometry at school. It was part of the curriculum at abacus-schools, which trained children in some of the skills required in business. The origins of abacus schools are not known, but it seems plausible to suggest that merchants set them up. Thus the fact that perspective was discovered at a particular place and time might ultimately be traced back to economic factors; but the emphasis should be on the word 'ultimately'.

Professor Lopez and his theory of 'hard times and investment in culture' (above, p. 31) may be vulnerable to similar criticisms; he suggests a correlation between cultural flowering and economic recession, and then explains the correlation in economic terms; merchants 'invested' in culture when there were fewer ways of placing their money than before. Suppose we take the case of Florence, where the existence of a recession seems fairly certain. The study of Florentine patronage (above, p. 106) suggests that merchants did not think in terms of 'investment' but of pride and piety when they commissioned works of art. Their style of life was changing, and they were coming to value conspicuous consumption more. It may be that this change in life-style can itself be explained in economic terms, that their shift from the role of entrepreneur to that of rentier was an unconscious adaptation to the economic recession. It might be a case of 'hard times and contempt for trade', a sort of 'sour grapes effect'. Even if this is so, the social factor, 'style of life' has to be inserted between economic changes and cultural ones.[48]

A number of twentieth-century sociologists have made points about social change which seem relevant to the impact of Italian society on Italian culture at this period. Durkheim advanced sociological explanations for modern man's self-consciousness and competitiveness, suggesting that they were the result of the division of labour, which emphasizes the differences between one human being and another and allows the survival of unusual individuals who might not have survived in simpler societies. Again, he argued that as population density rises, the struggle for existence becomes more acute, and so there is more competition and more stress on achievement. What Burckhardt described, Durkheim explains, although he does not mention fifteenth-century Italy at all.

Similar points were made by two American urban sociologists, Robert Park and Louis Wirth; each of them could be describing the Italy of this period, although neither mentions it. Park points out that the city 'offers a market for the special talents of individual men', and that competition tends to select for any given task the man best suited to perform it. To succeed, men need to specialize and to employ rational methods in their work. The effect of the division of labour is to break down family and local ties and to substitute occupational ties. Wirth adds the point that the juxtaposition of different kinds of man and styles of life tends to produce a tolerant outlook, even a relativist one. With the increase in social mobility comes 'the acceptance of instability and insecurity in the world at large as a norm', a point surely related to innovation in the arts. But the juxtaposition of individuals unrelated by family and local ties helps to foster the spirit of competition. This model of modernization suggests how a number of changes described separately elsewhere in this book may have interacted. It is a reminder that it is time to pull the different strands of the different chapters together, for, if this book has a fundamental thesis, it is that it is not possible to explain how works of art come to be as they are in terms of any single factor: economic, political or psychological; artist or patron; world-view or local tradition.[49]

Cultural and Social Change

> The natural change in worldly affairs makes
> poverty succeed riches . . . the man who first
> acquires a fortune takes greater care of it;
> having known how to make his money, he also
> knows how to keep it . . . his heirs are less
> attached to a fortune they have made no effort
> to acquire. They have been brought up to
> riches and have never learned the art of earning
> them. Is it any wonder that they let it slip
> through their fingers?
>
> *Guicciardini*

Most of this book has been concerned with cultural and social
'structures', that is, with factors which remain fairly constant
in the course of more than a century. They were not totally
static, but it makes for clarity to analyse them as if they were.
Artistic, ideological, political and economic elements have been
treated in relative isolation. Such a procedure of abstraction
has great advantages if the aim is to explain as well as to
describe, to construct plausible causal chains. But it is obvious
that at a given point in time the economic, the political, and
other elements all interact; we experience the whole conjunc-
ture, and it changes as we experience it. Hence it may be useful
to draw together here the themes of separate chapters and
sections, and to concentrate on the historian's traditional
business, the study of change over time.

It is convenient to distinguish two kinds of change, opposite
poles of a continuum. There is short-term change, of which
men are aware while it is happening, and long-term change,
which is visible to the historian but was usually invisible to
the men of the time.

GENERATIONS

A useful concept for the discussion of short-term changes is that of 'generation'. The concept is attractive because it seems to grow out of experience, the experience of identification with one group and of distance from others. It is often said that a generation lasts about thirty years, the period between maturity and retirement. One might therefore divide the period 1420–1540 into four generations, 1420–50; 1450–80; 1480–1510; 1510–40; classifying individuals according to the period in which their thirtieth birthday falls, and proceeding to test what Walter Friedländer, in a famous essay on Mannerism, called the 'grandfather law', that

> A generation with deliberate disregard for the views and feelings of the generation of its fathers and direct teachers skips back to the preceding period and takes up the very tendencies against which its fathers had so zealously struggled, albeit in a new sense.

In other words, the swing of the pendulum.

Such a division would be a convenient way of breaking down the problem of change into manageable units, but a dangerously mechanical one. It is not the fact that men are not born in batches every thirty years that counts; a generation, like a social class, is an ideal type or model, and to use it does not involve the assumption that everyone whose thirtieth birthday fell between 1420 and 1450, say, thought in the same way. The crucial objection to dividing the years 1420–1540 by thirty and producing four generations is of another kind. It is that generations are primarily subjective facts. The consciousness of belonging to a generation is part of the experience of belonging, just as class-consciousness is a necessary condition of belonging to a social class. But what creates this generation-consciousness? Karl Mannheim, in a well-known essay on the problem, found a happy formulation when he wrote of 'a common location in the social and historical process' as characteristic of generations as of social classes, a common location which encourages certain kinds of behaviour and inhibits others. If generation-consciousness is created by the historical process, then generations will not be equally long, and the gap between them will not be uniformly deep. This is the crucial objection to any mechanically regular division into thirty-year periods. Momentous events are likely to bind the members of an age-group together more closely than is normal. The Spanish writers known as the 'generation of 1898' were bound together by the war with the USA, and the loss of the remnants of the Spanish Empire; the need to explain these disasters led them to look hard at what was wrong with Spain and brought into a generation both Unamuno, who was born in 1864, and Ortega, born in 1883. It is equally apparent that a European generation was made conscious of itself, or rather created, by the political events of the later 1930s. It may be worth looking to see whether events in Italy around the years 1402, 1453, 1494 and 1527 made certain age-groups aware of themselves and their common location in history, and whether this awareness affected the arts.

In the necessarily compressed account which follows it will not be possible to reiterate certain qualifications, two in particular. First, it is important to avoid projecting on to the fifteenth and sixteenth centuries the acute generation-consciousness of today, the result of accelerating technological and social change. In a period when innovation was not generally considered legitimate (above, p. 225), any sense of breaking with the past was likely to be less acute and more disguised. In any case, in a period when men often considered themselves old when they reached their early thirties, there was little time for a revolution led by the self-consciously young. In the second place, in different activities men tend to do their best work at different ages. Fracastoro, the humanist-physician, and Giorgione were both born in 1478, but Fracastoro only made his reputation after Giorgione's death in 1511.[1]

The importance of political events in the early fifteenth century in creating a generation has been emphasized recently, notably by Hans Baron (above, p. 32). To summarize the argument briefly and a little freely: in the early fifteenth century there was a relatively sudden change of style in the visual arts in Florence, associated with Brunelleschi (born 1377); Ghiberti (born 1378); Masolino (born 1383); Donatello (born 1383/6); Michelozzo (born *c.* 1396); Uccello (born 1397); Luca della

Robbia (born 1400); and Masaccio (born 1401). There was a significant change in world-view, expressed by Leonardo Bruni (born *c*. 1370); Niccolò Niccoli (born 1364); Toscanelli (born 1397); Alberti (born 1404); and Palmieri (born 1406). The leading figures were closely linked as friends, colleagues, and pupils. In general, they were more prepared to innovate and more conscious of the value of classical antiquity than their predecessors had been.

Around 1400 there were certainly momentous political events in which Florence was involved. In the late fourteenth century, Giangaleazzo Visconti took over control of Milan and proceeded to build up an empire, seizing one after the other Verona, Vicenza, Padua, Pisa, Perugia, Siena and Bologna. The Florentines, virtually encircled, might well think that their turn was next. They went to war with Giangaleazzo, who was carried off by the plague in 1402 before he could attack Florence.

The Baron thesis suggests that there is a close relationship between the political crisis and the Florentine Renaissance; that political events made the Florentines aware of their fundamental values, such as liberty. Bruni presented the war between Florence and Milan as the struggle between liberty and tyranny. He identified Florence with republican Rome; this is the point of his remark (above, p. 15) that under the tyranny of the emperors, the brilliant minds of republican Rome vanished away. In his oration on the death of Nanni degli Strozzi (1428), Bruni illustrated his identification with the Athens of Pericles and the values expressed in the funeral speech.

The beauty of the thesis is that it provides an economical if partial explanation for a wide variety of phenomena. It is relevant to humanism and the visual arts. In the visual arts, it is relevant to form and content. The creation of a more 'antique' style came at the moment of identification with antiquity in politics, the 'grand manner' stressed the heroic at a time when heroism was needed, and such themes as David and St George (above, p. 203) carried political overtones. The theory brings in patrons as well as artists; Brunelleschi and Donatello were stimulated by civic patronage, and civic patriotism was stimulated by the crisis. An Englishman might ask himself whether Shakespeare's plays were a response to the crisis of 1588.

This interpretation is a little more ambiguous than it looks.

It is possible to argue, either that the events of the year 1402 were decisive in forming the new generation, or that this was done by the whole crisis period, from the 1390s to the 1420s. To argue that the one year was crucial involves the omission of Masaccio and Alberti, at least, simply because they were born too late; it involves technically controversial questions such as the dating of certain works by Bruni. It seems more plausible to argue that the whole struggle with Milan, not the events of one year alone, was the decisive factor in the education of this generation, and made it last unusually long – forty years from the birth of Niccoli to the birth of Palmieri. To widen the thesis in this way makes it more difficult to falsify, and to verify; but this price has to be paid. It must also be admitted that we know very little of the attitudes of leading creative figures to the political events of the time. Bruni does express the idea of a struggle for liberty, but Bruni was a professional rhetorician in the service of the Florentine Republic, and we do not know whether he was doing more than expressing an official attitude; whether he was personally committed to Florence, rather than his native Arezzo. We do not know how Brunelleschi, Donatello, Masaccio and others reacted to the political events of their day. The argument is a Florentine one; the Florentines were indeed culturally dominant at this time, but there were other important humanists, such as Vittorino da Feltre and Guarino da Verona, and other important painters, such as Pisanello, Domenico Veneziano and Jacopo Bellini. These two humanists did not show any marked dislike for courts and princes; Vittorino taught at the court of Mantua, Guarino at the court of Ferrara. It looks as if the development of art and ideas should not be explained in exclusively 'extrinsic' terms. There is a sense in which, illustrating Friedländer's 'grandfather law', Masaccio started where Giotto had left off, and the humanists where Petrarch left off, some sixty years before. The generation of 1402 had a cultural inheritance as well as a political education.[2]

The idea that the political events of the year 1453 made a great impact on Italian culture goes back at least to the fifteenth century itself, to the humanist Pier Candido Decembrio, and it was long embedded in school textbooks as 'the' explanation of the Renaissance. The fall of Constantinople, so the argument went, caused Greek scholars to migrate to Italy, bringing with them their knowledge of the Greek language and literature and so stimulating the 'Revival of Learning'. To this theory the objection has been made that Greek scholars in fact went to Italy before 1453. Gemistos Pletho and Bessarion went to the Council of Florence in 1439, and Bessarion stayed. In the 1440s, Demetrios Chalcondylas and Theodore Gaza arrived in Italy. As in the case of the year 1402, it is perhaps a mistake to focus attention too narrowly on a particular date. The relevant political event was the westward advance of the Turks, which was noticeable enough before 1453. The Council of Florence might not have been held but for this advance, and we know that Theodore Gaza went to Italy after Salonika had been taken by the Turks. After the fall of Constantinople, Janos Argyropoulos and Janos Lascaris came to Italy too.

These emigrants did have an important effect; Ficino, in his dedication to Lorenzo de'Medici of commentaries on Plotinus, is a witness that the coming of Gemistos Pletho to Florence was a stimulus to Greek studies. But the importance of the Greek scholars was that they could satisfy a demand which already existed. The advance of the Turks did not create a generation. True, the fall of Constantinople did strike contemporaries as a great disaster. Pope Nicholas V proclaimed a crusade the same year. His successors Calixtus III and Pius II also proclaimed crusades, no longer with the traditional aim of recapturing the Holy Places, but to protect Europe from further invasion. The first Venetian war with the Turks took place between 1463 and 1479. The difficulty is to find traces of political events on the arts. On the contrary, the artists and writers born between 1420 and 1450 and flourishing in the later fifteenth century seem a much less politically-minded generation than their predecessors. In Florence, there was Bertoldo (born c. 1420), Landino (born 1424), Baldovinetti (born 1425), Antonio Pollaiuolo (born c. 1431), Pulci (born 1432), Ficino (born 1433), Verrocchio (born 1436), Domenico Ghirlandaio (born 1449), Botticelli (born 1447) and Lorenzo de'Medici (born 1449). One might add Poliziano (born 1454) as a late but precocious member of the group. In Ferrara there was Tura (born 1430), Cossa (born c. 1436) and Boiardo (born c. 1440). Elsewhere this was the time of Mantegna, the Bellini brothers, Piero della Francesca, Perugino and Pontano, who share a mood of serenity, but nothing more specific. What the generation of

Ferrara-Florence have in common is a mood of escapism and a style of refinement, a great contrast to the mood of heroism and the forceful style of their fathers' time. It was an age of elegance in which private art tended to replace public; statuettes and busts tended to replace statues.* Ficino, in contrast to Bruni, put the contemplative life before the active, and Plato before Aristotle. In literature, the two most popular genres were the pastoral and the romance of chivalry, both far removed from everyday reality.

If it is possible to explain the heroic mood of one generation in terms of a conscious response to events, it ought to be possible to explain the escapist mood of another. In both cases, the political attitudes of the artists are unknown, and it is necessary to jump from events to style. One possible explanation is the swing of the pendulum, a reaction against the generation before; coupled with inheritance from them. In this period, Ferrara was ruled by Guarino's pupils, Mantua and Urbino by Vittorino's pupils. Lorenzo de'Medici was educated by Argyropoulos, Landino and Ficino. Lodovico Sforza was educated by Filelfo. The education of these prominent patrons was likely to make them more interested in literature and learning for its own sake than their fathers had been. As for artists, one might argue that Brunelleschi, Donatello and Masaccio had been too successful to create a tradition. They had not left enough for their successors to do. It may also be possible to suggest a political explanation for indifference to politics. It had often been said that the coming of the Medici to power discouraged Florentines from taking an interest in politics and so pushed them towards the values of contemplation. A difficulty here is that Ficino, Landino and Poliziano would have been political outsiders in the early fifteenth century too; another difficulty is that Lorenzo de'Medici, who was certainly interested in politics, tended to keep it out of his poetry. It may be more relevant to point out that in 1454 the peace of Lodi was made, an alliance between Milan, Florence and Venice. The result was forty years of a balance of power, forty years of relative peace in Italy. It was a time to which sixteenth-century Italians would look back nostalgically, calling it a golden age; a time when men could afford not to take

* One important exception, Verrocchio's Colleoni monument, was a Venetian commission.

much interest in politics. What united this generation, in a looser way than its predecessor, was not the political events of 1453 but the relative absence of momentous political events in Italy in the forty years which followed.[3]

After two essentially Florentine generations came one which was genuinely Italian. Of the 85 members of the creative élite born between 1460 and 1479, only 21 were Tuscans. It seems useful to group together the men born between about 1452 and about 1483. They include Leonardo, Savonarola (both born 1452), Piero di Cosimo, Pomponazzi (both born 1462), Pico (born 1463), Machiavelli (born 1469), Bembo (born 1470), Fra Bartolommeo (born 1472), Ariosto (born 1474), Michelangelo (born 1475), Titian (born c. 1477), Giorgione, Fracastoro and Castiglione (all born 1478), Raphael, Giovio and Guicciardini (all born 1483). For these men, political events were inescapable. From 1494 onwards, a succession of disasters overwhelmed Italy, and in the process helped make educated men at least aware of their common destiny as Italians. Three French kings invaded Italy in twenty years. First there was Charles VIII, who claimed the Kingdom of Naples as descendant of Alfonso of Aragon's unsuccessful rival René of Anjou. Second, there was Louis XII, who claimed Milan and also attacked Naples and Venice. Third, there was Francis I, who concentrated on Milan. Ferdinand the Catholic King of Spain and the Emperors Maximilian I and Charles V invaded Italy as well, which became the main theatre for the struggle for mastery between Habsburg and Valois, as well as the prize of the victors. In Italy the fifteenth century had been a time of relatively small-scale battles, but after 1494 came a succession of major ones: Fornovo, Novara, Cerignola, Agnadello, and Marignano. Many Italians were killed, whether serving with the French or Spanish or against them. Many cities were captured, and some were sacked. 'Crisis' is a term overworked by historians, but a strong term is needed to describe the conditions of Italy at this time; a 'time of troubles'.

The year 1494 has been taken as a break in the history of Italy from that day to this, and Guicciardini and Ranke are only two of the most famous historians who began their books with this date. But it should not be assumed without concrete evidence that a political event marks a break in cultural history. To start from the relatively narrow but relatively certain, it is possible to examine the impact of the invasion on the lives of individual artists and writers. Isaak left Florence in 1494; he had been in Medici service, and the Medici had been driven out. In Naples, Alfonso II's plans for improving the city were, as a contemporary put it, 'extinguished' by Charles VIII's invasion. But Charles took two artists back to France with him, Giocondo and Mazzoni. When the French invaded Milan in 1499, Lodovico Sforza fled and the artists at his court were dispersed. Bramante, Cristoforo Solari and Weerbecke all went to Rome; the historian Corio lost his offices and retired to a country villa. In 1509, it was the turn of Venice to be attacked by French, Spanish and imperial forces. Although Venice was not captured, the terraferma was overrun. The university of Padua closed for some years. After the sack of Brescia by the French in 1512, in which the young Tartaglia was injured, printing was not resumed there till 1521. In Venice itself there was a recession and the printers Aldus and Petrucci both left.

The dispersal of artists and writers in wartime is relatively easy to chart. The less tangible consequences of the invasions were probably more important, but it is harder to say anything certain about them. Savonarola presented his ideas as a conscious response to the time of troubles, a time which he had phophesied in the years immediately before 1494. He had a vision of the sword of God hanging over the earth. He declared that there would be a new flood, of foreign invaders, and a mystic ark, in which the Florentines could take refuge. After the invasion he declared that Charles VIII was God's instrument to reform the Church; he had been able to conquer Italy so easily because of her sins. He attacked blasphemy, cards, dice, drunkenness, low-cut dresses, painters who painted pagan goddesses, and humanists who studied the cure of souls in Virgil and in Cicero. It was probably under his influence that one leading humanist, Pico, and one Florentine painter, Baccio della Porta (better known as 'Fra Bartolommeo') became Dominican friars.

Another conscious response to the time of trouble is illustrated by Machiavelli. For him, as for Savonarola, Charles VIII's easy conquest of Italy was a lesson, but what he learned from it was something rather different. He learned that mercenaries cannot be trusted; that men are 'ungrateful, fickle, liars and deceivers'; that force, not reason, was decisive in politics. His work, like Guicciardini's, reflects what has been called a 'crisis of assumptions'. Events had called into question the conventional fifteenth-century wisdom, ideas about the perfectibility of man and the place of reason in politics. Like the Spanish generation of 1898, the Italian generation of 1494, however diverse their response, from Machiavelli to Savonarola, seem driven by the same need, to explain the disaster which had struck Italy, and Florence in particular.

It is natural to wonder whether this disaster affected styles of painting as well as styles of thought. Botticelli seems a case in point. Already in his late forties when the invasion occurred, his style nonetheless changed a great deal after it. The serenity of the *Birth of Venus* is replaced, in the *Mystical Nativity*, the S. Zenobio cycle, and the *Calumny*, by a much more unquiet quality. The inscription on the *Mystical Nativity* (above, p. 227) shows that Botticelli was thinking in apocalytic millenarian terms when he was painting it. In other cases, the essential clues about the painter's state of mind in 1494 are lacking. Leonardo's drawings of the destruction of the world date from the early sixteenth century, when the destruction of Italy was taking place around him, but his notebooks do not suggest any connexion. Nor did Leonardo's style change dramatically like Botticelli's; he continued in the 'grand manner', painting the *Last Supper* about 1497. Nor did he leave Milan when the French invaded. Piero di Cosimo's *Triumph of Death* and his now celebrated primitivism may be a response to the invasions; but his political opinions are not known. Fra Bartolommeo became a Dominican in 1500, but his style did not change. Michelangelo is known to have been sympathetic to Savonarola, but he was only nineteen in 1494, and so had no style to change. In the early sixteenth century he created the *David*, the lost *Battle of Cascina*, and the Sistine Chapel frescoes, all in the grand manner. One might argue, as in the case of Donatello and Masaccio, that the revival of the heroic ideal was a psychological response to the attack. There was a revival of civic commissions as well as civic ideals; Michelangelo created his *David* and his *Cascina* for the republic, and the works have obvious political meanings. But there is an obvious danger in explaining Botticelli's disturbed style and Michelangelo's heroic style as responses to the same events. Not that it is impossible to respond in different ways to the same events; Savonarola and Machiavelli did just that. What is impossible is to show that the different styles are in fact such responses. Other Italian artists and writers kept their serenity : Giorgione, Titian, Raphael, Ariosto, Bembo, Castiglione. But it may be significant that none of them were Tuscans, or worked in Milan or in Naples. In Venice and in the States of the Church the invasion did not lead to a change of regime.[4]

The sack of Rome by Charles V's troops in 1527 has some-times been taken to mark the end of a period. The sack, which followed Pope Clement VII's alliance with Charles's rival, Francis I, was probably the greatest disaster to happen to the city since its sack by Alaric and the Visigoths over eleven hundred years before. The Florentines took advantage of the plight of the pope, besieged in Castel St Angelo, to rebel against Medici rule, but found themselves besieged by an imperial army after the pope and the emperor had been reconciled. Florence was forced to surrender in 1530, and the Medici returned to stay till the eighteenth century. The 1520s and 1530s were also the time when the art style now called 'Mannerism' emerged (above, p. 47); a style which sometimes tended towards the restless, sometimes towards the elegant, but in any case broke with the rules of perspective and propor-tion which had been dominant. The aesthetic of the period (above, p. 157) was also one of the rejection of rules. It is natural to ask whether this rejection of rules, and so of reason, which can be found in the literature as well as the art of the time, is related to this second Italian 'time of troubles', creating a new generation. This generation might include Beccafumi (born c. 1486); Aretino (born 1492); Pontormo and Rosso (both born in 1494); Folengo (born 1496); Berni (born c. 1497); Gelli (born 1498); Giulio Romano (born c. 1499); Cellini (born 1500); Parmigianino (born 1503); Vasari (born 1511). The mood of this generation was characteristically an unstable, anxious one, veering between cynical acceptance and violent rejection of the world.

Like the invasion of Italy in 1494, the sack of Rome was seen by contemporaries as a cataclysm and it can be shown to have had limited but tangible effects on the arts. Rome had been a magnificent centre of patronage in the years immediately before 1527; artists and writers had flocked there, making their dispersal all the more spectacular when it came. Aretino,

Sebastiano del Piombo and Jacopo Sansovino all went to Venice, and Sammicheli entered Venetian service the year after. Parmigianino and Raimondi went to Bologna; Cellini went back to Florence; Perino del Vaga went to Genoa; Polidoro da Caravaggio to Naples; Giovanni da Udine returned to Udine. Those who stayed on suffered various unpleasant experiences. Cattaneo was imprisoned three times; Colocci's manuscripts and statues were destroyed, so was Sadoleto's library, and Tebaldeo's. Peruzzi and Perino del Vaga, before he left, were imprisoned and had to ransom themselves. It is no wonder that Valeriano was moved to write a book on the miseries of the *letterati*, 'especially at this time',

> Some killed by pestilence, others driven into exile, and oppressed with want; these butchered with the sword, those assailed with daily torments.

The sack put an end to the cultural predominance of Rome, and made considerable impact on the arts, of a precise and negative kind. Whether it stimulated changes in style is another matter. As in the case of the years 1402 and 1494, it would be a mistake to concentrate exclusively on 1527. It is better to look at the 1520s as a whole, and these were terrible years for the Italians, even by the standards of the period which began in 1494. In 1522, for example, Genoa was sacked and there was plague in Florence, whence Pontormo fled to the Certosa, and in Rome. In 1524 there was plague in Milan. In 1525 came the battle of Pavia, in 1526 the siege of Milan, in 1527 the sack of Rome, in 1528 the siege of Naples, in 1529 the siege of Florence. In Lombardy the whole period 1521–9 has been described by a modern historian as 'ruinous' because of war, famine and plague. In Venice, 1528 and 1529 were the years of the 'great hunger'. In Italy in general, the years 1527–31 were years of continuous plague. Of course there had been fearsome battles, sieges and plagues before this, but in this decade all the great cities of Italy suffered severe blows. Venice, where there was only famine, escaped most lightly, or at least the rich did; plagues and sieges were more egalitarian. One example of the economic impact of war will have to serve for the rest. Between April 1526 and May 1527, the Florentines spent 800,000 ducats on war. This sum was equivalent to the whole annual income of the Republic. And it was only then that the siege began. It is likely that the number of paintings made in the 1520s and 1530s was considerably less than in the previous two decades.

The 1520s were also years of spiritual crisis, or, if that term is too vague, of plans for the reform or destruction of the Church. In 1520, Paolo Giustiniani began to found reformed Camaldolese monasteries. In 1524 the Theatines were founded. During the 1520s, Matteo da Bascio worked for the reform of the Franciscans, and in 1528 his efforts culminated in the foundation of the Capuchins. In Rome in the 1520s, a group of priests and laymen, called the Oratory of Divine Love, used to meet on Sunday afternoons to discuss theology and practise spiritual exercises. Other reformers were less willing to stay within the framework of the Church. At the beginning of the decade, Luther criticized the Papacy more radically and more successfully than Savonarola had done; he was excommunicated in 1521. A number of other prophets arose to foretell the destruction of Rome and the punishment of the Church for her sins. During the Roman plague of 1522, a Greek magician called Demetrios told the people the plague was the work of demons, and sacrificed a bull to them in the Colosseum. More orthodox heresy, if the term be permitted, also spread in Italy; by 1524 the authorities were worried about the diffusion of Protestant books. In 1527 Cellario put forward a Zwinglian interpretation of the sacraments in his book *The works of God*, and in 1528 justification by faith was preached in public in Italy for the first time. These movements had in common, if no more than this, a rejection of reason and learning, a distrust of human nature. They were in contrast to the dominant world-view among the educated during the fifteenth century (above, p. 234).

An attractively simple account of the 1520s would suggest that changes in art style expressed changes in world-view, and that changes in world-view were a response to a decade of disasters. Unfortunately in this generation, as in the others, too little is known of the inner lives of artists, of their responses to the world around them. Michelangelo is an exception. A man of an older generation, he did change his style and reject Renaissance rules at the end of the 1520s. His letters and poems do communicate a sense of spiritual anguish. He was involved in the Catholic Reformation from Savonarola to Loyola. Paul Klee once suggested that the more fearful a place the world seems to be, the less realistic art becomes. Italian art of the 1520s and 1530s seems an example in favour of this hypothesis. A few remarkable paintings and buildings suggest that their creators had projected their distrust of men on to the world of objects, had lost faith not only in reason but also in matter and space.[5]

Looking back over four generations, it does seem that political events may have an effect on the form as well as the content of works of art. The strength of this effect seems to vary with the individual, with the period; and with the medium too; it does not appear possible to say anything about music in this section. However great the effect of politics on the arts, it does not seem so great as to exclude social preconditions on one side, or intrinsically artistic explanations on the other. The whole discussion again and again runs into two great obstacles. If in many cases the link between the events and the paintings of a decade appears obscure, the answer may be, not that the painter's inner world is immune from political influences, but that we simply do not know what that inner world was like. The second problem is that historical explanations imply generalizations; in this case, generalizations about the connexions between style, mood, and events. No doubt it is too simple to assume one-to-one correlations; in any case, a fully worked-out and empirically-based social psychology of art is needed to sustain, or refute, generalizations of the 'the more fearful a place the world seems to be, the less realistic art becomes.' We do not have such a social psychology of art yet.

STRUCTURAL CHANGES

If the Italian cultural and social scene in 1540 is compared with that of 1420, certain major differences spring to view. In a sentence, one might say that the Renaissance was a movement in 1420, but that it had become a period by 1540.[6] That is, around 1420 a small number of creative Florentines with ideals and enthusiasms in common, the Brunelleschi circle, made important innovations in the arts and elaborated a new world-view. But they were surrounded, even in Florence, by colleagues with traditional attitudes, patrons who made their customary demands, craftsmen who went on working in the old way. Gradually the new ideals spread through Tuscany and Italy. Fifty members of the creative élite were born between 1360 and 1399. Twenty-three came from Tuscany, 14 from the Veneto, only 13 from the rest of Italy. One hundred and seventy-six members of the élite were born between 1480 and 1520. Fifty came from Tuscany, 49 from the Veneto, 77 from elsewhere. One result of the spread of the new ideals was the ironing out of regional diversities, which had been important in the culture of the early fifteenth century. Beccafumi is not obviously a Sienese painter in the way that Neroccio was. Dialect literature was giving way to literature in Tuscan, written from Milan to Naples. Gradually the new art created a market for itself, patrons became aware that they could commission free-standing statues or classical mythologies, and a knowledge of Vitruvius, or at least of the differences between Doric, Ionic and Corinthian, became part of a gentleman's education. The new ideals spread, and changed in the spreading. In Giulio Romano's Palazzo del Te in Mantua there is a frieze with every third triglyph out of place. This kind of deliberate rule-breaking, not uncommon in the 1520s and 1530s, implies spectators who are educated enough to know what the rules are, to entertain certain visual expectations, and receive a shock when those expectations are falsified; to enjoy the sensation of shock, perhaps because long familiarity with the rules has made them rather blasé. Mannerist architecture is thus allusive architecture. In literature, the anti-Petrarchism of Aretino and Berni is equally allusive. To enjoy their parodies the reader must have some familiarity with Petrarch and his fifteenth-century imitators, a familiarity which breeds, if not contempt, at least boredom.

The invention of printing was responsible for familiarizing more people than before more quickly than before with new cultural ideals. Whereas in 1420 there were only manuscripts, by 1540 printing had been established in Italy for 70 years, and engraving had developed. Printing familiarized literate men and women all over Italy with Tuscan usage. At the end of the period, the illustrated treatises of Serlio and Palladio familiarized potential customers with the plans and elevations of churches, palaces and villas.

The differences between 1420 and 1540 cannot be reduced to the diffusion of the ideals of a small group, even allowing for the distortion inevitable on transmission. There were other trends too. Individualism of style was becoming more noticeable by the end of the period. There was a growing secularization of the arts. Taking dated paintings as a sample, in the 60 years from 1480 to 1540 every decade shows an increase in the proportion which have secular subjects:

1480–9	5 per cent
1490–9	9 per cent
1500–9	10 per cent
1510–19	11 per cent
1520–9	13 per cent
1530–9	22 per cent

source: Errera.

There was a growing separation between secular and religious pictures, so that it becomes easier to distinguish between St Jerome and a rocky landscape, between the birth of the Virgin and the interior of an Italian house. This separation parallels the growing distinction between sacred and profane in social life as a whole (above, p. 250). When, later in the sixteenth century, Veronese painted buffoons and halberdiers in the background of a *Last Supper*, the inquisition rapped him over the knuckles. Religious pictures were being purified of secular detail.

Another kind of purification was taking place at the same time. Wölfflin described it with a nice awareness of the sociology of gesture.

A great many gestures and movements disappear from pictures because they were felt to be too commonplace . . . St Peter, in Ghirlandaio's *Last Supper* of 1480, gestures with his thumb towards Christ, a gesture of the people, which High Art forthwith rejected as inadmissible . . . in the sixteenth century the universal search was for restraint and dignity of demeanour.

In other words, the meaning of the pictorial ideal of 'decorum' had changed, though the term continued to be used in writings on aesthetics. Decorum had meant suiting the gestures to the person gesturing, making an old man seem to move slowly and a young one quickly. Decorum came to mean making everyone in paintings behave as if they were heroes or gentlemen. The purification of paintings has a literary parallel. Castiglione advises his readers to pay attention to their gestures. Bembo advocated the separation of styles in literature, and the rejection of 'common' words from the high style (above, p. 167). Raphael, Castiglione and Bembo all knew one another. The spread of their ideals in the sixteenth century is attested by changes in fashionable adjectives. One cluster consists of terms like 'divine', 'grave', 'heroic' and 'majestic' and corresponds to the high or grand style in painting, and the use of mythology to glorify living men – Andrea Doria, for example, was painted as Neptune, and such apotheoses were to become common in the sixteenth century. The other cluster of terms of increasing importance includes 'elegant', 'graceful' and 'rare', and correspond to the paintings of Raphael and Parmigianino. For some people, even the heroic style was not really in good taste, because gentlemen were more restrained. There was a quip that 'Michelangelo painted stevedores, and Raphael painted gentlemen'.[7] The result of this movement of purification was that cultural differences between regions came to be replaced by cultural differences between classes. The split between Lombard and Tuscan narrowed, but the split between élite culture and popular culture widened.

These cultural changes seem to be related to other long-term changes within the milieu of artists and writers and their customers. There was a rise in the status of the artist, and a rise in his social origin. Suppose we compare 16 painters, sculptors and architects born between 1380 and 1419 with 16 born between 1500 and 1519. In the early group, nine are the sons of craftsmen, labourers or peasants; three are marginal; four of higher social origin or acquired status. In the late group, three are the sons of craftsmen; three are marginals; ten are of higher origin or status.[8] Most cases of ennobled painters date from the second half of the period, and so do most cases of painters who lived like gentlemen; Raphael, of whom it was rumoured that the Pope would make him a cardinal, or Peruzzi, who was taken for a nobleman when he was captured during the sack

of Rome. A consequence of this rise in the status of artists was
their reluctance to paint cassoni and such.

> In those times (the fifteenth century) . . . even the most
> excellent painters used to do that sort of work without being
> ashamed of it, as many are today, painting and gilding such
> things.

It is easy to replace Vasari's moralizing comment with a more
sociological one.[9] Another sign of the separation between art
and craft was the foundation of academies of art, at the very
end of the period, on the model of literary academies, which
were clubs of noble amateurs. So in 1420, the social status of
art was low; the social status of the artist was low; the social
origins of artists were low. Each of these facts helps explain
the others. By 1540, all three had risen together.

Patronage also changed during the period. By 1540 there
were relatively more private patrons, more educated patrons,
more humanist advisers (above, p. 121) and so more interest in
the details of symbolism and style. There seems also (p. 118)
to have been a shift in the balance of power between artist
and patron, in favour of the artist. His rising status improved
his bargaining position with the patron. Michelangelo, who
stood up to patrons in a way which most of his colleagues did
not emulate, was not the son of a craftsman but of a magistrate.
It may also be true that the artist's increasing independence,
which made him more like a poet than a carpenter, increased
his status. The roles of artist and patron were thus inter-
dependent and changed together. They were also part of a
much larger network of roles, the whole Italian social structure, affected by changes in that structure. Here two major
trends are visible.

The first trend might be described as 'commercialization'.
Towns were growing (above, p. 301) and this involved the
commercialization of agriculture. Speculators in farm leases
make their appearance in the fifteenth century. At the same
time, the art market became more important (p. 133) and the
professional writer, Aretino for example, emerged (p. 131).
Commercial relationships also affected war, politics and religion. Italy was a country where mercenaries did most of the

fighting; where the bureaucratic mode of domination (difficult to operate without the payment of officials in cash) was relatively well developed; and where the Church resembled a business in many ways – run, sometimes by a Medici, on the proceeds of alum and indulgences. In these three instances of war, politics and religion it is difficult to show that the situation in 1540 was substantially different from that in 1420; but it would be accurate to speak, if not of 'commercialization', at least of 'commercialism'.

The second major trend within the period has been conveniently if loosely summed up in one word: refeudalization.[10] The patricians of Florence and Venice, poised between bourgeoisie and nobility, opted by their changing style of life to be nobles. A famous description of the change at Venice was given by one of the patricians there, Priuli. He declared that the Venetians, having become rich, abandoned the sea which had made their fortunes and bought land and built houses, spending money freely in the pursuit of pleasure and magnificence. A moralizing literary source of this kind would be suspect if taken by itself, and counter-examples can be found – Alvise Cornaro, at least, bought land as an investment rather than as a piece of conspicuous consumption. However, in the course of the sixteenth century, the trend was as Priuli described it; the great Venetian families gradually withdrew from trade. In Florence, the trend was in the same direction. In the fifteenth century, some Florentine patricians had already begun to model their style of life on that of the nobility elsewhere; Lorenzo de'Medici and his brother Giuliano organized jousts and professed devotion to married ladies according to the conventions of courtly love. In the sixteenth century, more seriously, some great Florentine families withdrew from trade. It is impossible to say whether there was more capital invested in business in 1420 and more capital invested in land in 1540; the evidence does not exist which would verify or falsify this hypothesis. But individual families can be observed withdrawing from trade, and in sixteenth-century Italy, new families did not replace them. With these changes went an increasing prejudice against new men (barred from office in Brescia in 1488, for example) and a prejudice against manual labour. In other words, there was a crucial change in the attitudes of the ruling classes. They shifted from being entrepreneurs to being rentiers; from a dominant interest in profit to a dominant interest in consumption. The more elegant gestures of Florentine art in the sixteenth century reflect the attitudes of their patrons, men who were not prepared, as their fathers and grandfathers had been, to get their hands dirty.[11]

Why did this happen? It looks like an example of the shirtsleeves-to-shirtsleeves cycle, the third-generation syndrome, what the economist W. W. Rostow has called 'the pattern of Buddenbrooks dynamics'. The marginal utility of wealth, like that of other commodities, can diminish. But a society is not a family; it is composed of families some of whom will be in different phases of the Buddenbrooks cycle at any one time. Why should the style of life of the whole patriciate change in this way? Internal family dynamics is not a sufficient explanation and the historian has to turn to the environment for an explanation. Three possible explanations suggest themselves. The first is in terms of education and its effects, creative or destructive according to the value-system of the observer. In Florence in the early fifteenth century, for example, practical merchant fathers had their sons educated in the new learning (or at least given some tincture of the new learning) for practical reasons (p. 61). But the result was to make the pupils interested in learning for its own sake, more interested perhaps than they were in trade. A second possible explanation is political: there were fewer republics and more courts in Italy in 1540 than in 1420. In a republic it is easier for a patrician to remain a merchant. In a principality, a patrician is either for the regime or against. If he is for, he will be attracted into the orbit of the court, and if he does not turn courtier, his sons will. If he is against, he is likely to retire from the city altogether to live on his estates. Both processes can be illustrated from sixteenth-century Florence. A third possible explanation for the changing style of life at this time is economic; the 'sour grapes effect', or 'hard times and contempt for trade' (above, p. 316).

This change in style of life was likely to have two contrasting artistic consequences; the new style was good for the arts in the short-term, but not so good in the long term. It is likely that there was more patronage, though this cannot be measured, but in the long term patronage burned itself out as families spent their money and did not make more. The shift in values was probably bad for the arts. The emphasis on birth, the contempt for manual labour, both worked against the newly-risen status of the artist. The competitive spirit declined, and Florentine competitiveness, whatever its side-effects, seems to have been one of the conditions for the Florentine achievement. As Italy came to resemble other European societies, she lost her cultural lead.

The flourishing of the visual arts in Italy was inhibited by two other factors. One may speak of a 'brain drain' (brains being what an artist mixes his colours with) thanks to the diffusion of Renaissance ideals abroad, and the consequent demand for Italian artists to come to France, England, Spain, the Empire, and elsewhere. There was also a gradual shift of creativity from the visual arts into music during the sixteenth, seventeenth and eighteenth centuries, which may be related to the decline of the city-state, and increasing threats to freedom of expression from Church and State. But Italian art remained the envy of Europe until the death of Bernini in the later seventeenth century.[12]

COMPARISONS AND CONCLUSIONS

Historical explanations imply generalization and so comparisons, and the explanations advanced in this book are no exception. It may be useful to make some of these implied comparisons more explicit.

Specific features of Italian culture in the fifteenth and sixteenth centuries resemble features prominent at other places and times. In Western Europe, for example, Vasari was the first man to devote a book to the lives of artists; but in China, Chang Yen-Yuan had already written biographies of 370 artists. A world-view in which the values of order, symmetry, and utility all receive stress can be found in seventeenth-century France as in fifteenth-century Florence. A writer on the eighteenth-century English novel has found it useful to describe the innovations of that period in terms of individualism, realism and secularization, and notes that urbanization (that is, the growth of London) was an important social change in the age of Defoe, Fielding and Richardson. Civic pride was linked to artistic achievement and innovation in sixteenth-century

Nuremberg as in fifteenth-century Florence; Dürer was called in to design murals for the City Hall in 1521, and the post of city painter was created in 1531.[13]

The danger of isolating cultural traits lies in stressing similarities at the expense of differences. It may be more illuminating to compare whole cultural configurations in the hope of obtaining a more balanced picture. From the fifteenth century onwards, the comparison with ancient Greece, and more particularly Athens in about the fifth century BC, has proved irresistible; for not one but a whole cluster of cultural and social traits resemble Renaissance Italy. There was an emergence of artists as individuals with distinct styles, and anecdotes were recorded about the life and work of Apelles, Lysippos, Parrhasios, Polyklitos, Zeuxis and others. The competitive spirit was strong. Cities were large, governed themselves, and patronized the arts. In Greece, as in Italy, there was a linguistic unity but not a political one; hence culture had an important unifying function. The great age of Greek tragedy began shortly after the battle of Marathon, suggesting, as in the case of Florence *c*. 1402, that a crisis successfully surmounted is a stimulus to the arts.[14]

Two other 'configurations of culture growth' which bear some resemblance to the configuration in Italy 1420–1540 are the Netherlands in the same period, and Japan in the seventeenth and early eighteenth centuries. Marc Bloch made a helpful distinction between two kinds of comparative history. There are comparisons between societies which are fundamentally alike, such as England and France in a given century, and there are comparisons between the fundamentally unlike, for example between France and Japan.[15] This distinction suggests that comparisons between Italy and the Netherlands, Italy and Japan, may prove equally instructive, though in different ways.

Between 1420 and 1540 the Netherlands were a centre of cultural innovation equalled only, in Europe, by Italy. In the case of painting, it is possible to sustain a parallel between the two regions. In the Netherlands, as in Italy, there was a whole cluster of outstanding painters, including the Van Eycks, Roger van der Weyden, Gerard David, Hans Memlinc, Quinten Massys, Lucas van Leyden, and Pieter Brueghel the elder. As in Italy, there was conscious innovation, a *nouvelle pratique*, as it was called; one of the chief aims of artists was verisimilitude; and one of their chief means to this end was the employment of perspective. As in Italy, the subject-matter of painting was becoming secularized, and a differentiation of genres was taking place which included the portrait, even more popular than in Italy; the landscape, from the miniatures in the *Heures de Turin* at the beginning of the period to the work of Patenir, that 'good landscape painter' as Dürer called him, at the end; the scene of everyday life, such as the card-players and chess-players of Lucas van Leyden, or the market scenes in which Pieter Aertsen specialized. The still-life developed after 1540, but there is a surviving example from the fifteenth century, a vase of flowers painted on the back of a Memlinc portrait.

In other important respects, Italian and 'Flemish' culture (as it is convenient to call it, though Flanders was only one province of the Netherlands) were rather dissimilar.[16] As Panofsky once pointed out, a comparison of cultural innovation in the two regions reveals a 'chiastic pattern'. In Italy, innovation was greatest in architecture; then came sculpture, then painting, and finally music. In the Netherlands, innovation was greatest of all in music; Dufay, Binchois, Busnois, Ockeghem and Josquin des Près all fall within the period. In the second place came painting. A long way behind came sculpture; Claus Sluter died in 1406, and no major figure succeeded him. Architecture was also conservative; a typical example was the town hall at Leuven, built in 1448 in ornate Gothic style. The continuing importance of Gothic architecture, with great windows leaving little wall-space, helps explain why in the Netherlands frescoes did not have the importance they had in Italy. Instead, miniature-painting was more important in the fifteenth-century Netherlands than in Italy in the same period. This was not the only difference between the paintings of the two regions. Michelangelo's comparison, in which he says that the Flemings merely paint to deceive the 'outward eye', is both celebrated and unfair; it is understandable that he should underestimate a school of painters whose main interest was not the naked human body, who did not paint as if they were sculptors. For what interested the Italians in perspective was its making possible the illusion of solidity; what interested the Flemings was the illusion of space. Within the field of religious paintings, there are important differences between the two regions. In Flemish art, paintings of the Virgin Mary were relatively less numerous, paintings of Christ relatively more numerous, and more likely to represent scenes from his adult life before the Passion; Christ healing the sick, for example.[17]

There were economic and social as well as cultural parallels between Italy and the Netherlands. As a fifteenth-century Spanish traveller put it, 'two cities compete with each other for commercial supremacy, Bruges in Flanders in the West and Venice in the East.' These cities were set in the most urbanized parts of Europe. In the provinces of Flanders and Brabant, as much as two-thirds of the population lived in towns about the year 1500. In both areas, the commercialization of agriculture consequent on the growth of towns had led to the relatively early disappearance of serfdom. In both areas, the cloth industry was of great importance between the thirteenth and the fifteenth centuries. As in Italy, the cloth industry was not doing as well in the fifteenth century as it had been. Where the Italians were moving into silk-production, the Netherlanders, in Arras, Lille and Tournai, were concentrating on making tapestries. In both areas, the peak period for the visual arts coincided with the development of other luxury industries.

It is not difficult to relate Flemish painting to Flemish society. Here too artists had the status of craftsmen, were likely to be the sons of craftsmen, so that the more craftsmen there were in the population, the less chance there was of artistic ability being frustrated. Of 54 leading painters, the occupation of their father is known in 17 cases. One, Jan Mostaert, was of distinguished family; another, Marten van Heemskerck, was the son of a peasant; a third, Jan van Scorel, was the illegitimate son of a priest. The other 14 were all the sons of craftsmen. Roger van der Weyden was the son of a cutler, Pieter Aertsen the son of a weaver, Quinten Massys the son of a smith, and most of the others were the sons of painters. As in Italy, painting was a family business and 29 out of the 54 painters are known to have had relatives practising the visual arts. In two cases, the relatives were women: Cornelia, the wife of Gerard David, and Catherina, the daughter of Jan Sanders van Hemessen. There were several famous dynasties of artists, including the Bouts, Brueghel, Floris and Massys families. At least 32 of the 54 painters were born in sizeable towns, compared to 14 known to have come from small towns or villages – and some of these were near important towns; J. Cornelisz, for example, came from Oostsamen near Amsterdam. They tended to gravitate to a small number of important centres, especially Antwerp and Bruges, at each of which at least ten of the painters worked. There was in fact a noticeable drift of artists to the South; Key, from Breda, and Neymerswael, from a Zeeland village, worked in Antwerp.

Now Bruges and Antwerp were the greatest commercial cities of the Netherlands in the fifteenth and sixteenth centuries respectively. Bruges lost its commercial dominance about 1500 owing to the silting up of the River Zwijn, and at this time artistic as well as commercial dominance passed to Antwerp, a city with a population of about 100,000 by 1550. The correlation is not surprising, for merchants were among the most important patrons. Van Eyck's patrons included the merchants Giovanni Arnolfini, from Lucca, and Jodocus Vijdt. By the early sixteenth century, an art market had grown up at Bruges and Antwerp. Between 1515 and 1530, Albert Cornelis sold paintings from stalls in the market-place of Bruges. In 1540, an exhibition organized by the painters' guild was held in the main square of Antwerp.

In spite of their being craftsmen, some painters achieved a fairly high status. As in Italy, this was related to the existence of court patronage. Philip the Good appointed Jan van Eyck his official painter and valet de chambre, sent him on diplomatic missions, visited his studio at Bruges and sent him six silver cups on the baptism of the painter's son. But the painters of the Netherlands seem to have lacked the self-awareness of some of their Italian colleagues. Self-portraits are rarer – one example is that by Lucas van Leyden – and the Dutch Vasari, van Manders, did not publish his biographies, *Het Schilderboek*, till 1604, over fifty years later than the *Vite*.

It is less easy to relate the great age of Netherlands music to its social background; a more indirect approach is needed than in the case of painting. Most of the music of the time which has survived is church music – though it may be the case that secular compositions were increasing in numbers and have been lost. The great composers usually owed their musical training to the Church, to cathedral choir schools. Dufay was trained at Cambrai, for example, and Ockeghem at Antwerp. Some of the composers held benefices; Josquin was provost of the collegiate church at Condé. Ecclesiastical patronage was sometimes important; it was the bishop of Cambrai who 'discovered' Dufay.

However, the increasing size of church choirs in the period was made possible only by the gifts of the laity. The gifts were used in part to bring laymen into choirs; thus the cathedral chapter at Antwerp diverted income from some prebends to pay the salaries of professional singers who did not have to be clerics. Townsmen also founded confraternities, as in Italy, and some of them, the Confraternity of Our Lady at Antwerp, whose members included bankers, merchants and craftsmen, had a daily service with singers. The ecclesiastical culture of the fifteenth-century Netherlands was founded on urban wealth.

Much of the music that was not written for the Church was written for the Court, during the reigns of two dukes of Burgundy, Philip the Good and his son Charles the Bold. Philip made Binchois his chaplain and appointed Dufay music-tutor to his son. Charles the Bold sang, played the harp, and composed chansons and motets. He was the patron of Busnois, and he took his musicians with him even on campaign. We cannot be sure just how much difference court patronage made to the music, but it may be worth noting that the two most famous composers of secular music, Binchois and Busnois, were attached to the court, and that after the death of Charles the Bold in 1477, Josquin des Près and Isaak are found making their careers outside the Netherlands.[18]

The court had to be paid for. The Feast of the Pheasant, a Burgundian banquet where music played an important part, cost so much that even Olivier de la Marche, a courtier who took part in it, commented on the 'outrageous and unreasonable expense'. It was lucky for Philip the Good and Charles the Bold that they had towns like Ghent and Bruges, Brussels and Antwerp in their dominions, with rich merchants who could be taxed. The Court, like the Church, depended on urban wealth.[19]

In Japan in the seventeenth century, there was a cluster of cultural achievements and innovations at least as remarkable as the cases of Italy and the Netherlands.[20] The height of the period was the 'Genroku era' from 1688 to 1703. The great figures include the poet Bashō, the novelist Saikaku, the playwright Chikamatsu, and the artist Moronobu. Among the new genres were the wood-block print; a new kind of story, the kanazōshi; and two new kinds of theatre, the jōruri, in which the actors were puppets, and the kabuki, in which they were human. The samisen was introduced into Japanese music at this time, and was used to accompany dramatic performances.

As in the cases of Italy and the Netherlands, one important trend cutting across the arts was their secularization. The dominant form of drama before 1600, the Nō, was religious; but the jōruri and kabuki theatres were concerned with this world, either historical scenes or scenes from domestic life. In philosophy, the Japanese Confucians of the period, like the humanists of the fifteenth century, shifted their emphasis from knowing Heaven to knowing man. Whereas Japanese painting and sculpture before the year 1600 were mainly Buddhist in inspiration, secular works began to be popular in the seventeenth century. They included statuettes to ornament private houses, painted screens, and the wood-block print, which usually represented landscapes, actors, courtesans, or scenes from everyday life. At once an illustration and a symbol of this process of secularization is the term *ukiyo*, 'floating world'. Originally a Buddhist phrase referring to the transience of all worldly things, it took on hedonist overtones in the seventeenth century. It came to mean 'living only for the moment', more particularly in the pleasure-quarters of the three great cities, Edō, Kyōtō and Osaka. The 'floating trade' was prostitution. The world of pleasure was often represented in the wood-block prints, which came to be called *ukiyo-e*, 'pictures of the floating world'. This secularization of Buddhist values had a parallel in the fiction of the period, which was sometimes called *ukiyo-zōshi*, 'notes from the floating world'. Saikaku's most famous story, *The life of an amorous woman*, is an adaptation of a religious genre, Buddhist confession-literature. It resembles that genre as closely in form and as little in spirit as Defoe's *Moll Flanders* resembles *Grace Abounding*. Cultural innovation so often seems to come by way of creative adaptation rather than free invention, and the secularization of a religious theme seems one of the most common types of adaptation. In sixteenth-century Italy, the landscape was developing out of St Jerome in the wilderness. The still-life emerged as a 'corporeal metaphor of things spiritual' (above, p. 200). In

Japan, too, a secular subject might carry a hidden religious meaning. An eighteenth-century artist, Ekaku Hakuin, painted one of the rare still-lifes of the period, a lighted candle. The painting was inscribed: 'The light shines with a cut wick, the heart glows with the practice of Dharma.'

Another characteristic of more than one art in seventeenth-century Japan was realism, particularly in the sense of 'domestic realism' (above, p. 41). The equivalent Japanese term was *sewamono*, applied to kabuki plays about contemporary life as opposed to historical events. Thus Moronobu made prints of such subjects as a street scene in the Yoshiwara (the pleasure quarter of Edō), and a view of the Tokaido highway. Chikamatsu and Saikaku took scenes from everyday life and made plays and stories of them. Sometimes they based themselves on recent events, and did not even change the names and addresses. There is a story that Chikamatsu was in a restaurant when he was told that there had been a love suicide at Amijima, and was asked to write a puppet-play on the subject immediately, to be performed two days later. He did so, and the result is one of his best-known plays. Saikaku was fascinated by the true-to-life details of clothes and prices, and incorporated them into his stories.

Whether or no this is an illusion of a European observing from a distance and missing the detail, one has the impression that these changes in Japanese culture were more obviously and closely related to social changes than the equivalent changes in Italy and the Netherlands. The sixteenth century had been a period of civil war in Japan. At the end of the century peace was established by a succession of three strong rulers, the third of whom, Tokugawa Ieyasu, founded a dynasty of shōguns. Peace was followed by a rise in population, an improvement in communications, and rapid urbanization. Three towns in particular expanded: the old capital, Kyōtō, which had 410,000 inhabitants in 1634; Osaka, which had 280,000 in 1625; and Edō, now Tokyo, which was no more than a village till Tokugawa Ieyasu made it his capital, but numbered 500,000 people in 1721. The Tokugawa regime was not sympathetic to artisans and merchants, and treated them as socially inferior to peasants as well as to samurai. But the *chōnin*, the artisans and merchants of the towns, in practice prospered as never before, while many samurai, whose contempt for trade equalled that of seventeenth-century Spanish noblemen, found themselves in economic difficulties.

It seems plausible to argue that the rise of the chōnin and the cultural innovations of the seventeenth century are connected. Of the great writers and artists, Moronobu was the son of an embroiderer; Saikaku was the son of an Osaka merchant; Kiseki, the best-known of Saikaku's followers, was the son of a Kyōtō shopkeeper. The Nō plays had been for the samurai; no one else was allowed to watch them, and Tokugawa Ieyasu himself acted in them. But samurai were forbidden to go to the kabuki and jōruri plays, which were for the *chōnin*. It is their lives which are the subject of the domestic drama. The hero of the *Love suicides at Amijima*, for example, is a paper merchant called Jihei. Saikaku wrote about the same world. In his *Five women who loved love*, one of them loves a brewer; a second, a cooper; a third, a greengrocer; a fourth, a seller of calendars. Saikaku made entertainment, and literature, out of such utilitarian urban genres as the guide to wealth or the dictionary of courtesans – another case of innovation by adaptation. Not only the subject but the audience of his stories consisted of the townsmen, and their wives. His stories were called *kana-zōshi* because they were written not in ideograms but in the syllabic *kana* script, which meant that they could reach an audience much wider than that of the fully-educated. The seventeenth century was a period when bookselling became good business; there were 50 bookshops in Osaka in 1626, and so writing had become, to paraphrase Defoe, 'a very considerable part of the Japanese commerce'. Wood-block prints could be mass-produced, hence they were cheap and, unlike painted screens, say, within the means of craftsmen and small shop-keepers. One of their functions was a commercial one; to advertise the skills and charms of the actors and courtesans they so frequently portrayed.

There are two qualifications to be made to this picture of townsmen's culture. The first is that it is associated with merchants who are no longer accumulating but indulging in conspicuous consumption, as a number did at the end of the seventeenth century, some three generations after the *chōnin* began to prosper. It looks like another case of the 'Buddenbrooks dynamics'. Saikaku published a collection of business success stories, the *Family Storehouse*; one of his heroes, Jinbei, goes from rags to riches, but in later life decides that there is no point in continuing to save, that (as Cosimo de'Medici put it) it is sweeter to spend money than to gain it. Without men like Jinbei there might have been no Genroku era. The price to be paid was a decrease in economic growth in the eighteenth century. This parallel with Italian developments makes one wonder whether there is another syndrome besides that of the Buddenbrooks to be discerned; contempt for trade encourages conspicuous consumption by merchants – that is the only way in which they can achieve status, and so feel themselves successful.

The second qualification to make is to say that Genroku culture was not exclusively merchant-craftsman culture. Edō began as a court, even if court functions could not have supported all the half-million people living there in the early eighteenth century. The leisure class included samurai who did not fight, as well as merchants who were withdrawing from trade. Bashō the poet and Chikamatsu the playwright came from samurai families. Chikamatsu summarized his early career:

> I was born into a hereditary family of samurai but left the martial profession. I served in personal attendance on the nobility but never obtained the least court rank. I drifted in the market place but learned nothing of trade.

The new literary genres of the seventeenth century themselves owed something to aristocratic literary traditions, to the Nō plays and to the Tale of Genji, as well as portraying the problems of urban life.

This brief comparison of the Netherlands and Japan contains obvious and regrettable gaps; the available literature does not permit a systematic study of the milieu of Japanese artists, or of the merchant ethos in Flanders. But the cultural and social parallels may inspire confidence in the possibility of a sociology of art and literature. They make it a little easier to discuss, in this concluding paragraph, the question of the role of the 'bourgeoisie' in the Italian Renaissance. Is there a link between bourgeoisie and realism?[21] Once distinctions have been made between domestic, deceptive and psychological realism, it does seem possible to suggest an empirical connexion between the growth of towns and the emergence of an art of domestic realism. If the bourgeoisie is divided into merchants and craftsmen, it may be suggested that both groups have made important contributions to culture; craftsmen because they form the milieu from which artists often come, merchants because (more particularly when they are on the point of turning into nobles) they are often quick to patronize new arts. The emphasis on novelty is important. The argument is not that Church, King and nobility are insignificant patrons; this would be patently false. But the focus of this study has been on cultural innovation, and both the Flemish and the Japanese examples suggest that innovations need the support, initially at least, of new kinds of patron. In culture as well as in economic life there are rentiers and there are entrepreneurs.

Appendix: the Creative Élite

The 600 painters, sculptors, architects, writers, humanists, scientists and musicians were selected as follows:

1. 313 painters and sculptors from Vigni's article, 'Italian art' in the *Encyclopaedia of World Art* (organized by region, this list seemed less likely than others to emphasize the Florentine achievement at the expense of the rest of Italy).
2. 88 writers from E. Wilkins, *A History of Italian Literature*, London, 1954. These men wrote mostly in Italian.
3. 50 musicians from G. Reese, *Music in the Renaissance*, London, 1959. Unlike cases 1, 2, 4 and 5 I did not use his whole list but omitted anyone he mentions who did not receive an entry in the latest edition of Groves.
4. 55 scientists from Taton; revised with the advice of Marshall Clagett. R. Taton (ed.) *A General History of the Sciences*, vol. 2, London, 1965.
5. 74 humanists from E. Garin, *Italian Humanism*, Oxford, 1965. These wrote mostly in Italian.

These five sources produced a total of 581 people. I rounded this off to 600 by adding writers and humanists whom I had been surprised not to find in Wilkins and Garin: theirs are the last 19 names.

The names marked by an asterisk are those of the 32 non-Florentine humanists, discussed on p. 67 above.

Such a compilation is inevitably arbitrary; ten historians of the Renaissance, each asked to produce a list of 600 names, would no doubt produce considerably different lists. The men of the period, who might well have been in sympathy with the idea of a biographical collection, would have found the criterion of selection, 'creativity', somewhat odd. There are no kings and no generals here, and not even theologians, though S. Bernardino finds a place among the writers. However I have simply made explicit the implicit criteria of most modern historians. A more serious danger than that of being arbitrary is that of being biased. It is possible that, even after making a special effort not to discriminate in favour of Florence, I have done so, because we are so much better informed about Florentines. There may have been some excellent artists in Venice whose names are not recorded; such discoveries were made as recently as the nineteenth century. Thus the Florentine culture lead may be to some extent a myth, the creation of a circular argument. But it would be impossible to explain the whole Florentine lead in this way.

The object of the exercise was to conduct something like a social survey of the lead; to look for biographical patterns. In order for the data to be processed, I had to ask a small number of precise questions and to classify the answers. The questions concerned recruitment, training, organization, period of birth, and lay or clerical status.

1. Region of birth. 9 answers. Lombardy: Veneto: Tuscany: State of the Church; South Italy; Liguria; Piedmont; outside Italy; not known.

2. Size of birthplace. 4 answers. Large; medium; small; not known.

3. Father's occupation. 9 answers. There would have been only 6 answers if I had simply used the social classification employed throughout this book, i.e. noble; merchant/professional; artisan/shopkeeper; cleric; peasant; not known. But it seemed useful to split the artisan/shopkeeper group into three, into artists; those connected with the arts; those unconnected with the arts, and to separate humanists from other professionals.

4. Training. 6 answers. University of Padua; other universities; a humanist education outside the universities; apprenticeship; a musical education; not known. A man who went to Padua and other universities appears as 'Padua' only, so that the two categories added produce the total of university men.

5. Main art practised. 7 answers. Painter; sculpture; architect; writer; humanist; scientist; musician.

6. Specialization. 3 answers. An individual is known to have practised one art from the list in 5, above; or two; or three or more.

7. Relatives practising the arts. 5 answers. No relatives known to have done so; 1 relative; 2 relatives; 3 relatives; 4 or more.

8. Geographical mobility. 5 answers. Extremely sedentary; fairly sedentary; fairly mobile; extremely mobile; not known.

9. Patronage. Regrettably it did not prove possible to make a quantitative study of types of patronage. This category was reduced to 2 answers, known Medici patronage; no known Medici patronage.

10. Period of birth. 10 answers, derived by dividing the possible time of birth into nine 20-year periods, 1340–1519, and adding a 'not known'.

Using these categories I transferred the data to coding sheets, from which the Data Processing Unit of the University of Sussex prepared punched cards, which were then used (using a survey analysis programme) and fed into a computer (ICT 1900). The results were printed out in tabular form, the 63 categories (the total number of answers to the 11 questions) making 63 columns and 63 rows, so that correlations could be read off. The 600 names are the following with dates and places of birth:

1. Painters and Sculptors

Niccolò dell'Abbate, *1512–71, Modena*

Agostino di Duccio, *1418–c1481, Florence*

Macrino d'Alba, *c1470–c1528, Alba*

Mariotto Albertinelli, *1474–1515, Florence*

Galeazzo Alessi, *1512–72, Perugia*

Domenico Alfani, *c1480–c1553, Perugia*

Girolamo Alibrando, *1470–c1524, Messina*

Giovani Amadeo, *1447–1522, Pavia*

Cola dall' Amatrice, *c1485–c1547, Amatrice*

Bartolommeo Ammannati, *1511–92, Settignano*

Fra Angelico, *c1400–1455, Vicchio*

Antoniazzo Romano, *c1461–1508, Rome*

Antonio da Fabriano, *Fabriano*

Andrea dell'Aquila, *c1420–96, Aquila*

Silvestro Aquilano, *d.1504, Sulmona*

Arcangelo da Camerino, *Camerino*

Niccolò dall'Arco, *d.1494, Bari*

Antonio Baboccio, *1351-1435, Piperno*

Jacomart Baçó, *d.1461, Valencia*

Alesso Baldovinetti, *1425–99, Florence*

Baccio Bandinelli, *1493–1560, Florence*

Jacopo de' Barbari, *Venice?*

Fra Bartolommeo, *1472–1517, Florence*

Bartolomeo da Foligno, *Foligno?*

Marco Basaiti, *c1470–c1530*

Jacopo Bassano, *c1517–1592, Bassano*

Lazzaro Bastiani, *c1425–c1512, Venice?*

Giovanni Battaggio, *Lodi*

Domenico Beccafumi, *c1486–1551, Le Cortine*

Belbello da Pavia, *Pavia*

Bartolommeo Bellano, *1434–97, Padua*

Gentile Bellini, *1429–1507, Venice*

Giovanni Bellini, *c1430–1516, Venice*

Jacopo Bellini, *c1400–c1470, Venice*

Benedetto Bembo, *Brescia*

Bonifazio Bembo, *Brescia*

Francesco Benaglio, *d.c1492, Verona*

il Bergognone, *c1455–c1522, Fossano?*

Bertoldo di Giovanni, *c1420–91, Florence*

Leonardo da Besozzo, *c1400–c1488*

Michelino da Besozzo, *c1388–1450, Pavia*

Francesco Bissolo, *c1492–1554*

Boccaccio Boccaccino, *1467–1524, Ferrara*

Giovanni Boccati, *c1420–c1480, Camerino*

Giovanni Boltraffio, *1467–1516, Milan*

Bartolomeo Bon, *d.1529, Bergamo*

Benedetto Bonfigli, *c1420–96*

Bonifazio Veronese, *1487–1553, Verona*

Bartolomeo Bono, *d.1464, Venice*

Giovanni Bono, *c1382–1442*

Paris Bordone, *1500–71, Treviso*

Sandro Botticelli, *1447–1510, Florence*

Carlo Braccesco, *c1451–c1501, Milan?*

Donato Bramante, *1444–1514, Urbino*

Ludovico Brea, *c1443–c1520, Nice*

Andrea Bregno, *1421–1506, Osteno*

Antonio Bregno, *Righeggia*

Moretto da Brescia, *1498–1554, Brescia*

Benedetto Briosco, *Ardizola da Briosco*

Angelo Bronzino, *1503–72, Monticelli*

Filippo Brunelleschi, *1377–1446, Florence*

Giuliano Bugiardini, *1475–1554, Florence*

Giovanni Buonconsiglio, *Vicenza*

Agostini Busti, *1483–1548, Busto Arsizio*

Bernardino Butinone, *c1445–c1507, Treviglio*

Domenico Campagnola, *c1517–62*

Giulio Campagnola, *1482–, Padua*

Galeazzo Campi, *1477–1536, Cremona*

Giulio Campi, *c1502–1572, Cremona*

Bartolomeo Caporali, *c1442–c1509*

Luigi Capponi, *Milan*

Meo del Caprino, *1430–1501, Florence*

Cristoforo Caradosso, *1452–c1527, Mondonico*

Polidoro Caldara, *c1490–1543, Caravaggio*

Giovanni Cariani, *c1485–c1547, Venice?*

Matteo Carnevale, *Noto*

Giovanni Caroto, *c1480–1555, Verona*

Vittore Carpaccio, *c1465–c1526, Venice?*

Andrea dal Castagno, *c1419–1457, Castagno*

Giovanni Castello, *c1509–c1569, Gandino*

Vincenzo Catena, *c1470–1531, Venice*

Danese Cattaneo, *1509–73, Colonnata*

Mirabello Cavalori, *c1510–c1572*

Paolo Cavazzola, *1486–1522, Verona*

Benvenuto Cellini, *1500–71, Florence*

Cima da Conegliano, *c1459–c1517, Conegliano*

Vincenzo Civerchio, c1470–1544, Crema

Mauro Conducci, 1440–1504, Lenna

Colantonio, *Naples?*

Jacopino del Conte, 1510–98, Florence

Antonio Correggio, c1489–1534, Correggio

Francesco del Cossa, c1436–78, Ferrara

Lorenzo Costa, c1460–1535, Ferrara

Giacomo Cozzarelli, 1453–1515, Siena

Lorenzo di Credi, c1459–1537, Florence

Gerolamo da Cremona, Cremona?

Giovan Criscuolo, c1500–c1584, Gaeta

Carlo Crivelli, c1430–c1495, Venice

Simone Cronaca, 1457–1508, Florence

Giovanni Dalmata (Ivan Duknovic), c1440–1509, Trogir

Andrea Delitio, *Guardiagrele*

Desiderio da Settignano, c1430–64, *Settignano*

Benedetto Diana, c1460–1525, Venice

Giovanni Dolcebuono, 1440–1506, Milan

Donatello, 1386–1466, *Florence*

Dosso Dossi, c1479–1542, *Trent?*

Eusebio di San Giorgio, c1465–c1539, *Perugia?*

Evangelista di Pian di Meleto, 1458–1549, *Pian di Meleto*

Gentile da Fabriano, c1390–1427, *Fabriano*

Defendente Ferrari, c1490–c1535, Chivasso

Gaudenzio Ferrari, c1470–1546, Valduggia

Andrea Ferrucci, 1465–1526, Fiesole

Antonio Filarete, c1400–c1469, Florence

Jacobello del Fiore, d.1439, Venice

Fiorenzo di Lorenzo, c1445–c1525, Perugia

Marcello Fogolino, *S. Vito*

Agostino dei Fonduti, c1450–1522, Crema

Vincenzo Foppa, c1428–c1515, Brescia

Francesco dei Franceschi, Venice

Francesco Francia, c1450–1517, Bologna

Francesco Franciabigio, 1482–1525, *Florence*

Francesco di Gentile, *Fabriano*

Gianbattista Franco, c1498–1561, Venice

Domenico Gaggini, d.1492, Bissone

Nicola Gallucci, c1395–c1462, Guardiagrele

Raffaellino del Garbo, c1470–1524, *Florence*

Benvenuto Garofalo, 1481–1559, Ferrara

Girolamo Genga, c1476–1551, Urbino

Domenico Ghezzi, c1400–c1444, Asciano

Lorenzo Ghiberti, 1378–1455, Florence

Domenico Ghirlandaio, 1449–94, Florence

Michele Giambono, ?

Giovanni Giocondo, c1433–1515, Verona?

Francesco di Giorgio, 1439–1501, Siena

Giorgione, 1478–1511,
  Castelfranco

Giovanni di Paolo, c1403–83,
  Siena

Girolamo da Camerino, ?

Antonio Giuffrè, ?

Giulio Romano, c1499–1546,
  Rome

Benozzo Gozzoli, 1420–98,
  Florence

Francesco Granacci, 1477–1543,
  Florence

Gualtiero di Alemagna, Germany

Isaia da Pisa, Pisa

Niccolò di Piero Lamberti,
  c1370–1450, Florence

Piero Lamberti, c1393–1435,
  Florence

Francesco Laurana, c1430–1502,
  La Vrana

Luciano Laurana, d.1479,
  La Vrana

Mario di Laureto, Laureto

Leonardo da Vinci, 1452–1519,
  Vinci

Leone Leoni, 1509–90, Menaggio

Liberale da Verona, c1445–c1526,
  Verona

Girolamo dai libri, 1474–1555,
  Verona

Bernardino Licinio, c1469–1565,
  Poscante

Pirro Ligorio, c1513–83, Naples

Fra Lippo Lippi, c1406–69,
  Florence

Filippino Lippi, c1457–1504,
  Prato

Antonio Lombardo, c1458–1516,
  Venice

Pietro Lombardo, c1435–1515,
  Carona

Tullio Lombardo, c1455–1532,
  Venice

Lorenzo da Severino,
  c1445–c1503, Severino

Lorenzo Lotti, 1490–1541,
  Florence

Lorenzo Lotto, c1480–1546,
  Venice

Bernardino Luini, c1480–1532

Benedetto da Maiano, 1442–1497,
  Maiano

Giuliano da Maiano, 1432–1490,
  Maiano

Giovanni Mansueti, d.1527

Antonio Mantegazza, Milan

Andrea Mantegna, 1431–1506,
  Isola di Cartura

Marco di Costanzo, ?

Marco Marziale, Venice

Masaccio, 1401–28,
  Castello S. Giovani

Masolino, 1383–c1447, Panicale

Matteo di Giovanni, c1430–95,
  Borgo S. Sepolcro

Matteo da Gualdo, c1430–c1503

Lodovico Mazzolino,
  c1480–c1528, Ferrara

Guido Mazzoni, d.1518, Modena

Melozzo da Forlì, 1438–94,
  Forlì

Altobello Meloni, Cremona

Francesco Melzi, 1493–c1570,
  Milan

Antonello da Messina, c1430–79,
  Messina

Pierantonio Mezzastris,
  c1430–c1506, Foligno

Michelangelo, 1475–1564,
  Caprese

Michelozzo, c1396–1472,
  Florence

Mino da Fiesole, 1429–84,
  Papiano

Bartolomeo Montagna,
  c1450–1523, Orzinuovi

Jacopo Montagnana, c1440–99,
  Montagnana

Raffaele da Montelupo,
  c1505–66, Montelupo

Giovanni Montorsoli, *c1507–63*,
  Montorsoli

Domenico Morone, *c1440–c1517*,
  Verona

Francesco Morone, *1471–1529*,
  Verona

Ottaviano Nelli, *c1370–c1432*,
  Gubbio

Neroccio de'Landi, *1447–1500*,
  Siena

Niccolò Alunno, *c1425–1502*,
  Foligno

Marco d'Oggiono, *c1475–c1530*,
  Oggiono

Gianbattista Ortolano,
  c1488–c1525, *Ferrara*

Andrea Palladio, *1508–80*, *Padua*

Palma Vecchio, *c1480–1528*,
  Serinalta

Marco Palmezzano, *c1458–1539*,
  Forlì

Bernardo Parentino, *c1437–1531*,
  Parenzo

Francesco Parmigianino,
  1503–40, *Parma*

Pastura, *Viterbo*

Vincenzo de Pavia, *d.1557*

Giovanni Pedrino, *c.1519–40*

Giovanni Francesco Penni,
  c1488–c1529, *Florence*

Pietro Perugino, *c1445–1523*,
  Città delle Pieve

Baldassare Peruzzi, *1481–1536*,
  Siena

Francesco Pesellino, *c1422–c1472*,
  Florence

Callisto Piazza, *1500–61*, *Lodi*

Martino Piazza, *d.1527*, *Lodi*

Pietro Alemanno, *Göttweib*

Piero di Cosimo, *1462–1521*,
  Florence

Piero della Francesca, *c1420–92*,
  Borgo S. Sepolcro

Bernardino Pinturicchio,
  c1454–1513, *Perugia*

Sebastiano del Piombo,
  c1485–1547, *Venice*

Antonio Pisanello, *c1395–1455*,
  Pisa

Nicolò Pizzolo, *1421–53*,
  Villa Ganzerla

Antonio Pollaiuolo, *c1431–98*,
  Florence

Piero Pollaiuolo, *c1443–96*,
  Florence

Baccio Pontelli, *1450–95*,
  Florence

Jacopo Pontormo, *1494–1557*,
  Pontormo

Giovanni da Pordenone,
  c1484–1539, *Pordenone*

Ambrogio de Predis, *1455–c1522*,
  Milan

Cristoforo de Predis, *d.1486*,
  Milan

Andrea Previtali, *c1470–1528*,
  Bergamo

Francesco Primaticcio, *1504–70*,
  Bologna

Ercole Procaccini, *1515–95*,
  Bologna

Domenico Puligo, *1492–1527*,
  Florence

Riccardo Quartararo, *?*

Jacopo della Quercia,
  c1374–1438, *Quercia*

Raffaello, *1483–1520*, *Urbino*

Marcantonio Raimondi,
  c1480–c1534, *Argini*

Matteo de'Raverti, *Milan?*

Andrea Riccio, *c1470–1532*,
  Trent

Lattanzio da Rimini, *Rimini*

Antonio Rizzo, *d.c1500*,
  Verona

Luca della Robbia, *1400–82*,
  Florence

Tommaso Rodari, *Maroggia*

Girolamo Romani, *c1484–c1566*,
  Brescia

Gian Cristoforo Romano,
c1470–1512, Rome

Cosimo Rosselli, 1439–1507,
Florence

Antonio Rossellino, 1427–79,
Settignano

Bernardo Rossellino, 1409–64,
Settignano

Biagio Rossetti, c1447–1516

Nanni il Rosso, Florence

Giovanni Battista Rosso,
1494–1540, Florence

Benedetto da Rovezzano,
1474–1552, Pistoia

Giovan Francesco Rustici,
1474–1554, Florence

Andrea Sabatini, c1484–1530,
Salerno

Guillén Sagrera, d.1456, Inca

Antonello de Saliba,
c1466–c1535, Messina

Francesco Salviati, 1510–63,
Florence

Salvo di Antonio, ?

Antonio di San Gallo, the elder,
1455–1534, Florence

Antonio di San Gallo, the
younger, 1483–1546, Florence

Giuliano di San Gallo,
c1445–1516, Florence

Michel Sammicheli, 1484–1559,
Verona

Sano di Pietro, 1406–81, Siena

Andrea Sansovino, c1460–1529,
Monte San Savino

Jacopo Sansovino, 1486–1570,
Florence

Girolamo da Santacroce, d.1556,
Santacroce

Giovanni Santi, c1435–94,
Urbino

Andrea del Sarto, 1486–1530,
Florence

Stefano Sassetta, 1392–1450,
Siena

Giovanni Savoldo, c1480–1550,
Brescia

Cristoforo Scacco, Verona

Giorgio Schiavone, c1436–1504,
Scadrin

Giorgio da Sebenico (Sibenik),
d.1475

Jacopo del Sellaio, 1441–93,
Florence

Vincenzo Seregni, c1404–94

Sebastiano Serlio, 1475–1554,
Bologna

Cesare da Sesto, 1477–1523, Sesto

Luca Signorelli, c1441–1523,
Cortona

Giovanni Sodoma, 1477–1549,
Vercelli

Giovanantonio Sogliani,
1492–1544, Florence

Andrea Solari, c1460–1520, Milan

Cristoforo Solari, c1460–1527,
Angera

Guiniforte Solari, 1429–1481,
Milan

Pietro Antonio Solari, c1450–93,
Milan

Antonio Solario, Venice

Giovanni lo Spagna, c1450–1528

Giovanni Martino Spanzotti,
c1450–c1526, Casale

Francesco Squarcione, 1397–1468,
Padua

Bartolommeo Suardi

Paolo Taccone, Sezze

Jacopo Tintoretto, c1518–94,
Venice

Titian, c1477–1576, Pieve

Gian Francesco da Tolmezzo,
c1450–c1510, Tolmezzo

Francesco Torbido, c1482–1562,
Venice

Pietro Torrigiano, 1472–1528,
Florence

Niccolò Tribolo, 1500–50,
Florence

Cosimo Tura, 1430–95

Francesco Ubertini, 1494–1557,
Florence

Paolo Uccello, 1397–1475,
Florence

Giovanni da Udine, 1487–1564,
Udine

Perino del Vaga, 1501–47,
Florence

Francesco Valdambrino, ?

Giorgio Vasari, 1511–74, Arezzo

Lorenzo Vecchietta, c1412–80,
Castiglione

Bartolomeo Veneto, ?

Domenico Veneziano, c1400–61,
Venice

Marcello Venusti, c1512–79,
Como

Andrea del Verrocchio, 1436–80,
Florence

Tommaso de Vigilia, Palermo

Lorenzo da Viterbo, c1437–c1476,
Viterbo

Alvise Vivarini, c1445–c1504,
Venice

Antonio Vivarini, c1415–c1476,
Murano

Bartolommeo Vivarini,
c1432–c1499, Murano

Daniele da Volterra, c1509–66,
Volterra

Bernardino Zaccagni,
c1455–c1529, Rivalta

Francesco Zaganelli, c1470–1531,
Cotignola

Bernardo Zenale, c1436–1526,
Treviso

Stefano da Zevio, c1374–1438,
Verona

Marco Zoppo, 1433–78, Cento

2. Writers

Luigi Alamanni, 1495–1556,
Florence

Leon Battista Alberti, c1404–72,
Genoa

Andrea Alciati*, 1492–1550,
Alzate

Pietro Aretino, 1492–1556,
Arezzo

Ludovico Ariosto, 1474–1533,
Reggio

Matteo Bandello, c1480–1561,
Castelnuovo

Andrea da Barberino,
c1370–c1431, Barberino

Feo Belcari, 1410–84, Florence

Pietro Bembo, 1470–1547,
Venice

S. Bernardino, 1380–1444,
Massa Marittima

Francesco Berni, c1497–1535,
Lamporecchia

Flavio Biondo*, c1392–1463,
Forlì

Matteo Maria Boiardo, c1440–94,
Scandiano

Leonardo Bruni, c1370–c1444,
Arezzo

Domenico Burchiello, 1404–49,
Florence

Andrea Calmo, c1510–71, Venice

Annibale Caro, 1507–66,
Cittanova

Giovanni dall Casa, 1503–56,
Mugello

Lodovico Castelvetro, c1505–71,
Castelvetro

Baldassare Castiglione,
1478–1529, Villa Casatico

Giovanni Cavalcanti, 1444–1509,
Florence

Giovanni Maria Cecchi, 1518–87,
Florence

Benedetto Gareth ('Chariteo'),
c1450–1514, *Barcelona*

Francesco Colonna, c1432–
c1527

Vittoria Colonna, 1492–1547,
Marino

Alvise Cornaro, 1475–1566,
Venice

Angelo di Costanzo, c1507–90,
Naples

Lodovico Dolce, 1508–68, *Venice*

Anton Francesco Doni, 1513–74,
Florence

Marsilio Ficino, 1433–99, *Figline*

Francesco Filelfo*, 1398–1481,
Tolentino

Agnolo Firenzuola, 1493–1545,
Florence

Marcantonio Flaminio,
1498–1550

Teofilo Folengo, 1496–1544,
Mantua

Girolamo Fracastoro,
1478–1553, *Verona*

Galeazzo di Tarsia, c1520–53,
Naples

Veronica Gambara, 1485–1550,
Brescia

Giambattista Gelli, 1458–1563,
Florence

Paolo Giovio, 1483–1552, *Como*

Giambattista Giraldi, 1504–73,
Ferrara

Leonardo Giustinian, c1388–1446,
Venice

Anton Francesco Grazzini,
1503–84, *Florence*

Guarino Veronese*, c1370–1460,
Verona

Francesco Guicciardini,
1483–1540, *Florence*

Cristoforo Landino, 1424–c1492,
Florence

Niccolò Machiavelli, 1469–1527,
Florence

Giovanni Battista Spagnuolo,
1448–1516, *Mantua*

Pietro Martire d'Anghiera*,
c1457–1526, *Arona*

Michele Marullo, c1440–1500,

Alessandro de'Medici, 1483–1530,
Florence

Lorenzino de'Medici, 1514–48,
Florence

Lorenzo de'Medici, 1449–92,
Florence

Francesco Maria Molza,
1489–1544, *Modena*

Jacopo Nardi, 1476–1563,
Florence

Andrea Navagero*, 1483–1529,
Venice

Matteo Palmieri, 1406–75,
Florence

Giovanni Pico*, 1463–94,
Mirandola

Antonio il Pistoia, 1436–1502,
Pistoia

Pius II*, 1405–64, *Pienza*

Poggio, 1380–1459, *Terranova*

Angiolo Poliziano, 1454–94,
Montepulciano

Giovanni Pontano*, 1426–1503,
Ponte

Luigi da Porto, 1485–1529,
Vicenza

Luigi Pulci, 1432–84, *Florence*

Francesco Robortello, 1516–67,
Udine

Bernardino Rota, c1508–75,
Naples

Giovanni Rucellai, 1475–1525,
Florence

Angelo il Ruzzante, c1502–42,
Padua

Masuccio Salernitano, *Salerno*

Jacopo Sannazzaro, c1456–1530,
Naples

Marino Sanudo, 1466–1535,
Venice

Girolamo Savonarola, 1452–98,
Ferrara

Giulio Cesare Scaligero,
1484–1558, Riva

Serafino Aquilano, 1466–1500,
Aquila

Sperone Speroni*, 1500–88,
Padua

Gian Francesco Strapparola,
Caravaggio

Luigi Tansillo, 1510–68, Venosa

Bernardo Tasso, 1493–1569,
Venice

Antonio Tebaldeo, 1463–,
Ferrara

Claudio Tolomei, 1492–c1555,
Siena

Gian Giorgio Trissino, 1478–1550,
Vicenza

Lorenzo Valla*, 1407–57, Rome

Benedetto Varchi, 1503–65,
Florence

Polidoro Vergilio, c1470–1555,
Urbino

Vespasiano da Bisticci, 1421–98,
Bisticci

Girolamo Vida, 1485–1566,
Cremona

Vittorino da Feltre*, c1378–1446,
Feltre

3. Musicians

Pietro Aaron, c1490–1545,
Florence

Alexander Agricola, Flanders

Francesco d'Ana, d.c1503, Venice

Andrea Antico, c1470–c1537,
Montona

Marco Dall'Aquila, Aquila

Jacques Arcadelt, c1505–c1567,
Liège

Antoine Brumel, c1460–c1525

Niccolò Burci, c1450–c1518,
Parma

Marchetto Cara, d.c1527, Verona

Girolamo Cavazzoni, c1500–60,
Urbino

Marc Antonio Cavazzoni,
c1480–c1569, Urbino

Loyset Compère, c1455–1518,
Flanders

Juan Cornago, Spain

Francesco Corteccia, 1504–71,
Arezzo

Guillaume Dufay, c1400–74
Flanders

Domenico Maria Ferrabosco,
1513–74, Bologna

Costanzo Festa, 1490–1545,
Villafranca Sabauda

Lodovico Fogliano, d.1539,
Modena

Pierre de Fossis, d.1527, Flanders

Andrea Gabrieli, c1520–86,
Venice

Franchino Gaffurio, 1451–1522,
Ospitaletto

Elzéar Genet, c1470–1548,
Carpentras

John Hothby, c1415–87, England

Heinrich Isaak, c1450–1517,
Flanders

Maistre Jhan, ?

Josquin des Prez, c1450–1521,
Flanders

Erasmus Lapicida, ?

François Layolle the younger,
Lyons

Filippo da Luprano, ?

Jean Mouton, c1475–1522, France

Jacob Obrecht, c1450–1505,
Berg-op-Zoom

Marbriano de Orto, d.1527,
Flanders

Michele Pesenti, *Verona*

Johannes Prioris, *?*

Bartolomé Ramos de Pareja, *c1440–c1491, Baeza*

Cyprien de Rore, *1516–65, Mechlin*

Vincenzo Ruffo, *c1510–87, Verona*

Francesco Santacroce, *c1487–c1556, Padua*

Giovanni Spataro, *c1458–1541, Bologna*

Antonio Squarcialupi, *1416–80, Florence*

Johannes de Tinctoris, *c1436–1511, Nivelles*

Bartolommeo Tromboncino, *Verona*

Philippe Verdelot, *d.c1567, Flanders*

Nicola Vicentino, *c1511–72, Vicenza*

Alfonso dell Viola, *Ferrara*

Gaspar van Weerbecke, *c1440–1514, Oudenarde*

Adriaan Willaert, *c1490–1562, Bruges*

Antonio Zachario da Teramo, *Teramo*

Nicola Zacharia, *?*

Gioseffe Zarlino, *1517–90, Chioggia*

4. Scientists

Alessandro d'Alessandro, *c1461–1523, Naples*

Giovanni Battista Amico, *1512–38, Cosenza*

Ugo Benzi, *1376–1439, Siena*

Jacopo Berengario da Carpi, *c1460–1530, Carpi*

Giovanni Bianchini, *Bologna*

Vannoccio Biringuccio, *1480–c1539, Siena*

Pompeo Bolognetti, *?*

Raffaele Bombelli, *Bologna*

Antonio Brassavolo, *1500–55*

Francesco Buonafede, *1474–1558*

Celio Calcagnini, *1479–1541, Ferrara*

Girolamo Cardano, *1501–76, Pavia*

Cennino Cennini, *c1370–c1440, Colle di Valdelsa*

Andrea Cesalpino, *1519–1603, Arezzo*

Gherardo Cibo, *?*

Bartolommeo della Rocca, *1467–1504*

Realdo Colombo, *1516–c1577, Cremona*

Federico Commandino, *1509–75, Urbino*

Giacomo Antonio Cortuso, *1513–1603, Padua*

Nicholas of Cusa, *c1400–64, Cues*

Bartolommeo Eustachio, *c1500–74, San Severino*

Scipione dal Ferro, *c1465–1526*

Giovanni da Fondi, *c1400–c1473*

Giovanni da Fontana, *c1395–c1455, Venice*

Gaetano da Thiene, *1387–1465, Thiere*

Luca Gaurico, *1476–1558, Giffoni*

Luca Ghini, *c1450–1556, Croaro d'Imola*

Guglielmo Grataroli, *1516–68, Bergamo*

Guido Guidi, *c1500–69, Florence*

Jacopo da Cremona, *Cremona*

Niccolò Leoniceno, *1428–1524, Lonigo*

Luigi Lilio, c1510–76, Cirò

Leonardo Mainardi, Cremona

Giovanni Manardi, 1462–1536,
Cremona

Giovanni Marliani, Milan

Pierandrea Mattioli, 1500–77,
Siena

Francesco Maurolico, 1494–1575,
Messina

Domenico Maria da Novara,
1454–1504, Ferrara

Luca Pacioli, c1445–c1514,
Borgo S. Sepolcro

Antonio Francesco Piccioli, ?

Alessandro Piccolomi, 1508–78,
Siena

Ippolito Salviani, 1514–72,
Città di Castello

Michele Savonarola, c1384–1468,
Padua

Scipione of Mantua, Mantua

Mariano Taccola, 1381–c1450,
Siena

Niccolò Tartaglia, c1499–1557,
Brescia

Bernardo Torni, 1452–97

Giovanni Battista della Torre,
Verona

Marcantonio della Torre,
1481-1511, Verona

Paolo Toscanelli, 1397–1482,
Florence

George of Trebizond, 1396–1484,
Crete

Paolo Veneto, c1372–1429,
Udine

Andreas Vesalius, 1514–64,
Brussels

Benedetto Vittori, d.1561, Faenza

Bartolommeo Zamberti, d.c1460
Venice

5. Humanists

Donato Acciaiuoli, 1429–78,
Florence

Benedetto Accolti, 1415–64,
Arezzo

Alessandro Achillini, c1461–1512,
Bologna

S. Antonino, 1389–1459, Florence

Tullia d'Aragona, 1508–65, Rome

Janos Argyropoulos*, c1415–87,
Constantinople

Bessarion*, c1403–72, Trebizond

Giuseppe Betussi, c1515–c1573,
Bassano

Antonio Brucioli, d.1556,
Florence

Gian Michele Bruto, 1516–94,
Venice

Filippo Buonaccorsi*, 1437–96
S. Gimignano

Lazzaro Buonamici, 1479–1552,
Bassano

Giulio Camillo, c1480–1544,
Portogruaro

Giovanni Antonio Campano,
c1427–77, Cavelli

Ciriaco d'Ancona, 1391–c1452,
Ancona

Gasparino Contarini, 1483–1542,
Venice

Angelo Decembrio*, c1415–
66

Francesco da Diacceto,
1466–1522, Diacceto

Girolamo Donato, c1454–c1511,
Venice

Egidio da Viterbo*, 1469–1532,
Viterbo

Elia of Crete, 1460–97, Crete

Mario Equicola*, c1470–1525,
Alvito

Bartolomeo Fazio*, 1400–57,
La Spezia

Antonio de Ferrariis, *1444-1517,*
   Galatone
Galeazzo Florimonte, *1478-1567*
Niccolò Franco, *1515-70,*
   Benevento
Donato Giannotti, *1492-1573,*
   Florence
Francesco Giorgi, *1460-1540*
Giovanni Crisostomo Javelli,
   c1470-c1538, Casole
Giovanni Lamola, *c1407-49,*
   Bologna
Lapo Castiglionchio, *c1405-38,*
   Castiglione
Lodovico Lazzarelli, *1450-1500*
Leone Ebreo*, *c1465-c1535,*
   Lisbon
Pomponio Leto*, *1428-97, Diano*
Bartolommeo Lombardi, *d.1540,*
   Verona
Antonio Loschi*, *1368-1441,*
   Vicenza
Vincenzo Maggi,*d.c1564*
Giannozzo Manetti, *1396-1459,*
   Florence
Carlo Marsuppini, *1398-1453,*
   Genoa
Giorgio Merula, *c1424-94, Acqui*
Antonio Minturno, *c1500-74,*
   Traetto
Girolamo Muzio, *1496-1576,*
   Padua
Giovanni Nesi, *c1456-1520,*
   Florence
Niccolò Niccoli, *1364-1437,*
   Florence
Agostino Nifo*, *c1473-1538,*
   Jopoli
Mario Nizzoli, *1489-1566,*
   Brescello
Marcello Palingenio,
   c1500-c1543, La Stellata
Antonio Panormita*, *1394-1471,*
   Palermo

Marcantonio Passero, *1491-1563*
Alessandro de Pazzi, *1483-c1530,*
   Florence
Francesco Piccolomini,
   1520-1604, Siena
Giovanni Francesco Pico,
   1470-1533
Bartolommeo Platina*, *1421-81*
Georgios Gemistos Pletho*,
   c1355-
Pietro Pomponazzi*, *1462-1525*
Simone Porzio, *c1496-1554,*
   Naples
Cosimo Raimondi, *d.1435,*
   Cremona
Giovanni Battista Ramusio, *1485-*
Alamanno Rinuccini,*1426-1504*
Girolamo Ruscelli, *c1500-66,*
   Viterbo
Jacopo Sadoleto, *1477-1547,*
   Modena
Alberto Sartiano, *1385-1450,*
   Sarteano
Agostino Steuco, *1496-1549,*
   Gubbio
Antonio Telesio, *1482-1534,*
   Cosenza
Niccolò Tignosi, *1402-74, Foligno*
Niccolò Leonico Tomeo,
   1456-1531, Venice
Bernardino Tomitano, *1517-76*
Giovanni Tortelli, *c1400-66,*
   Arezzo
Ambrogio Traversari, *1386-1439,*
   Portici
Giorgio Valla*, *1447-99,*
   Piacenza
Maffeo Vegio, *1407-58, Lodi*
Pietro Paolo Vergerio*,
   1370-1444, Capodistria
Nicoletto Vernia, *c1420-99,*
   Chieti
Francesco Vicomercati, *d.1570,*
   Vimercate

Additional

Jacopo Aconcio*, 1492–1565,
Trent

Giovanni Battista Adriani,
1511–79, Florence

Giovanni Aurispa, 1376–1459,
Noto

Francesco Barbaro*, 1390–1454,
Venice

Gasparino Barzizza, c1360–1431,
Barzizza

Girolamo Benivieni, 1453–1542,
Florence

Filippo Beroaldo il vecchio,
c1453–c1505, Bologna

Bernardo da Bibbiena, 1470–1520,
Bibbiena

Antonio Bonfini*, 1427–1502,
Montalto

Vincenzo Calmeta, c1460–1508,
Castelnuovo

Jacopo Caviceo, 1443–1511,
Parma

Bernardino Corio, 1459–c1519,
Milan

Ludovico Domenichi, 1515–64,
Piacenza

Aldo Manuzio, 1444–1515,
Bassiano

Filippo de'Nerli, 1485–1556,
Florence

Bernardo Rucellai, 1448–1514,
Florence

Marcantonio Sabellico,
c1436–1506

Bartolommeo della Scala,
1428–96, Colle

Bernardo Segni, 1504–58,
Florence

Abbreviations

AB: The Art Bulletin (New York).

Alberti, architecture: L. B. Alberti,, *De re aedificatoria*: many editions and translations. I used the Latin/Italian parallel texts ed. by P. Portoghesi, Milan, 1966. The eighteenth century English translation has been reprinted.

Alberti, family: L. B. Alberti, *I libri della famiglia*. Many editions: I used the one in Alberti's *Opere volgari*, ed. C. Grayson, Bari 1960.

Alberti, painting: L. B. Alberti, *Della pittura*. I have given references to the translation by J. R. Spencer, London, 1956.

Antal: F. Antal, *Florentine painting and its social background*, London, 1947.

Annales E.S.C.: *Annales: économies: sociétés: civilisation* (Paris).

ASL: Archivio storico lombardo (Milan).

Baron (1938): H. Baron, 'the historical background of the Florentine Renaissance' in *History*, 1938.

Baron (1955): H. Baron, *The crisis of the early Italian Renaissance*. 2 vols, Princeton 1955. I have given references to the one-volume revised edition, Princeton, 1966.

Bridgman: N. Bridgman, *La vie musicale au quattrocento*, Paris, 1964.

Cennini: Cennino d'Andrea Cennini, *Il libro dell'arte* (written between *c*. 1396 and 1437) ed. D. V. Thompson, New Haven, 1932. Translated by D. V. Thompson, New Haven, 1933.

Chastel: A. Chastel, *Art et humanisme à Florence au temps de Laurent le magnifique*, Paris, 1961.

Condivi: A. Condivi, *Vita di Michelangnolo Buonarroti*, ed. E. S. Barelli, Milan, 1964.

Dolce: L. Dolce, *Aretino*, ed. M. W. Roskill, New York, 1968 (text and English translation).

EI: Enciclopedia italiana, (Rome, 1948–52).

EWA: Encyclopaedia of World Art, English trans. New York/Toronto/London 1959–68.

Ferguson: W. K. Ferguson, *The Renaissance in historical thought*, Cambridge, Mass., 1948.

Filarete: Antonio Averlino 'Filarete' *Treatise on architecture*, ed. and trans. J. R. Spencer, 2 vols, New Haven, 1965.

Gauricus: P. Gauricus, *De sculptura* ed. and trans. into German by H. Brockhaus, Leipzig, 1886: There is a French translation, Geneva, 1969.

Gaye: G. Gaye, *Carteggio inedito d'artisti*, vol. 1, Florence, 1839.

GBA: Gazette des Beaux-Arts (Paris).

Gombrich (1963): E. H. Gombrich, *Meditations on a hobby horse*, London, 1963.

Gombrich (1966): E. H. Gombrich, *Norm and Form*, London, 1966.

Ghiberti: I commentari, ed. O. Morisani, Naples, 1957.

Groves: G. Groves, *Dictionary of music and musicians* 5th ed., London, 1954.

Huizinga: J. Huizinga, *Men and ideas*, New York, 1959.

JHI: Journal of the History of Ideas (New York).

JWCI: Journal of the Warburg and Courtauld Institutes (London).

Leonardo: Literary works, ed. J. P. Richter, 2nd ed., 2 vols, Oxford 1939.

Lopez: R. S. Lopez, 'hard times and investment in culture' in W. K. Ferguson et al., *The Renaissance*, New York, 1953.

Manetti: the life of Filippo Brunelleschi, attributed to A. Manetti. ed. H. Holtzinger, Stuttgart, 1887.

von Martin: Soziologie der Renaissance (1932). English trans., London, 1944; new ed. New York 1963; references are to the 1963 edition.

Martines: L. Martines, *The social world of the Florentine humanists*, Princeton 1963.

Rubinstein: N. Rubinstein (ed) *Florentine studies*, London, 1968.

T–B: U. Thieme/F. Becker, Allgemeine Lexikon der bildenden Künstler, Leipzig, 1907–50.

Vasari: G. Vasari, *Vite*, ed. G. Milanesi, Florence, 1878–81.

Wackernagel: M. Wackernagel, *Der Lebensraum des Künstlers in der florentinischen Renaissance*, Leipzig, 1938.

Warburg: A. Warburg, *La Rinascita del pagansimo antico*, Florence 1966. References are to this translation of his essays. For German texts see his *Gesammelte Schriften*, I, Leipzig/Berlin 1932.

Wittkower (1949): R. Wittkower, *Architectural principles in the age of humanism*, London 1949: references are to the 3rd edition, London, 1962.

Wittkower (1963): R. Wittkower and M. Wittkower, *Born under Saturn*, London, 1963.

References

Chapter one: The Historians

1. A useful general discussion of creative epochs in A. L. Kroeber, *Configurations of Culture Growth*, Berkeley and L.A., 1944, critically discussed by T. Munro, 'what causes creative epochs in the arts?' in *Journal of Aesthetics and Art Criticism*, 1962–3.
2. An invaluable general survey of interpretations of the Renaissance is Ferguson, although in the later chapters the wood cannot always be seen for the trees. Bruni quoted by Baron (1955), p. 58.
3. Machiavelli, *History of Florence*, the opening of Book 5; Vasari, life of Masaccio.
4. Vasari, life of Perugino, puts the explanation into the mouth of Perugino's master; *c.* 1400, G. Dati gave a similar explanation for the prosperity of Florence.
5. Huizinga, p. 249.
6. Quotations from E. Gibbon, *Memoirs*, London, 1966, 122ff; A. Ferguson, *Principles of moral and political science*, Edinburgh, 1792, p. 291; A. Smith, *Wealth of Nations* (1776), London 1904 edition, p. 308, and C. Burney, *A general history of music*, 4 vols., London 1776–1789, vol. 2, p. 584. On eighteenth century views see H. Weisinger, 'the English origins of the sociological interpretations of Renaissance' in *JHI*, 1950.
7. The quotations from Winckelmann, Goethe and Schlegel are translated from the chapter on Winckelmann in U. Kultermann, *Geschichte der Kunstgeschichte*, Vienna and Düsseldorf, 1966, pp. 102, 107. Winckelmann's social interpretations of Greek art is to be found in his *Geschichte der Kunst des Altertums*, 1764; English trans., London, 1881, 1.285ff.
8. On Herder see I. Berlin, 'Herder and the Enlightenment' in E. Wasserman, ed., *Aspects of the eighteenth century*, Baltimore, 1965. The quotation is on p. 67. The comparison between Herder and modern anthropology is developed in Grawe, *Herder's Kulturanthropologie*, Bonn 1967. Herder discussed the rise of Italian cities in Book xx of his *Ideen zur Philosophie der Geschichte der Menschheit*.
9. G. W. F. Hegel, *Philosophie der Geschichte*, first published 1837.

For the Greeks, see part 2; for the end of the Middle Ages, part 4, the end of the second section.

10. J. Huizinga, *Men and Ideas*, New York 1959, p. 249.

11. The quotation from Burckhardt comes from chapter 5 of his *Die Kultur der Renaissance in Italien*, the first sentence. Burckhardt's method is compared to Hegel's by E. H. Gombrich, *In search of Cultural History*, Oxford, 1969.
   W. Kaegi, *J. Burckhardt*, vol. 3, Basel/Stuttgart 1956, has a chapter on the *Renaissance in Italy*.

12. A remark recorded by Wölfflin, and quoted by Peter Murray in the introduction to his translation of Wölfflin's *Renaissance und Barock*, London, 1964.

13. J. Burckhardt, *Weltgeschichtliche Betrachtungen*, first published 1906, especially chapter 3. I have quoted the English translation, London, 1943.

14. J. Burckhardt, *Beiträge zur Kunstgeschichte von Italien*, Basel 1898. I take the information about his manuscripts from Wölfflin's introduction.

15. This explanation of Burckhardt's intellectual retreat in terms of his personal retreat is suggested by H. Baron, 'Burckhardt's *Civilisation of the Renaissance* a century after its publication' in *Renaissance News*, 1960.

16. The quotations are taken from Wölfflin's *Renaissance und Barock* 1888, English trans., London, 1964, pp. 79, 76. An interesting discussion of Wölfflin from a Crocean point of view is to be found in C. Antoni, *Dallo storicismo alla sociologia*, Florence, 1940. English trans., Detroit, 1959, p. 207ff.

17. Burckhardt's letter to Warburg is printed in W. Kaegi, 'Das Werk Aby Warburgs' in *Neue Schweize Rundschau*, 1933, p. 285. On Warburg see G. Bing, 'A. M. Warburg' in *JWCI*, 1965; F. Saxl, 'three Florentines' in his *Lectures*, London, 1957; and E. H. Gombrich, *Aby Warburg*, London, 1971.

18. The quotation is from a letter of Burckhardt's to Bernhard Kugler, 21 August 1874, no. 644 in Max Burckhardt's edition of Jacob Burckhardt's letters — *Briefe*, vol. v, Basel/Stuttgart 1963.

19. This criticism of German philosophy comes from K. Marx and F. Engels, *Die Deutsche Ideologie*, English trans., Moscow 1964, p. 37.

20. *Ibid.*, p. 430. The classic discussion of 'superstructure' and 'base' comes from the preface to *A contribution to the critique of Political Economy*, Berlin, 1859.

21. A. von Martin. A brief discussion by W. K. Ferguson in his *The Renaissance in Historical Thought*, Cambridge, Mass., 1948, p. 228ff. and in his introduction to the Harper Torchbook edition of von Martin.

22. F. Antal. Important reviews by M. Meiss *AB* 1948, 143ff, and Y. Renouard, *Annales E.S.C.* 1950, 361ff.

23. For criticisms of Hauser's method, see E. H. Gombrich, 'the social history of art' in Gombrich (1963) Hauser himself discusses method in his *Philosophie der Kunstgeschichte*, Munich, 1958, English trans. Cleveland and New York, 1963.

24. Wackernagel. The definition of *Lebensraum* comes from his *Vier Aufsätze*, Wattenscheid 1963, 5. See also E. H. Gombrich, 'the early Medici as patrons of art' in Gombrich (1966).

25. L. Martines, N. Bridgman.

26. R. S. Lopez, 'hard times'. See also his 'économie et architecture médiévales' in *Annales E.S.C.*, 1952. The Lopez thesis has been criticized by C. M. Cipolla: see p. 311 below.

27. H. Baron, (1955). The quotation is from the 1966 edition, xxv.

28. C. Wright Mills, *The sociological imagination*, New York, 1959. esp. chapters 1-3.

29. See V. Kavolis, *Artistic expression: a sociological analysis*, Ithaca, 1968, p. 124ff.

30. F. Galton, *Hereditary Genius*, London 1869, 2nd ed., London 1892, p. 239-40; E. Müntz, *Histoire de l'art pendant la Renaissance*, vol. I, Paris, 1889, pp. 50-51.

Chapter two: A Profile of Italian Culture

1. The case for and the case against the cultural unity of an age are elegantly and briefly presented in J. Huizinga, 'the task of cultural history' (esp. section d) in Huizinga, and E. H. Gombrich, *In search of cultural history*, Oxford, 1969.

2. For 'clusters' see A. L. Kroeber, *Configurations of culture growth*, Berkeley and L.A., 1944. He writes as if 'culture growth' could be measured like economic growth.

3. Vasari at Naples, Vasari-Milanesi 7.674. Tinctoris qu. E. E. Lowinsky, 'music of the Renaissance as viewed by Renaissance musicians' in B. O'Kelly, ed., *The Renaissance image of man and the world*, Ohio, 1966.

4. R. W. Lee, 'ut pictura poesis', *AB* 1940, notes how in the Renaissance, theorists 'cavalierly applied to painting doctrine intended in antiquity to apply to dramatic and epic poetry'. E. H. Wilkins, 'on the nature and extent of the Italian Renaissance', in his *The invention of the Sonnet*, Rome 1959, makes a useful distinction between 'Naissance' (cultural 'strands' in which the classical element is secondary or non-existent) and Renaissance, where the classical is important.

5. The Renaissance 'hybrid' is discussed by E. Wind, *Pagan Mys-*

teries in the Renaissance, new ed., London, 968, p. 24ff. 'Additive' and 'substitutive' cultural changes are discussed in M. J. Herskovits, *The human factor in changing Africa*, London, 1962, ch. 13. The Botticelli 'Birth of Venus' example is mentioned in C. Gould, *An introduction to Italian R·‑naissance painting*, London, 1957, p. 48.

6. For Burckhardt's use of *Realismus* and *Naturalismus*, see his *Cicerone*, Basel, 1855, p. 553ff. On the problem of realism, the following studies are valuable: E. Auerbach, *Mimesis*, English trans. Princeton, 1953; E. H. Gombrich, *Art and illusion*, London 1960; J. Huizinga, 'Renaissance and realism' in *Men and Ideas*: R. Wellek, the concept of realism in literary scholarship' in his *Concepts of Criticism*, New Haven 1963; and 'Auerbach's special realism' in *Kenyon Review*, 1954.

7. The point about the 'family luggage' is made by H. Wölfflin, *Classic Art*, English trans. London, 1952, p. 218. The play, 'Della Natività di Cristo' in A. D'Ancona, ed., *Sacre Rappresentazioni*, vol. I, Florence 1872; see esp. pp. 197–8.

8 See, above all, Gombrich (as note 6) who quotes Riegl (p. 16). Wölfflin's point comes from his *Principles of Art History*, English trans. New York, 1950 ed., p. 13. Francastel's point trans. from his *Peinture et société*, 2nd ed., Paris, 1965, pp. 7, 79.

9. On wax images, see Warburg, p. 117ff. Instructions how to make a life-mask in Cennini, p. 124. Vasari's criticism of Uccello in his life of Uccello.

10. Similar distinctions to the one between realism of structure and realism of detail have often been made. Lukács, for example, distinguishes 'realism' from 'naturalism' in literature (e.g. in *The Meaning of contemporary realism*, English trans., London 1963, p. 34). Huizinga distinguishes 'emphatic' from 'illustrative' realism (see note 6 for reference) and F. Chabod *Machiavelli and the Renaissance*, English trans., Cambridge, 1958, p. 175ff. Needless to say all these terms are simply English equivalents of the actual distinctions.

11. The sample taken was that of dated paintings, as listed in I. Errera, *Répertoire des Peintures Datés*, vol. I, Brussels, 1920. The dangers of bias in the sample are discussed in chapter 7 below, p. 180. Details of the pattern for each decade are discussed in chapter 10 below p. 333. The significance of the contrast between Innocent III and Manetti is a matter of controversy. It was emphasised by G. Gentile, 'il concetto dell'uomo nel Rinascimento' in his *Il pensiero italiano del Rinascimento*, 3rd ed., Florence 1940. It is minimized by C. Trinkhaus, *In our image and likeness*, London 1970, part 2. A balanced discussion of Machiavelli and medieval writers is A. H. Gilbert, *Machia-*

velli's Prince and its forerunners, Durham, N.C., 1938.

12. The idea of crypto-secularisation is in B. Berenson, *The Italian painter of the Renaissance*, London, 1952, and Warburg, p. 115.

13. The point about Bertoldo's relief is made by E. H. Gombrich in 'the early Medici as patrons of art' in Gombrich (1966), p. 56. Croce's remark about Machiavelli comes from the *Elementi di politica*, Bari 1925, qu. in De Lamar Jensen, *Machiavelli*, Boston, 1960, p. 13. The case for the non-subject in Renaissance paintings is made by C. Gilbert 'on subject and non-subject in Italian Renaissance pictures', in *AB* 1952.

14. R. Wittkower, 'individualism in art and artists' in *Journal of the History of Ideas*, 1961, is an important discussion of Renaissance Italy, emphasizing the changes of style by arists and the prizing of unfinished works as evidence. Cennini, p. 15. Castiglione, *Courtier*, Book I, chapter 37. de Hollanda, *Da Pintura Antigua*, Porto, 1918, p. 243.

15. On the court dance and the popular dance, see Bridgman, p. 62. On aristocratic art and popular art, H. Wölfflin, *Classic Art*, English trans. London 1952, p. 213. On literature, G. Cocchiara, *Le origini della poesia popolare*, Turin 1966, p. 29ff., emphasizes the connexion rather than the split between the two cultures.

16. A useful bound-up volume of early sixteenth-century Italian chap-books is in the British Museum, shelf-mark C.57.1.7. It would be fascinating to have for sixteenth-century Italy a study like the one R. Mandrou has made for France in the seventeenth and eighteenth centuries, *De la culture populaire aux 17e et 18e siècles*, Paris, 1964. The 'trenta vecchie' are mentioned by G. Dominici, *c.* 1400: *regola del governo di cura familiare*, Florence 1860, p. 151.

17. I have deliberately avoided the term 'mannerism' to describe this trend because art-historians have used it to describe two different styles, one serene and one disturbed. But see chapter 10, below p. 332.

18. On 'decompartmentalization' see E. Panofsky, 'artist, scientist, genius' in W. K. Ferguson *et al.*, *The Renaissance*, New York 1962 edition, p. 128. A. Chastel uses a similar formula, 'décloisonnement' in his 'art et humanisme au quattrocento' in V. Brancha, ed., *Umanesimo europeo e umanesimo veneziano*, Florence, 1964. E. Zilsel emphasizes the relations between artisans and humanists in his 'genesis of the concept of scientific progress' in *JHI*, 1945.

19. A succinct survey of regional styles in the Italian Renaissance is to be found in *EWA*, s.v. 'Italian art'.

Chapter three: Artists and Writers

No references are given for biographical information about the élite derived from the following four sources: *DIH: EI:* Groves: *T–B*.

1. See Vasari's lives of Brunelleschi, Baldovinetti and Michelangelo; Manetti: Condivi.
2. See Vasari's lives of Giotto, Castagno, Beccafumi, Sansovino; and K. Frey, ed., *Il libro di Antonio Billi*, Berlin, 1892. The comparison with myths of the birth of the hero in E. Kris, *Psychoanalytic explorations in art*, London, 1953, p. 64ff.
3. The three kinds of school are a generalization to Italy in the period of Villani's famous distinction between three kinds of school for Florence *c*. 1340, which is consistent with the descriptions of education given in diaries and memoirs. For a picture of Italian education based on local and documentary sources, see A. Zanelli, *Del pubblico insegnamento in Pistoia dal xiv al xvi secolo*, Rome, 1900.
4. Cennini, p. 65.
5. Barzizza quoted by M. Baxandall in *JWCI*, 1965, 183n. Vasari's description of training from his life of Beccafumi. On workshop organization, see Wackernagel on Florence; on Venice, H. Tietze, 'master and workshop in the Venetian Renaissance' in *Parnassus*, Dec. 1939. On trade secrets in the Ghiberti workshop, F. D. Prager and G. Scaglia, *Brunelleschi*, Cambridge, Mass., 1970, p. 65ff.
6. There has been a great deal of recent research on the history of individual Italian universities, and the university of Padua even has a journal devoted to its history, but there is no general synthesis, and one has to go back to H. Rashdall, *The universities of Europe*, ed. F. M. Powicke and A. B. Emden, Oxford, 1936. Rashdall lists 20 Italian universities founded before 1420 but seven were probably extinct: Arezzo, Reggio, the City of Rome, Treviso, Vercelli, Verona, Vicenza. An example of college statutes from the period, Ferrara 1485, is printed in V. Caputi, *Il collegi dottorali*, Ferrara, 1962, p. 104ff: there are some obvious resemblances to guild statutes.
7. On the training of architects, see J. Ackerman, 'architectural practice in the Italian Renaissance' in *Journal of the Society of Architectural Historians*, XIII, no. 3.
8. Alberti, *On architecture*, Book 9, chapter 10, Filarete, p. 198.
9. Chastel, p. 19ff, discusses the 'academy' of Bertoldo, and N.

Pevsner, *Academies of art*, Cambridge 1940, chapter 1, discusses those of Leonardo and Bandinelli.

10. On the library of the da Maianos, L. Cendali, *Giuliano e Benedetto da Maiano*, Florence 1926, p. 182ff. On Neroccio, G. Coor, *Neroccio*, Princeton 1961, p. 107. On Leonardo, L. Reti 'the 2 unpublished mss of Leonardo' in *Burlington Magazine*, vol. 110 1968, p. 81ff.

11. The idea of art as a family business is stressed by Tietze, cited in note 5 above.

12. Companies of artists discussed by U. Procacci, 'compagnie di pittori' in *Rivista d'Arte*, 1960.

13. On the organization of the sculptor's workshop, C. Seymour, *Sculpture in Italy*, Harmondsworth 1966, p. 11ff. On marble supplies, C. Klapisch, 'le commerce des marbres de Carrare entre 1450 et 1550' in *Nuova Rivista Storica*, 1966.

14. On the role of the architect, Ackerman (note 7 above) on Rome; N. Pevsner, 'the term "architect" in the Middle Ages', *Speculum*, 1942; A. Wirobisz, 'l'attività edilizia a Venezia' in *Studi Veneziani*, 1965.

15. On the relation between architects and masons, Ackerman (note 7 above); C. Ricci, *Il tempio malatestiano*, Milan/Rome 1924, p. 588ff. (on Alberti at Rimini); H. Saalman, 'Filippo Brunelleschi' in *A.B.* 1958, and 'Antonio Filarete' in *A.B.*, 1959.

16. S. Thrupp has good discussions of the medieval guild system in M. M. Postan *et al.*, eds, *Cambridge Economic History of Europe*, vol. III, and D. L. Sills, ed., *International Encyclopaedia of the Social Sciences*, under 'gilds'.

17. The Paduan statutes have been published in Gaye, vol. 2, p. 43ff, and in the *Archivo Veneto* for 1874.

18. A. de la Mare, *Vespasiano da Bisticci*, Ph.D thesis, London 1965, (on deposit at the Warburg Institute) notes that one or two illuminators worked regularly in Vespasiano's shop, but that it was too small to be a proper scriptorium, and that Vespasiano's letters to scribes show that mss. were copied for him elsewhere.

19. L. Martines, p. 97, argues that the stay-at-home humanists were as important as the wandering ones.

20. C. Dionisotti, 'chierici e laici' in his *Geografia e storia della letteratura italiana*, Turin 1967, looks at a hundred writers active between 1500 and 1550 and talks of the 'clericalization' of Italian literature in the period; half his group are clerics.

21. Acciarini's complaint to Poliziano about his 'evil star' quoted in Usmiani, 'Marulic', *Harvard Slavic Studies*, 1957, p. 19.

22. General discussions of the status of the artist in Antal, Wackernagel, and Wittkower (1963).

23. Cennini, p. 91; Leonardo, p. 91; St Antonio quoted by C. Gilbert, 'the archbishop on the painters of Florence' in *AB*, 1959; Venetian patrician painters quoted by Dolce, p. 106ff. Giulio Romano documents assembled in C. D'Arco, *Giulio Pippi Romano*, second ed. Mantua 1842, appendix; the translations are F. Hartt's from his *Giulio Romano*, New Haven 1958. Dürer's letter, often quoted, 13 October 1506 to W. Pirckheimer.

24. Federico's patent is quoted and discussed by P. Murray, 'the Italian Renaissance architect' in *Journal of the Royal Society of Arts*, 1966, p. 589ff.

25. Tinctoris discussed by E. Lowinsky, 'music of the Renaissance as viewed by Renaissance musicians' in B. O'Kelly, ed., *The Renaissance image of man and the world*, Ohio, 1906. See also Bridgman, and C. Anthon, 'social status of Italian musicians' in *Journal of Renaissance and Baroque Music*, 1946.

26. This question discussed by Martines.

27. Leonardo, pp. 57 and 91.

28. Michelangelo, letter of 2 May 1548: trans E. H. Ramsden in *The letters of Michelangelo*, London 1963. Vasari, life of Perino del Vaga.

29. Condivi, p. 45.

30. Benvenuto quoted by Coor (as note 10) p. 10. Vasari, preface to part 3.

31. C. Trinkaus, *Adversity's Noblemen*, especially preface to second edition, New York, 1965.

32. Wittkower (1963) discusses six deviant traits – obsession with work; melancholy; suicide; crime; homosexuality; general eccentricity.

33. Gauricus p. 110 describes Donatello. One might compare the contempt of the jazz musician for the 'squares' he plays for, discussed in H. Becker, *Outsiders*, New York, 1963, p. 90ff.

Chapter four: Patrons and Clients

1. On art patronage in general, see Antal; J. Burckhardt, 'Die Sammler' in his *Beiträge zur Kunstgeschichte*, Basel, 1898; Wackernagel (section, 'Die Auftraggeber'); Wittkower (1963), p. 34ff. M. Baxandall *Painting and experience in 15th century Italy*, Oxford 1972. I have not given references for contracts where they can be found in standard lives of the artists concerned. D. S. Chambers has edited a volume of translated sources, *Patrons and artists in the Italian Renaissance*, London 1970. The typology of patronage is taken from J. M. B. Edwards, 'Creativity: social aspects' in D. L. Sills, ed., *International En-*

cyclopaedia of the Social Sciences, vol. 3, but I have divided his first category, the 'personalized' into two.

2. The importance of Florentine civic patronage is stressed by Baron (1938). Some documents available in G. Poggi, ed., *Il duomo di Firenze*, Berlin, 1909.

3. Patronage of Venetian confraternities studied in P. Molmenti and G. Ludwig, *Vittore Carpaccio et la confrérie de St Ursule*, Florence, 1903, and G. Ludwig, 'Archivalische Beiträge zur Geschichte der Venezianische Malerei in *Jahrbuch der königlich preussischer kunstammlungen*, 1905, Beiheft.

4. Vivarini's commission and other documents about Venetian state patronage in G. B. Lorenzi, ed., *Monumenti per servire alla storia del Palazzo Ducal di Venezia*, part 1, Venice, 1868.

5. Patronage at the court of Milan studied in F. Malaguzzi-Valeri, *La corte di Lodovico il Moro*, 4 vols., Milan 1913–23.

6. On Federico of Mantua and Alfonso of Ferrara respectively see F. Hart, *Giulio Romano*, New Haven, 1958, and J. A. Crowe and G. B. Cavalcaselle, *The life and times of Titian*, 2nd ed., London, 1881.

7. The suggestion that Mantegna found moving to Mantua a difficult decision to make comes from E. Tietze-Conrat, *Mantegna*, London 1955, p. 11.

8. Wackernagel, p. 6.

9. 'the marble itself' quoted by Wackernagel, p. 245. Filarete, p. 106. Machiavelli's *Prince*, chapter 21.

10. Domenico's letter in Gay 1.136; Milanese negotiations in C. J. ffoulkes and R. Maiocchi, *Vincenzo Foppa*, London 1909, p. 300ff; Vasari, life of Bandinelli; E. Rud, *Vasari's life and lives*, London, 1963.

11. Professor Gombrich has reminded me that the system of competitions for commissions, here explained as a characteristic of societies dominated by merchants, could have been a deliberate imitation of classical antiquity, as described by Pliny.

12. Titian's letter quoted by Crowe and Cavalcaselle (as note 6), 1.181.

13. Gay 1.191ff, translated by Grote in *JWCI*, 1964, p. 321ff. Vasari gives this incident as a possible reason for Michelangelo's leaving Rome.

14. On Isabella as a patroness, see W. Braghirolli, ed., 'Carteggio' in *Archivo Veneto*, 1877; J. Cartwright, *Isabella d'Este*, 2nd ed., London 1903; E. Wind, *Bellini's Feast of the Gods*, Harvard, 1948; Caro's letter quoted by Gombrich, 'icones symbolicae' in *JWCI*, 1948.

15. Humanist advisers discussed by Warburg, pp. 36, 43; R. Kraut-

heimer and T. Krautheimer-Hess, *Lorenzo Ghiberti*, Princeton, 1956, p. 169ff; M. Baxandall, 'Guarino' in *JWCI*, 1965; E. H. Gombrich, 'Botticelli's mythologies' in *JWCI*, 1945; E. Wind, as note 14, p. 14ff.

16. E. H. Gombrich, 'the early Medici' in Gombrich, (1966).

17. General discussions of music patronage in C. Anthon, 'social status of Italian musicians' in *Journal of Renaissance and baroque music*, 1947; N. Bridgman, *La vie musicale au quattrocento*, Paris 1964; A. Einstein, 'early concert life' in his *Essays on music*, London, 1958. On G. M. Sforza, see E. Motta, 'musici alla corte degli Sforza' in *ASL*, 1887; the letter to Ercole d'Este printed in E. van der Straeten, ed., *La musique aux pays bas*, vol 6, Brussels, 1882.

18. R. Sabbadini, 'come il Panormita diventò poeta aulico' in *ASL*, 1916. G. Cozzi, 'cultura politica nella "pubblica storiografia" Veneziana' in *Studi Veneziani*, 1963. V. Calmeta's life of Serafino, prefixed to Serafino, *Opere*, Venice, 1505.

19. The advertisement in S. Venezian, *Olimpo da Sassoferrato*, Bologna, 1921, p. 121. The activities of Serragli discussed in G. Corti and F. Hartt, 'new documents concerning Donatello' in *AB*, 1962. Isabella's letter quoted by M. Conway, *Giorgione*, London 1929, p. 13ff. Della Palla's activities discussed in Wackernagel and in Vasari's life of Pontormo. On exhibitions see K. Luckhurst, *The story of exhibitions*, London and New York, 1951, and Koch, *Die Kunstanstellung*, Berlin, 1967. The quotation comes from Vasari's life of Bandinelli, which Koch cites.

20. Medici patronage, inflated by propaganda, has been cut down to size by Chastel; D. Gnoli, *La Roma di Leon X*, Milan, 1938; and Gombrich, 'the early Medici' in Gombrich (1966).

Chapter five: Functions

1. The classic essay on the use of the concept of 'function' in sociology is R. Merton, 'manifest and latent functions' reprinted in Merton, *Social theory and social structure*, revised edition, Glencoe, 1957. The Strozzi will is quoted, but mistranslated, in R. G. Goldthwaite, *Private wealth in Renaissance Florence*, Princeton, 1968, p. 102n.

2. W. Bombe, 'Die Tafelbilder des Benedetto Bonfigli' in *Repertorium für Kunstwissenschaft*, 1909. L. Kriss-Rettenbeck, *Das Votivbild*, Munich, 1958, is a general study of ex votos, and L. Novelli and M. Massaccesi, *Ex voto del santuario della Madonna del Monte di Cesena*, Forlì, 1961, an extremely specific one.

3. On Botticelli and magic, see F. A. Yates, *Giordano Bruno and the hermetic tradition*, London, 1964, p. 76ff. On magic and astrology, see chapter 8, below.

4. Gregory the Great on images and devotion in Migne, *Patrologia Latina* vol. 77, columns 990ff. For the domestic devotional image, Wackernagel, p. 180ff, and S. Ringbom, *Icon to narrative*, Abo. 1965. Gerhard von Kaiserberg is quoted by Ringbom, p. 29n; I have adapted the translation. Two Florentine inventories are edited by W. Bombe, *Nachlass-inventare*, Leipzig/Berlin, 1928.

5. Gregory the Great on the didactic function, as note 4, columns p. 1027ff. Dominici, *Regola del governo*, Florence 1860, p. 131ff. On Korah, see below, chapter 7, p. 204.

6. Filarete, p. 130. The political function of early fifteenth-century Florentine art discussed by F. Hartt, 'art and freedom in quattrocento Florence' in L. F. Sandler, ed., *Essays in memory of K. Lehmann* New York 1964. For a more detailed discussion of the meaning of these images, chapter 7, below, p. 202.

7. The private functions are illustrated by the inventories printed by Bombe, as note 4.

8. Political functions of literature are discussed in F. Flamini, *La lirica toscana del Rinascimento*, Pisa, 1891, and exemplified by the collection of A. Medin and L. Frati, *Lamenti storici*, vols 2 and 3, Bologna 1888, 1890.

9. J. S. Ackerman, *The architecture of Michelangelo*, London, 1961, the chapter, 'the Farnese Palace' discusses the functions of domestic architecture; so does J. S. Ackerman, *Palladio*, Harmsworth, 1966, chapter on 'villas'. See also B. Rupprecht, 'villa' in *Probleme der Kunstwissenschaft*, vol. 2, Berlin, 1966.

10. Tinctoris discusses the functions of music in his 'complexus effectuum musices' in E. de Coussemaker, ed., *Scriptorum de musica . . .* vol. IV Paris 1876, p. 191ff. For modern discussions, see Bridgman; E. Lowinsky, 'music of the Renaissance as viewed by Renaissance musicians' in B. O'Kelly, ed., *The Renaissance image of man and the world*, Ohio, 1966. On Ficino, music and astrology, D. P. Walker, *Spiritual and demonic magic*, London, 1958, chapter 1.

Chapter six: Taste

1. For an analysis with very similar aims to those of this chapter, see M. Baxandall *Painting and experience in 15th-century Italy*, Oxford 1972, 109f. Good introductions to a subject closely

connected to taste, that of art theory, are A. Blunt, *Artistic theory in Italy*, Oxford, 1940 and E. Panofsky, *Idea*, 1924, English trans., Columbia, S.C., 1968.

On the concept of 'taste' see Dolce. p. 103, and J. Reynolds, *Discourses*, number seven. Two famous demonstrations that taste has a history were made by A. O. Lovejoy, 'the first Gothic revival' in his *Essays in the history of ideas*, Baltimore 1948; G. Boas, 'the Mona Lisa in the history of taste' in *JHI*, 1940.

2. In this chapter extensive use will be made of Vasari, although his *Lives* were first published in 1550, and additions made for the 1568 edition. But Vasari wrote the book in the 1540s, he was an adult by 1540, so that his ideas are relevant when discussing the later part of the period. Fazio is translated and discussed by M. Baxandall in *JWCI*, 1964.. G. Savonarola, *Semplicità della vita christiana*, in M. Ferrara, ed., *prediche e scritti*, Florence 1952, vol. 2, p. 47. G. B. Gelli, *Vite d'artisti*, *Archivio Storico Italiano* 1896, p. 37. Alberti, *painting*, Book Two. Michelangelo's remark, recorded by N. Martelli, in R. J. Clements, ed., *Michelangelo*, Englewood Cliffs 1963, p. 19.

3. The importance of order, symmetry and related values is to be found almost on every page of treatises on art theory; a famous passage is Alberti, *Architecture*, Book 6, chapter 2. The orderly arrangement of trees, *ibid.* Book 9, chapter 4. The significance of gardens as a clue to the history of taste and other ideas is discussed in Lovejoy, (as note 1). See J. Cartwright, *Italian gardens of the Renaissance*, London, 1914, 23ff. The Sannazzaro quotation comes from the opening of his *Arcadia*, of which there are many editions: a similar aesthetic ideal was expressed by Theocritus. Michelangelo, recorded by Lomazzo, in Clements (as note 2); compare Dolce, p. 103.

4. An important general discussion of the concepts of 'richness' and simplicity' in E. H. Gombrich, 'visual metaphors of value in art' in Gombrich (1963). G. Weise has discussed the rise of 'grandeur' several times; see his *L'ideale eroico del Rinascimento*, Naples 1961, part 1. Alberti, *Architecture*, Book 7, chapter 10, Pius II, Commentarii, Frankfurt 1614, p. 234ff. C. Landino, *Commento sopra la Comedia di Dante*, 'proemio': I used the Venice, 1507 edition; on him as art critic see O. Morisani, 'C. Landino' in *Burlington Magazine*, 1953, p. 267ff, and P. Murray, *ibid.*, 391ff.

5. On expressiveness, see Fazio (as note 2); Alberti, *Painting*, p. 77; Leonardo, p. 341ff; Dolce, p 97ff.

6. On facility, Dolce, p. 156ff (using the term *sprezzatura*, like Castiglione); on surprise, Dolce, p. 146ff; on mystery, P. Pino,

Dialoghi di pittura (1548), Milan, 1954 ed., p. 45. Modern discussions of the use of the term *maniera* in the period are C. H. Smyth, *Mannerism and maniera*, Locust Valley, New York, 1962, and G. Weise, 'maniera und *pellegrino*' in *Romanistisches Jahrbuch*, 1950.

7. Alberti's letter quoted by Wittkower (1949), p. 117ff. Important modern discussions of music theory are A. Einstein, *The Italian madrigal*, Princeton 1949, vol. I, p. 212ff; E. E. Lowinsky, 'music in the culture of the Renaissance' in *JHI*, 1954. From taste point of view, three important treatises of the period are J. Tinctoris, *De arte contrapuncti*, 1477, in E. de Coussemaker, ed., *Scriptorum de musica . . .* vol. IV (esp. 78, 120, 144, 147); P. Aron, *Toscanello* (1523) esp. book 2, chapters 16–18; and, late but important, N. Vicentino, *L'antica musica*, 1555. The Castiglione passage from his *Courtier*, Book I, chapter 37. The Zarlino passage from his *Institutioni Harmoniche*, 1558, Book 4, chapter 32; the translation is Lowinsky's.

8. 'A certain great affinity' in Fazio (as note 2), p. 43. The links between art theory and literary theory are discussed by R. W. Lee, 'ut pictura poesis' in *AB*, 1940. Modern discussions of sixteenth-century Italian literary theory are V. Hall jr, *Renaissance literary criticism*, New York 1945, and B. Weinberg, *A History of Literary Criticism in the Italian Renaissance*, Chicago, 1961. For the fifteenth century, one important source is Poliziano's letter to Federico of Aragon (sometimes attributed to Lorenzo de'Medici) printed and discussed in I. Maier, *Ange Politien*, Geneva, 1966, p. 232ff. Important treatises of the early sixteenth century include P. Bembo, *Prose* (1525), M. Vida, *De arte poetica* (1527) and B. Daniello, *Poetica* (1536). The verse translations of Vida are from the version by C. Pitt, London, 1725. Gauricus and Britannico are quoted by Weinberg, pp. 90n, 93n.

9. G. Savonarola, eighteenth sermon on Amos and Zacharias, 1496, quoted in Ferrara (as note 2) vol. 2, p. 49. G. F. Pico, *De rerum praenotione* (1506) quoted in Weinberg (as note 8), p. 255.

10. The debt of art criticism to rhetoric is discussed by E. H. Gombrich, in *JWCI*, 1960, 1966, and J. R. Spencer, *JWCI*, 1957. Its debt to manuals of behaviour, especially Castiglione, is discussed in Blunt (as note 1) p. 92ff. See also M. Baxandall, *Giotto and the orators*, London, 1971.

11. See K. F. Schuessler, 'social background and musical taste' in *American Sociological Review*, 1948.

12. Filarete, books 11 and 12, discusses this question. N. Vicentino is quoted by Einstein (as note 7) p. 228. Boccaccio's audience

in the early fifteenth century discussed by C. Bec, *Les Marchands écrivains*, Paris/The Hague, 1967, and Petrarch's audience by A. Graf, *Attraversa il cinquecento*, Turin, 1888 (the essay on Petrarchism).

Chapter seven: Iconography

1. See J. Bialostocki, 'iconography and iconology 'in *EWA*, and E. Panofsky, *Studies in iconology*, New York, 1939, introduction. What Panofsky calls 'conventional' and 'intrinsic' I here refer to as 'manifest' and 'latent'. Some writers reserve the term 'iconography' for the study of the first level, and the term 'iconology' for the study of the second.

2. I. Errera, *Repertoire des peintures datées*, vol. 1, Brussels, 1920.

3. Only paintings are scored, not woodcuts or drawings. Attributions are not unchallengeable: I followed Pope-Hennessy on Uccello, Vigni on Antonello, Cipriani on Mantegna, Salvini on Botticelli, Lauts on Carpaccio, della Chiesa on Luini, and Gibbons on Dossi.

4. E. Mâle, *L'art religieux du XIIIe siècle en France*, Paris, 1925. It is surprising how often one can describe fifteenth-century Italy in the same terms Mâle used for thirteenth-century France. See especially p. 176ff of the New York 1958 edition of the English translation, called *The Gothic image*.

5. L. Réau, *Iconographie de l'art chrétien*, Paris 1955, vol. 3, R. H. P. Crawfurd, *Plague and pestilence in literature and art*, Oxford, 1914.

6. For Federico Gonzaga, see Gaye, vol. 2, p. 179; for Aretino, G. G. Bottari, *Raccolta di lettere*, 8 vols. Milan, 1822–5, vol. 3, p. 136.

7. Modern art historians can be divided into iconoclasts and iconodules. C. Gilbert, 'on subject and not-subject in Italian Renaissance pictures' in *AB* 1952, is a critique of Panofsky's iconographical approach; the quotation from Giovio comes from this article, p. 204. For Giorgione contrast L. Venturi, 'Giorgione' in *EWA*, with E. Wind, *Giorgione's Tempestà*, Oxford, 1969.

8. For the emergence of landscape, see E. H. Gombrich, 'the Renaissance theory of art and the rise of landscape' in Gombrich (1966), an essay which makes it as embarrassing as superfluous to utter a word on the same subject; A. R. Turner, *The vision of landscape in Renaissance Italy*, Princeton 1966; R. Wittkower, 'L' Arcadia ed il Giorgionismo' in V. Branca, ed., *Umanesimo europeo ed umanesimo veneziano*, Florence, 1964. On

still-life, E. H. Gombrich, 'tradition and expression in the Western still-life' in Gombrich (1963).

9. For medieval architecture, see R. Krautheimer, 'iconography of medieval architecture' in *JWCI*, 1942, and O. von Simson, *The Gothic Cathedral*, London, 1956, esp. pp. 37ff, 113ff. On Renaissance architecture, Wittkower (1949) especially p. 27ff; the quotation from Giorgi *ibid.*, p. 154. See also Filarete, book 7, and R. Klein, 'l'urbanisme utopique' in Lameere, ed., *Les utopies à la Renaissance*, Brussels/Paris, 1963.

10. Landino and Vellutello are quoted by B. Weinberg, *A History of Literary criticism in the Italian Renaissance*, Chicago 1961, pp. 80, 101. I used the Venice, 1497 edition of the Italian translation of Ovid's *Metamorphoses*. On *Orpheus*, E. Wind, *Pagan mysteries in the Renaissance*, London 1958, chapter on 'Amor as a god of death'.

11. H. Caplan, 'the four senses of scriptural interpretation' in *Speculum* 1929 gives a history of this approach, and E. Auerbach, 'figura' in his *Scenes from the drama of European literature*, New York, 1959 explains the principles of figural interpretation. The Tobias story in Réau, (as note 5) vol. 2, Fra Pietro's interpretation in J. Cartwright, *Isabella d'Este*, 2nd ed., London 1903, vol. 1, p. 319 (the text in A. Luzio, *Precettori d'Isabella d'Este*, Ancona 1887). The Ficino passage discussed by E. H. Gombrich, 'Botticelli's mythologies' in *JWCI*, 1945. Alberti's emblem discussed by Wind (as note 10) p. 186ff. For Vasari, J. Rouchette, 'la domestication de l'ésoterisme dans l'oeuvre de Vasari' in E. Castelli, ed., *Umanesimo e esoterismo*, Padua, 1960. For his portrait of Lorenzo, see his *Literarische Nachlass*, ed. K. Frey, vol. 1, Munich 1923, p. 17ff.

12. E. Panofsky, *Early Netherlandish painting*, Cambridge, Mass., 1953, chapter five; the Piero della Francesca discussed by C. Gilbert, (as note 7) p. 209; the Crivelli, by H. Friedmann, 'the symbolism of Crivelli's Madonna and Child' in *GBA*, 1947; the Dossi by F. Gibbons, *D. and B. Dossi*, Princeton, 1968; the Leonardo aqueduct by E. Wind in an Oxford lecture, *c.* 1960.

13. Machiavelli's *Prince*, Chapter 17; Lorenzo de' Medici, *S.S. Giovanni e Paolo*, in A. d'Ancona, ed., *Sacre Rappresentazioni*, vol. 1, Florence 1872, p. 257; E. H. Gombrich, 'the social history of art' in Gombrich, 1963 (Donatello's *Judith*); F. Hartt, 'art and freedom' in L. F. Sandler, ed., *Essays in memory of K. Lehmann*, New York, 1964 (on Donatello and Masaccio); M. Meiss, 'Masaccio and the early Renaissance' in I. E. Rubin, ed. *Renaissance and Mannerism*. On the rebellion of Korah, L. Ettlinger, *The Sistine Chapel before Michelangelo*, Oxford 1965.

14. Vasari's comments in his life of Giorgione, but see Wind's com-

ment (as note 7), on them. The classic discussion of the manuals of mythology is J. Seznec, *La survivance des dieux antiques*, London, 1940 (there is an English translation).

Chapter eight: World Views: Some dominant traits

1. On 'outillage mental' see L. Febvre, *Le problème de l'incroyance*, Paris 1942, p. 384ff; on 'Weltanschauung' see K. Mannheim, *Essays on the sociology of knowledge*, London, 1952, p. 33ff.
2. B. Berelson, *Content analysis in communication research*, Glencoe, 1952 is an introductory survey. A similar approach to Machiavelli offered by J. H. Hexter, 'the loom of language' in *American Historical Review*, 1964. For 'fashionable terms', G. Weise, 'vom Menschenideal und von den Modewörtern der Gotik und der Renaissance', in *Deutsche Vierteljahrschrift*, 1936 and his *L'Ideale eroico del Rinascimento*, Naples, 1961.
3. Useful models for the organization of this chapter were C. S. Lewis, *The discarded image*, Cambridge, 1964, and E. M. W. Tillyard, *The Elizabethan world picture*, London, 1943.
4. Leonardo, *Literary works*, ed. Richter, 2nd ed., Oxford, 1939, no. 1000. Leone Ebreo, *Dialoghi d'amore*, Bari, 1929, second dialogue, part 1.
5. Fontana quoted by L. Thorndike, *History of Magic*, vol. 4, New York, 1934, p. 169n. On this aspect of Leonardo's thought, see E. J. Dijksterhuis, *De Mechanisering van het Wereldbeeld*, English trans. Oxford, 1961, p. 253ff.
6. Bernardino da Siena, *Prediche volgari*, Florence, 1958, 'del nome di Gesù'. On the fourfold interpretation of Scripture, below p. 194.
7. F. Guicciardini, *Storia d'Italia*, Bari 1929, vol. 1, p. 63ff.
8. The best introduction to the image of the heavens at this time is to read Dante. Modern work on astrology includes J. Seznec, *La survivance des dieux antiques*, London, 1940, Book 1, chapter 2; Warburg, who discusses the Palazzo Schifanoia; D. P. Walker, *Spiritual and demonic magic*, London, 1958, who discusses Ficino. The quotation from Vasari comes from his life of Leonardo, the first paragraph.
9. Lorenzo de'Medici, 'SS. Giovanni e Paolo' in A. D'Ancona, ed., *Sacre Rappresentazioni*, vol. 1, Florence 1872, pp. 264, 267.
10. Cavalcanti quoted by C. Varese, *Storia e politica nella prosa del' 400*, Turin 1961, p. 109. F. Guicciardini, *Ricordi*, series C, no 207.
11. A. Strozzi's image of God in her *Lettere*, ed. C. Guasti, Florence,

1877, p. 56ff. God as man's steward, Brandolini's image, quoted by C. Trinkhaus, *In our image and likeness*, London 1970, vol. 1, p. 301; Lorenzo de Medici's image in his *Scritti spirituali*, Milan 1958, p. 51; Machiavelli's rejection of a supernatural explanation in his *Prince*, chapter 12.

12. The classic discussion is A. O. Lovejoy, *The great chain of being*, Cambridge, Mass., 1936; see also Lewis and Tillyard (above, note 3). On Vasari, J. Rouchette, 'La domestication de l'esotérisme' in E. Castelli, ed., *Umanesimo e esoterismo*, Padua, 1960.

13. A. Doren, *Fortuna im Mittelalter*, Hamburg, 1922; F. Gilbert, 'Bernardo Rucellai' in *JWCI*, 1949.

14. On alchemy, L. Thorndike (as note 5) also S. Toulmin and J. Goodfield, *The architecture of matter*, London 1962, chapter 6. On Parmigianino and alchemy, M. Fagiolo Dell'Arco, *Il Parmigianino*, Rome, 1970; many symbols are ambiguous, and it cannot be said that the author has found the key to Parmiagianino, as elusive as the philosopher's stone itself.

15. Giovanni Pico della Mirandola, *Oration of the dignity of man*, translated in E. Cassirer et al. eds., *The Renaissance philosophy of man*, Chicago, 1948, p. 246ff.

16. On demons, L. Thorndike, (as note 5); on miraculous images, below p. 256. P. Pomponazzi *De incantationibus*, Basel, 1556 (written 1520) lacks a modern editor and translator, but deserves both.

17. On witchcraft in Italy, G. Bonomo, *Caccia alle streghe*, Palermo, 1959; a collection of fifteenth-century Italian texts on the subject in J. Hansen, *Quellen zur Geschichte des Hexenwahns*, Bonn 1901, p. 17ff; I am preparing a new edition of G. F. Pico, *La Strega*, last reprinted a hundred years ago; the Signorini case discussed by C. Ginzburg, in *Annali della scuola normale superiore di Pisa*, 1961.

18. This defence of monarchy in Castiglione's *Courtier*, Book 4, chapter 19; Machiavelli on political 'illness' in his *Prince*, chapter 3; for uses of 'stato' see Lorenzo de'Medici (as note 9) p. 244, and J. H. Hexter (as note 2) p. 953.

19. Concepts of stratification discussed by F. Gilbert, *Machiavelli and Guicciardini*, Princeton 1965, p. 19ff. For Machiavelli, his *History of Florence*, Book 2, chapters 34, 36, 40, 42. The analogy with horses and trees in Castiglione, *Courtier*, Book 1, chapter 14.

20. More detail and references in P. Burke, 'the sense of historical perspective in Renaissance Italy' in *Journal of World History*, 1969. Dolce, p. 124ff, on Raphael's research. Vasari quoted by Gombrich (1966) p. 124, and by E. Panofsky, *Meaning in the*

visual arts, New York 1955, p. 212. F. Guicciardini, *Ricordi*, series C, no. 110.

21. Alberti's *Family*, book 3, entitled 'economicus'.

22. Savonarola quoted by D. Weinstein, 'millenarianism in a civic setting' in S. Thrupp, ed., *Millennial dreams in action*, The Hague, 1962, p. 1965; Botticelli quoted by D. Weinstein, 'the myth of Florence' in N. Rubinstein, ed., *Florentine Studies*, London, 1968, p. 15. Ariosto, *Orlando Furioso*, Canto 15, section 26.

23. For the 'Triumph of the four complexions', C. S. Singleton, ed., *Canti Carnascialeschi*, Bari, 1963, p. 148ff; on melancholy, R. Klibansky, E. Panofsky, F. Saxl, *Saturn and melancholy*, London, 1964, p. 241ff; Ficino's 'anatomy of melancholy' is his *De vita triplici*, (1489): I used the Venice edition of c. 1525.

24. On physiognomy, P. Meller, 'physiognomical theory in Renaissance heroic portraits' in I. E. Rubin, ed., *Renaissance and Mannerism*.

25. Pico (as note 15) p. 225; Castiglione, *Courtier*, Book 1, chapter 26; Aretino, *Ragionamenti*, Book 2, chapter 29.

26. This point is abundantly documented by G. Weise, '*maniera und pellegrino*' in *Romanistisches* Jahrbuch, 1950.

27. C. Varese, ed., *Prosatori volgari del '400*, Milan/Naples, 1955, p. 767ff, 'la novella del grasso legnaiuolo'.

28. For Gelli, Singleton (as note 23), p. 351ff. For mirrors, E. Eng, 'the significance of the mirror and the self-portrait' in *Actes du Xe Congrès internationale d'histoire des sciences*, p. 1045ff.

29. Huizinga, 70. D. McClelland, 'achievement drive and economic growth' in his *The roots of consciousness*, is a brief statement of his attempt to measure the relative strength of the achievement drive in different societies by an analysis of literary texts.

30. L. Bruni, *Epistolae*, Florence 1741, I. 137; Albert, *Family*, p. 139; Leonardo (as note 4) p. 307; Vasari, life of Castagno (incorrectly translated in the Everyman edition).

31. Castiglione, Courtier, Book 2, chapter 8. Pius II, *De curialium miseriis*, Baltimore 1928, p. 32. L. Landucci, *Diario*, Florence 1883, entries for 1482, 1492.

32. On the significance of signatures on paintings, H. Tietze, 'master and workshop in the Venetian Renaissance', in *Parnassus*, December, 1939.

33. Manetti's argument in Vespasiano's life of him; the reference seems to be to Luke, chapter 16, which is about a landlord and his steward, but the businessman Manetti has transposed the passage into commercial terms. Vespasiano da Bisticci, *Vite di uomini illustri*, Milan, 1951. On space and time, P. Francastel, 'valeurs socio-psychologiques de l'espace-temps figuratif de la

Renaissance' in *L'Année Sociologique*, 1965.

34. F. Guicciardini, *Ricordi*, series C, numbers 74, 25.

35. On the irrational in Renaissance thought, there is no general study, but on one aspect, see E. Wind, *Pagan mysteries in the Renaissance*, London, 1958, chapter 'Orpheus in praise of blind love'.

36. For guidance through the literature of the period on the dignity of man, the reader may entrust himself to C. Trinkaus, *In our image and likeness*, London, 1970.

37. G. Weise, *L'Ideale eroico del Rinascimento*, Naples, 1961.

38. Attitudes to death are surveyed in two books by A. Tenenti, *La vie et la mort à travers l'art du 15e siècle*, Paris, 1952, and *Il senso della morte e l'amore della vita nel Rinascimento*, Turin, 1957. For the corpses at Carnival, Singleton (as note 23), p. 238ff. The Strozzi letters (as note 11) p. 178ff, 189.

39. Gauricus, and, for the Candide-like advice, B. Taegio, *La villa*, Milan 1559, p. 140.

40. Poggio quoted in G. Holmes, *The Florentine enlightenment*, London, 1969, p. 147. Cosimo de'Medici's views quoted by Vespasiano (as note 33).

41. Honour and loyalty. Two very different attitudes expressed by Ariosto, *Orlando Furioso*, cantos 45, 46, and Machiavelli, *Prince*, chapter 18.

42. Well-known versions of this thesis are presented by Antal and by von Martin.

43. I have borrowed the concept and definition of 'syndrome' from W. T. Jones, *The romantic syndrome*, The Hague, 1961, but his 'axes of bias' are along much more general lines, such as order/disorder and inner/outer.

Chapter nine: The Social Framework

1. Burckhardt's survey of Italian religion in the last chapter of his 'essay' has scarcely been followed up; there is a need for studies of popular religion like Febvre's on France and Toussaert's on Flanders, or for studies of the Italian church as an institution like Pantin, Knowles and Hamilton Thompson on England. No doubt Denys Hay's Birkbeck lectures will do much to fill the gap when they are published.

2. P. Tacchi-Venturi, *Storia della compagnia di Gesù in Italia*, vol. 1, Rome, 1910, p. 179ff (a much more general survey than the title implies). The Mantua visitation published by R. Putelli, *Vita, storia ed arte mantovana nel' 500*, vol. 2, Mantua, 1935 (the quotation from p. 16).

3. Tacchi-Venturi, p. 36ff; the point about the numbers of Italian bishops made by D. Hay, *The Italian Renaissance*, Cambridge 1961, p. 49; N. Caturegli, 'le condizioni della chiesa di Pisa' in *Bollettino Storico Pisano* 1950, uses the visitations of the diocese, and so does M. Berengo, *Nobili e mercanti nella Lucca del '500*, Turin 1965, chapter 6.

4. Italian bishops discussed in G. Alberigo, *I vescovi italiani al concilio de Trento*, Florence 1959. The same predominance of lawyers is to be found among the English bishops of the early sixteenth century.

5. J. R. H. Moorman, *A history of the Franciscan order*, Oxford, 1968, discusses Italy, and offers some statistics on pp. 465, 489, 581. The impact of the Dominicans on fourteenth-century art is treated by M. Meiss, *Painting in Florence and Siena*, Princeton, 1951; nothing comparable for the fifteenth and sixteenth centuries, nor for the Franciscans, although the influence of St Francis on the arts is discussed by P. Francastel in an article in *Annales E.S.C.*, 1955.

6. Tacchi-Venturi (as note 2), p. 36ff.

7. Pius III, *Commentarii*, Frankfurt 1614. Book 8 discusses the feast of Corpus Christi.

8. The cautious definition of the Veronica is Pius II's, Book 8. Arnold van Harff, *Pilgrimage*, London 1946, discusses the pilgrims at St John Lateran (p. 19) and the Passion Play (p. 40).

9. *Miracoli della gloriosa vergine Maria*, Venice, 1545 (there are many other editions). Documents about the Genazano shrine collected in *Analecta Augustiniana*, 1945. S. Maria Impruneta studied by G. B. Casotti, *Memorie istoriche*, Florence, 1714. See also R. C. Trexler, 'Florentine religious experience: the sacred image' in *Studies in the Renaissance*, 1972. S. Infessura, *Diario*, Rome, 1890, p. 72, reports the miracles at Rome in 1470, but does not make it clear whether the image was the cause or the result of the miracles. L. Novelli and M. Massaccesi, *Ex voto del santuario della Madonna del Monte di Cesena*, Forlì, 1961, is a catalogue with introduction.

10. Editions of the *Golden legend* and the *Transito* are from the British Museum Catalogue, so probably represent only a fraction of the true total. The relation between saints and civic sentiment studied by H. C. Peyer, *Stadt und stadtpatron im mittelalterlichen Italien*, Zürich, 1955. Lists of Italian saints in Count de Mas-Latrie, *Trésor de chronologie*, Paris, 1889, and L. Pastor, *History of the Popes*, English trans., vol. 5, p. 86ff; the point that this illustrates the pressure for canonization in Italy made by D. Hay (as note 3), p. 48.

11. Figures for the foundation of confraternities in G. M. Monti,

Le confraternite medievali, Venice, 1927. Monti has also edited a collection of fifteenth-century Umbrian *laude*, Città di Castello, 1920. The cultural function of confraternities is studied by P. O. Kristeller, 'lay religious traditions and Florentine Platonism' in his *Studies in Renaissance thought and letters*, Rome, 1956. On the confraternity of the Magi, see R. Hatfield in *JWCI*, 1970.

12. The 'seven works' from Bernardino da Feltre, *Confessionale*, Milan, 1519. The concept of 'civic christianity' and the figures for Pistoia in D. Herlihy, *Medieval and Renaissance Pistoia*, New Haven 1967, p. 246ff. The table in Pastor (as note 10), p. 66. *The works of mercy* reproduced in A. G. Dickens, *The counter reformation*, London, 1968, p. 127.

13. Church property in Tuscany discussed by G. Brucker, *Renaissance Florence*, New York, 1969, p. 176ff; in Lombardy, by C. Cipolla, 'une crise ignorée' in *Annales E.S.C.*, 1947.

14. Burckhardt's chapter on 'the state as a work of art' is a famous introduction to the political history of the period. More recent criticisms of this approach are fairly represented by F. Chabod, 'was there a Renaissance state?' in H. Lubasz, ed., *The development of the modern state*, New York, 1964. D. Waley, *The Italian city-republics*, London, 1969, pp. 18–19 has a map marking 75 city-republics.

15. Useful surveys of the Venetian political system in H. F. Brown, *Studies in the history of Venice*, vol. 1, London, 1907, 'the Venetian constitution' and D. S. Chambers, *The imperial age of Venice*, London, 1970.

16. Accounts of the Florentine system include a chapter of G. Brucker, *Renaissance Florence*, New York,, 1969; A. Molho, 'politics and the ruling class in early Renaissance Florence' in *Nuova Rivista Storica*, 1968; N. Rubinstein, 'Florentine constitutionalism and Medici ascendancy in the fifteenth century' in Rubinstein; N. Rubinstein, *The government of Florence under the Medici*, Oxford, 1966. The Venetian comment in A. Segarizzi, ed., *Relazioni degli ambasciatori veneti*, vol. 3, Bari, 1916, p. 39.

17. On Milan, F. Chabod, 'usi e abusi' in *Studi storici in onore di G. Volpe*, Florence, 1958; F. Malaguzzi Valeri, *La corte di Lodovico il Moro*, vol. 1, Milan, 1913, esp. chapter 3. On Rome, M. Mallett, *The Borgias*, London, 1969, chapter 3, and P. Partner, *The papal state under Martin V*, London, 1958. On Naples, Coniglio, *Il regno di Napoli al tempo di Carlo V*, Naples, 1951, and A. J. Ryder, 'the evolution of imperial government in Naples under Alfonso v' in J. R. Hale, R. Highfield, B. Smalley, *Europe in the later Middle ages*, London, 1965.

18. For the 'iron law of oligarchy', R. Michels, *Zur Soziologie des Parteiwesens*, 1910, English trans. London, 1915. P. Jones, 'communes and despots' in *Transactions of the Royal Historical Society*, 1965, looks at both as oligarchies.

19. Harff (as note 8), p. 59.

20. G. Cavalcanti, *Istorie fiorentine*, Milan, 1944, Book 2, chapter 1. He was writing in the 1420s.

21. For Weber's types, see his *Wirtschaft und Gesellschaft*, trans. as *Economy and Society*, New York, 1968 (part 2, chapters 10–14).

22. Alberti, *Family*, p. 181.

23. Quoted in Chabod (as note 14), p. 109.

24. F. Guicciardini, 'dialogo del reggimento di Firenze' in his *Opere*, ed., V. de Caprariis, Milan/Naples, 1961, p. 281; Bernardo del Nero is speaking.

25. Pius II, *De curialium miserii epistola*, Baltimore 1928, p. 35.

26. R. Mousnier, 'le trafic des offices à Venise' in his *La plume, la faucille et le marteau*, Paris, 1970. For Milan, see Chabod, and for Naples, Coniglio (as note 17). I have found no evidence for sale of offices in Florence, not even the posts in the permanent civil service which were not filled by lot.

27. Pius II (as note 25), p. 39. Bruni and Conversino quoted by Baron (1955), pp. 58, 139.

28. Where Baron relates civic humanism to the war against Milan, Becker relates it to internal political developments in Florence. M. Becker, 'The Florentine territorial state and civic humanism' in Rubinstein. The point about bureaucracy and the literate layman made by D. Herlihy, (as note 12), p. 214.

29. The complaint about assessment from Cavalcanti (as note 20), p. 15.

30. I know of no general survey of the Italian social structure in the early modern period, only of studies of regions. For Tuscany in the early fifteenth century there is one source of capital importance, the *catasto* records of 1427, only now (1970) being studied with this aim in mind by D. Herlihy and C. Klapisch. I am grateful to Professor Herlihy for commenting on this section in draft.

31. For the clergy, see above, p. 250.

32. Machiavelli, *Discourses*, Book 1, chapter 55.

33. Studies of the Italian nobility include F. R. Bryson, *The point of honour in sixteenth-century Italy*, New York, 1935; R. Goldthwaite, *Private Wealth in Renaissance Florence*, Princeton, 1968; J. C. Davis, *The decline of the Venetian nobility as a ruling class*, Baltimore, 1962; J. Heers, 'les deux aristocraties gênoises' in his *Gènes au 15e siècle*, Paris 1961; A. Ventura,

Nobiltà e popolo nella società veneta, Bari, 1964.

34. Studies of merchants and professional men hardly exist except for Tuscany: C. Bec, *Les marchands écrivains*, Paris/The Hague, 1967; M. Berengo (as note 3); Martines; L. Martines, *Lawyers and state-craft in Renaissance Florence*, Princeton, 1968, esp. 'the profession'.

35. Still less has been written about artisans and shopkeepers. Berengo (as note 3), p. 64ff; G. Brucker and R. de Roover in Rubinstein; J. Delumeau, *Vie économique et sociale de Rome dans la second moitié du 16e siècle*, 2 vols., Paris, 1957–9. The Roman census of c. 1526 was edited by D. Gnoli in *Archivio della R. Società Romana di Storia Patria*, 1894. Da Porto quoted by B. Pullan, 'the famine in Venice and the new poor law' in *Studi veneziani*, 1963–4, p. 153.

36. Least of all is known about the peasants, but a start can be made from Herlihy (as note 12); P. Jones, 'Italy' in M. M. Postan, ed., *Cambridge Economic History of Europe*, vol. I, 2nd ed. Cambridge 1966; and the contributions of both Herlihy and Jones to Rubinstein. See also P. S. Leicht, *Operai, artigiani, agricultori in Italia*, Milan, 1946. The 1415 statute quoted in R. Poehlmann, *Die Wirthschaftspolitik der Florentiner Renaissance*, Leipzig 1878, p. 7n.

37. G. Barbieri, *Economia e politica nel ducato di Milano*, Milan 1938; F. Chabod, *L'epoca di Carlo V*, Milan 1961; F. Fossati, 'Lavor: a Milano nel 1438' in *Archivio storico Lombardo*, 1928; F. C. Lane, *Venetian Ships and Shipbuilders of the Renaissance*, Baltimore, 1934; P. Sardella, *Nouvelles et spéculations à Venise*, Paris, 1948; R. de Roover, *The rise and decline of the Medici bank*, Cambridge, Mass. 1963.

38. quoted by Berengo (as note 3) p. 124. The idea that social mobility declined in the period is put forward in von Martin; Martines; Goldthwaite (as note 33); Ventura (as note 33).

39. Most examples from Leicht (as note 36); the song about mezzadria in D'Ancona, *Origini del teatro in Italia*, Florence, vol. I, 1877, p. 605.

40. N. Tamassia, *La famiglia italiana*, Milan, 1911; Heers (as note 33) on the *albergo*; Goldthwaite (as note 33) on Florence, criticized by L. Martines in his review, *Renaissance Quarterly*, 1966; D. Herlihy, 'vieillir au quattrocento' in *Annales E.S.C.*, 1969, and C. Klapisch, 'fiscalité et démographie en Toscane', *ibid.*, on Tuscan demography. 'We are four brothers' from C. Clough, review of Ventura in *Studi veneziani* 1966, p. 543; Berengo (as note 3), p. 31ff, 84ff, 132.

41. K. J. Beloch, *Bevölkerungsgeschichte Italiens*, 3 vols., Berlin, 1937/1940, 1961 (vol. 2 on Tuscany, vol. 3 on the Veneto) Lower

population estimates in C. M. Cipolla, 'Four centuries of Italian demographic development' in D. V. Glass and D. E. C. Eversley, eds., *Population in History*, London, 1965; and J. C. Russell, *Late ancient and medieval population*, Philadelphia, 1958, the last chapter.

42. Lombard industry and trade discussed in G. Barbieri, *Economia e politica nel ducato di Milano*, Milan, 1938; E. Chinea, 'antiche botteghe d'arti' in *ASL*, 1932; D. F. Dowd, 'the economic expansion of Lombardy' in *Journal of Economic History*, 1961. The quotation about arms from Segarizzi (as note 16), vol. 2, p. 18.

43. Venetian industry and trade discussed in F. Braudel, 'la vita economica di Venezia nel secolo 16' *La civiltà veneziana del Rinascimento*, Florence, 1958; V. M. Godinho, 'le répli vénitien et la route du Cap' in *Hommage à Lucien Febvre*, Paris, 1953; F. C. Lane, *Venetian ships and ship-builders of the Renaissance*, Baltimore, 1934; G. Luzzatto, *Storia economica di Venezia*, Venice, 1961.

44. Genoese trade and industry discussed in Heers (as note 33), p. 218ff. R. S. Lopez, 'quattrocento genovese' in *Rivista Storica Italiana* 1963.

45. As Martines (p. 289) comments, studies of Florentine trade and industry in the fifteenth century are lacking. But on cloth there is A. Doren, *Die Florentiner Wollentuchindustrie*, Stuttgart, 1901. R. de Roover, *The rise and decline of the Medici Bank*, Cambridge, Mass., 1963; and his 'a Florentine firm of cloth-manufacturers' in *Speculum*, 1941.

46. On agriculture, Dowd (as note 42); Jones (as note 36); P. Jones, 'the agrarian development of medieval Italy' in *Second international conference of economic history*, Paris/The Hague, 1965. The quotation from A. Cornaro, *Discorsi intorno alle vita sobria*, Florence, 1943, p. 66.

47. A useful survey is N. S. B. Gras, 'capitalism – concepts and history' in F. C. Lane/J. Riemersma (eds.) *Enterprise and secular change*, London, 1953. Discussions of the structure of Italian industry and trade in M. Carmona, 'aspects du capitalisme Toscan' in *Revue d'Histoire Moderne*, 1964; Doren (as note 45); Heers (as note 33); G. Hermes, 'Der Kapitalismus in der Florentiner Wollenindustrie' in *Zeitschrift für die gesamte Staatswissenschaft*, 1961; Lopez (as note 44); de Roover (as note 45).

48. For the relationship between economic and cultural change, Lopez, 'hard times', and his *The three ages of the Italian Renaissance*, Charlottesville, 1970.

49. E. Durkheim, *De la division du travail social*, 1893: Glencoe, 1964 edition of the English trans., 256ff. R. E. Park, 'the city' in his *Human Communities*, Glencoe, 1952; L. Wirth, 'urbanism

as a way of life' in P. K. Hatt and A. J. Reiss, eds., *Cities and society*, revised ed., Glencoe, 1957.

Chapter ten: Cultural and Social Change

1. For a decade-by-decade analysis of trends in the arts, Chastel; and C. Seymour, *Sculpture in Italy*, Harmondsworth, 1966. On the concept of generation, K. Mannheim, 'the problem of generations' in his *Essays on the sociology of knowledge*, London, 1952. For the 'grandfather law', W. Friedlaender, *Mannerism and anti-mannerism in Italian painting*, New York, 1965, p. 54. Generations in the Italian Renaissance are discussed by H. Peyre, *Les générations littéraires*, Paris, 1948, p. 107ff; R. S. Lopez, *The three ages of the Italian Renaissance*, Charlottesville, 1970; and P. Burke, 'art humanism and society 1377–1559' in D. Mack Smith et al., *An illustrated history of Italy*, London, 1966.

2. For the Baron thesis, below, p. 32. Applications to the visual arts by F. Hartt, 'art and liberty' in L. F. Sandler, ed. *Essays in memory of K. Lehmann*, New York, 1964, and J. Pope-Hennessy, *Italian Renaissance sculpture*, London, 1958, 'introduction'; criticisms of the thesis by J. Seigel in *Past and Present*, 1966, and J. Larner, *Culture and Society in Italy 1290–1420*, London, 1971, p. 244f.

3. On the balance of power, peace and the Italian Renaissance, G. Mattingly, *Renaissance diplomacy*, London, 1955, p. 96.

4. F. Gilbert, 'Bernardo Rucellai' in *JWCI*, 1949; F. Gilbert, *Machiavelli and Guicciardini*, Princeton, 1965; G. Weise, *L'ideale eroico del Rinascimento*, Naples, 1961.

5. Changes in the arts discussed by K. Clark, *A failure of nerve*, Oxford, 1967 (a lecture on Italian art 1520–35); A. Hauser, *Mannerism*, London 1965; N. Pevsner, 'the Counter-Reformation and Mannerism' in his *Studies in art, architecture and design*, vol. 1, London, 1968. The economy discussed by C. Barbagallo in *Nuova Rivista Storica* 1950, 1951, and by F. Chabod in the Treccani *Storia di Milano IX*, Milan, 1961. Valerianus quoted by C. Trinkaus, *Adversity's noblemen*, 2nd ed. New York, 1965, p. 137. Heresy discussed by D. Cantimori, *Eretici italiani del '500*, Florence, 1939. The decline in numbers of paintings: I. Errera, *Répertoire des peintures datées*, vol. 1, Brussels, 1920, gives 441 dated paintings 1510–19; 314 for 1520–9; 195 for 1530–9. The idea expressed in the Klee quotation had been developed by W. Worringer, *Abstraktion und Einfühlung*, English trans. London, 1953, and was to be developed by P.

Sorokin, *Fluctuations of forms of art*, New York, 1937.

6. The distinction between 'movement' and 'period' is made in E. H. Gombrich, *In search of cultural history*, Oxford, 1969 (but for him the Renaissance is a movement and never a period).

7. H. Wölfflin, *Die klassische Kunst*, 1899, English trans. London, 1952, p. 213ff. The quip from Dolce, p. 172.

8. The criterion of selection is membership of the creative élite and some information about origin or achieved status. (i) high are Pisanello, Luca della Robbia, Masaccio, B. Rosselino. Low are Angelico, J. Bellini, Castagno, Agostino di Duccio, Donatello, Lippi, Masolino, Michelozzo, A. Vivarini. Marginal are Piero della Francesca, Squarcione and Uccello. (ii) high are Alessi, P. Bordone, Bronzino, Castello, Cattaneo, Cellini, N. dell'Abate, Leoni, Ligorio, Primaticcio. Low are Salviati, Tintoretto, Tribolo. Marginal are J. Bassano, Palladio, Parmigianino.

9. Vasari, life of Dello.

10. The concept of 'refeudalization' comes from F. Antal, 'the social background of Mannerism' in *AB*, 1948. Allowing for the wide Marxian sense of 'feudal' this point seems a valid one; similar interpretations have been offered by von Martin (see above, p. 27); Weise (as note 4, above); E. Loos, *Baldassare Castigliones libro del Cortegiano*, Frankfurt 1955; F. Zeri, *Pittura e controriforma*, Turin, 1957; and F. Braudel, *La Méditerranée*, 2nd ed. Paris, 1966, vol. 2, p. 50ff.

11. The return to the land is discussed by H. Baron and D. Hicks in *Comparative studies in society and history*, 1959–60; R. Goldthwaite, *Private wealth in Renaissance Florence*, Princeton, 1968; S. Woolf, 'Venice and the terraferma' in *Studi veneziani*, 1962.

12. For the 'brain drain', Chastel, p. 191; for the shift into music after the decline of city-states, H. Koenigsberger, 'decadence or shift?' in *Transactions of the Royal Historical Society*, 1960.

13. I. Watt, *The rise of the novel*, London, 1957; C. C. Christensen, 'municipal patronage in Reformation Nuremberg' in *Church History*, 1967.

14. M. Finley, *The ancient Greeks*, London, 1963; A. Gouldner, *Enter Plato*, New York, 1965; and the anecdotes about Greek artists in Pliny's *Natural History*, Book 30.

15. M. Bloch, 'pour une histoire comparée des sociétés européennes' translated in his *Land and work in medieval Europe*, London, 1967.

16. See esp. J. Lestocquoy, *Les villes de Flandre et d'Italie*, Paris, 1952; E. E. Lowinsky, 'music in the culture of the Renaissance' in *JHI*, 1954; E. Panofsky, *Renaissance and renascences*, Stock-

holm, 1960, chapter 4; E. Panofsky, *Early Netherlandish paint-ing*, Cambridge, Mass., 1953, chapter 1; H. Floerke, *Studien zu niederländischen Kunst–und Kulturgeschichte*, Munich/Leipzig, 1905 (esp. on the art market).

17. Flemish paintings from Errera (as note 5). There are only 213 of them (compared with 2,229 for Italy in the same period), too few to break down usefully by decades. Of these 213, 79 were secular (63 being portraits). The religious pictures were 35 per cent Mary, 35 per cent Christ, 24 per cent saints, 6 per cent the rest (compare Italy: 50 per cent Mary, 25 per cent Christ, 23 per cent saints, 2 per cent the rest).

18. Flemish painters from *EWA* (the same source as was used in the case of Italy: see appendix) which gave only these 54. Biographical details in T–B. By 'sizeable towns' I mean the following 15: Aalst, Amsterdam, Antwerp, Breda, Bruges, Brussels, Dinant, Ghent, Gouda, Haarlem, Leyden, Liège, Louvain, Tournai, Utrecht.

19. See P. Burke, 'the sheep hath paid for all' in *The Listener*, March, 1966.

20. See esp. R. N. Bellah, *Tokugawa religion*, Glencoe, 1957; H. Hibbett, *The floating World in Japanese fiction*, London, 1959; D. Keene, *Major plays of Chikamatsu*, New York, 1961; 'intro-duction'; R. Lane, *Masters of the Japanese print*, London, 1962; C. D. Sheldon, *The rise of the merchant class in Tokugawa Japan*, New York, 1958. It is only fair to add that the inter-pretation of Tokugawa social history followed here is essen-tially that of the 'Kyoto school'. For criticisms, see E. S. Craw-cour in *Journal of Asian Studies*, 1963.

21. On the connexion between realism and the bourgeoisie, see esp. E. H. Gombrich, 'the social history of art' in Gombrich (1963).

Index

Some Modern Classics in Fontana

The Fontana History of Europe

Praised by academics, teachers and general readers alike, this series aims to provide an account, based on the latest research, that combines narrative and explanation. Each volume has been specially commissioned from a leading English, American or European scholar, and is complete in itself. The general editor of the series is J. H. Plumb, lately Professor of Modern History at Cambridge University, and Fellow of Christ's College, Cambridge.

Fontana History

Fontana History includes the well-known History of Europe, editied by J. H. Plumb and the Fontana Economic History of Europe, edited by Carlo Cipolla. Other books available include:

Lectures on Modern History   Lord Acton

The Conservative Party from Peel to Churchill
Robert Blake

A Short History of the Second World War
Basil Collier

American Presidents and the Presidency
Marcus Cunliffe

The English Reformation   A. G. Dickens

The Norman Achievement   David C. Douglas

The Practice of History   G. R. Elton

Politics and the Nation, 1450-1660   D. M. Loades

Ireland Since the Famine   F. S. L. Lyons

Britain and the Second World War   Henry Pelling

Foundations of American Independence   J. R. Pole

A History of the Scottish People   T. C. Smout

The Ancien Regime and the French Revolution
Tocqueville

The King's Peace 1637-1641   C. V. Wedgwood

The King's War 1641-1647   C. V. Wedgwood